AA

KEYGUIDE

NORMANDY

71

CONTENTS

98

40

160

130

CONTENTS NORMANDY

3

UNDERSTANDING NORMANDY

Understanding Normandy is an introduction to the region, its geography, economy, history and its people, giving a real insight into the area. Living Normandy gets under the skin of Normandy today, while The Story of Normandy takes you through the region's past.

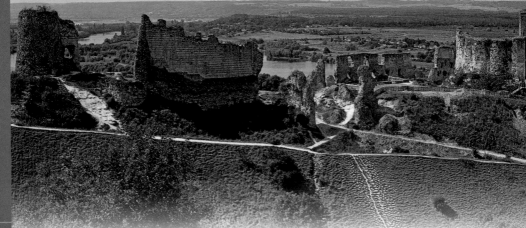

This most peaceful of regions, with its seemingly endless coastline and sleepy hinterland of half-timbered cottages, fast-flowing streams and lush green fields, was born of centuries of conflict. Every city of looming gables and turrets, each hamlet or village, and almost every port and beach has a tale to tell. This may be a story of knights and dukes, chivalry and kingship, it may be a seafarer's yarn of exploration, discovery and piracy, or it may be a memory of more recent battles and invasion from land, sea or air. And each chapter in Normandy's story is illustrated, whether in 11th-century needlework at Bayeux, through stained glass in Rouen's churches and cathedrals, or by the late 19th-century Impressionists whose trail stretches from Honfleur to Le Havre and back to Giverny.

IDENTITY

Normandy has the patience to tell its stories at a gentle pace. Just far enough away from the French capital, Paris, to retain a sense of its own identity, this one-time dukedom—for centuries foreign to France—has a quiet, self-sufficient spirit. Although lacking the fiery independence of neighbouring Celtic Brittany, Normandy retains an awareness of its past and its potential. A Viking land, colonised by Norsemen from whom it took its name and spirit of adventure, the region retains the self-reliance of its colonial past.

Not long after the original Scandinavian settlers claimed the land for themselves, Normandy looked out to sea to make further conquests. England was its most enduring trophy (the monarch still retains title to the duchy of Normandy), but the Norman empire stretched as far as Sicily and southern Italy. Even after Normandy became part of France at the end of the Hundred Years War in 1453, its sea captains pursued the path of colonisation, being among the original settlers of Canada.

Traders, sailors, farmers and fighters: thanks to centuries of outside influences, Normans can't be pigeonholed. But when a patriotic Norman talks of *mon pays* (my land) he is more likely to be referring to his region than to his country.

LANDSCAPE

Normandy has a dramatic coastline, thrusting symbolically through the English Channel towards the Atlantic Ocean. Even in this age of pan-European budget air travel, this is still a region that regards seaports as its principal gateways, just as when William Shakespeare wrote of England's King Henry V famously laying siege to Harfleur as the first step in his invasion of France. Honfleur, Barfleur and Dieppe are attractive enough to lure visitors as destinations in their own right, while Le Havre, Cherbourg and Rouen remain very much trading posts. Between the ports are beaches of every type and, at Étretat, some of Europe's most dramatic cliffs.

Inland, the pastoral nature of the region means that agriculture defines the land. Here, dairy farms and apple orchards dominate the landscape, much as vineyards do in regions further south. Rich forests in areas furthest from the coast provide areas of unspoiled tranquillity.

While many towns—especially those in coastal areas—suffered terribly from wartime bombings, leaving a legacy of harsh concrete post-war rebuilding, other areas were miraculously saved. There are fine manor houses in a splendid range of architectural styles, from Renaissance to the traditional half-timbered houses of the Suisse Normande, and the many chateaux and fortifications that survived the air raids are matched by the remarkable religious heritage of Gothic abbeys and cathedrals.

TOURISM AND THE ECONOMY

Those ports that once proved so lucrative as homes to privateers, pirates and adventurers continue to play a crucial role in France's transatlantic trade. Alongside the container ships at the docks are cruise liners and car ferries, a sign that the biggest modern boom is in tourism.

The traditional tourist lures of the French regions are augmented in Normandy by its World War II sites, which attract visitors from the UK, the US and Canada, and increasingly from other European countries. Annual return visits by veterans themselves are declining, as is inevitable more than 65 years after D-Day, but interest in the sites and lessons learned from the war continues to grow as families and descendants of combatants come to pay their own respects.

Tourism flourished in Normandy in the mid-19th century, as Cabourg, Deauville and Trouville grew to meet the demands of fashionable Paris society needing a Riviera within easy reach of the capital. Once the region was adopted by the Impressionists, its success among the well-to-do was assured. Even today, a certain chic element defines several resorts, and the image of the playground of the wealthy is reinforced by casinos, spas and racecourses. Horses play a part in both tourism and business in the Orne, home of the Percheron breed and countless riding stables.

Clockwise from left to right *The view from the ruins of Château Gaillard; the British Military Cemetery; Normandy's flag*

The agricultural legacy of a land of dairy farms supports a new style of gastronomic tourism that reflects a revived interest in traditional rather than faddish foods. Creamy sauces, full-flavoured cheeses, ciders and seafood are on menus in country inns and city-centre restaurants. Despite this interest, agriculture on its own has been affected by the politics of modern farming, with European Union (EU) quotas on milk production and regulations on the use of unpasteurised milk having put paid to many small, independent dairies. As a result, there is much rural unemployment in the heartland away from the cities and tourist resorts of the coast.

POLITICS

Normandy's long-time dependence on farming and fishing means that the influence of the European Union (EU) colours local politics, with views polarized between those who blame Europe for their woes and those dependent on subsidies. Voters move to the right and even the Front Nationale when fearing for their livelihoods, and tend towards the left, from socialism

some commentators have debated the effects of the Allied bombings.

SOCIETY

The native Norman reserve should not be taken as an anti-social sign. Good manners are valued and it is always worth making the effort to get to know the hosts at your inn or *chambre d'hôte* (bed-and-breakfast). A genuine interest in the local area and traditions will be rewarded with a very warm welcome, even an invitation to share a *goutte* (drop) of farmhouse Calvados, cider or Poiré. A sure indication of a welcome in winter is the offer of a *goutte* of Calva in your black coffee.

to communism, when remembering the wartime occupation. Whatever the individual leaning, politics plays a lively role in local life and conversations. Elected mayors have wide-ranging powers that often come as a shock to visitors from the UK or US, who are surprised at the large scale of local events and campaigns.

Political action is widespread, whether protests at ports by environmental campaigners or lorry drivers opposing a new EU directive. These can spill over to the days before and after the official industrial action. Since France has a long tradition of street-corner gatherings during political and social unrest, bystanders usually repair to the nearest café to pass the time.

Even when other parts of France are caught in a passing wave of nationalism or slight xenophobia, Normandy has affection for its visitors, especially those from the Allied liberating nations of D-Day. In commemoration season in June, newsagents sell thank you cards for locals to give to visiting veterans, and the British, American and Canadian flags fly in most villages. In recent years, however, in a lifting of earlier taboos,

Outside the cities and university towns, Normans may not live the Latin late-night lifestyle, but for family occasions, confirmations and weddings, they do like to let their hair down. If you encounter a procession of cars with ribbons streaming from their door handles or aerials and their horns tooting incessantly, this is a traditional wedding parade travelling from the home town or village of the bride to that of the groom. The partying may continue for two or three days, as dispersed families unite around the table from Saturday afternoon until late on Sunday, irrigating the endless meal with shots of Calvados.

A more public form of merrymaking may be shared by visitors during Normandy's festivals, which celebrate local produce. These food fairs, along with musical and other cultural events, provide excellent excuses for sharing a drink with locals, and are a good chance for outsiders to see the people of Normandy at their best.

Above *Heads of state at the 2004 commemoration of D-Day*
Below *Fishing boats moored at low tide in Barfleur's port*

NORMANDY'S REGIONS

Officially, Normandy consists of two autonomous regions: Basse-Normandie (Lower Normandy) and Haute-Normandie (Upper Normandy), each subdivided into administrative *départements*. Essentially, Basse-Normandie is the western half of Normandy, containing the *départements* of Manche, Orne and Calvados; Haute-Normandie, meanwhile, is the region to the north and east, split between the *départements* of Eure and Seine-Maritime.

In truth, however, modern-day Normans regard Normandy as one regional entity, and it is probably only the decision as to where a joint capital city would lie that presents the principal stumbling block to unification. Caen (William the Conqueror's city) is capital of Basse-Normandie, while Rouen (the more romantic city on the Seine, with its own legacy of dukes, kings and bishops) is capital of Haute-Normandie. Choosing between them would be difficult.

Normandy's *départements* are distinguished by the first two numbers of an address's post code). These number pairs are as follows: Calvados—14; Eure—27; Manche—50, Orne—61; and Seine-Maritime—76. Each *département* also has its own well-defined character.

La Manche This coastal *département* is flanked on one side by the Cotentin beaches of World War II and on the other by Mont-St-Michel. Its seafaring past and present are represented in harbours as diverse as William the Conqueror's Barfleur and the resort of Granville. The principal port is Cherbourg, at the top of the peninsula, and the capital is St-Lô.

Orne The lush hinterland of Normandy is known as the country of the horse, and the main attractions for visitors are its stud farms and forests. It is an area known for good country food, and it has Alençon as its capital

Calvados Sprawling out from its capital of Caen, Calvados includes the D-Day landing beaches and the picturesque inland regions of the Pays d'Auge and Suisse Normande. Here, country lanes are dotted with signs inviting passers-by to taste the eponymous apple brandy of the region's farmyard producers.

Eure Administered from the picturesque capital of Évreux, Eure was the frontier between old Normandy and France. It has a centuries-old legacy of abbeys and castles, and a newer artistic heritage thanks to Claude Monet's residence at Giverny.

Seine-Maritime Rouen, on the banks of the Seine, is the capital of this *département*. It's an area of historic ports, ranging from the rebuilt Le Havre to the picturesque towns and villages along the Côte d'Albâtre. Manor houses and abbeys, ruined and intact, are among the lures away from the coast and rivers.

THE BEST OF NORMANDY

LA MANCHE

Au P'tit Quinquin (▷ 62) Dine on local Mont-St-Michel lamb in a simple country restaurant.

Avranches (▷ 42) With views towards Mont-St-Michel, this town's history is entwined with that of the abbey.

Barfleur (▷ 43) A typical Cotentin fishing town with a fascinating history. The nearby Gatteville lighthouse is a must-see.

Cité de la Mer, Cherbourg (▷ 45) More than a mere aquarium, this is a celebration of Normandy's relationship with the sea.

Maison Gosselin Buy provisions and souvenirs at St Vaast-la-Hougue's legendary grocery store (▷ 60).

Mont-St-Michel (▷ 48–51) Out of season, ideally in winter, is the best time to experience the amazing abbey and town perched on a granite rock in the bay.

Musée de Christian Dior, Granville (▷ 47 and 55) Visit the home of the man who devised post-war cool.

Patinoire Chantereyne Go late night ice skating in this complex in Cherbourg (▷ 59).

Tatihou, St-Vaast-la-Hougue (▷ 53) An island of timeless calm, just offshore from a bustling pleasure port.

ORNE

Haras National du Pin (▷ 72) Anyone who loves horses should visit this elegant royal stud farm.

Jean-Claude Lebaron, Bagnoles-de-l'Orne (▷ 78) Another vice of the resort of Bagnoles—aside from spa pampering and casino gambling—is indulging in delicious chocolate swans from this shop.

Mortagne au Perche. (▷ 72) Taste the distinctive local *boudin noir* sausage.

Parc Naturel Régional Normandie-Maine (▷ 73) The flora and fauna of the park's four forests provide pure escapism for nature lovers.

La Poêlerie, Joué-du-Bois (▷ 79) Beer makes a refreshing alternative to cider at this farmhouse brewery.

Sées (▷ 73 and 79) Gothic cathedral and December turkey fair.

CALVADOS

Au Repos des Chineurs Never mind the soap, at this hotel you can take your bedroom furniture home with you (▷ 117).

Bayeux Tapestry (▷ 86–87) No matter how many times you see it reproduced in print, the original needlework remains an impressive sight.

Beuvron-en-Auge (▷ 88) One of the prettiest corners of this picture-book region.

Château St-Germain-de-Livet (▷ 93) A fairy-tale chateau reflected in a river.

Deauville (▷ 95) Kicking off with its 'Swing In' festival in July and ending with the film festival in September, the chic resort becomes Paris-on-sea during the summer season.

Honfleur (▷ 98–99) Unquestionably the most picturesque port in Normandy is made for strolling.

Isigny-sur-Mer (▷ 112) Discover France's best-loved butter and cream at the world-famous dairy.

Mémorial de la Paix, Caen (▷ 91) This peace museum is a powerful indictment of the 20th century's rush to war.

Mulberry Harbour, Arromanches-les-Bains (▷ 85) The awe-inspiring remains of the floating harbour that launched the D-Day landings can still be seen.

Suisse Normande This area has the most rugged landscapes of Normandy and is a haven of adventure sports (▷ 113).

EURE

Abbaye du Bec-Hellouin (▷ 121) The calm of the abbey and its grounds exudes a powerful spirituality.

Château Gaillard, Les Andelys (▷ 122–123) Richard the Lionheart's final stronghold dominates Les Andelys and the surrounding countryside.

Évreux (▷ 128–129) Come here for waterside strolls along the river Iton and to admire the floral displays.

Grain de Café. The finest cup of tea in Normandy is served in this tiny café in Louviers (▷ 140).

Léry (▷ 140) Enjoy a day on the water at the lakeside leisure complex here.

Lyons-la-Fôret (▷ 132), a delightful town of timber framed houses in the midst of a beautiful beechwood forest.

Restaurant Baudy, Giverny (▷ 131) Before the crowds arrive or after they leave, dine in the restaurant that was the meeting place of Claude Monet and his fellow Impressionists.

Val de Risle Pit yourself against the white waters of the river Risle in a kayak (▷ 140).

SEINE-MARITIME

Abbaye de Jumièges (▷ 149) The perfect backdrop to a concert on a summer evening.

Abbaye de St-Wandrille Listen to the Gregorian chants at a service at this abbey (▷ 150).

L'Auberge du Val au Cesne. (▷ 179) Ducks, chicks and cats greet arrivals at this charming inn.

Cathédrale de Notre-Dame, Rouen (▷ 162) The night-time summer light show projected on the cathedral's façade is spectacular.

Château du Champ-de-Bataille (▷ 17) The restoration of this castle and its grounds is a labour of love.

Église Jeanne-d'Arc, Rouen (▷ 163) Modern church architecture at its most inspiring.

Étretat (▷ 154) See magnificent cliffs and caves at one of France's most dramatic beaches.

Fêtes Jeanne d'Arc. Visit Rouen during the Joan of Arc festivities in May (▷ 175).

Musée des Beaux-Arts André Malraux, Le Havre (▷ 158) The natural light that inspired the Impressionists fills this modern art museum.

Palais Bénédictine, Fécamp (▷ 155) This distillery almost upstages the region's abbeys and cathedrals for sheer grandeur.

Clockwise from left to right The Bayeux Tapestry; Palais Bénédictine; the Christian Dior Museum

TOP EXPERIENCES

Drink apple juice in all its forms—Calvados, cider and Pommeau—down on the farm. Just stop the car when you see a sign for *Dégustation* (tastings) or visit Domaine Fougeray-Duclos (▷ 175) if you're in the vicinity.

Tour the D-Day beaches to experience the raw emotion of remembrance. Take a drive from Caen or Bayeux (▷ 106–109) or join an organized tour.

Explore ruined castles, the least restored of which provide a potent link with the past (Château de Pirou ▷ 44).

Eat an omelette whisked in copper bowls on Mont-St-Michel (▷ 48–51); the generations-old recipe of Mère Poulard is generally believed to be the best in France.

Skip the diet and indulge in cream and cheese, especially Camembert, to get a real taste of Normandy.

Go to the market to buy food and craftwork direct from the producers. Every town will have one, each with its own flavour, but Rouen's Place St-Marc (▷ 174) and Honfleur's market (▷ 112) are worth a detour.

Visit a monastery at St-Wandrille (▷ 150) or Bec-Hellouin (▷ 121) to discover the serenity of the past.

Buy the past as you go antiques hunting in the upmarket shops of Honfleur and Rouen, in bric-a-brac stalls and at auction sales.

Go fishing for trout and carp along the river Orne or put to sea with fishermen from coastal ports to land mackerel, herring, sole or bass (▷ 199).

Ride the rails and set off from Gare du Pont Erambourg (▷ 79) on a two- or four-man rail-bike or on an historic scenic train to explore the hinterland.

Get festive at the region's numerous food (autumn's herring festival in Étretat, ▷ 175) and cultural events (the spring jazz festival in Countances, ▷ 61), the best times to meet locals.

Be pampered at a health spa by the coast (▷ 199).

Have a flutter one night at the gaming tables of the casinos in Deauville (▷ 111), Bagnoles-de-l'Orne (▷ 78) or Dieppe (▷ 172).

Relax on the beach, choosing from the sands of the Cotentin peninsula, *les planches* of Deauville or the pebble strands of the Côte d'Albâtre.

Go clubbing in Caen (New Club, ▷ 110) or Rouen (Le Chakra, ▷ 174), Évreux or Le Havre and be prepared to party until dawn.

Enjoy a round a golf at the Golf Club Dieppe-Pourville (▷ 173) or the Golf Barrière de Deauville (▷ 111).

Saddle up and explore the region on horseback. Village Équestre d'Étretat (▷ 173).

Get active on the beaches and have a go at sea-kayaking or sand yachting at Station de Voile de Granville (▷ 59).

Dance with the locals at a Sunday afternoon Guinguette at Jouy-sur-Eure (▷ 139).

Take a river cruise and explore the countryside as you eat a traditional Norman meal aboard the *Val d'Orne* or *Guillaume le Conquérant*.

Make a day trip from Granville to Jersey, largest of the Channel Islands, which has pretty bays, castles and World War II monuments to explore.

Left *The fortified battlements of Château du Pirou*
Below *Striped tents offer shelter on the beach at Cabourg*

LIVING NORMANDY

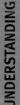

FOOD AND DRINK

Normandy remains fiercely proud of its culinary identity. And this is more than just a regional quality, as towns are defined by their specialities, such that a blindfolded diner could tell you his location by the dish of the day. In Caen, tripe is on every menu; Rouen has its tradition of preparing duck, complete with table-top rituals; in the villages that dot the bay of Mont-St-Michel, *gigot d'agneau* (leg of lamb) is prepared from the young sheep that graze on the salty grass; and on the Mount itself, restaurant walls are decked with shiny copper bowls for preparing omlettes. Along the Cotentin, oysters from St-Vaast-la-Hougue are served; in Dieppe, sole is the speciality; and in Mortagne-au-Perche, black *boudin* sausages are a local staple. Rich, creamy fare in hearty portions is standard. Wedding feasts can last days, the eating punctuated by a *trou normand*—a swig of Calvados that aids digestion. Four of France's most well-known cheeses are made in Normandy: creamy Pont-l'Eveque and pungent Livarot, both from towns in Calvados); Neufchâtel produced in the northeast corner of Normandy and often moulded into a heart-shape; and, of course, the famous Camembert from the Orne. In a land of such fabulous cheeses, seafood and ciders, food fairs, festivals and markets are firmly part of Normandy's calendar.

CONTROVERSIAL CAMEMBERT

Everyone knows what France's most famous cheese looks like—round, soft and squidgy when ripe—but what goes into it has become the subject of fierce argument. Traditionally, *appellation d'origine controllée* (AOC) Camembert has to be made from untreated milk.

Now the big industrial producers of the cheese want the AOC rules changed to allow them to make it with pasteurized milk 'for health reasons'.

Small producers say this is just a pretext: no one has ever died from eating an unpasteurized Camembert, they argue. The rule change, they claim, has more to do with prolonging shelf life and selling into foreign markets which ban the use of raw milk but it would take away the character of the cheese.

DISAPPEARING PEARS

It is easy to find cider in Normandy, and Calvados is the very essence of hospitality, but one of the great orchard tipples of the region is in danger of extinction. Poiré, or perry, brewed from pears, was once a popular alternative to cider, served in the farmhouses and taverns around Domfront and Mortain. Pear orchards were a common sight in the Perche, offering contrasting blossom in springtime to that of the ubiquitous apple trees. However, as countryfolk believe it takes 35 years to grow a pear tree suitable for making Poiré, farmers started to replace their pear trees with more lucrative apple trees, which yield fruit and profits in a fraction of the time. As the drink disappears from shops, visitors are most likely to find it in family-run guesthouses, where commercial farmers continue to make the drink for personal consumption.

SPRING BUTTER IS GOOD FOR YOU

Butter is often demonized by dieticians in debates about natural foods versus cholesterol, but scientists have discovered that *beurre d'Isigny* churned in April and May could be good for your heart.

Since AOC *(appellation d'origine contrôllée)* products are banned from using artificial additives, the cardiovascular and anti-stress benefits of the butter must come directly from the natural environment.

It seems that Isigny's butters are boosted with iodine from pastures that are located close to the Cotentin coast, and are also a natural source of Omega 3, usually found in oily fish such as mackerel. The highest proportion of antioxidants is to be found in butter made in April and May, when the dairy product may be labelled as naturally rich in Omega 3.

In other words, it's creamy yet guilt-free!

SWANSONG OF A DUCK

While many Normandy restaurants acknowledge vegetarian diners, one table-top tradition strictly for hard-core carnivores has flourished since a 1980s revival: *caneton à la Rouennaise*. A sauce of Beaune red wine, veal stock, shallots, thyme and bay leaves is made up, while a suffocated duckling is cooked rare for less than 20 minutes. The bird's organs are added to the sauce and, at the table, cognac and port are poured in and flambéed. The final test of the true carnivore is watching as the duck's bones are crushed in a silver press to squeeze the final drops of blood into the sauce. Not for the squeamish, this Rouen delicacy may be prepared only by a chef initiated into the Order of Canardiers, created in 1986 by *maître canardier* Michel Gueret.

Clockwise from opposite *French cheeses; Tarte Normande, a local specialty; Normandy cider and Poiré bottles*

THIS LITTLE PIGGY

Normandy is proud of its cattle and treats its cows as bovine VIPs, but the region's pigs have long been the poor relations, with the pink tinged white and black Cochon de Bayeux little more than a fleeting image in the memories of elderly farmers. The breed was virtually wiped out over decades of industry standardization and the demands of productivity that made keeping free-range pigs for twice as long as usual uneconomical. Then, in 1998, the breed was rediscovered. A herby-flavoured cross between domestic Normandy and Berkshire breeds, a true Bayeux pig must be born in the Bessin (straddling Calvados, Manche and Orne). Litters of piglets are weaned at seven weeks then raised in the open air on a diet of whey, barley and nettles. At eight months they're sacrificed to gastronomy. So successful has the revival been that the breed now has its own annual show in October.

SOCIETY AND FASHION

Don't think of Normandy as a simple rural region, for high society has long been alive and well here. A strong ducal heritage led to a close relationship with the court, so, come the Revolution, Normandy became home to a hardcore royalist resistance. Even after the Terror had faded, aristocrats lived in the region. Generations of paternalistic concern for the workers on their estates meant that many Norman nobles retained the respect of fellow citizens. Various art movements grew up in Normandy and inevitably attracted fashionable salons of fellow artists and wealthy patrons: Impressionist Claude Monet's Giverny years saw the painter entertaining statesmen for lunch. The railways guaranteed the success of the seaside resorts, a mid-19th-century phenomenon that brought Parisians to the coast and led to the building of grand hotels and *résidences secondaires*. Normandy's proximity to Paris, together with the vibrant life of the Seine-side cities of Rouen and Le Havre, and the perennial attractions of seaside resorts like Deauville, Honfleur, Granville and Etretat, have kept the region from becoming a social backwater.

MARIANNE UNFAITHFUL

Marianne is the symbol of France. The bare-breasted figure featured on statues in every town, whose warrior-like pose is stamped on French coins and stamps is as much an image of France as the tricolour flag itself. For four memorable years, Marianne embodied the independent spirit of Normandy. Every few years a new model is chosen for Marianne. A new Marianne was voted by the 36,000 mayors of France for the new millennium. The 21-year-old model from Pont Audemer, Laetitia Casta, was nominated as Marianne. She proudly described her figure as 'made in Normandy from butter and cream'. Soon after, however, scandal broke out in the media when it was revealed that she had demonstrated her independence by leaving France to live in London.

Clockwise from left to right *Yachts in the marina opposite the casino at Deauville; beach huts on the seafront at Deauville carry the names of celebrities; Château du Champ-de-Bataille near Évreux*

A 21ST-CENTURY SUN KING

Jacques Garcia, long France's golden boy of interior design and responsible for the grand luxury of such hotels as the Hôtel Royale in Deauville, bought the Château du Champ-de-Bataille, northeast of Évreux (▷ 128–129), in 1992 and set about restoring it. The interior is splendidly furnished throughout, but Garcia's creative masterpiece has been the reconstruction of the castle's gardens in the fashion of those at King Louis XIV's Versailles, which were designed by landscape architect André Le Nôtre. With their chequerboard *parterres*, splendid architectural features and perfect perspectives of planting and waterways, the gardens at Champ-de-Bataille were completed in 2005. As befits Garcia's status as an arbiter of taste, the event was celebrated with a typically grand gesture—a production of Verdi's *La Traviata* in the chateau grounds.

DONKEYS HAVE THEIR DAY

Normandy is a land of horses, and, from the studs of the Perche to the millionaires who mill around the racecourse of Deauville, horses are the regions's very symbol of high society. Thus, there is a pleasant irony in the fact that the resort of Trouville-sur-Mer (▷ 103), once a playground of the rich and famous but now eclipsed by its glitzier neighbours, holds a variation on the theme; here, donkeys take to the tracks rather than racehorses.

Each August, Trouville's gambling fraternity eschews the expensive hats and tailcoats of rival race tracks across the estuary and makes its way to the beach, where carefully selected donkeys race along the sands. It may be an informal affair with free admission, but big money still changes hands, as cafés and bars are abuzz with talk, and rumours of favourites and definite winners—all, of course, straight from the donkey's mouth.

CANNIER THAN CANNES

The paparazzi may swarm over the stars at the Cannes Film Festival in May, but the first fortnight of September in Normandy sees a much more civilized Hollywood invasion of France. There may be fewer staged media moments and less in the way of velvet ropes, but there is certainly no reduction in glamour as Hollywood steps out on the famous Les Planches boardwalk at Deauville's American Film Festival, which famously rounds off the resort's summer season. Since 1984, the event has reflected the special relationship between America and the people of Normandy after the D-Day landings. Whereas other festivals attract ephemeral starlets, Deauville reels in the big names: The turn-of-the-millennium roll call included actors Kirk Douglas, Lauren Bacall, directors Steven Spielberg, Clint Eastwood and regular visitor the actor Tom Hanks.

DIOR—THE SEQUEL?

Could the inspiration for the next 'New Look' in fashion come from Christian Dior's home town of Granville (▷ 47)? It's a possibility.

In 2005, to celebrate the centenary of Dior's birth, the designer's childhood home— the Villa les Rhumbs, now a museum dedicated to the couturier who shaped women's style through the 1940s and 1950s—launched an annual programme of weekly summer workshops on the art of couture, aimed at youngsters with an interest in fashion.

The museum looks at the Norman and maritime influences on the young Christian Dior and how it affected his work in later life. In a different twist, the links between designing stylish clothes and creating attractive aromas are explored in the gardens of the Villa les Rhumbs, which are planted with fragrant flowers used by parfumiers.

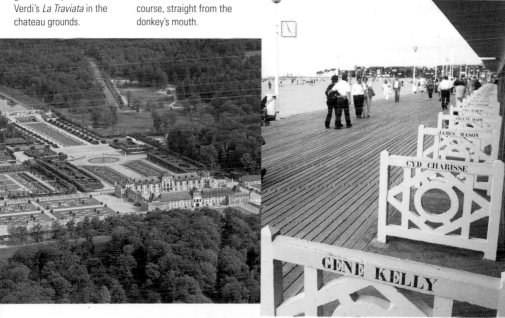

Normandy is defined by its landscapes. It takes particular pride in its blending of nature with domestic and vernacular architecture in a way that identifies each community. Although scarred by wartime bombing, this is the home of Norman architecture, with great monasteries, churches and castles. The temperate summer sunshine and healthy rainfall create a land where pastures nurture the indigenous dairy and drinks traditions. A postwar revival of traditional landscaping means that about 40 special gardens are now open to visitors, and a new concept in weekend breaks has emerged with the creation of *gîtes au jardins*, bed-and-breakfast or self-catering accommodation in private homes with beautiful gardens.

HOT OFF THE PRESS

Blow your nose in France, sit down to dinner or lay your head on the pressed pillow of any decent hotel and you will probably be grateful for, but unaware of, Normandy's latest success story: linen, which is making a comeback against cotton and man-made fabrics. French linen is considered to be among the world's finest and 60 per cent is now produced in Normandy. As well as being used in domestic fabrics, linen is used for artist's canvases and as an ingredient in banknotes.

FLOODING THE MONT

It isn't easy to push an abbey into the sea, but by 2010 Mont-St-Michel should be surrounded by water once more. Over the centuries, the silting of the bay has led to the Mount becoming moored to the mainland. The causeway often remains above the water at high tide. In 2005, a five-year project involving a dam and bridge was started in order to contain the sea around the abbey. A ban on cars within 2km (1 mile) of the Mount will also be put in place.

ROSES OF REMEMBRANCE

Love and grief may be measured in blooms and thorns in Normandy's most remarkable rose garden, a moving memorial to the death of a child.

The Lebret family knew nothing of gardening when their beloved daughter Angélique died, but the planting of a rose in her memory grew into one of the most beautiful 'English' rose gardens in France.

Since 1990, the rose garden at Les Jardins d'Angélique in Montmain, just outside Rouen, has evolved into a complex and lovingly landscaped estate around the manor house. Unlike the irises and water-lilies of Giverny, which are frozen forever to preserve a moment of time, Les Jardins d'Angélique are an ever-growing, vibrant, living testament to enduring love.

Above left *Detail of a window in a medieval stone and timber building in Domfront*
Right *The green landscape of the Suisse Normande*

THE STORY OF NORMANDY

The region that we know as Normandy was Celtic for 800 years, before the Romans conquered Amorica in 51–58BC. They linked the land with Brittany and founded ports and towns. Christianity arrived in the second century AD, with the formation of the Bishopric of Rouen in AD206 by St. Nicaise. The region's reputation as a Christian heartland grew from the monasteries that were built in the seventh and eighth centuries AD. From the second century AD, there were periodic invasions by Saxons, Franks and Norsemen, the latter arriving in force after AD800. In AD911, Normandy, the land of Norsemen, was established, with Rollo becoming the region's first duke. His successor, William Longsword, extended the dukedom to the Cotentin peninsula, and during the 11th century Norman armies conquered Sicily and southern Italy. In 1027, William the Conqueror was born at Falaise. Invading England in 1066, William started a line of English kings. From the 12th to the 15th centuries, England and France fought for control of Normandy. King Henry II of England married Eleanor of Aquitaine in 1152, claiming much of western France by the union, but the lands were regained by France in 1204. England's King Edward III invaded in 1346, sparking the Hundred Years War, which ended in 1453, when Normandy was returned to France for good.

ANGELIC PERSUASION

Visitors often wonder what inspired the feat of engineering that is Mont-St-Michel (▷ 48–51). The original chapel may have been built by faith, yet its founder, Aubert, Bishop of Avranches, required a prod to get started.

It is said that the archangel St. Michael appeared to Aubert and ordered him to build the chapel. Aubert was sceptical about the vision and did not hurry to start the task. St. Michael returned once more, poking his finger into the bishop's head for emphasis. Aubert swiftly ordered construction to begin in AD709.

The importance of listening to angels is seen only too clearly at Avranche's Église St-Gervais, where Aubert's skull is displayed, complete with the hole made by St. Michael's finger (▷ 42).

A VIKING HANDSHAKE

What do you get if you refrain from seizing power in France? The answer, if you are a Scandinavian ruler with a penchant for pillage, looting and compromise, is Normandy.

The Vikings had spent most of a century attacking France's Channel coast and persecuting the region's Christians, when pagan raider Rolf the Walker led his forces along the Seine and into Paris at the turn of the 10th century. Rather than engage in long-term conventional battle, King Charles III of France decided to pay off the would-be invader by handing over the land known today as Normandy (after the Norsemen) following a simple handshake at the Treaty of St-Clair-sur-Epte in AD911. In return, Rolf agreed to Latinize his name to Rollo and run his newfound dukedom as a Christian.

LION HEART, ACHILLES HEEL

Richard the Lionheart, King of England and Duke of Normandy (1157–99), was feared across Europe as a bold crusading warrior. Yet his legacy in Normandy is a reminder that a lion's heart is no protection against an Achilles heel. At the end of his reign, this scourge of Saracens was less concerned with war in the Holy Land than in keeping France out of Normandy. Thus, in just one year from 1195 to 1196, he built the supposedly impenetrable Château Gaillard at Les Andelys to protect Normandy (▷ 122–123). Gaillard stood fast while Richard spent his last three years defending lands further south. But, after his death, French soldiers entered Gaillard by the sewers and, just a decade after the castle's construction, Rouen was in French hands.

BRAND LEADERS

Leaders' nicknames are like marketing brands. 'Lionheart' and 'Brave' are certainly invaluable political assets, but Duke William began his career with a less fortunate tag in 1035 when he inherited Normandy. Since his father, Robert the Magnificent, didn't marry William's mother, Herleva, William was dubbed 'The Bastard'. During his early years, William's nickname did seem a hindrance—he lacked support and faced assassination plots, which he survived only by forming an alliance with France's King Henri I. He wooed and wed his cousin Mathilde but the union courted controversy amid whispers of incest. Even the 1066 invasion risked negative spin, when William fell from his boat onto English soil. William went on to win the Battle of Hastings and the safer soubriquet of 'Conqueror'—and with it 21 years of peace.

THE WRONG TROUSERS

Joan of Arc might have cheated the stake had prison guards not stolen her clothes. History tells of Joan's imprisonment and trial in Rouen, and how in 1431 she was sentenced to death as a heretic. On 24 May, in St-Ouen Abbey cemetery, Joan finally recanted, her death sentence commuted to life in prison. But English anger at her escape from execution led to devious attempts to reverse the decision. Having conceded that wearing men's clothes was heresy, Joan agreed to wear a dress, but on Trinity Sunday that dress mysteriously vanished. Leaving her cell, she was forced to don her masculine attire. As a result, she was accused by the English of rejecting her own recantation, and was led to the stake and martyrdom on 30 May, less than a week after her life had been spared.

Clockwise from opposite *Effigy on the tomb of Richard the Lionheart in Rouen; Mont-St-Michel; Joan of Arc by Sir John Gilbert*

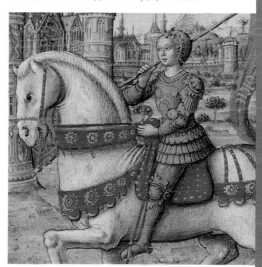

CENTURIES OF WAR

By 1453 Normandy was French once more. Normandy's mercantile future was assured with the founding of Le Havre in 1517. Rouen, already the seat of Normandy's parliament since 1514, became a self-governing city in 1542. From 1562, France was torn by Wars of Religion. Protestant King Henri IV defeated the Catholics at Arques-la-Bataille (▷ 150) and Ivry-la-Bataille in 1589. The Edict of Nantes (1598) enshrined the civil rights of Protestants, until it was revoked by King Louis XIV in 1685, when pogroms led to the mass emigration of Huguenots from Norman ports. Other departures included that of explorer Samuel de Champlain, who sailed from Honfleur in the early 17th century to found Québec. In 1789, thoughts turned to conflict again with the French Revolution. Normandy, apart from Caen, sympathized with the Royalist cause in the struggle. In 1793, republican Girondins rose up against Chouan royalists at Granville. The 19th century saw the rise in popularity of Normandy's seaside resorts. The area's popularity was given an extra boost in 1874, when artist Claude Monet exhibited the first Impressionist painting, of a sunrise at Le Havre. Monet lived in Giverny from 1883 until his death in 1926, and attracted many other artists to the region. From 1940 Normandy fell under German occupation, until the Allied liberation of France began with the landings on the Cotentin beaches on D-Day, 6 June 1944.

AMERICA'S NORMAN CONQUESTS

Just as the Normans had crossed the Channel to invade Britain, so the region's mariners sailed the Atlantic to reach North America in the 16th and 17th centuries. An Honfleur sailor, Jean Denis, found the mouth of the St. Lawrence river in 1506, a century before countryman Samuel de Champlain established Québec on behalf of the governor of Dieppe. It was from Dieppe that King François I's explorer Giovanni da Verrazano set sail for New France, discovering the site of New York in 1524. He also moored off what is now North Carolina, starting a tradition of Norman exploration of the Deep South. Réné de la Laudonnière tried to colonize Florida with Protestants from Dieppe and Le Havre in 1564. In 1682, Rouen's Cavalier de La Salle seized Louisiana for King Louis XIV.

A BETTER CLASS OF PIRATE

In the 16th century, after centuries of battles with European neighbours, France realised a money-saving alternative to war was the use of self-employed pirates. Rather than declare outright war, King François I commissioned Dieppe's sailors to seize cargoes from the merchant ships of rivals. When Portugal declared sovereignty over African waters, François I issued letters of marque to Norman shipbuilder Jean Ango, a financier of expeditions. Ango's captains became privateers, looting Portuguese vessels, keeping a healthy commission for themselves and Ango, and giving the bulk of the plunder to the King. Ango flourished, becoming a patron of Renaissance art and entertaining royalty at his lavish manor house in Varengeville, which he built from his bounty (▷ 165). Not all privateers' cargo came from raids—the expeditions to North America brought tobacco to France.

HOLLOW VICTORY

The quick thinking of a village teacher saved France's two most unusual chapels from becoming a pile of firewood. The community of Allouville-Bellefoss, near Yvetot in Seine-Maritime, is famous for a remarkable 1,200-year-old oak tree with a grand girth measuring 10m (33ft). In 1696, the local parish priest built two chapels within the hollow trunk of the tree, the lower chapel was dedicated to Notre Dame de la Paix and the upper room is known as the hermit's chamber. The tree is topped with a steeple and an iron cross.

During the French Revolution, when churches across the country were threatened with attack, verger and local schoolteacher Jean-Baptiste Bonheure placed a sign on the tree declaring it to be a Temple of Reason. His action spared the chapel-oak, which still hosts a Mass service held twice each year.

WHO'S THE DADDY?

The first Impressionist picture was painted at Le Havre, but its inspiration came further along the estuary in Honfleur. Claude Monet's iconic canvas of sunrise in Le Havre, *Impression: Soleil Levant*, gave the name to the Impressionist movement when it was exhibited in 1874. Monet's haste to capture a particular moment of sunlight was the result of lessons learnt from his tutor, Eugène Boudin (1824–98), son of an Honfleur boatman. Boudin introduced Monet to the idea of painting outdoors, and a technique for adapting to the changing light and weather of the Normandy coast. Monet's tutor recorded not only the dates and times of his paintings, but prevailing wind speed and weather conditions as well. Although Boudin remained faithful to classical traditions of colour in his own work, his instinct for interpretation made this lesser known artist the true father of Impressionism

THE HIGHEST PRICE

D-Day pioneers were able to transport huge military harbours across the sea and land silent gliders on target, next to Pegasus Bridge, but the best strategic brains of the 1940s were nearly outwitted by the modest hedge. The hedgerows that mark out the distinctive Norman landscape, known as *bocage*, proved the toughest obstacle for American forces fighting their way across the Cotentin peninsula in World War II. With lanes sunk below the level of fields, and bramble-thick hedges and trees surrounding each pasture, conventional vehicles and modern artillery proved ineffective, and progress could be made only by foot soldiers until tanks could be adapted with agricultural-style equipment. This quirk of the landscape cost one life for every metre advanced during the liberation of Lessay, and the lives of thousands of other soldiers across Normandy in 1944.

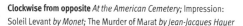

Clockwise from opposite *At the American Cemetery*; Impression: Soleil Levant *by Monet*; The Murder of Marat *by Jean-Jacques Hauer*

INTO THE MODERN AGE

Post-war Normandy was inevitably most characterized by reconstruction. Since then Normandy has moved forward. The region entered the atomic age with the opening of a nuclear processing plant at la Hague. France's enthusiasm for nuclear power increased and power stations were built at Paluel and Flamanville in the early 1980s. The first French nuclear submarine, was launched at Cherbourg in 1971 (▷45). On a greener note, the Parc Naturel Régional Brotonne was created in 1974, with Normandie-Maine Natural Regional Park following in the next year. In 1991, the Cotentin and Bessin area also achieved nature park status. The second half of the 20th century saw another achievement: suspension bridges across the Seine estuary; the Pont de Tancarville opened in 1959.

Above *The special Armada of the Century was held in Rouen in 1999; a similar event is held every four or five years in the port*

HISTORIC CONCRETE
What do France's Gothic cathedrals, medieval towns, royal palaces and the pre-fab port of Le Havre have in common? They are all listed World Heritage Sites, with Le Havre being a good 200 years younger than anywhere else on the list. In 2005 UNESCO singled out Le Havre for its post-war reconstruction 'It is an outstanding post-war example of urban planning…and the innovative exploitation of the potential of concrete.'

BRIDGES OVER UNTROUBLED WATERS
One thing they know how to do in Normandy is build bridges. Two of the newest and most impressive structures are the Pont de Normandie and the Pont Gustave Flaubert. Pont de Normandie links Le Havre and Honfleur across the Seine and when it opened in 1995 it was the longest cable-stayed bridge in the world and the one with the longest central span (856m/2,803ft). In 2008 Pont Gustave Flaubert opened as Rouen's sixth river crossing. This is a vertical lift bridge in which the central section rises 55m (180ft) between the two piers.

NORMAN RULE
It took several centuries, but on 23 December 1953 a Norman finally found himself in charge of France. Réné Coty was born in Le Havre in 1882. His finest hour came after World War II, when he became the second President of the Fourth Republic, a post he held until 1958 before handing power to Charles de Gaulle.

ON THE MOVE

On the Move gives you detailed advice and information about the various options for travelling to Normandy before explaining the best ways to get around the region once you are there. Handy tips help you with everything from buying tickets to renting a car.

BY AIR

Patterns of air travel to northwestern France have fluctuated. After a period of expansion, when low-cost operators began using small regional airports, the network suddenly contracted. This hit the short-break market and left many holiday-home owners unexpectedly stranded with no direct local flights. The picture is changing again as new operators fill the gaps.

There are some small airports in Normandy, but at present they handle few direct international flights. To get there by air from long-haul destinations such as North America or Australasia you have to route your journey via Paris, France's main air-gate, and take a connecting domestic flight. Lyon, Marseille, Nice and Nantes also have internal air-links with Normandy and Brittany. It may be cheaper to fly to London and continue your journey from there.

» There are no direct scheduled flights to Normandy from the UK. Low-cost airline Flybe currently flies to Brest and Rennes in Brittany. Beauvais Tillé airport (often billed as Paris) is 90km (56 miles) north of Paris and handy for travel to Rouen and Giverny (avoiding Paris). It is used by low-cost airlines, including Ryanair from Glasgow and Dublin.

» Paris has three airports. Busiest is Roissy–Charles de Gaulle, 23km (14 miles) from the city centre. It has three terminals, all connected with each other and with central Paris and its main railway stations by bus or train (RER Line B). The smaller Orly airport, 14km (8.5 miles) south of central Paris, takes mainly domestic but also some international flights. Its two terminals are linked by bus and train with Paris.

» At busy holiday periods (eg Christmas/New Year, Easter or July–August), flights into Paris get very booked up.

» From Paris, Air France provides domestic flights to Norman airports (Rouen, Caen, Le Havre) from Lyon. Independent airline Twin Jet has scheduled flights to Cherbourg from Paris–Orly.

» It is often more convenient, just as quick, and almost certainly cheaper to continue your onward journey to Normandy by train or rental car from a Parisian airport. From the Périphérique ring road, take the A13 motorway towards Caen for the D-Day beaches and the Cotentin. For Rouen, exit at junction for the D7 and N15.

» Flight prices usually increase the nearer you book to departure date, and are more expensive at weekends than mid-week. Book online to get the best deals. Don't assume that 'no-frills' airlines are invariably cheaper.

» Exceptionally low fares imply some degree of inconvenience in terms of flight times, baggage allowances or airport location. Check whether prices quoted include departure tax, fuel surcharges and other charges, and what penalties are involved if you change your booking.

» Check newspaper advertisements and specialist agencies for possible bargains.

AIRLINE CONTACTS

Aer Arann	0818 210 210 (Ireland)	www.aerarann.ie
Aer Lingus	0818 365 000 (Ireland)	www.aerlingus.com
Air France/Brit Air	0871 663 3777 (UK);	
	0820 820 820 (France)	www.airfrance.co.uk
American Airlines	1-800/223-5436 (US)	www.aa.com
Aurigny Air Services	0871 871 0717 (UK)	www.aurigny.com
British Airways	0845 450 2245 (UK)	www.ba.com
Bmibaby	0871 224 0224 (UK)	www.bmibaby.com
British Midland	0870 60 70 555 (UK)	www.flybmi.com
Continental	1 800 231 0856 (US)	www.continental.com
Delta	1 800 241 4141 (US)	www.delta.com
EasyJet	0871 244 2366 (UK)	www.easyjet.com
Flybe	0871 700 2000 (UK)	www.flybe.com
Twin Jet	08 92 70 77 37 (FR)	www.twinjet.fr
United Airlines	1 800 538 2929 (US)	www.united.com

AIRPORT CONTACTS

General airport information	www.worldairportguide.com	
Information on all French airports	www.aeroport.fr or www.french-airports.com	
PARIS		
Roissy-Charles de Gaulle	3950	www.adp.fr
Paris-Orly	3950	www.adp.fr
Beauvais Tillé	0892 682 066	www.aeroportbeauvais.com
Orlybus	3246	
Paris Métro and RER information	3246	www.ratp.fr
Air France bus to Paris	0892 350 820	www.cars-airfrance.com
NORMANDY		
Caen–Carpiquet	02 31 71 20 10	www.caen.aeroport.fr
Cherbourg–Maupertus	02 33 88 57 60	www.aeroport-cherbourg.com
Deauville–St-Gatien	02 31 65 65 65	www.deauville.aeroport.fr
Le Havre–Ste-Adresse	02 35 54 65 00	www.havre.aeroport.fr
Rouen–Boos	02 35 79 41 00	www.rouen.aeroport.fr

BY CAR

If you are taking your car from the UK to France you can either catch a ferry to a choice of ports on France's northwestern coast or take the Eurotunnel shuttle train through the Channel Tunnel. Driving to France from neighbouring countries on mainland Europe is straightforward.

FERRIES

Numerous cross-Channel ferries link France with the UK.

» It is generally cheaper to take a short crossing and drive down. Longer sea crossings are more expensive, but you save time and energy, as well as the cost of fuel and motorway tolls. From Calais, Dunkirk or Boulogne, allow 2 to 3 hours to reach Normandy.

» Look out for special offers, and good-value deals for short breaks. Expect to pay between £50 and £100 standard return for a car plus up to five passengers on a short crossing and anywhere from £150 to £350 on a longer crossing. On the short sea routes, Speed Ferries has introduced low-cost airline-style pricing, with one-way crossing from £25.

» Ferry Savers (0870 066 9612; www.ferrysavers.com) can book crossings with principal operators and has a best-price guarantee.

» Confirm sailing times before setting off. Most companies require you to check in at least 45 minutes before departure. Don't fill your fuel tank to the brim before boarding.

» Access to the car decks is restricted. Don't leave valuables in your car. Lock up with the car in gear and the handbrake on.

» In 2005 LD Lines took over the Portsmouth to Le Havre crossing from P&O, which also axed its service from Portsmouth to Cherbourg. Brittany Ferries has taken up some of the slack for Cherbourg. LD Lines (0844 576 8836; www.ldlines.co.uk) will operate a daily, no-frills service.

TAKING YOUR PET

UK visitors are allowed to take cats and dogs to France, subject to compliance with the DEFRA PETS scheme. You need the following:

» Before setting off—a DEFRA-approved pet passport (tel: 020 7238 6951; www.defra.gov.uk) or veterinary certificate showing that your pet has been microchipped, vaccinated and blood-tested for rabies antibodies (allow 7 months before travel to arrange all this).

» On returning—a pet passport or certificate showing that your pet has been treated against ticks and fox tapeworm before re-entering.

» If documentation is not in order, your pet could be refused entry to the UK and placed in quarantine at your expense.

» If you are caught smuggling an animal, you risk severe penalties.

SAILING ROUTES

All timings are approximate and may take longer in bad weather.

» Norfolkline operates from Dover to Dunkirk (journey time 2 hours).

» P&O Ferries and SeaFrance sail from Dover to Calais (70–90 minutes). Hoverspeed's catamaran cuts the time to 50 minutes.

» SpeedFerries operates a fastcraft service between Dover and Boulogne (50 minutes).

» Transmanche Ferries runs a year-round service (4 hours) between Newhaven and Dieppe.

» Brittany Ferries sails from Portsmouth to Caen (6 hours); from Poole to Cherbourg (4 hours 15 mins; Fastcraft 2 hours 15 minutes, summer only).

» Condor Ferries has seasonal sailings from Weymouth/Poole to St-Malo (4 hours 30 minutes).

» Irish Ferries sails from Cork/Rosslare to Roscoff (12 hours).

EUROTUNNEL

Eurotunnel is a shuttle train running along the Channel Tunnel.

» Drive your vehicle on to the shuttle train as directed, and you will arrive at the French terminal at Coquelles, near Calais in 35 minutes.

» Eurotunnel shuttle trains depart up to five times per hour, 24 hours a day, 365 days a year; the price is charged per vehicle (reserve ahead). LPG and CNG vehicles are not allowed for safety reasons.

» French border controls take place on the UK side.

» Eurotunnel contact details: 08705 35 35 35 (UK) www.eurotunnel.com.

ONWARD TRAVEL

» The quickest route from Calais is to take the A16 via Boulogne and Le Touquet to Abbeville, then the A28 into Normandy. To continue towards Lower Normandy, it is more straightforward to take the A29 towards Le Havre, avoiding Rouen. South of the Seine, the A13 takes you to Caen, and from here the A84 (known as the Autoroute des Estuaires) leads on to Rennes.

TRAVEL WEBSITES

Cheap Flights	www.cheapflights.co.uk
E Bookers	www.ebookers.com
Expedia	www.expedia.com
Flight Centre	www.flightcentre.com
Last Minute	www.lastminute.com
STA Travel	www.statravel.com
Trailfinders	www.trailfinders.com
Travel Cuts	www.travelcuts.com
Travelocity	www.travelocity.co.uk

FERRY CONTACT DETAILS

Brittany Ferries	0871 244 0744	www.brittany-ferries.com
Condor Ferries	01202 20716	www.condorferries.co.uk
Hoverspeed	0870 164 2114	www.hoverspeed.com
LD Lines	0844 576 8836	www.ldlines.co.uk
Norfolkline	0844 499007	www.norfolkline.com
P&O Ferries	0871 664 5645	www.poferries.com
SeaFrance	08705 711 711	www.seafrance.com
SpeedFerries	0871 222 7456	www.speedferries.com
Transmanche Ferries	0800 917 1201	www.transmancheferries.com

BY RAIL OR COACH

France is justly proud of its railway system, particularly its world-renowned TGV (high-speed) service, which cuts overland journey times to ribbons. There are excellent train links between France and its European neighbours. Thalys, for example, operates high-tech rail services connecting Paris Gare du Nord with Brussels, Amsterdam and Cologne. Going to France by long-distance bus (coach) is worth considering if you're on a tight budget, and by no means as irksome as you might imagine. The main European operator from the UK is Eurolines.

BY TRAIN
The Channel Tunnel

The Channel Tunnel has revolutionized both road and rail travel between the UK and Continental Europe. The tunnel finally opened in 1994, almost 200 years after the first designs were submitted for a permanent link between England and France. It is the longest undersea tunnel in the world, with 39km (24 miles) of its 50km (31 miles) length under the Channel.

» It emerges on the British side near Folkestone, and meets the French coast at Sangatte (about 7km/4 miles southwest of Calais).

» Two separate rail systems operate through the tunnel, Eurostar and Eurotunnel.

» Both the French and UK terminals link directly with the motorway system.

Eurostar

Eurostar is a sophisticated high-speed passenger train connecting London directly with Paris and Brussels.

» From London, up to 16 Eurostar trains per day pass through the Channel Tunnel into France. The introduction of upgraded track has cut the journey time to Paris to 2 hours 35 minutes on the fastest services.

» Some trains stop en route at Ashford International (UK), Calais–Fréthun (France) and Lille, where the line splits, one branch heading for Brussels, the other for Paris.

» Trains leaving London currently depart from the Eurostar terminal at St. Pancras international.

» You can check in automatically with certain types of tickets, otherwise check in at the desks. You must do this at least 30 minutes before your train is due to leave.

» Before you reach the departure lounge you must go through airport-style security checks and passport control (immigration procedures for your destination country are carried out at the Eurostar departure station). Once in the departure lounge there are newspaper and gift shops, cafés, lavatories, Internet points and a mail box.

» Boarding begins around 20 minutes before departure. Information screens tell you where and when to board. Each train has 18 carriages (cars) so you could face a long walk along the platform. Trolleys (carts) for luggage are available, although you need a £1 coin as a deposit. Once on board, large cases must be stored on the luggage racks at the end of each carriage, but you can put smaller bags in the racks above your seat.

» A buffet car serves drinks, snacks and light meals on board. Inform Eurostar of any special dietary requirements 48 hours before you travel. Upgrades are inexpensive, costing about £30. There are lavatories and a designated baby-changing area. The journey through the Channel Tunnel itself takes around 20 minutes; an announcement is made just before you enter it.

Onward Travel

» Calais or Lille are good starting points for non-TGV trains to north Normandy (Le Tréport or Dieppe). If Lower Normandy (Caen, Cherbourg) is your final destination, you may find it easier to enter Paris, where you will have to change stations from Gare du Nord to Gare St-Lazare (allow an hour to do this).

» If you are planning to travel to Brittany, you can leave the Eurostar at Lille and catch a high-speed TGV Atlantique Ouest connection directly to Rennes (3 hours 50 minutes) or Quimper (6 hours 50 minutes). This will save you the bother and expense of crossing Paris.

» When you arrive at Paris's Gare du Nord station you do not need to go through passport control as immigration checks have already been carried out in London. Watch out for pickpockets at the stations in Paris.

» Trains for Normandy depart from Paris's Gare St-Lazare. From Gare du Nord, take Métro Line 4 (Porte d'Orléans) and change at Réaumur-Sébastopol to Métro Line 3 (Pont de

Levallois-Bécon). Better still, take the high-speed underground express RER Line E from Magenta (Gare du Nord) one stop to the terminus Haussmann St-Lazare.

» The Paris-Rouen intercity (Corail) service takes just over an hour from St-Lazare. The trip to Cherbourg takes around 3 hours.

Rail Passes

» Rail passes for visitors intending to travel extensively by train in France or Europe are good value, but they must be bought in advance in your home country. To buy certain passes you must have been resident in Europe for at least six months, and have a valid passport with you.

» If you are staying in France for a long time, you may want to buy an annual rail pass. This entitles you to a 50 per cent discount and is available to those aged 12 to 25 (Carte 12–25), those with a child under 12 (an Enfant+ card) and the over-60s (senior card).

» If your visit is confined simply to Brittany or Normandy, consider how much use you will make of a rail pass. The railway network is relatively limited in these regions.

In the UK and Ireland

» EuroDomino and InterRail passes give unlimited travel in France for specified periods to anyone resident in the EU for more than six months (available to any age group, but cheaper for under 26s).

» Both passes are available from Rail Europe UK.

In the US and Canada

» Eurail passes allow unlimited first-class travel within 17 European countries (excluding the UK).

» The France Railpass gives four days' travel in France within a one-month period.

» France Rail 'n' Drive gives 4 days' rail travel plus 2 days' car rental.

BY LONG-DISTANCE BUS

» Eurolines buses are modern and comfortable, with plenty of leg-room, safety belts, reclining seats, air-conditioning and on-board washrooms (WCs). All services are non-smoking.

» Eurolines has a scheduled route from London to Ouistreham (the port of Caen) via Portsmouth using Brittany Ferries for the Channel crossing. You can make a through-booking to Caen, with the last leg on a local shuttle bus. The standard return fare is £77 including the ferry crossing. There is a day time journey (depart 11.30am arrive 10.30pm) and an overnight journey (depart 7.30pm and arrive 7.30am).

» An alternative is to take the Eurolines service to Paris and take a Ze Bus hop-on, hop off minibus from there to Normandy (www.ze-bus. com). A booking fee of £3 is charged on all fares (check whether it is included in any price quoted).

» Through-tickets are easy to arrange from any National Express destination in the UK. A simple add-on fare of £15 (single or return) is charged for any connecting service to London.

» Check in at least one hour before the departure time; the Eurolines check-in desk is located near departure gate 19 at London's Victoria Coach Station.

» Luggage space is limited; you are allowed two suitcases per person plus hand luggage. Excess baggage cannot be carried.

» Eurolines buses arrive and depart from the city centre; you don't have to arrange transfers.

» Eurolines Contact Details 0071 781 8177 (UK) www. nationalexpress.com/eurolines

TIPS

» You can book Eurostar tickets through Rail Europe. In central London, the Rail Europe Travel Centre shares premises with the French tourist office (Maison de la France, ▷ 193). Telephone bookings can be made every day including Sundays and Bank Holidays (Mon–Fri 8am–9pm, Sat 9am–6pm, Sun/hols 10am–5pm). Online reservations are generally cheaper, and include no booking fees.

» Eurostar Plus fares are a package deal including Eurostar and one journey within France. You can break your journey for 24 hours en route.

» You'll pay less for your Eurostar ticket if you reserve it in advance. It is highly recommended that you do this, since non-booked seats are limited. The train is split into Premium, First and Standard class. Premium and First class give you a meal, extra leg-room, a reclining seat and free newspapers. Certain tickets also allow admission to business lounges at both ends of the journey.

» Remember that you need your passport to travel between Britain and France (Visas ▷ 184).

» The official luggage allowance is two suitcases and one piece of hand luggage. Luggage must be clearly labelled with your name and seat number.

» Trolleys (carts) are available on the platforms in London and at Gare du Nord, but you need a £1 or €1 coin (refundable). If you have a heavy case a trolley (cart) is a good idea as the walk along the platform can be long if your carriage (car) happens to be the last of 18.

RAIL CONTACT DETAILS		
Eurostar	08705 186 186 (UK)	www.eurostar.com
Rail Europe		
(UK) 1 Regent Street, London SW1	0844 848 4064	www.raileurope.co.uk
		www.sncf.com
Rail Europe (US)		
226 Westchester Avenue,		
White Plains, NY 10064	1 877 257 2887	www.eurail.com
Thalys	02 548 06 00 (France)	www.thalys.com
Lost luggage (Waterloo, UK)	0207 401 7861	
(Gare du Nord, Paris)	01 55 31 58 40	

DRIVING IN NORTHWEST FRANCE

Driving is the best way to tour rural areas of Normandy. It is less enjoyable in larger cities such as Caen or Rouen, where the traffic is heavy, the one-way systems confusing and parking sometimes difficult and expensive. Coastal resorts can also present driving problems in high season. The roads in France are always busy at the beginning of the summer school holidays (mid-July), and when the holidays end at the beginning of September (la grande rentrée).

BRINGING YOUR OWN CAR

Legal Requirements

» Private vehicles registered in another country can be taken into France for up to six months without customs formalities.

» You must always carry: a passport or national ID card, a full, valid national driver's licence (even if you have an International Driving Permit), a certificate of motor insurance, and the vehicle's registration document.

» Check your motor insurance is valid for driving in France, and against damage in transit, for example on the train or ferry. Third-party motor insurance is the minimum requirement in France but fully comprehensive cover is strongly advised.

» Display an international sticker or distinguishing sign plate as near as possible to the national registration plate at the rear of your car. If you don't, you risk an on-the-spot fine. Registration plates displaying the Euro-symbol of an EU country mean displaying a sticker is unnecessary.

» To avoid dazzling oncoming drivers, adjust the headlights of left-hand-drive vehicles. On older cars, use simple headlamp beam converters that stick onto the glass. But don't use these on cars with halogen headlamps. If your vehicle has Xenon or High Intensity Discharge (HID) headlamps, your dealer may need to make the adjustment.

Breakdown Cover

If you are taking your own car, make sure you have adequate breakdown cover for your trip to France. For information on AA breakdown cover, call 0800 085 2721 or visit www.theAA.com.

Renting a Car

» Renting a car in France can be expensive due to high taxes. Arranging a fly-drive package is generally a less expensive option. SNCF, the national railway firm, has inclusive train and car-rental deals from mainline stations.

» To rent a car in France you must be at least 20 years old and have held a full driver's licence for at least a year. However, some companies either do not rent to, or else add a surcharge for, drivers under the age of 25. The maximum age limit varies, but the average is 70.

» Your rental agreement should include the following: unlimited mileage, insurance cover, theft protection, 24-hour emergency roadside assistance, a replacement vehicle if the one you have rented becomes unusable.

» Some agencies may charge extra above a certain mileage.

» Most international rental companies will let you return your car to other French cities, and even other countries, but there may be an extra charge. Always agree the drop-off point first.

» Make sure you have adequate insurance and that you are aware of what you are covered for in the event of an accident.

» Low-cost operators may have a very high excess charge for damage.

» Most companies supply vehicles with breakdown cover.

» If your car breaks down on an autoroute, look for emergency telephones on the roadside.

GENERAL DRIVING

Roads

» The autoroute is the French counterpart of the British motorway and is marked by an 'A' on maps and road signs. Sections around cities or ports may be free of charge, but tolls are levied elsewhere (autoroutes à péage). Always have cash available as foreign credit cards may not be accepted. For information on autoroute conditions throughout France call: 0800 10020 (www.bison-fute.gouv.fr) or look at www.autoroutes.fr.

» Other roads in Brittany and Normandy may be almost as fast as motorways. The next level in France's road hierarchy is occupied by routes nationales (code-marked N). The fastest of these key routes are dual carriageways called voies express, notably the N13. The next grade of road is the route départementale (D), often surprisingly wide and fast. Minor rural lanes are labelled C roads.

» Beware of traffic-calming measures in built-up areas.

The Law

» In France you drive on the right (serrez à droite).

» The legal age to drive is 18.

» In built-up areas vehicles should give way to traffic from the right (Priorité à droite), unless signs advise otherwise. At roundabouts (traffic circles) with signs saying Cédez le passage or Vous n'avez pas la priorité, traffic already on the roundabout has priority. On roundabouts without signs, traffic entering has priority. A priority road can also be shown by a white diamond-shaped sign with a yellow diamond within it. A black line through the diamond indicates the end of priority. A red-bordered triangle with a black cross on a white background, with the words passage protégé, also shows priority.

» Holders of EU driver's licences who exceed the speed limit by more than 25kph (16mph) may have their licences confiscated on the spot.

» You must wear a seatbelt. Children under 10 must travel in the back, with a booster seat, except babies under nine months with a rear-facing front seat.

» Do not overtake where there is a solid single central line on the road.

» There are harsh penalties if the level of alcohol in the blood is 0.05 per cent or more.

» Always stop completely at STOP signs, or you may be fined.

Road Signs

» Road signs are split into three categories. Triangular signs with a red border are warnings, circular signs are mandatory (such as speed limits or No Entry); square signs display text information.

» Common signs include: *déviation* (diversion), *sortie* (exit), *gravillons* (loose chippings), *chaussée déformée* (uneven road and temporary surface) and *nids de poules* (potholes).

» Study the French highway code on www.legifrance.gouv.fr.

» For more information on road signs: www.permisenligne.com.

Equipment

» Carry a red warning triangle in case you break down and a reflective jacket in the front of the car. Don't rely simply on hazard warning lights.

» Keep a spare-bulb kit, as it is illegal to drive with faulty lights.

Fuel

» Fuel *(essence)* comes as unleaded (95 and 98 octane), lead replacement petrol (LRP or *supercarburant*), diesel *(gasoil* or *gazole)* and LPG.

» Many filling stations close on Sunday and at 6pm the rest of the week. Some automatic pumps may not accept foreign credit cards.

» Prices are highest at filling stations on autoroutes, and lowest at large chain supermarkets.

» Filling stations can be far apart in rural areas.

Parking

» Authorized parking spaces are indicated by road markings (white dotted lines). Blue markings, or those marked *Payant*, indicate a charge is due. Watch out for any signs indicating parking restrictions.

» Charges usually apply from about 9 to 6.30, Monday to Saturday. There may be a free period at lunchtime (12.30–2). Sundays and holidays are often free, but check.

» To pay for parking, buy a timed ticket from a meter *(horodateur)* at the side of the road and display it in your car. Some towns operate on an honesty system and allow you some free time, but you must display a 'clock' showing when you arrived. You can get one in local shops or *tabacs*—or ask in the tourist office.

Car Breakdown

» If your car breaks down on an autoroute, look for an emergency telephone along the roadside.

» If you break down on the Paris *Périphérique* or an *autoroute*, you must call the police or the area's official breakdown service.

SPEED LIMITS	
Urban roads	50kph (31mph)
Outside built-up areas	90kph (56mph)
	80kph (49mph) in wet weather
Dual carriageways (divided highways), and non-toll motorways	110kph (68mph) 100kph (62mph) in wet weather
Toll motorways (autoroutes)	130kph (80mph) 110kph (68mph) in wet weather
Visiting drivers who have held a licence for less than two years are not allowed to exceed the wet-weather limits, even in good weather	

Road Conditions

» To find out about traffic conditions, for example on the congested coastal routes in high season, visit www.bison-fute.equipement.gouv.fr (in French only). Queues can build up, particularly at weekends or towards the end of the day when people leave the beaches.

» For weather information before travelling visit www.meteo.fr.

» For road conditions on autoroutes and local roads call and local roads, call 0800 100 200.

» Autoroute FM provides useful traffic bulletins on the radio.

CAR RENTAL COMPANIES		
COMPANY	TELEPHONE NUMBER	WEBSITE
Avis	0820 050 505	www.avis.com
Budget	0825 003564	www.budget.com
Europcar	0825 352 352	www.europcar.com
Hertz	01 41 91 95 25	www.hertz.com
Sixt	0820 007 498	www.sixt.com

ROAD SIGNS	
Allumez vos phares	Switch on your lights
Cédez le passage	Give way
Chantier	Road works
Péage	Toll
Priorité à droite/gauche	Priority to the right/left
Rappel	Reminder (continue with the previous instruction)
Route barrée	Road closed
Sens interdit	No entry
Sens unique	One way
Serrez à droite/gauche	Keep to the right/left
Stationnement interdit	No parking
Travaux	Roadworks

OTHER WAYS TO GET AROUND

Driving may be the most convenient way to tour Normandy, but if you are without a car there are other reliable ways to see at least the region's larger towns. Even if you have a car, you may sometimes wish to leave it at home and make a trip by train, bus or boat.

TRAINS

In general, France has excellent trains—fast, comfortable and usually punctual. France's state railway, the Société Nationale des Chemins de Fer (SNCF), runs the services. These include *Grandes Lignes* (mainline routes) such as the ultra-modern, high-speed TGV *(Train à Grande Vitesse)* which can operate at speeds of up to 320kph/200mph, and Corail (fast intercity trains). TER trains *(Trains Express Régionaux)* operate on regional journeys. That said, the rail network in Normandy is not extensive, and while you can reach main towns easily by train, smaller places are served infrequently, if at all.

Tickets

» Most trains have first- and second-class carriages.
» Fares are split into blue (normal) and red (peak). Reduced-rate fares are generally available for normal travel on mainline routes, excluding TGV and *couchette* services.
» Ticket prices vary according to the level of comfort and departure time. First-class fares are roughly 50 per cent more expensive than second class.
» You can buy tickets in stations, at SNCF offices or *boutiques*, which you'll find in major cities like Rouen, and through some travel agents. Tickets for TGV trains must be reserved. You can do this up to a few minutes before departure, but in peak season book in advance. *Couchettes* must be booked at least 75 minutes before the train leaves its first station.
» Stamp your ticket *(composter)* in the orange machines on the platforms before you start your journey. You risk a fine if you forget to do this.
» Four rail cards are available, entitling the holder to fares discounted by between 25 per cent and 60 per cent:
Carte Enfant for children
Carte 12–25 for those under 26
Carte Senior for older people
Carte Escapades for those who intend to travel often by train.
» SNCF also offers a range of promotional tickets depending on where and when you are going, and availability. Train tickets are generally cheaper when bought online rather than over the counter and when bought two weeks to three months prior to departure.
» Some discounted tickets require you to spend a Saturday night at your destination.
» Ticket machines accept notes, coins and credit cards. They can also be used to collect tickets you have ordered on the Internet, by telephone or Minitel.
» In France it may be difficult to change bookings made abroad.

Catering Service

» Catering facilities—ranging from sandwiches and salads to hot meals—are available on most TGV and mainline services, but can be quite expensive.
» A benefit of first-class travel is that you can have food served at your seat on most TGV trains. You'll need to reserve in advance.
» You can order meals when you buy your train ticket. Ticket machines dispense vouchers.
» Hot and cold drinks, sandwiches and snacks are served on most trains.

Station Assistance

» Larger stations will have an information kiosk.
» If you need assistance or a porter, look for a member of the station staff, identifiable by their red waistcoats.
» You need a €1 coin deposit to use the luggage trolleys (carts).

» Some stations have a left-luggage office or coin-operated lockers. Electronic locks issue a printed ticket with a code number, which you'll need to keep. Don't store valuables in lockers.

Understanding Railway Timetables

» You can pick up free timetables *(horaires)* at stations, at tourist offices, or at SNCF offices.
» SNCF timetables are published twice a year.
» There are two timetables: one for the *Grandes Lignes*, covering high-speed TGV and other mainline services, and another for the regional TER trains.
» On *Grandes Lignes* timetables, two rows of boxed numbers at the top refer to the *numéro de train* (train number) and to the *notes à consulter* (footnotes). In TER timetables, the train number is not listed.
» Footnotes explain when a particular train runs *(circule)*. *Tous les jours* means it runs every day; *sauf dimanche et fêtes* means it doesn't run on Sundays and holidays. *Jusqu'au*, followed by a date, indicates the service runs only up until that date.

Timetable, Fare and Other Information

» Timetable, fare and service information is available from SNCF train stations and travel agencies, by telephone (tel 08 92 30 83 08 or at www.voyages-sncf.com).
» The relevant TGV brochure for northwestern France is Atlantique Ouest.
» *Train + Auto*, *Train + Vélo* and *Train + Hotel* schemes include car rental, bicycle transfer or accommodation bookings respectively in the price of your ticket. Ask for leaflets outlining these package deals.
» A booklet called *Le Guide du Voyageur* gives you the A–Z (in French) of all you need to know on French railway travel (available at rail agents, tourist offices, station booking offices).

BUSES

» Buses in Normandy cover a much wider network of destinations than the trains, but most individual routes are quite short. Long-distance bus travel is not very widespread in France; most people use the train for longer journeys. Buses are slightly less expensive than trains, and journey times are sometimes just as quick, but in rural parts of Normandy services may be infrequent, erratic or very seasonal.

» Buses are operated by a confusing number of different companies, some of which act as umbrella co-ordinators in certain areas. Since franchises may be up for renewal at any time it is not unusual for a new company to take over a route and sometimes change route numbers. Ask tourist offices for information, and you will be showered with little leaflets outlining separate routes.

» Bus or coach stations (gares routières) are often located close to railway stations, and some attempt is made to co-ordinate train and bus services. Smaller towns without train stations are often linked by bus to the nearest railway station. These buses may be operated by Keolis, a partner of SNCF as a replacement for uneconomic rail services. Rail passes are valid on most SNCF buses, but check before you travel. For information on buses, telephone 01 71 18 00 00, or look at www.keolis.com.

» Bus transport within cities is usually excellent and cheap, whereas rural areas are less well served. Many routes operate for schoolchildren or commuters, with long gaps during the day or complete breaks in holidays. But look out for market-day buses.

» You can generally buy tickets for short distances on board, but for longer journeys, buy tickets in advance at the bus station to reserve a seat.

» Few bus stations have a designated left-luggage office. Some have information desks that can double as luggage rooms.

TAXIS

» Taking a taxi is not the most cost-effective way of getting about but it may be the only convenient option.

» The fare consists of an initial pick-up charge plus a charge per kilometre, (0.6 mile), and any extra charges for luggage and journeys during the evening or on Sundays. All taxis use a meter (compteur).

» The best way to find a taxi is to head to a taxi stand, marked by a blue Taxis sign (often near railway stations, ferry terminals or main squares). If you phone for a taxi the meter may start running as soon as the taxi sets off to collect you.

» Taxis taken from expensive hotels often charge more.

» Smoking is not allowed in some taxis—look for the sign.

» Always check the meter is reset before you set off.

» It is best to have cash available for the fare. Tip around 10 per cent.

» For a receipt, ask for un reçu.

BOATS

Normandy's offshore excursions are mostly limited to the Channel Islands and the Îles Chausey, accessible from Granville and one or two smaller ports on the Cherbourg peninsula.

» Compagnie Corsaire (08 25 13 81 10; www.compagniecorsaire.com): excursions to Granville and Îles Chausey.

» Manche Iles Express (02 33 61 08 88, www.manche-iles-express.com): Trips to Jersey, Guernsey, Aurigny and Sark.

BY BICYCLE

France is an attractive destination for cyclists, and nowhere more so than Normandy and Brittany, with plenty of glorious countryside, not too many mountains, and good facilities. Tourist offices supply maps and touring guides for cyclists, and there are lots of places to rent or repair a bike. Bicycles can be taken on most trains, often free of charge (check the SNCF website). There are high rates of theft, so check insurance cover.

GETTING AROUND IN NORMANDY'S CITIES

Even Normandy's largest cities are modest in size compared with, say, Paris or Lyon, but they can still be confusing and harassing for motorists. However, most have excellent bus and train links to other bases in the region, along with exemplary networks of internal public transport. The areas most visitors want to see are usually compact, and manageable on foot. In smaller cities, visit the Gare Routière bus depot near the train station to check city bus routes, or look for local timetables at the main railway station or tourist office.

CAEN

Caen has had an integrated public transport system since the mid-19th century, with horse-drawn bus routes plying for trade in 1860. An electric tramway was introduced in 1901, and the network expanded until it was destroyed by bombing in 1944. A post-war bus network was introduced and developed with video screens installed in modern buses in the 1980s. The 21st century saw the Twisto transport network extending to 24 communes between Caen and the coast and the inauguration of the next-generation Caen Tramway in 2002. Tickets are interchangeable between buses and trams, should be validated on boarding and are valid for an hour's travel. One-way single tickets and day passes may be purchased aboard buses. Otherwise buy tickets from machines at stations or the two Twisto outlets.

Trams

Caen is proud of its tramway. Two routes, running north–south (Line A: Caen Campus 2–Ifs Jean Villar) and east–west (Line B: Herouville St Clair–Caen Grâce de Dieu), each have a departure every 7 minutes. In the key central area around the main sites the lines run in tandem so tourists can expect to wait no longer than three and a half minutes for a tram. The tramway runs from 5.30–0.30 Mon–Sat, 9–midnight on Sundays. A single ticket costs €1.27 and a 10-trip ticket costs €10.10. Tourists should opt for the day pass at €3.35 per person, or €4.40 for a family.

Buses

The Twisto bus network is vast. Most visitors will find four routes particularly useful. Lines 1, 2 and 3 cover the city, along with the two tram routes. Bus number 2 goes out to the Mémorial Museum. Line 62 takes you to the beaches at the seaside resorts of Lion-sur-Mer and Hermanville-sur-Mer.

Information

The two Twisto shops sell tickets and offer free route maps (also available from the tourist office).
» Boutique Château
15, rue de Geôle
» Boutique Théâtre
Boulevard Maréchal Leclerc
Open Mon–Fri 9–12.30, 1.30–5
Tel 02 31 15 55 55, www.twisto.fr.

Taxis

Taxis may be found at the city's two principal ranks at the main station and place de la République. Tel 02 31 52 17 89 (Abbeilles Taxis).

Bicycles

From 2005, the tourist office hires bikes at €10 for half a day and €15 for a full day.

LE HAVRE

The biggest city and seaport in the region is served by a network of buses running from 6am until as late as midnight on some key routes.

Since nightlife may be located some distance from city-centre hotels, remember that taxis may be the only option in the small hours.

Buses

Bus Océane run services in the city centre, out to the modern port district and beyond to Harfleur and the suburbs. Tickets are available from the tourist office and newspaper and tobacco kiosks. However the two types of ticket most useful to tourists may be bought from the bus driver when you board. As soon as you step on the bus, you should validate your ticket in the machine by the door. A simple return ticket costs €1.50 and a Ticket Ville, day pass, costs €3.30 and is valid on all journeys until midnight on the day of purchase. Information: 02 35 22 35 00; www.bus-oceane.com.

Taxis

You'll find 27 taxi ranks at various convenient points around the city, including the station and seafront; call 02 35 25 81 81 (Radio Taxi). A taxi service for disabled visitors is available on 02 35 21 52 51.

Bicycles

Bike hire in Le Havre is excellent value: two hours for €2, a half day for €3 and a full day for €5. Hire bikes from the Hôtel de Ville (02 35 22 35 00) Mon–Sat 10.30–7.30 year round. In summer you may also hire cycles from the tourist office's outlet at the beach (02 35 43 18 59), open daily May–Oct 10–6.

ROUEN

Rouen sprawls along the Seine and spills over into a network of suburbs. The main areas of interest to visitors however can be found within a 20-minute radius of the cathedral. Once in the city centre, everywhere may be visited on foot, and the inevitable tourist 'mini-train' works its way around the principal sites. The local Métro-Bus is run by the public transport network ICAR (Transports en Commun de l'Agglomeration de

Rouen) with a principal metro line that runs north–south though the centre and buses to the rest of the city. Tickets may be used on both buses and metros. Each ticket is valid for one hour's travel, so you may change from bus to metro to complete a journey. Buy your ticket before boarding. Tickets are sold at the tourist office, tobacconists and from machines at metro stations.

Métro

Officially, Rouen has two metro lines. In fact it is a forked route with one northern terminus at Boulingrin and two southern termini, across the Seine, Georges Braques and Technopole. Most visitors will need just three stations, served by both 'lines': Théâtre des Arts, Palais de Justice and the Gare Rue Verte (for the mainline SNCF railway station).

All stations are to be found along the rue Jeanne d'Arc, between the Pont Jeanne d'Arc and the station. Leading artists have been invited to give each station its individual style. At Palais de Justice, train arrival indicators form part of Philippe Kauffmann's artwork L'Horloge du Temps, which plays with the concept of time itself. Rouen-born Jean-Pierre Bourquin is amongst several artists whose works are displayed at Théâtre des Arts.

The metro runs from 5am to 11pm. Tickets cost €1.40 for a single journey, a Carte à 10 Voyages, 10-trip pass is €10.70. Visitors planning to explore further afield than the centre might consider buying a special pass. The Carte Découverte

one day is €3.80, 2 days €5.50 and 3 days €7.20

Buses

Smart, blue, energy-efficient buses in varying shapes and sizes serve the wider city and suburban area. Hop on and off, remembering to frank your ticket (prices as for the metro above) for each journey. As well as its conventional buses, Rouen is proud of the TEOR (Transport Est-Ouest Rouennais), a concept midway between a bus and a tram without tramlines. The TEOR is an environmentally friendly vehicle which stops at 41 special platforms in the streets on three east–west routes across the city.

For more information call 02 35 52 52 52, or visit the website www.tcar.fr.

Taxis

Taxi ranks can be found at the railway station and on rue Général Leclerc. Or telephone 02 35 88 50 50.

Bicycles

Bike hire is not offered from Rouen's tourist office and there is nowhere to hire a bicycle in the city, but if you have not arranged cycles through SNCF, you can rent a bicycle for €15 per day from:
Etretat Aventure
Route Gonneville
Le Chateau du Bois
76790 Les Loges (5km/3 miles from Etretat)
Tel 02 35 29 84 45
www.etretat-aventure.fr

VISITORS WITH A DISABILITY

Getting around France is gradually becoming easier, thanks to the improved design of buses and trains. Any recently constructed public building, including airports and stations, will have facilities for people with disabilities and mobility problems. But you'll still find challenges in Normandy, especially in towns with cobbled streets.

Before you travel, check what facilities are available, for example, at your arrival airport (www.aeroport.fr) and your hotel; many older buildings do not have an elevator. If you have mobility problems and may require help during a flight, tell your airline when you reserve your ticket. You may also find useful information on airline websites. The easiest way for visitors with disabilities to reach France from Britain is by using Eurotunnel, where you remain in a vehicle for the whole journey. If you are taking a ferry, make sure you arrive early so that you can have help with boarding.

AIRPORTS
Caen and Le Havre airports have facilities for disabled travellers, including adapted WCs. In Paris, both Roissy–Charles de Gaulle and Orly airports are equipped for people with reduced mobility. Shuttle buses between terminals have ramps for wheelchairs, as well as voice

announcements for people with visual impairments. The terminals have adapted lavatories, low-level telephones and reserved parking spaces. For details ask for the publication *Guides des Aeroports Français pour les Passagers à Mobilité Réduite* (Aeroguide Editions, tel 0146 559 343). It costs €18 and it has information about accessibility in French airports. You can also look at www.aeroguide.fr. The organization Handicap has information about companies offering special transport services for disabled passengers—see www.tourisme.handicap.fr (in French). The Orlyval train has wheelchair access.
» For information on facilities at airports in Normandy, contact Aeroguides (tel 01 46 55 93 43; www.aeroguide.fr).

TRAINS
Eurostar trains and terminals are wheelchair-friendly and wheelchair-users can also benefit from discounted tickets. France's long-distance trains are equipped for people with reduced mobility. On TGV and Corail trains, spaces for wheelchair-users are reserved in first class, although only a second-class fare is payable. Reserve at least 24 hours in advance. There are also adapted lavatories. Most large stations have elevators or ramps. If you need assistance, request it when you reserve your ticket. Facilities on regional trains tend to be more varied so check before you travel. For more information, call 08 90 64 06 50, look up SNCF's website (www.accesibilite.sncf.com) or see the pamphlet *Guide du Voyageur Handicapé*.

FURTHER INFORMATION
See the French tourist office website, www.franceguide.com for information on facilities for disabled visitors. The French volume of the *Smooth Ride Guides* series is

Association des Paralysés de France
Tel 01 53 80 92 97 (Paris)
www.apf.asso.fr
This French organization for the disabled is represented in each *département*. See the website for more information on local facilities.

Holiday Care Service
Tel 08451 249 971 (UK)
www.holidaycare.org.uk
Travel and holiday information for people with disabilities.

Mobile en Ville
www.mobile-en-ville.asso.fr
A website packed with information on disability access and related issues.

Mobility International USA
www.miusa.org
Promotes international travel and exchange schemes for people with disabilities.

RADAR (Royal Association for Disability and Rehabilitation)
Tel 020 7250 3222
www.radar.org.uk
Literature on travelling with disabilities.

Society for Accessible Travel and Hospitality (SATH)
Tel 212 447 7284 (from US)
www.sath.org
A US-based organization offering advice for visitors with disabilities and promoting awareness of their travel requirements.

DLM
Tel 03 20 12 13 33
www.dlm.fr
Rents adapted vehicles.

available (free) in English from the Maison de la France (▷ 193). This handbook has been compiled by disability organizations and tourist boards throughout France. Venues, including airports, ferries, railways, museums and accommodation, are rated for their user-friendliness.

REGIONS

This chapter is divided into five regions of Normandy (▷ 9). Places of interest are listed alphabetically in each region.

LA MANCHE

You're never more than 50km (30 miles) from the sea in Normandy's westernmost *département* which protrudes into the English Channel (Manche in French) as the rugged Presqu'ile Cotentin peninsula. And it is wind and tide that here determines geography and history. Nowhere is this more evident than in the extraordinary tidal island of Mont-St-Michel, legendary place of pilgrimage and one of the most visited sights of France, which rises like a vision out of a vast shallow bay. Equally dramatic, but in different way, are the cliffs, promontories and bays of Cap de la Hague at the seaward tip of Cotentin. Nearby, Cherbourg, meanwhile, is the epitome of the maritime tradition of La Manche. This port built to shelter transatlantic liners, warships and cross-Channel ferries, is now home to the quayside City of the Sea, which includes the world's biggest visitable submarine. Other coastal towns—Barfleur, Granville and St-Vaast-la-Hougue—combine the roles of working fishing port and low-key holiday resort. The menus of their harbourside restaurants are inevitably dominated by fresh fish and seafood.

Inland, the Manche gets fewer visitors and while there may be only a sprinkling of sights they are still worth seeking out. The prefecture town of St-Lô was razed during World War II and had to be rebuilt but it does have a good museum explaining the traditional farming methods of Normandy. Coutances is arranged around a splendid Norman Gothic cathedral and Villedieu-les-Poêles has one of the world's last surviving bell foundries. Of several abbeys that dot the countryside the most atmospheric, after Mont-St-Michel is Hambye.

If you want to escape from mainland Normandy altogether you can always take a day trip to an island: Chaussey (off Granville), Tatihou (off St-Vaast-la-Hougue) or Jersey in the Channel Islands, or Iles-Normandes as they are known locally.

ABBAYE DE CERISY-LA-FORÊT

The well-maintained remains of a 12th-century Benedictine abbey stand at the edge of the Cerisy woods on a site that has been home to monks since the sixth century AD. The limestone abbey church was scaled down from its original grandeur in 1812, when it proved too large to serve as a parish church. The building nonetheless retains its original carved choir stalls as well as splendid vaulting. Fissures in the transept have led to a schedule of reinforcement—similar projects date back to the 15th century. Visit the museum to see tiles and statuary from the original abbey. Between Easter and the end of October the buildings are illuminated at nightfall to beautiful effect.

✚ 213 F5 ✉ 50680 Cerisy-la-Forêt
☎ 002 33 57 34 63 ⏰ Daily 9–6.30. Guided tours: Easter–end Sep daily 10.30–12.30, 2.30–6.30; Oct Sat, Sun, public holidays 10.30–12, 2.30–6 🚌 17km (10.5 miles) from St-Lô via the D6, D92 and D34

ABBAYE DE HAMBYE

Second only to Mont-St-Michel (▷ 48–51), the Benedictine Abbey of Hambye, in the woods of the Sienne valley, is among Normandy's most complete monastic buildings. Despite the air of desolation and the crows nesting in the ruined church, the surrounding buildings are in good condition. The restoration of the sacristy, chapter house, parlour, scriptorium, kitchens and stables is now complete. The site offers a glimpse into the days of the abbey's founding in 1145 by Guillaume Paysnel, without the detraction of the hordes of visitors. Discover Norman tapestries, frescoes, religious objects and paintings of the abbey from centuries past. But the most powerful image is of the ruined abbey church itself, its flying buttresses emerging from the woods and its tower poised against the sky.

✚ 218 E6 ✉ 50450 Hambye ☎ 02 33 61 76 92 ⏰ Apr–end Oct daily 10–12, 2–6 💰 Adult €4.20, child (7–15) €1.75 🚌 From Villedieu-les-Poêles, take the D9 for 4.5km (3

miles), turn right onto the D51 for 9km (5.5 miles), then right again onto the D13

ABBAYE DE LA LUCERNE

www.abbaye-lucerne.fr

The ruined 12th-century Abbey of Lucerne, set on the sandy soil of the Cotentin peninsula, has been undergoing restoration since 1959. On Sunday mornings, however, the stones echo to the sound of a traditional Mass, and on summer evenings music fills the air during concert season.

Lucerne was founded by William the Conqueror's nephew, Hasculfe de Subligny, in 1164, and in the intervening centuries the surrounding countryside has hardly changed. Highlights still to be seen include a Romanesque doorway and an 18th-century organ. There are traces of a 19th-century aqueduct, constructed to serve a watermill, along with the abbot's residence, a tithe barn and a section of the original cloisters. A Romanesque lavatorium, a washing area with four small arches, is next to the entrance to the former refectory. Best of all is the traditional Norman *colombier* (dovecote), near the porter's lodge, a striking round tower with entrances for 1,500 birds.

✚ 218 D7 ✉ 50320 La Lucerne d'Outremer ☎ 02 33 48 83 56 ⏰ Apr–end Sep daily 10–12, 2–6.30; Oct–end Mar Wed–Mon 10–12, 2–6.30. Closed Jan to mid-Feb 💰 Adult €4–€5, youth (14–21) €3, child (7–14) €2 🚌 From La Haye-Pesnel, take the D309 to La Lucerne d'Outremer, and then turn left onto the D35 to reach the abbey

Opposite *The ruins of the Abbaye de la Lucerne at La Haye-Pesnel are under restoration*
Below *The Benedictine Abbaye de Cerisy-la-Forêt*

AVRANCHES

www.ville-avranches.fr

This city of art and history is linked with Mont-St-Michel (▷ 48–51), a view of which can be had from the gardens at the top of the town. The town looks after the abbey's library of parchment manuscripts (some dating back to the eighth century AD) and 14,000 ancient books, stored at the Bibliothèque du Fonds Ancien in the town hall (tel 02 33 89 29 50; Jul, Aug daily 10–6; Jun, Sep daily 10–12, 2–6).

Originally settled by the Gauls and Romans, it became a key citadel under the Normans. The main remnant of the Norman castle is the Tour St-Louis, a tower built in the 13th century and garlanded with cannonballs from a 16th-century siege. Follow traces of the ramparts from the Jardins du Donjon for views across the Vallée de la Sée and the Baie du Mont-St-Michel.

Another restored site is the Palais Episcopal, a testament to the power of the bishops who controlled the city. The most famous was St. Aubert, who founded Mont-St-Michel (▷ 20).

Narrow cobbled streets have timbered house fronts from the 16th century. The Monument Patton commemorates the town's liberation on 31 July 1944.

✚ 218 E8 ℹ️ 2 rue du Général de Gaulle, 50300 Avranches ☎ 02 33 58 00 22 🕐 Jul, Aug daily 9–12, 2–7; mid-Jun to end Jun, 1–15 Sep Mon–Sat 9–12, 2–7; mid-Sep to mid-Jun Mon–Fri 9–12, 2–6, Sat 10–12, 2–5 �")" Avranches

BARNEVILLE CARTERET

www.barneville-carteret.net

This traditional resort, on the west coast of the Cotentin peninsula, is the union of the three towns of Barneville, Barneville-Plage and Carteret, and offers two styles of holiday within a mile of coastline. Barneville itself is the simpler option, a quiet residential town dominated by an austere 11th-century church. Restaurants are found here rather than along the neighbouring stretch of seaside. The beach at Barneville-Plage is a basic stretch of seafront. Carteret has a livelier beachfront, with shops, bars, seafood restaurants and a port. Cap Carteret's resort, to the west, still retains its Edwardian style.

✚ 212 C4 ℹ️ 10 rue des Écoles, 50270 Barneville-Carteret ☎ 02 33 04 90 58 🕐 Mon–Sat 9–12.30, 2–6 ℹ️ Place Flandres Dunkerque, 50270 Barneville-Carteret ☎ 02 33 04 94 54 🕐 Jul, Aug daily 10–12.30, 3–7 🚌 From Cherbourg

BRICQUEBEC

www.ville-bricquebec.fr

The pleasant market town of Bricquebec would probably have remained unnoticed by the outside world but for its legacy of monastic cheese-making. Named by Vikings as Brekkubekk, Norse for 'the brook of the slopes', it is topped by the ruins of a 14th-century chateau. The main street leads up to the gatehouse of the castle, whose 11-sided keep still stands. Visitors can explore the fortifications, walls and towers, the vaulted cellars and a 13th-century crypt.

The Abbaye Notre-Dame-de-Grâce, a Trappist monastery (tel 02 33 87 56 12; services daily 8.15, 2.15, 6, 8), was founded in 1824 by Dom Augustin Onfroy and is the town's main claim to fame. The second abbot, Dom Germain, decreed that the monks' self-sufficiency would best be guaranteed by cheese production, as in other Trappist communities such as Port Salut and Mont des Cats. The monks signed an agreement with the Maison de la Providence society to sell their cheese across France. The Providence brand became nationally popular and by World War II the monks were collecting milk from around 230 Cotentin farmers. Competition from industrial factories resulted in the sale of the brand in 1961 to a commercial operation. The holy cheese is sold in the abbey shop.

✚ 212 D4 ℹ️ Place Ste-Anne, 50260 Bricquebec ☎ 02 33 52 21 65 🕐 Mid-May to mid-Oct daily 9–12, 1.30–6.30; mid-Oct to mid-May daily 9–12, 1.30–5.30

CAP DE LA HAGUE

www.lahague.org

This northwestern tip of the Cotentin peninsula is marked by landscaped parks and gardens, while windswept walks take you along rocky cliffs and through stone villages. The house in Gréville-Hague where painter Jean-François Millet was born in 1814 is open to visitors (tel 02 33 01 81 91; Jun–Sep daily 11–7; school holidays daily 1–6). A bust of Millet is all that remains of a statue after wartime bombings, although a new sculpture of the artist by Louis Derbré stands in the village square. The 19th-century church at Gréville displays 15th-century statuary.

The Château et Parc de Nacqueville, whose distinctive granite walls and stone roofs date from the 18th century, is listed as a national historic monument (tel 02 33 03 21 12; tours Easter–end Sep Tue, Thu–Sun 12–5) and can be found at Urville Nacqueville, 5km (3 miles) west of Cherbourg. In 1830, Hippolyte de Tocqueville commissioned a romantic English garden here. Today, colourful ornamental trees, hydrangeas, azaleas and rhododendrons, waterfalls and a lake liven up the chateau's grey façade.

✚ 212 C2 ℹ️ 45 rue Jallot, 50440 Beaumont-Hague ☎ 02 33 52 74 94 🕐 Mar–end Sep Sun–Fri 10–12, 2–5, Sat 10–12; Nov–end Feb Sun–Fri 10–12, 2–5; also office at Goury: mid-Jun to end Sep daily 10–1, 2–7; Oct to mid-Sep daily 1.30–5.30 🚌 Cherbourg (20km/12 miles)

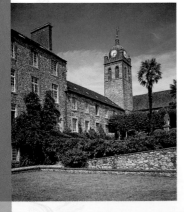

BARFLEUR

This pretty fishing port has excellent seafood and historical links with the kings of England. Barfleur is a short drive from Cherbourg, on a stretch of the eastern side of the Cotentin peninsula popularly known as the Viking coast. The town has been putting boats to sea since the days of the Vikings and in the Middle Ages it was the peninsula's principal port. A plaque at the port entrance reminds visitors that the boat that took William the Conqueror to England in 1066 was built in Barfleur's shipyards. The town's tradition of shipping English monarchs continued in 1194, when Richard the Lionheart set sail from here to be crowned king.

DANGEROUS WATERS

In 1120, a royal tragedy occurred when the *White Ship* sank offshore with 300 members of the Anglo-Norman nobility aboard. William Atheling, heir to England's King Henry I and grandson of William the Conqueror, drowned in the treacherous currents that have claimed many ships over the centuries, an incident that led to fresh warring over the English succession. In 1348, King Edward III of England burned Barfleur, and in the 15th and 16th centuries further attacks from the English and their allies destroyed the ramparts.

Today, the neat granite and slate buildings that stand around the port are modest and simple. The prettiest and oldest district is Cour Ste-Cathérine, entered through a stone arch next to the harbour. A stroll around Barfleur's unpretentious harbour and on seaside paths takes in a couple of small lighthouses, these dwarfed by the massive Gatteville-le-Phare at Pointe de Barfleur, 4km (2.5 miles) north of the town. At 75m (246ft), it is the second-tallest lighthouse in France, and the light can be seen for 56km (35 miles). A museum at the foot of the tower recounts its history and explains modern lighthouse technology (closed mid-Nov to Jan). The lighthouse has stunning coastal views. Barfleur is also home to France's first lifeboat station and there is a lifeboat museum in the harbour.

SAINTLY HEROINE

Before you leave Barfleur, visit the Bretonne quarter to pay homage to St. Marie-Madeleine Postel. Born in 1756, Julie Postel was a post-Revolution heroine who hid priests fleeing France in her schoolhouse. While she taught pupils in the kitchen, she persuaded fishermen to carry the fugitives across the Channel to England. Stained-glass windows in the local chapel depict scenes from her life.

INFORMATION

www.ville-barfleur.fr
✚ 212 E3 ℹ 2 Rond-point Guillaume le Conquérant, 50760 Barfleur ☎ 02 33 54 02 48 🕐 Jun–end Aug daily 9.30–12, 2–6.30; Sun, Bank Holidays 10–12, 2–5; Feb–end May, Sep–end Nov Mon–Sat 10–12.30, 2.30–5.30; Dec, Jan 10–12, 2–4. Closed 2 weeks at Christmas 🚌 Regular service from Cherbourg

TIPS

» Don't leave town without trying the famous local mussels, known as *blondes de Barfleur*.
» Visit on Saturday mornings to enjoy the small market.

Above *Barfleur's harbour*
Opposite *The gardens outside the Abbaye Notre-Dame-de-Grâce at Briquebec*

43

Above *The fortified keep and battlements of Château de Pirou*
Right *A row of tile-roofed beach huts on the promenade at Carolles*

CAROLLES

www.ville-carolles.fr

A low-key alternative to busier holiday resorts in Granville and Avranches, Carolles-Plage has summer bathing huts and beach bars, yet outside peak months it retains the peace and quiet of a simple coastal village. Walk from the heart of Carolles through woodland and along the Vallée du Lude to reach the seashore. The best view of the Baie de Mont-St-Michel is from Le Pignon Butor. From here you can walk along the cliffs or follow a Grand Randonnée trail into the Vallée des Peintres, which was found by artists in the 1860s, as bathers embraced the seaside.

✚ 218 D7 🛈 2 rue de la Poste, 50740 Carolles ☎ 02 33 61 92 88 🕐 Jul, Aug daily 9–12.30, 2–6; Sep–end Jun Mon–Sat 9–12.30, 2–6

CHÂTEAU DE GRATOT

The romantic ruins of a castle where a knight is said to have wooed, won and wed a fairy are being rescued from centuries of neglect and an army of weeds. Seat of the Argouges family for 500 years, the chateau is most famous for its Tour de la Fée (Fairy Tower). Legend has it that a knight came to drink at the waters of Gratot and saw a beautiful fairy, who disappeared when she caught sight of him looking at her. He returned each night and on the fifth visit saw her

again. He proposed, and she agreed to marry him on the condition that he never spoke the word 'death'. Years later, at a tournament, the knight uttered the fatal word and his wife fell from the window of the Fairy Tower, never to be seen again, although locals say you can hear her whispering the word *'mort'* (death) on stormy nights.

The octagonal Fairy Tower, with its square bedroom, spiral staircase and balustraded walkways, is among the most ambitious of the restoration projects now taking place. The castle's four towers date from the 14th and 15th centuries, while a 17th-century lodge and mansarded house have also been renovated.

✚ 218 D6 ✉ Centre d'Animation du Château de Gratot, 50200 Gratot ☎ 02 33 45 18 49 🕐 Daily 10–7 ✋ Adult €3, child (10–18) €1.50, under 10 free 🚊 Coutances (4km/2.5 miles)

CHÂTEAU DE PIROU

www.chateau-pirou.org

Normandy's oldest fortified castle gave its name to the most graceful move in ballet, the pirouette, and also provided a hero of the Norman Conquest and a Shakespearean character. During a Viking siege of the original wooden fortress, the defenders of the castle were said to have magically turned themselves into geese and flown away. For centuries, geese nested there each

spring and were fed by locals, who named the birds after the castle. The spinning and twisiting of the geese as they launched themselves into flight gave rise to the title of the dance move.

The stone fort, near Cotentin's sand dunes, dates from the 12th century. A knight from Pirou took part in the Norman Conquest of England in 1066, and was rewarded with Stoke-Pirou, an estate in Somerset. A lord of Pirou in the 15th century was English knight Jehan Falstoff, later caricatured by William Shakespeare as Sir John Falstaff, hero of the plays *King Henry IV* and *Merry Wives of Windsor*.

By the 19th century, the castle was a modest farm. However, in 1968 it was listed as an historic monument by the State and work began on restoring the building, which now stands on an island in an artificial lake. The original 12th- and 14th-century ramparts remain, protected by five fortified gates. Later additions, including a chapel, kitchens and living quarters, are also open to visitors.

Son et lumière shows with a medieval theme are held in July and August.

✚ 212 D5 ✉ 50770 Pirou ☎ 02 33 46 34 71 🕐 Jul, Aug Thu 10–12, 2–6.30; mid-Oct to end Mar daily 10–12, 2–5 ✋ Adult €5, child (7–14) €3 🍴 Pirou village and Plage (2km/1 mile) 🚊 Coutances (20min drive)

CHERBOURG

The ferry port, with a maritime history museum, leads directly to the D-Day beaches trail. Flattened by air raids and unimaginatively reconstructed after World War II, Cherbourg has never been an obvious visitor destination. King Louis XIV's architect, the Marquis de Vauban, planned a major naval base here in the 17th century, although the navy did not establish itself at the port until 1858, nor did it play an important military role until Liberation on 27 June 1944, three weeks after D-Day. Allied divers cleared the port of wrecks and mines so that Cherbourg could replace the makeshift Mulberry Harbour at Arromanches.

The town's main claim to fame since 1969 has been as an Atlantic gateway, where passengers have boarded the greatest oceangoing liners of the modern age. Funnels of the SS *France* and Cunard's *Queen Elizabeth* and *QE2* were once familiar features on the Cherbourg skyline, even if today's port mostly welcomes the more humble cross-Channel ferries.

CITÉ DE LA MER

The art deco Gare Maritime Transatlantique terminal has been reinvented as the Cité de la Mer, a celebration of man's conquest of the deep. Besides aquariums and displays on ocean exploration, the main attraction in the port is *Le Redoutable*, France's first nuclear submarine, launched here in 1967. It is the largest submarine in the world open to the public. The amazing 'undersea' trail at the Cité de la Mer brings the visitor face to face with marine life at Europe's largest aquarium.

BEYOND THE SEA

The Musée d'Ethnographie 'Emmanuel Liais' (tel 02 33 53 51 61; May–end Sep Tue–Sat 10–12, 2–6, Sun, Mon 2–6; Oct–end Apr Wed–Sun 2–6), has exhibitions on Inuit life. Or admire the works of Jean-François Millet (1814–75) at the Musée Thomas-Henry (tel 02 33 23 39 30; May–end Sep Tue–Sat 10–12, 2–6, Sun, Mon 2–6; Oct–end Apr Wed–Sun 2–6), near the port. Historians can see World War II exhibits at Fort du Roule (tel 02 33 20 14 12; May–end Sep Tue–Sat 10–12, 2–6, Sun, Mon 2–6; Oct–end Apr Wed–Sun 2–6). There are markets at place de Gaulle (Tue, Sat morning, Thu all day) and Octeville's avenue de Normandy (Sun morning).

INFORMATION

www.ot-cherbourg-cotentin.fr
🔲 212 D3 ℹ️ 2 quai Alexandre III, 50100 Cherbourg ☎ 02 33 93 52 02
🕐 Jul–Aug Mon–Sat 9–6.30, Sun 10–12.30; Sep–May Mon–Sat 9–12.30, 2–6; Jun Mon–Sat 9–12.30, 2–6.30
🚆 Cherbourg

CITÉ DE LA MER

✉️ Gare Maritime Transatlantique, 50100 Cherbourg ☎ 02 33 20 26 69
🕐 Jul–end Aug daily 9.30–7; May, Jun, Sep daily 9.30–6.30, Feb–end Apr daily 10–6 ♿ Feb–end Mar; Oct–end Dec adult €15.50, child (5–17) €15.50, under 5 free; Apr–end Sep adult €18, child (5–17) €13, under 5 free

Below *Fishermen coming home after mooring to a pontoon in the harbour at Cherbourg*

COTENTIN

www.ot-cherbourg-cotentin.fr

The unspoiled landscape of the Cotentin peninsula suggests a remote region far removed from Normandy's commercial towns and the more gentle beauty of the hinterland. Cotentin offers an authentic glimpse of French rural life, with farming and fishing very much to the fore. On the west of the peninsula, the stark rugged coastline around Cap de La Hague (▷ 42) and Nez de Jobourg is almost Breton in its craggy majesty, perfect for windswept walks and views out to the Channel Islands. In contrast, the eastern side has a lusher, more verdant landscape, where green fields and rich woodland mark the countryside around the Val de Saire stretch to the dunes of the D-Day beaches. The hedgerows of the man-made Cotentin *bocage* landscape proved an obstacle to Allied troops in 1944, and provided cover for guerrilla resistance.

Neither as glitzy or sophisticated as such popular coastal destinations as Deauville, as picturesque as the Suisse Normande region, nor as established on the tourist trail as Étretat and Honfleur, Cotentin offers a simpler glimpse of country life by the sea. The bathing may be excellent around Flamanville on the west coast, but, safety assurances aside, some holidaymakers may feel uncomfortable about swimming in the shadow of a nuclear power plant. Highlights of the region include the views from the top of Gatteville lighthouse by Barfleur (▷ 43); and La Pernelle, with a panoramic observation point overlooking the Val de Saire and a tiny *mairie* (town hall), claimed by locals to be the smallest in France.

✚ 212 D4–E4 ℹ 2 quai Alexandre III, 50100 Cherbourg ☎ 02 33 93 52 02 ◷ Jul, Aug Mon–Sat 9–6.30, Sun 10–12.30; Sep–end May 9–12.30, 2–6; Jun Mon–Sat 9–12.30, 2–6.30 🚃 Cherbourg, Valognes

COUTANCES

www.ville-coutances.fr

Hailed as a masterpiece of Norman Gothic architecture, the cathedral at Coutances is cunningly grafted onto the remains of a Romanesque church. The 13th-century construction is beautifully proportioned, with strong buttresses, elegant spires and an octagonal lantern tower. Stained-glass windows tell the story of Archbishop of Canterbury Thomas Becket (c1118–70); King Henry II of England, who was responsible for Becket's murder, did penance for his crime in Normandy.

The origin of the town lies in the third century AD, when a settlement here was dubbed Constantia, after the Roman Emperor Constantius-Chlorus (c AD250–306). The name Constantia subsequently evolved into both Coutances and Cotentin (see left). The seat of a bishop and a political centre until the French Revolution, Coutances is sleepier today than in times past. It is essentially a peaceful and well-to-do town, away from the seaside tourist trail. Among other traces of the town's glory days are three arches, all that remains of the original 14th-century aqueduct.

The Musée Quesnel-Morinière (tel 02 33 07 07 88; Jul, Aug Mon, Wed–Sun 11–6; Sep–end Jun Mon, Wed–Sat 10–12, 2–5, Sun 2–5. Closed public holidays and mornings Nov–end Mar), housed in the former Hôtel Poupinel, has a collection of local art, crafts and clothes, although these are gloriously outshone by the splendid *Lions and Dogs Fighting* by painter Peter Paul Rubens (1577–1640). The nearby Jardin des Plantes is a pleasant spot for a walk or picnic on a summer's day. If you're here in spring, catch the Jazz Sous les Pommiers festival (▷ 61).

✚ 218 D6 ℹ Place Georges Leclerc, 50200 Coutances ☎ 02 33 19 08 10 ◷ Jul, Aug Mon–Fri 9.30–6.30, Sat 10–12.30, 2–6, Sun 10–1; Sep–end Jun Mon–Fri 9.30–12.30, 2–6, Sat 10–12.30, 2–5 🚃 Coutances

GENÊTS

www.decouvertebaie.com

Dominated on misty mornings by the silhouette of Mont-St-Michel, this former fishing port shares its modest history with the monastery across the bay. Nowadays, flocks of sheep, prized for their meat, graze on the salt marshes here, except during the great seasonal tides. Yet, until the bay silted up after the 15th century and the rival town of Granville (see below) found favour, Genêts was Normandy's most prosperous port. As gateway to the Mount, Genêts sent food, wine, clothes and even building materials to the inhabitants of Mont-St-Michel. Today, visitors gather by the bridge next to the 12th-century church to take guided walks across the treacherous sands to the abbey, and the town is also home to one of the Maisons de la Baie (▷ 51). Opposite the village is the island of Tombelaine, a staging post for the escorted pilgrimage and a bird sanctuary, home to gulls and egrets. The rock was used by England's King Henry V as a fortress in his unsuccessful campaign to take over the Mount following his victory over the French at Agincourt in 1415.

➕ 218 D8 ❗ Relais de Genêts, La Maison du Guide Decouverte de la Baie du Mont-St-Michel, 1 rue Montoise, 50530 Genêts ☎ 02 33 70 83 49 🕓 Apr–end Oct daily 9.30–12.30, 1.30–7; Nov–end Mar Mon–Fri 9–12.30, 2–5.30 🚌 From Avranches

GRANVILLE

www.ville-granville.fr

This busy port and lively summer resort, on the bay of Mont-St-Michel, retains its 15th-century battlements, built by Englishman Thomas Scales. The main entrance to the upper town is still via the original drawbridge of the Grand'Porte. Climb to the Musée du Vieux Granville (tel 02 33 50 44 10; Apr–end Sep Wed–Mon 10–12, 2–6; Oct–end Mar Wed, Sat–Sun 2–6) to see local crafts and learn about the history of the fishing port. Modern art at the Musée Richard Anacréon (tel 02 33 51 02 94; Jun–end Sep

Tue–Sun 11–6; Oct–end May Tue–Sun 2–6) includes works by Pablo Picasso (1881–1973).

The Musée Christian Dior is in the fashion designer's childhood home (tel 02 33 61 48 21; late May–end Sep daily 10–6.30; ▷ 55).

➕ 218 D7 ❗ 4 cours Jonville, 50406 Granville ☎ 02 33 91 30 03 🕓 Jul, Aug Mon–Sat 9–1, 2–7, Sun, Bank Holidays 10–1, 3–6; Sep–end Jun Mon–Sat 9–12, 2–6 🚉 Granville

LA HAYE-PESNEL

Within half an hour of Mont-St-Michel, between Avranches and Granville, is La Haye-Pesnel, the perfect base for a couple of days' exploration on horseback. The pretty little market town in the *bocage* landscape of fields and hedgerows is celebrated for its flowers, which spill out onto the streets from window boxes, pots and tubs set outside the brick and stone cottages. On 1 May, La Haye-Pesnel holds its flower market, and every third August (next date 2010) the summer Triennale Fleurie festival sees flowers on every spare ledge, wall and street corner.

In the summer, artists open the doors to their workshops and galleries, and many set up stalls during the Wednesday morning market. Visit the church of Ste-Madeleine, whose bell dates back to 1793. The Ecu-Musée du Cidre (tel 02 33 61 31 51; Jul, Aug Mon–Sat 10–12, 1.30–6; Easter and Jun, Sep Mon–Fri 2–6), at the Ferme l'Hermitière in St-Jean-des-Champs, north of the town, offers tastings and shows farmhouse skills.

➕ 218 D7 ❗ Rue de la Libération, 50320 La Haye Pesnel ☎ 02 33 00 75 02 🕓 Jul, Aug Tue–Thu 9–12, 1.30–5.30, Fri 9–12, 1.30–5, Sat 10–12; Sep–end Jun Tue 9–12, Wed 10–12, 2–5.30, Fri 8.30–12, 1.30–4.30, Sat 10–noon 🚉 Folighy (4km/2.5 miles)

LESSAY

www.canton-lessay.com

Lessay is famous for its abbey (daily 9–7), which was founded by Baron Turstin Haldup of La Haye-au-Puits

in 1056. The Benedictine monks and abbot came to the small town just north of Coutances from the Abbaye du Bec-Hellouin. The original 12th-century abbey buildings that once surrounded the church fell victim to religious conflicts and the Hundred Years War (1337–1453). They were completely rebuilt in the 18th century, but destroyed in the bombings of 1944. The church was also seriously damaged by the bombardments of the Battle of Normandy. However, it was reconstructed to its original design between 1945 to 1958 using traditional local materials, and is regarded as a typical example of Normandy's Romanesque style. The honey-toned limestone walls and lichen-coated roof slates from La Hague seem as mellow and timeless as ever. The three-tiered nave has a gallery connecting the topmost windows. Light from the stained-glass windows provides a contemplative atmosphere inside.

The Foire de Ste-Croix (Holy Cross Fair) is held in the town of Lessay in September.

➕ 212 D5 ✉ 11 place St-Cloud, 50430 Lessay ☎ 02 33 45 14 34 🕓 Jul, Aug Mon–Fri 9–12.15, 1.30–6, Sat 10–12.15, 2.30–6; Sep–end Jun Mon–Fri 9–12.15, 1.30–5.30 🚌 From Cherbourg

Opposite *The east coast of the Contentin peninsula seen from Barfleur*
Below *The abbey church of Lessay*

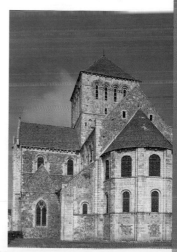

MONT-ST-MICHEL

INTRODUCTION

If the Eiffel Tower is one iconic silhouette of France, the other is Mont-St-Michel with its elegant spire pointing skyward from an ancient abbey which looks seamlessly joined to the conical granite rock beneath it. Standing in a vast tidal bay and reached by a causeway, Mont St Michel always stirs the imagination. Seen from the shore rising out of a mist, there is something distinctly otherworldy about it.

Even when the place is crowded in the height of summer it resonates with 1,300 years of its eventful history. In AD 708, St. Aubert, Bishop of Avranches, was inspired by repeated visions of the archangel Michael to build a modest chapel on the 79m (260ft) granite Mont-Tombe (so named because it was believed to be an ancient graveyard). Benedictine monks settled here in 966 at the invitation of the Duke of Normandy and a village soon formed around them on the southeast side of the rock. A Romanesque church was constructed in the 11th century and work continued on other buildings over the following centuries. In the 13th century, the finest Gothic buildings, an ensemble known as the Merveille (the Marvel), were added to the abbey. Meanwhile, Mont-St-Michel grew to be a famous place of medieval pilgrimage with pilgrims following roads called the 'paths to paradise'.

The Mount was fortified against attacks by the English during the Hundred Years' War (mid-14th to mid-15th centuries) and managed to resist 30 years of siege. After the Revolution the shrine was rudely transformed into a prison. In 1874, the Mount's cultural and artistic merit was recognized and it opened to visitors as a national monument. Three years later Emmanuel Frémlet's gilded statue of St. Michael was placed on top of a new steeple, 157m (515ft) high. A monastic community returned to the site in 1966, the 1,000th anniversary of the installation of the original abbey and today the members of the Fraternités Monastiques de Jerusalem continue to provide a spiritual counterbalance to what might otherwise be merely a hub of commercialism and tourism.

INFORMATION

www.ot-montsaintmichel.com

✚ 218 D8 ✉ 50170 Le Mont-St-Michel ☎ 02 33 60 14 30 ⏰ Jul, Aug daily 9–7; Apr–end Jun, Sep Mon–Sat 9–12.30, 2–6.30, Sun 9–12, 2–6; Oct–end Mar Mon–Sat 9–12, 2–6, Sun 10–12, 2–5 🍴 La Mère Poulard, on the Mount, serves world-famous omelettes beaten in age-old copper bowls that have fortified pilgrims and visitors alike for years (☎ 02 33 89 68 68) 🚌 From Rennes, St-Malo 🚆 TGV to Rennes, then morning bus link to the Mount. Pontorson station, 9km (6 miles) away, has bus services 🅿 The visitors' car park alongside the present causeway is to be replaced with parking for 4,200 cars, 2km (1 mile) south of the coast road on the mainland. Parking costs €4 📖 Free English-language leaflets

Opposite *Buildings huddled below the abbey*
Below *The abbey's double row of cloisters*

TIPS

» If the main street is packed with people, climb the steps to the less crowded ramparts to look down on the village and across the sea.

» Rather than pay €8 to visit the abbey, you could time your visit to coincide with the midday Mass, when tickets are free. You can take your time walking through the monument after the service.

» *Son et lumière* shows are staged in the summer.

If you're planning to visit during the peak summer months it's worth arriving very early (around 8am) or late in the day (after 5pm) to get a sense of the atmosphere of the place. Another option is to stay overnight in one of the four hotels in the village.

WHAT TO SEE

ABBAYE

www.monum.fr

You can join a guided tour around the abbey and its grounds and discover the huge treadmill in which prisoners once trudged to work a system of pulleys to haul building materials up the side of the Mount. The original name of the rock island beneath the abbey was Mont Tombé, suggesting it was used as a burial ground.

The abbey is often referred to as *La Merveille* (the Wonder), but this epithet actually applies to a Gothic extension commissioned by King Philippe Auguste of France in the 13th century to celebrate his conquest of Normandy. The name reflected the amazing feat of the architects and builders who created it in just 20 years. The Merveille, with its three floors of dining rooms for pilgrims, nobles and monks, is topped by a tranquil cloister garden, with a window looking out to sea.

✉ 50170 Le Mont-St-Michel ☎ 02 33 89 80 00 🕐 May–end Aug daily 9–7 (last entry 6pm); Sep–end Apr daily 9.30–6 (last entry 5pm) 🖐 Adult €8.50, youth (18–25) €5, under 18 free

THE VILLAGE

You may be tempted to hurry through the village along the Grande Rue below the abbey, and you'll probably use it for its shops and restaurants, but it has several attractions of its own worth stopping for, including four museums, ramparts, gardens and a church.

The village may seem incongruously commercial for such a sacred spot, but its traders will tell you that they are merely continuing a medieval tradition. Hundreds of years ago, the final stretch of the pilgrimage route would be lined with souvenir stalls not all that different from those of today.

Below *The Great Wheel was used for raising provisions from below*
Below right *A side-chapel in the abbey*

Above *Tourists walk through the narrow streets*

THE BAY

The bay experiences the most extreme tidal movements in Europe. In exceptional low tide the sea withdraws 15km (9 miles) and the difference between the high and low water marks reaches 15m (50 ft). The sea comes back in at a surprisingly fast pace although comparisons to a galloping horse are poetic exaggeration. The phenomenon of an incoming tide is worth witnessing at leisure from a good vantage point.

The most spectacular movements of water are the spring tides 36 to 48 hours after full and new moons, when the sun, earth and moon are in syzygy (alignment). You need to be on the Mount a good two and a half hours before the high-water mark is reached. Ask the tourist office for a tide table.

A plan is underway to reduce the silting up of the bay and thus reduce the extreme differences in high and low water marks. It is due for completion by 2012 and as part of it the causeway will be replaced with a pedestrian bridge.

MAISONS DE LA BAIE

www.maison-baie.com

Back on the mainland, you can enjoy wonderful views of the Mount from the Maison de la Baie vantage points at Le-Vivier-sur-Mer, Courtils and St-Léonard. These individually themed mini-museums offer a perspective on the daily life of the abbey in times past, along with excellent displays of local wildlife. They also organize escorted treks across the sands to the Mount, on foot and horseback, and guided tours of up to 7 hours long to explore the mussel and oyster beds and tidal shallows.

⊠ Courtils ☎ 02 99 48 84 38 ⊠ Le-Vivier-sur-Mer ☎ 02 99 48 84 38 ⊠ St Léonard ☎ 02 33 09 06 06 🕐 Jul, Aug daily 9–12.30, 2–6.30; Sep–end Jun 9–12.30, 2–5.30 (closed on weekends in winter)

Above *The Romanesque cloisters of Abbaye Blanche in Mortain*

MORTAIN

www.ville-mortain.fr

Churches and waterfalls bring visitors to this town on a high ridge overlooking the Sélune valley and the Mortain forest. To reach the Grand Cascade, follow signs out of town and park on the roadside; here, the waters of the Cance tumble 20m (65ft), and in early summer the scene is coloured by rhododendrons.

The Petit Cascade, closer to the town, is an easy walk from Mortain's architectural attractions.

The latter include the 12th-century Abbaye Blanche and the Église St-Evroult, in the centre of Mortain, dating from the 11th century (tours Jul–Aug, Tue at 10). The church's treasure is the Chrismale reliquary, an eighth-century AD casket. Mortain's Petite Chapelle has painted biblical scenes and commands views to Mont-St-Michel. The chapel has a tourist information desk (Jul, Aug daily 2–6.30; May, Jun Sat–Sun 2–6.30). 🚩 218 F8 🛈 La Collegiale, 50140 Mortain ☎ 02 33 59 19 74 🕐 Jul, Aug Mon–Sat 9.30–12.30, 2–6.30, Sun 9.30–12.30, 2–5; Apr–end Jun, Sep, Oct Mon–Sat 9.30–12.30, 2–6 (closed on Mon in Oct); Nov–end Mar Tue–Sat 10–12.30, 2–5.30

ST-LÔ

www.saint-lo.fr

St-Lô was razed to the ground on 6 June 1944, four years after its occupation by the Germans. The

Grande Brûlerie (Great Burning) began at 8pm and continued all night, destroying 95 percent of the town and killing 500 of its 1,200 inhabitants. Despite calls to leave the town in ruins as a memorial and create a new city elsewhere, the citizens insisted on rebuilding St-Lô around the *enclos*, or hilltop fortification. The destruction had revealed the foundations of the original Gaul *castrum* (military camp), on which the new town was laid out.

Vestiges of the old ramparts remain today. The Tour des Beaux Regards lookout tower has views over the Vire. The only surviving relic of the citadel is La Poudrière (Powder Magazine), with a thick fragment of the city wall at one side. The Église Notre-Dame has modern bronze doors, although one bomb-damaged façade has been left as testament to the wartime devastation.

A museum within the Centre Culturel Jean Lurçat on place Champ-de-Mars (tel 02 33 72 52 55; Wed–Sun 2–6) houses the municipal art collection; there are also some fine tapestries dating from the 16th century. The Musée du Bocage Normand (tel 02 33 56 26 98; Jun–end Sep Wed–Fri 10–12, 2–6, Sat–Sun 2–6; Oct, Mar–end May Wed– Sun 2–6; Nov–end Feb Thu–Sun 2–6) is a grand farmyard ringed by 17th- and 19th-century

stone farm buildings, with stables, a bakery and cider press illustrating traditional Normandy farming life. 🚩 213 F6 🛈 Place Général de Gaulle, 50010 St-Lô ☎ 02 33 77 60 35 🕐 Jul, Aug Mon–Sat 9–6; Sep–end Jun Mon 2–6, Tue–Fri 9.30–12.30, Sat 9.30–1

STE-MÈRE-ÉGLISE

www.sainte-mere-eglise.info

A mannequin of a parachutist hanging from the town's church tower recalls D-Day and acts as a reminder that this corner of the Cotentin has a history of conflict. During the Hundred Years War (1337–1453), fortified farms witnessed fighting between France and England, and through the 16th- and 17th-century Wars of Religion Ste-Mère became a Protestant fiefdom. During the French Revolution, the town was renamed as Mère Libre.

Occupied by the Germans from 18 June 1940 during World War II, Ste-Mère was liberated at midnight on 5 June 1944, when an American parachutist was left dangling from the church tower by his parachute; he survived the battle and spent the rest of his life in the town.

D-Day memorials dominate the church square, with the Musée des Troupes Aéroportées (tel 02 33 41 41 35; Feb–Nov) home to a Douglas C-47 aircraft. The church dates from the 11th to the 15th centuries but a stained-glass window shows the Virgin Mary surrounded by aeroplanes and parachutists. Another window was donated by veterans of the 505th Regiment of the US 82nd Airborne Division. The statue of Iron Mike erected in 1997, named for the patron saint of parachutists, is 2.5km (1-mile) out of town. On D-Day, American troops captured the bridge over the Merderet stream, a scene depicted in a map on the excellent, parachute-shaped bronze memorial table.

Ste-Mère has peaceful stories, too. The Fontaine St-Méen, next to the church, is dedicated to the English-born St. Méen, who struck the ground with his staff to bring forth healing waters. There is also a museum of farming, Ferme-Musée du Cotentin (tel 02 33 95 40 20).  212 E4  6 rue Eisenhower, 50480 Ste-Mère-Église ☎ 02 33 21 00 33 Jul, Aug daily 9–6; Sep–end Jun Mon–Fri 9–4 From Cherbourg

ST-VAAST-LA-HOUGUE
www.saint-vaast-reville.com
This smart little harbour is famous for its oysters.

The modest port sits at the top of the Cotentin peninsula a half-hour drive from Cherbourg, and makes an ideal base for those wishing to explore offshore Normandy. At the tip of the natural southern causeway linking St-Vaast with the former island of La Hougue is the distinctive silhouette of architect Marquis de Vauban's fort and a mariners' chapel of local stone.

Just offshore lies St-Vaast's key attraction, the tiny island of Tatihou, which played its part in the town's most famous hours. In 1346, the English King Edward II landed here to claim the French throne, then in 1692 King James II gathered a fleet at La Hougue in order to invade England and regain the crown from William and Mary. Overwhelmed first by the Anglo-Dutch fleet at Barfleur, then by treacherous currents at Cap de la Hague, James II's ships retreated, only to be set alight by the English off Tatihou.

More recently, in an act of D-Day heroism, two local men, Charles Moncuit and Auguste Contamine, defied German gunfire and swam from St-Vaast to the island. There they raised the French flag to welcome the Allies, thus saving Tatihou from bombing.

Today, no more than 500 visitors a day may cross to Tatihou, due to strict environmental-protection rules. The trip can be made either on foot at low tide or on an amphibious boat, the price of which is included in the admission charges to the island's fort and maritime heritage museum.

The best time to visit St-Vaast is August for the international open-air music festival, with free fringe entertainment on the quayside and music in the port bars until late.

The former pirate haunts of the St-Marcouf islands, l'Ile de Terre and l'Ile du Large are now home to thousands of gulls, cormorants and herons, perching on derelict military buildings. During summer months, local fishermen and lifeboat crews take visitors out to sea for a closer view of these uninhabited seabird sanctuaries.

Maison Gosselin (▷ 60) is a famed Norman grocer.
 212 E3  1 place du Général de Gaulle, 50550 St-Vaast-la-Hougue ☎ 02 33 23 19 32 Jul, Aug Mon–Sat 9.30–12.30, 2.30–6.30, Sun 2.30–6; Sep–end Jun Mon–Sat 9.30–12, 2.30–6, Sun 2.30–6 From Cherbourg Valognes (18km/11miles)

VALOGNES
Although Valognes was seriously damaged during wartime air raids, its centre harbours some architectural delights. The Hôtel de Beaumont re-creates 18th-century life in a splendidly decorated merchant's house of the period (tel 02 33 40 12 30; Jul to mid-Sep Mon–Sat 10.30–12, 2.30– 6.30; and Sun 2.30–5.30).

The interesting Musée Régional de Cidre (tel 02 33 40 22 73) is dedicated to cider-making, and the Musée de l'Eau-de-Vie et des Vieux Métiers (02 33 40 26 25), has displays on Calvados.
 2112 D3  Place du Château, 50700 Valognes ☎ 02 33 40 11 55 Jul, Aug daily 10–12, 2–6.30; Sep–end Jun Mon–Sat 10–12, 3–6 Valognes

VILLEDIEU-LES-POÊLES
www.ot-villedieu.fr
Don't let the name fool you: They make more than poêles (pots and pans) at Villedieu. The town still manufactures church bells in the traditional manner, yet it was the workshops beating out kitchen implements that gave it its name.

At the Musée de la Poeslerie (tel 06 80 45 51 08) you can learn how copper workshops were first established in the 12th century by the Knights of the Order of St. John of Jerusalem. One of the world's last surviving bell foundries, the Fonderie de Cloches, is open to the public (tel 02 33 61 00 56).

Other museums in town are the Maison de l'Étain, with pewterwork displays (tel 02 33 51 05 08) and the Musée du Meuble Normand (tel 02 33 61 11 78), where you can admire a collection of traditional Norman furniture.
 218 E7  43 place de la République, 50800 Villedieu-les-Poêles ☎ 02 33 61 05 69 Jul, Aug daily 9–1, 1.30–7; Sep–end Jun Mon–Sat 9–12, 2–5.30 Villedieu-les-Poêles

Below *Small fishing craft tied up to the breakwater near the port at St-Vaast-la-Hougue*

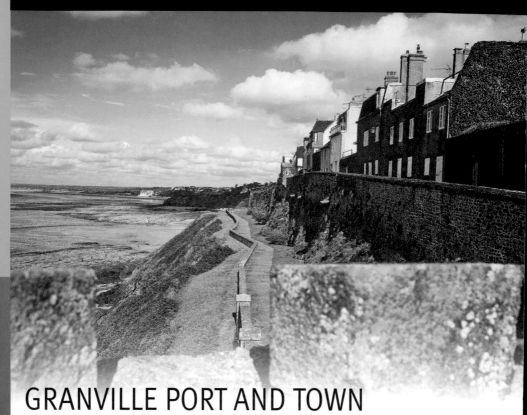

GRANVILLE PORT AND TOWN

This circuit takes in the ports and waterfront of Granville (▷ 47), as well as the ramparts and steep streets of the old town, with the opportunity to break the journey in attractively landscaped parks and gardens. Comfortable walking shoes are essential.

THE WALK

Distance: 5km (3 miles)
Allow: 2 hours, excluding visits
Start/end at: Place d'Orléans

HOW TO GET THERE

Arriving at Granville from the south on the D911, follow boulevard des Amiraux Granvillais through place Albert Godal to place d'Orléans. You can park in place d'Orléans, place Guepratte or in Granville's main port.

★ The walk begins at place d'Orléans, looking out over the sailing port. Follow the quai d'Orléans to your left and then turn left again onto rue d'Orléans. At a crossroads, turn right along boulevard des Amiraux Granvillais to reach the Station Nautique.

❶ The Station Nautique is Granville's principal pleasure port, and is the perfect place for hiring all types of boat, from kayaks to catamarans. A sailing school offers long courses or half-day lessons, and boat-hire outlets and tour operators run excursions to the Îles Chausey.

At the square de la Bisquine, turn left, climbing up to rue St-Gaud. On your right, around 50m (55yds) along the road, is the chemin de la Huguette. At the top of this road turn left onto rue St-Paul, then take the second road on your right, rue

Ste-Marie. Another 50m (55yds) on your left, take rue Tardif, then follow the passage Gautier on your right. At the end of the passage, cross the main road (rue Couraye) and follow the gently curving chemin de Val des Fleurs into the Parc de Val des Fleurs.

Pause for a stroll under the trees in the park, which provide welcome shade on a sunny day, then leave via the winding allée des Daimes. Turn right along boulevard Girard Desprairies past the Catholic school and turn left on rue de la Croix de Lude. Cross over avenue de la Libération onto rue d'Estoutville.

② The Musée de Christian Dior is on your right in the Villa les Rhumbs. The childhood home of one of the most influential fashion designers of the 20th century hosts enthralling exhibitions and is a perfect example of a 1920s domestic villa. A tearoom in the museum's gardens provides refreshment.

Follow chemin du Noroit, then bear right onto rue de la Falaise. Turn right when you come to rue Michelet. Cross place Maréchal Foch, taking the steps by the casino to place de l'Isthme.

③ Place de l'Isthme provides a perfect photo-opportunity: From here you look out over the town itself, and have a superb panorama over the sea to the north and south, with clear views of the Îles Chausey.

While you are in place de l'Isthme, check out the modern art collection at the Musée Richard Anacréon (▷ 47), which includes works by Pablo Picasso, Raoul Dufy and Paul Signac. There are often interesting temporary exhibitions here, and the museum library has an acclaimed collection of original manuscripts and photos of key literary figures of the early 20th century, among them Jean Genet and Colette.

Walk along the ramparts that follow rue du Nord. Turn left on rue Platriers and right along rue St-Jean. The Montée du Parvis leads to place Notre-Dame and its church.

④ The 15th-century Église Notre Dame may have an austere granite exterior, but appearances can be deceptive. Inside, modern stained-glass images of Old Testament characters illuminate the chancel.

From the church, follow boulevard du 2ème and 202ème de Ligne to the Grand'Porte, original gateway to the fortified town.

⑤ The Musée du Vieux Granville (▷ 47), above the gateway, has displays of traditional maritime costumes and tells the story of the port from the days of pirates to the golden age of seaside holidays.

Follow rue des Juifs from the Grand'Porte. Steps on your right lead to place Pleville and the start point on place d'Orléans.

PLACES TO VISIT
STATION NAUTIQUE
www.station-nautique-granville.com
✉ Centre Régional de Nautisme, 260 boulevard des Amiraux, 50400 Granville
☎ 02 33 91 83 72

MUSÉE DE CHRISTIAN DIOR
✉ Villa les Rhumbs, 50400 Granville
☎ 02 33 61 48 21 🕐 Late May–end Sep daily 10–6.30 👆 Adult €6, child €4

WHEN TO GO
The walk is best undertaken from spring to September, when the sights are open and the weather—and hence the views—are most likely to be at their best. Note that the stairs along the route may become slippery in rain.

WHERE TO EAT
LA CITADELLE
▷ 63.

Opposite *Part of the ramparts that still surround the Haute Ville*
Below *A residential area of the Haute Ville*

A DAY TRIP TO JERSEY

Jersey, the largest of the Channel Islands, is only an hour by high-speed catamaran from the coast of Normandy. It's packed with visitor attractions so you'll need to be selective to make the best of your day — or stay overnight. This is a driving tour but most of the stops on it can be reached by bus.

Above Corbière lighthouse at St-Ouens

THE DRIVE
Distance: 45 km (27 miles)
Allow: 1 day
Start and finish: St. Helier, capital of Jersey
Information: A valid ID or passport is needed to visit Jersey. Certain nationalities need a visa: Check before sailing. Jersey time is one hour behind France. To park, you will need to buy prepaid scratchcards, which are widely available.

HOW TO GET THERE
A regular ferry service connects Granville and Barneville–Carteret on the west coast of Normandy with St. Helier. Sailing times vary according to the tides (▷ 33).

★ In St. Helier get your bearings, visit the tourist information office and change money.

❶ Once in your rental car, follow the signs out of town for 'the east' onto the 'coast route', the A4. This follows the sweep of St. Clement's Bay, passing one of the island's many Martello towers at La Hocq. These mini-forts were built in the late 18th and early 19th century to protect the island against an attack

by the French. There's another tower, atypically square and built on offshore rocks, to be seen as you round Jersey's southeast corner, La Roque. Continue on the A4 to Gorey. The village here is pretty but the harbour is even prettier.

❷ The colourful façades on Gorey harbourside are overshadowed by Mont Orgueil castle, Jersey's most emblematic building. It was built in the 13th century to defend Jersey from the French after England's King John had lost Normandy to king Philip of France. It was made obsolete by the introduction of gunpowder in the 16th century.

Back in your car, take the road uphill from the harbour, the B30 towards St. Martin's Church. Turn off right on the B38 and follow the signs for Rozel Bay.

❸ This charming harbour and beach gives a good flavour of the north coast with its secluded coves and rugged grandeur. The Hungry Man Café on the quayside is an informal but very popular place to eat.

Leave Rozel in the direction you

were travelling, uphill on Le Mont de Rozel (the C93) towards Trinity. Turn right at the T-junction with the B31. Immediately you come to Durrell Wildlife on your left.

❹ The naturalist Gerald Durrell (1925–95) conceived this menagerie as a 'stationary ark' rather than a conventional zoo and its primary purpose is still to foster understanding of conservation work. The animal enclosures and landscaped grounds between them make a peaceful place to stroll.

Turn left out of Durrell Wildlife. and turn right on the A8 at the next junction by the church. This road becomes the A9 and leads to the village of St. John. Turn left here on the A10 heading south towards St. Helier. Some way after St. Lawrence Church, look out for an inconspicuous right turning (next to Sonella House) to the Jersey War Tunnels on rue de la Ville Emphire. Follow the signs into the Tunnels car park.

❺ Jersey was occupied by the Germans throughout World War II

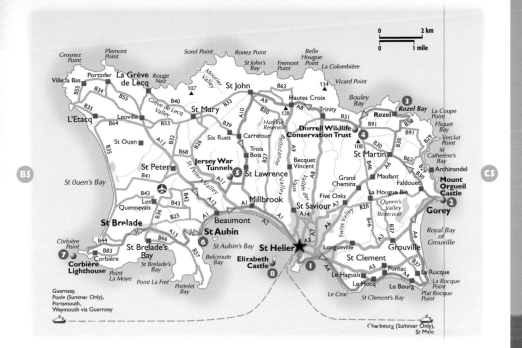

and the island heavily fortified. This extensive subterranean complex was dug out of the rock by forced labour. It is a stupendous feat of engineering which now houses an exhibition aboutf life in wartime.

Leave the Tunnels and bear right at the bottom of the hill on the Rue des Pres Sorsoleil (also called Meadowbank). Turn right on to the A11 and left off this road towards St. Aubin up Le Mont Fallu. Turn left on the A12 and keep going downhill at the roundabout to reach the south coast. Turn right on the A1 beside the beautiful bay of St. Aubin.

6 St. Aubin harbour was used by merchants and privateers until it silted up and trade moved to St. Helier. The fort guarding the bay was built in the 1540s.

Follow the main road around St. Aubin village, the A13, towards La Corbière. Go straight over the crossroads dominated by Marks & Spencer (behind St. Brelade's Bay) and take the left turning for Corbière lighthouse.

7 From the small car park in the southwest corner of the islands you have a view of both Corbière lighthouse and of the 5km (3-mile) long beach of St. Ouen's Bay, which takes up almost the entire west coast of the island, and is a popular place for windsurfing and blokarting.

To return to St. Helier, resume the road in the direction you were travelling in and you will be back on the A13. At St. Aubin take the A1 round the bay.

8 As you approach St. Helier, you have a good view of Elizabeth Castle on its tidal island. It was built in the 1590s and named in honour of Queen Elizabeth I by the then governor, Sir Walter Raleigh.

PLACES TO VISIT
MONT ORGUEIL CASTLE
✉ Gorey Harbour ☎ 01534 853292
◷ Apr–Oct daily 10–6; Nov–Mar Fri–Mon 10–4 ♿ Adult £9.30, child (6–16) £5.50

DURRELL WILDLIFE
www.durrell.org
✉ Les Augrès Manor, La Profonde Rue,

Trinity ☎ 01534 860000 ◷ Daily 9.30–6 (closes 5pm in winter) ♿ Adult £11.90, child (4–16) £8.40

JERSEY WAR TUNNELS
www.jerseywartunnels.com
✉ Meadowbank, St. Lawrence ☎ 01534 860808 ◷ Daily 10–6 ♿ Adult £9.85, child £5.75

CAR RENTAL
ZEBRA
✉ 9 Esplanade St. Helier ☎ 01534 736556 ❓ Also bicycle rental

WHERE TO EAT
OLD COURT HOUSE INN
www.oldcourthousejersey.com
A 17th-century merchant's house is now a bistro, restaurant and hotel.
✉ St. Aubin ☎ 01534 746433

WHEN TO GO
If you want to avoid queues and traffic, this route is best done outside the summer tourist season.

TOURIST INFORMATION OFFICE
www.jersey.com
✉ Liberation Place, St. Helier, Jersey, JE1 1BB ☎ 01534 448877

BARNEVILLE-CARTERET
LA MAISON DU BISCUIT
www.maisondubiscuit.fr
The Burnouf family has been baking traditional biscuits for more than 100 years. The old bakery in La Haye-du-Puits has been surpassed by this new factory, whose shop stocks other local delicacies.

✉ Sortosville-en-Beaumont, 50270 Barneville-Carteret ☎ 02 33 04 09 04 ⓒ Tue–Sat 9–12.30, 2–6.30, closed Jan 🍷

LE TRAIN TOURISTIQUE DU COTENTIN
www.ttcontentin.mousite.wanadoo.fr
The vintage diesel locomotive runs along 10km (6 miles) of track between Carteret and Portbail. The summer Sunday service is augmented by Tuesday and Thursday runs between local market towns.

✉ Clos St-Jean, St-Jean-de-la-Rivière, 50270 Barneville-Carteret ☎ 02 33 04 70 08 ⓒ End Jun–early Sep Sun and bank hols depart Carteret at 3pm and Portbail at 5pm; Jul, Aug depart Carteret Sun 10.30, 3, Sat 3, Tue 10, Thu 8.30, 12.30 and depart Portbail

Sun 12, 5, Sat 3, Tue 12.30, Thu 2 ✋ Adult €8, child (4–12) €4

CHAMPREPUS
ZOO DE CHAMPREPUS
www.zoo-champrepus.com
Wild animals roam in these gardens, between Villedieu-les-Poêles and Granville, with flamingos on the marshlands and ostriches on the savannah. Feeding time for the lemurs is a highlight of this zoo, whose collection of the Madagascan primates is famed across France. The big cats include lions, cheetahs and leopards.

✉ Parc Zoologique, 50800 Champrepus ☎ 02 33 61 30 74 ⓒ Apr–end Sep daily 10–7, 10 Feb–9 Mar daily 1.30–6, 24 Oct–5 Nov daily 11–6, 1–24 Oct Sat–Sun 11–6. Closed 6 Nov–9 Feb ✋ Adult €12.40, child (3–12) €6.80, (13–18) €10.40

THE CHANNEL ISLANDS (ÎLES ANGLO-NORMANDES)
MANCHE ILES EXPRESS
www.manche-iles-express.com
History may have left this group

of islands feeling closer to Britain than France, but geographically they are far closer to the coast of Normandy than of southern England. As well as the Granville-Jersey route described on page 33, there are sailings, weather permitting, from Barneville–Carteret to St. Helier (capital of Jersey, crossing 60 minutes) or Gorey (on the east coast of Jersey, 45 minutes) and from Diélette to St. Peter Port (capital of Guernsey, 60 minutes) and Diélette to Alderney (45 minutes).

✉ Gare Maritime, Rue des îles 50400 Granville ☎ 08 25 13 30 50 ⓒ Varies from month to month, frequent in summer, infrequent in winter ✋ Adult €38–€49 round-trip; child €24.50–€31.50; under 4 free

CHERBOURG
L'ANTIDOTE
Try wine by the glass from one of hundreds of vintages here. The bright designer interior is all wood and brass, and there's a pleasant terrace, open in fine weather.

Opposite A passenger ferry is almost hidden behind other craft at Cherbourg

✉ 41 rue au Blé, 50100 Cherbourg
☎ 02 33 78 01 28 🕐 Tue–Sat and public holidays 12–3, 7–11. Closed Sun, Mon

ART'S CAFÉ
Reggae and rock are pumped through the sound system here and there are live bands too. The walls are hung with works by young artists, there are theme nights on Fridays and Saturdays, and the house punch is the drink of choice. Although open all day, the hip crowd arrives after 11pm.
✉ 69 rue du Blé, 50100 Cherbourg ☎ 02 33 53 55 11 🕐 Mon–Sat 11am–1am

LE BAYOU
www.lebayou.fr
Despite the traditional New Orleans frontage, this is a good place to hang out at the weekend and hear new bands perform live. On hot summer nights, try to find a table in the little courtyard for a breath of fresh air. It's not too expensive either, with beers around the €2 mark.
✉ 5 rue Tour Carré, 50100 Cherbourg ☎ 02 33 53 04 55 🕐 Sep–end Jun Mon–Sat 5pm–1am, Sun 5–midnight; Jul, Aug Mon–Sat 5pm–2am, Sun 5–midnight

LE CRABE-TAMBOUR
Don't line up outside the garish murals of this popular disco on the pedestrianized rue de l'Union much before 1am, as the party crowd doesn't arrive until the neighbouring bars have shut up for the night. But the mood is lively, with the mixture of pop and rock attacting a mixed group who bop until dawn.
✉ 5 rue de l'Union, 50100 Cherbourg ☎ 02 33 53 15 74 🕐 Wed–Sun midnight–5am

ESPACE JACQUES FEREY
This corner site is home to a huge showroom where you can find popular menswear and women's fashion labels. The sportswear, leisurewear and formal outfits are from designer houses such as Burberry and Marlboro Classic.

✉ 7–17 rue au Blé, 50100 Cherbourg
☎ 02 33 53 14 18 🕐 Tue–Sat 10–12, 2–7

LE FREEDOM CAFÉ
The essential gay rendezvous in Cherbourg, a scene stalwart, attracts a mixed crowd of men and women.
✉ 9 rue Charles-Blondeau, 50100 Cherbourg ☎ 02 33 94 08 88 🕐 Tue–Sun 5pm–2am

FIFTY'S DINER
Go back to the future with this retro 1950s American-style diner. Most evenings the television screens live sport, but on Friday nights this is the place for karaoke, with cheerful clusters of friends taking the mike to sing American pop classics in French accents.
✉ Place de Gaulle, 50100 Cherbourg
☎ 02 33 43 58 20 🕐 Mon–Sat 8am–1am, Sun 10am–1am (food served 12–2.30, 7–11) 🍴 Burger, coffee and drink from €9

MARCHÉ AUX PUCES
Everything from antiques to old toys, books, second-hand clothes, china and glassware can be found at the sprawling flea market in Cherbourg's centre. Traders set up stalls on the place de la Révolution, rue d'Espagne and the Parvis de la Basilique Ste-Trinité.
✉ Town centre, 50100 Cherbourg 🕐 First Sat of month 8–6

PATINOIRE CHANTEREYNE
Cherbourg's ice-skating rink welcomes families in the afternoon, while evening sessions appeal to couples. The rink is part of a sports complex with a dance hall and swimming pool. No credit cards.
✉ Port Chantereyne, 50100 Cherbourg
☎ 02 33 53 60 50 🕐 4 Sep–end May Tue 9pm–10.45pm, Wed, Sat 2.30–5, Sun 3–6 Open all afternoons during French school holidays 2.30–5 🍴 Adult €5.50, child €4, including skate rental

LE TRIDENT
www.trident-sn.com
Cherbourg's national theatre is a union of three separate venues in the city. The Classic Théâtre à l'Italienne, on place du Général

de Gaulle, is a traditional 600-seat 19th-century playhouse. Le Théâtre de la Butte, on place René Cassin, was built in 1986 and has 400 unreserved places, so arrive early to choose your seat. Both of these theatres stage a vibrant schedule of new and classic performance. On avenue de Paris is Le Vox, which was renovated in 2000 and has free unreserved seating for 240. This venue hosts jazz cabaret evenings.

The Trident operates a car-pool scheme and theatregoers staying outside Cherbourg may be asked to offer a lift to other out-of-town customers.
✉ B.P. 807, 50108 Cherbourg ☎ 02 33 88 55 55 🕐 Times vary according to performance schedule 🍴 Admission varies depending on performance

GRANVILLE
ANTIQUITÉS BROCANTE DE LA FORGE CORNON
Re-create a rustic Norman garden at home thanks to this second-hand shop. It sells Norman artefacts, including farm carts, water pumps and urns, 19th-century farm tools and pre-war milk churns.
✉ Route de Villedieu, 50400 Granville
☎ 02 33 51 53 76 🕐 Daily 9–7

ILES CHAUSEY
www.vedettejoliefrance.com
The only part of the Channel Islands which belongs to France, this archipelago lies 16km (10 miles) off the Normany coast in front of Granville. A regular ferry service takes day-trippers to the largest island, Grande Ile for a leisurely day out to enjoy the wildlife (you may even see dolphins) and to collect shellfish on its tidal beaches.
✉ Vedette Jolie France Gare Maritime, 50400 Granville ☎ 02 33 50 31 81 🕐 1 to 5 sailings in each direction daily, more frequent at weekends and in summer 🍴 Adult €21 round-trip, child (3–14) €12.90, under 3 €5

STATION DE VOILE DE GRANVILLE
www.station-nautique-granville.com
The water and beach sports on offer

here include windsurfing, catamaran sailing, sea kayaking and sand yachting, but be warned that the bay of Granville has some of Europe's strongest tides. You may also hire or charter a sailing boat and set off for the Channel Islands, or visit the health spa.

✉ 260 boulevard des Amiraux, 50400 Granville ☎ 02 33 91 38 62 ⏰ Reserve ahead 🖐 From €12 to €35 per 1 hour session of catamaran sailing, windsurfing or kayaking

GRATOT
LA SOIFFERIE
For a great night out in the Coutances area, this nightclub appeals to those who prefer to sit around the swimming pool sipping the house gin fizz as much as to the young crowd shaking their stuff on the dance floor. It is lively, without the intensity of city clubs.

✉ 117 rue Argouges, 50200 Gratot ☎ 02 33 47 88 34 ⏰ Fri–Sat and eve of public holidays 11pm–5am

HAMBYE
ANTIQUITÉS FARRADECHE CHRISTIAN
Best known for its displays of antique Norman furniture, cherrywood grandfather clocks, 19th-century chestnut dressers and Louis XV oak wardrobes, this antiques shop and furniture-restoration centre also does a nice line in smaller *bibelots* (curiosities and ornaments) from the region.

✉ Route de Granville, 50450 Hambye ☎ 02 33 90 40 36 ⏰ Mon–Sat 9–7, Sun 2–7

LESSAY
LE GIPSY
This lively club is a favourite with locals from across the Manche for its music policy, which stretches from the 1980s retro tracks that are the staple of French nightlife to more contemporary urban sounds. There are house and techno nights, and a welcoming young team runs the door and bar with friendly efficiency.

✉ 59 route Marais, 50430 Lessay ☎ 02 33 46 30 07 ⏰ Fri–Sun 11pm–5am

LAITERIE FROMAGERIE DE VAL D'AY
Before you stock up on the fabulous cheeses, crème fraîche and butter from this dairy, take the guided tour to see how milk is moulded, salted and packaged into Camembert. A video presentation and visit to the modern production line are complemented by an exhibition of traditional cheese-making tools and a tasting of the finished product.

✉ 1 rue des Planquettes, 50430 Lessay ☎ 02 33 46 41 33 ⏰ Tours: Jul, Aug Mon–Fri 9.15, 10.15, 11.15, 12.15, 1.15; during school terms Fri 2; Sep–end Jun by appointment for groups only 🖐 Adult €2.40, under 14 free

MONT-ST-MICHEL
ÉCOLE DE CUISINE
www.mere-poulard.fr

The most famous restaurant on Mont-St-Michel now has its own cookery school. Two-hour classes on preparing classic Norman dishes are followed by a chef's demonstration of Mère Poulard's legendary omelettes, whisked in copper bowls, and the chance to taste this delicious dish with a celebration glass of local cider. Booking is essential.

✉ La Mère Poulard, 50170 Le Mont-St-Michel ☎ 02 33 89 68 68 ⏰ Variable 🖐 €50 per person 🍴

ST-DENIS-LE-GAST
ANDOUILLERIE DE LA VALLÉE DE LA SIENNE
Bernard and Jacqueline Boscher are among the last artisanal sausage-makers to create the real *andouille de Vire* in the traditional manner, and all their products are made by hand and cured in authentic smokehouses. The sausages are sold in this shop in St-Denis-la-Gast (between Coutances and Villedieu-les-Poêles) alongside hams, *poitrines fumés* (smoked breast meat) and *rillettes à l'ancienne* (traditional coarse pâtés). Sausage-making demonstrations are held in summer. The opening times may vary, so phone ahead of your visit.

✉ Pont de la Balaeine, 2 les Planches,

50450 St-Denis-le-Gast ☎ 02 33 61 44 20 ⏰ Shop open all year Tue–Sat 9–12.30, 2–7. Demonstrations: Jul, Aug Mon–Fri 11, 3.30, 4.30, 5.30, Sat 11.30 🖐 Demonstrations and visits: adult €2.20, under 14 free

ST-LÔ
LE DRAKKAR
This cinema has four screens showing the latest releases, mainly Hollywood blockbusters but occasionally independent films shown in their original language. Movies for children are shown on Wednesday.

✉ 29 rue Alsace-Lorraine, 50000 St-Lô ☎ 08 92 68 06 17 ⏰ Phone for schedule, times and prices

ST-VAAST-LA-HOUGUE
MAISON GOSSELIN
www.maison-gosselin.fr

This family-run grocer's store in the main shopping street of St-Vaast is known throughout the region, and its vintage delivery vans are something of a local icon. Besides an excellent range of Norman delicacies, from coarse *rillettes* (pâtés) to cheese, the shop has a superb wine cellar and vast selection of spirits.

✉ 27 rue de Verrüe, 50550 St-Vaast-la-Hougue ☎ 02 33 54 40 06 ⏰ Mon 9.30–12.30, Tue–Sat 9–12.30, 2.30–7, Sun 9–12.30

TATIHOU
Buy your oysters from the fishing shed on rue des Parcs on Tatihou island, and learn about the famed seafood, *les huîtres de St-Vaast*, with an exhibition, video presentation and regular tastings. See the freshly caught shellfish being cleaned and packaged. Groups can enjoy escorted trips out to the extensive oysterbeds.

✉ 6 rue des Parcs, 50550 St-Vaast-la-Hougue ☎ 02 33 54 43 04 ⏰ Shop Mon–Fri 8–noon; visits and exhibition by appointment

VALCANVILLE
LA TRICOTERIE DU VAL DE SAIRE
Behind the traditional stone walls

of this unassuming house is the headquarters of a knitwear company with shops across the Cotentin peninsula. The stylish jumpers and cardigans for men, women and children are firm favourites with the sailing community in the nearby pleasure port of St-Vaast-la-Hougue, and the tailored woollen suits for women are also sought after.

A free guided tour of the factory on Thursdays may be booked by prior arrangement (in July and August only).

✉ 36 rue Doncanville, 50760 Valcanville ☎ 02 33 54 02 06 ⏰ Jul, Aug Mon–Sat 10–12, 2–6; Sep–end Jun Tue–Sat 10–12, 2–6

VILLEDIEU-LES-POÊLES
GENEVIÈVE PERRUT
www.gene-perrut.com
Geneviève Perrut creates jewellery from glass and paper protected by a clear resin. Her pieces are almost weightless but hard-wearing and come in distinctive designs.

✉ 39 rue du Docteur Havard, 50800 Villedieu-les-Poêles ☎ 06 88 31 30 46/ 02 33 90 77 87 ⏰ Mid May to end Sep Tue–Sun 10–7

VILLIERS-FOSSARD
FERME MINIATURE
www.perso.wanadoo.fr/thierry.durel/ Claude.htm
A tiny, perfectly scaled model of a traditional Normandy farm has been the passion of retired gendarme Claude Delaunay, who has been working on his miniature creation for more than 20 years. Farm buildings, animals, equipment and even people are all made at 1:20 scale, and they offer a glimpse into the heritage of the region.

✉ 1 Hôtel Durant, 50680 Villiers-Fossard ☎ 02 33 57 06 41 ⏰ Mar–end Oct Sun and public holidays 3–7 ✋ Free

FESTIVALS AND EVENTS

FEBRUARY
CARNIVAL
Winter is officially on its way out when Granville stages its Mardi Gras carnival. This essential date since the mid-19th century sees parades, live music and merrymaking in the streets of the port, resort and old town, a colourful treat and a great chance to see the townsfolk enjoying themselves to the full outside the holiday season.

✉ Granville ☎ 02 33 91 30 03 ⏰ Long weekend closest to Shrove Tue

MAY
JAZZ SOUS LES POMMIERS
www.jazzsouslespommiers.com
France's first major jazz event of the year is the music in the orchards festival at Coutances. It's a packed programme, with plenty of fringe events in the streets and bars of the town.

✉ Coutances ☎ 02 33 19 08 10 (tourist office) ⏰ One week early in the month

AUGUST
LES TRAVERSÉES TATIHOU
This convivial music festival is held on the island of Tatihou and in the seafront cafés and restaurants of St-Vaast.

✉ St-Vaast-la-Hougue ☎ 02 33 05 95 88 ⏰ Third weekend in Aug

SEPTEMBER
VOIX DU MONDE
Concerts across the *département* and hikes and rambles to local beauty spots characterize this wide-ranging celebration of music and the great outdoors.

✉ Across La Manche ☎ 02 33 05 95 88 ⏰ Second or third weekend in Sep

Right *Normandy is renowned for the quality of its oysters*

EATING

PRICES AND SYMBOLS

The restaurants are listed alphabetically (excluding Le, La and Les) by town. The prices given are the average for a two-course lunch (L) and a three-course dinner (D) for one person, without drinks. The wine price is for the least expensive bottle. All the restaurants listed accept credit cards unless otherwise stated.

For a key to the symbols, ▷ 2.

AVRANCHES
CROIX D'OR

This 17th-century coach house is built in the timbered style of the area. Chef Franck Baulieu is passionate about using the best local produce and freshly caught fish. A favourite among diners eating à la carte is the *bavaroise de tourteaux et marinade de coquillages au jus de langoustines* (crab and marinated shellfish bavarois with a langoustine sauce). The Croix d'Or has a well-judged wine list and specializes in bottles from the Loire valley. Service is smart and efficient.
✉ 83 rue de la Constitution, 50300 Avranches ☎ 02 33 58 04 88 🕐 Apr–end Sep daily 12–1.45, 7.15–9.15. Closed Sun eve Oct–Mar, Jan ✋ L €25, D €40, Wine €15

BARNEVILLE-CARTERET
LA MARINE

www.hotelmarine.com
This family-run hotel restaurant overlooks the sea. Savour the local catch in the dining room, which is decorated with pastel colours and cane chairs. Apart from the obvious fish dishes, try the appetizing *mille-feuille de saumon cru* (raw salmon pastry) or the *carré d'agneau en croûte de niora* (rack of lamb). Service is attentive.
✉ 11 rue de Paris, 50270 Barneville-Carteret ☎ 02 33 53 83 31 🕐 Tue, Wed Fri–Sat 12–2, 7–9.30, Sun 12–2; Mon, Thu 7–9.30. Closed mid-Nov to Feb ✋ L €35, D €50, Wine €25

CÉAUX
AU P'TIT QUINQUIN

This modest service station restaurant is a perfect place to stop for a good-value meal on the road to Mont-St-Michel. Enjoy honest and basic *cuisine de terroir* (local food) on the regularly changing menu, with dishes such as *gigot d'agneau de pays* (leg of lamb). Allow enough time to appreciate the meal and the friendly service.
✉ 9 Les Forges, 50220 Céaux ☎ 02 33 70 97 20 🕐 Tue–Sat 12–2, 7–9.30, Sun 12–2.

Closed Sun eve, Mon, Tue lunch and early Jan–mid-Feb ✋ L €18, D €30, Wine €5.50 per pitcher

CHERBOURG
FIFTY'S DINER

Come to this 1950s American-style diner for a quick bite. The kids will love the Hollywood design theme, and it is a great place for a one-course refuelling stop for the family. Friday night is karaoke night.
✉ Place de Gaulle, 50100 Cherbourg ☎ 02 33 43 58 20 🕐 Mon–Sat 8am–1am, Sun 10am–1am (food served 12–2.30, 7–11) ✋ Burger, coffee and drink €10

LA RÉGENCE

www.laregence.com
La Régence overlooks the port of Cherbourg and its fishing fleet. Inside, the fine bistro-style furniture and tableware give the place a touch of class. The menu includes regional specials, especially seafood. There is a children's menu.
✉ 42 quai de Caligny, 50100 Cherbourg ☎ 02 33 43 05 16 🕐 Daily 12–2.30, 7.30–10. Closed Christmas and New Year ✋ L €20, D €40, Wine €16

Above *The rustic interior of the Croix d'Or restaurant in Avranches*

RESTAURANT CAFÉ DE PARIS

The owners of this long-standing brasserie, facing the fishing port of Cherbourg, pay particular attention to food quality. The imaginative menu features such local specialties as *huîtres pochées en habit vert* (poached oysters) and *filet de st-pierre rôti* (roast fillet of John Dory). ✉ 40 quai de Caligny, 50100 Cherbourg ☎ 02 33 43 12 36 🕐 Mon–Sat 12–2, 7–10. Closed mid-Jan to early Feb, early Nov–end Nov 🍴 L €25, D €30, Wine €15

COURTILS
MANOIR DE LA ROCHE TORIN

www.manoir-rochetorin.com
This lovely old manor house facing Mont-St-Michel is set in beautiful parkland, with a dining room that has stone walls and wood beams. It is famed for its local lamb dishes. ✉ 34 route de la Roche, 50220 Courtils ☎ 02 33 70 96 55 🕐 Tue–Sun 7.30–8.30. Closed Nov–Apr 🍴 D €50, Wine €16

COUTANCES
LE CLOS DES SENS

The owners of this old restaurant have injected a modern and lively feel to the menu while maintaining the traditional approach to good food which has served it well. ✉ 55 rue Geoffroy-de-Montbray, 50200 Coutances ☎ 02 33 47 94 78 🕐 Tue–Sat 12–1.30, 7.30–9.30, Wed 12–1.30 🍴 L €20, D €40, Wine €18

ÉQUEURDREVILLE-HAINNEVILLE
LA GOURMANDINE

Regarded by local foodies as one of the best choices in the Cherbourg area, this restaurant is run by Stéphanie and Sylvain Lebas. Regular diners suggest the *bouillon de volaille aux champignons et langoustines* (chicken soup with mushrooms and langoustines) as a starter. The desserts are renowned. There is access for visitors with disabilities; dogs are allowed. ✉ 24 rue Surcouf, 50120 Équeurdreville-Hainneville ☎ 02 33 93 41 26 🕐 Tue–Sat 12–2.15, 7.15–9.15, Closed mid-Jul to early Aug, late Dec–early Jan 🍴 L €50, D €50, Wine €17

GRANVILLE
LA CITADELLE

www.restaurant-la-citadelle.com
La Citadelle, a seafood restaurant opposite the port, has a pretty dining room, or you can relax and enjoy your food on a veranda. Oysters with a Camembert cream are praised. ✉ 34 rue du Port, 50400 Granville ☎ 02 33 50 34 10 🕐 Thu–Tue 12–2, 7–9.30. Closed mid-Dec to mid-Jan 🍴 L €20, D €30, Wine €15

LA GENTILHOMMIÈRE

Franck Baumert has cooked at this restaurant for more than 25 years. His cooking is a mix of contemporary and regional style, the *citron vert avec la côte de veau au beurre demi-sel* (veal ribs with lime and salted butter) being a terrific example. ✉ 152 rue Couraye, 50400 Granville ☎ 02 33 50 17 99 🕐 Wed–Sat 12–2, 7–9, Tue–Wed 7–9 🍴 L €15, D €27, Wine €26

LE GUÉ DU HOLME

www.le-gue-du-holme.com
Anne and Michel Leroux offer you a friendly welcome at the restaurant of their family-run hotel. The two dining rooms provide a perfect backdrop to the dishes prepared by chef Guillaume Leroux. The owners are proud of their 'Bonne Table 2003' award, earned through the kitchen's flair with fresh fish and seafood. ✉ 14 rue des Estuaires, St Quentin-sur-le Holme, 50220 Ducey ☎ 02 33 60 63 76 🕐 Tue–Fri 12.30–1.30, 7.30–9, Sat 7.30–9, Sun 12.30–1.30 and evenings Jul–Aug. Closed mid- to end Nov and Feb school holidays 🍴 L €27, D €30, Wine €17

MONT-ST-MICHEL
DU GUESCLIN

Du Guesclin has wonderful panoramic views across the bay. There's plenty of seafood and the grilled local lamb is recommended. There is also a children's menu. ✉ Grande Rue, 50170 Le Mont-St-Michel ☎ 02 33 60 14 10 🕐 Thu–Mon 12–2, 7–9, Tue 12–2; Aug open daily; closed Nov to mid-Mar 🍴 L and D €17.50–€36 menus; more if you go a la carte, Wine €16

ST-GERMAIN-DES-VAUX
LE MOULIN À VENT

The rough exterior of the building contrasts with the fine dining room. Chef Antoine Fernandes believes in good, honest food, such as organic salmon served with a *tartare d'algues* (seaweed tartar). ✉ Hameau Danneville, 50440 St-Germain-des-Vaux ☎ 02 33 52 75 20 🕐 Tue–Sat 12–2, 7–9, Sun 12–2. Closed Jan 🍴 L €30, D €30, Wine €17

ST-LÔ
LA GONIVIÈRE

www.restaurant-goniviere.fr
Chef Emilian Rose follows the traditional style of French and Norman cuisine and likes to use local meat and game produce—savour *filet de boeuf en cocotte et au soja* (beef stew with soya). ✉ 1 rue d'Alsace-Lorraine, 50180 St-Lô ☎ 02 33 05 15 36 🕐 Mon–Sat 12–2, 7–9.30. Closed Sat L, Sun D and early Jan 🍴 L €20, D €34, Wine €15

ST-PIERRE-DE-SEMILLY
LA FLEUR DE THYM

www.lafleurdethym.com
Yann Auger's cuisine is refreshingly different. Having travelled widely, Auger has infused his dishes with a distinct Mediterranean flavour, as you will taste in the *calamari* stuffed with fennel. Service is attentive and there is a classic wine list. ✉ Le Calvaire, 50810 St-Pierre-de-Semilly ☎ 02 33 05 02 40 🕐 Tue–Fri 12–2, 7–9.30, Sat 7–10, Sun 12–2. Closed Mon, Sat L and Sun D 🍴 L €30, D €45, Wine €18

ST-VAAST-LA-HOUGUE
RESTAURANT LES FUCHSIAS

www.france-fuchsias.com
Managed by one family for 50 years, this restaurant is named for the fuchsias around the building. The chef's *choucroute de la mer* (seafood sauerkraut) is famous. There is access for wheelchair-users, and bedrooms (▷ 65). ✉ 20 rue du Maréchal-Foch, 50550 St-Vaast-la-Hougue ☎ 02 33 54 42 26 🕐 Daily Jul–Aug 12–2, 7–9.45. Closed Mon rest of year, Tue Nov–Mar, Jan, Feb 🍴 L €30, D €45, Wine €12

For a key to the symbols, ▷ 2.

PRICES AND SYMBOLS

The prices are the lowest and highest for a double room for one night including breakfast, unless otherwise stated. All the hotels listed accept credit cards unless otherwise stated. Note that rates can vary widely throughout the year.

AGNEAUX
LE CHÂTEAU D'AGNEAUX

This fairy-tale turreted chateau, restored to its former glory, has spacious bedrooms with whitewashed stone walls that are furnished with four-poster beds. The lounge has views of the garden through wooden-shuttered windows. There is wheelchair access and dogs are welcome. A playground and tennis are some of the leisure activities on site.
✉ Avenue Ste-Marie, 50180 Agneaux ☎ 02 33 57 65 88 ⊕ Year-round ⬚ €99–€212, excluding breakfast (€12) ⓘ 12

AVRANCHES
LA RAMADE

www.laramade.fr

A three-star, family-run hotel between the sea and the countryside, the Ramade is close to Mont-St-Michel. There is a separate granite guesthouse accommodating up to three people. After a winter walk you can enjoy a drink by the open fireplace in the lounge. Madame Morvan can organize trips for her guests. As it has no restaurant, try the Croix d'Or in town (▷ 62).
✉ 2–4 rue de la Côte, Marcey-les-Grèves, 50300 Avranches ☎ 02 33 58 27 40 ⊕ Closed mid to end Nov, Jan ⬚ €67–€116, excluding breakfast (€10) ⓘ 10, 1 guesthouse (non-smoking)

BARNEVILLE-CARTERET
HÔTEL DES ORMES

www.hoteldesormes.fr

An ivy-covered *maison bourgeoise*, facing the port on one side and a garden on the other, this hotel is ideal for a romantic break. The upgrading of the bedrooms blends the antique and modern. Enjoy golf, tennis, horseback-riding and water sports.
✉ 13 promenade Barbey-d'Aurevilly, 50270 Barneville-Carteret ☎ 02 33 52 23 50 ⊕ Closed Jan ⬚ €75–€175, excluding breakfast (€14) ⓘ 10

BRÉVILLE-SUR-MER
LA BEAUMONDERIE

www.la-beaumonderie.com

La Beaumonderie is a smart country house on the bay of Mont-St-Michel, overlooking a nearby harbour. Spacious bedrooms are classically furnished, with large beds. The restaurant is open to non-residents.
✉ 20 rue de Coutances, 50290 Bréville-sur-Mer ☎ 02 33 50 36 36 ⊕ Year-round ⬚ €82–€179, excluding breakfast (€12) ⓘ 15

DUCEY
AUBERGE DE LA SÉLUNE

www.selune.com

This family-run hotel is close to Mont-St-Michel. An award-winning garden and idyllic countryside are the main reasons to choose this Logis de France hideaway. Bedrooms are modestly furnished and a restaurant serves traditional food. The owner is happy to instruct guests in the art of fly fishing on the Sélune river.
✉ 2 rue St-Germain, 50220 Ducey ☎ 02 33 48 53 62 ⊕ Closed late Nov to mid-Dec, late Jan to mid-Feb, Mon Oct–Mar ⬚ €61–€65, excluding breakfast (€8.60) ⓘ 20

GRANVILLE

HOTEL DES BAINS

www.hoteldesbains-granville.com

A restored 1920s hotel on the seafront. This is a good choice if you want to stay in the middle of town. They don't have a restaurant but you can eat in the casino next door. Some of the rooms have a sea view.

✉ 19 rue Georges Clémenceau, 50400 Granville ☎ 02 33 50 17 31 🛏 €44–€112, excluding breakfast (€8) ⓘ 47

MONT-ST-MICHEL

AUBERGE ST-PIERRE

www.auberge-saint-pierre.fr

This 15th-century *auberge* is on the main street of Mont-St-Michel. Despite a picture-book exterior, it has modern fittings. This is an ideal spot for visiting the Mount, and is especially pleasant late at night and early in the morning, when the Mount is deserted.

✉ Grande rue, 50170 Mont-St-Michel ☎ 02 33 60 14 03 🕐 Year-round 🛏 €97–€128, excluding breakfast (€13) ⓘ 21

DE LA DIGUE

www.ladigue.fr

One of a cluster of hotels in a tourist 'village' at the landward end of the causeway, about 2km (one and a half miles) from the Mount itself. Other hotels nearby are cheaper if you can do without a view.

✉ La Caserne, 50170 Mont-St-Michel ☎ 02 33 60 14 02 🛏 €65–€86 ⓘ 35

LA MERE POULARD

www.merepoulard.com

The classic place to eat or stay in Mont-St-Michel is at the bottom of the village on the main street. Established in 1888, it has received many distinguished visitors.

✉ Grande rue, 50116 Mont-St-Michel ☎ 02 33 89 68 68 🛏 €140–€370 ⓘ 27

QUINÉVILLE

LE CHÂTEAU DE QUINÉVILLE

www.chateau-de-quineville.com

Château de Quinéville, once home to King James II of England, has extensive grounds to walk around and a heated swimming pool

to enjoy. The dining room and bedrooms are exquisitely furnished.

✉ 18 rue de l'Église, 50310 Quinéville ☎ 02 33 21 42 67 🕐 Closed Jan–Mar 🛏 €62–€130, excluding breakfast (€11) ⓘ 20 ⚓ Outdoors 🏊

ST-VAAST-LA-HOUGUE

HÔTEL DE FRANCE

www.france-fuchsias.com

This popular hotel is near the harbour. Guest rooms are tastefully furnished and most look onto an exotic garden which is the setting for chamber-music concerts in August. Cookery courses in Les Fuchsias restaurant (▷ 63) are offered out of season.

✉ 20 rue du Maréchal-Foch, 50550 St-Vaast-la-Hougue ☎ 02 33 54 40 41 🕐 Closed Jan, Feb, Mon out of season 🛏 €50–€132, excluding breakfast (€9.50–€10.50) ⓘ 36 rooms, 1 suite

Opposite *Breakfast on a croissant*
Below *Inside the bar of the Auberge St-Pierre on Mont-St Michel*

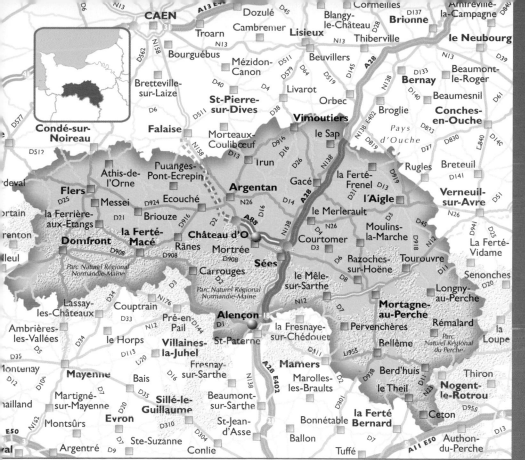

ORNE

The landlocked, green, southern hinterland of Normandy, the Orne, is a rural *département* away from major communication routes, with no major cities and only a few large towns —the *préfecture* of Alençon has a population of just 30,000 inhabitants. But it is precisely the low population density and the sense of space which are its main attractions. Half the Orne's territory lies within two regional natural parks, Normandie-Maine and the Perche, which exist to protect the landscapes, wildlife and traditional livelihoods within their borders. The *département* is divided into five river basins, one feeding the Loire to the south and one supplying the Orne, Normandy's second longest river after the Seine. Normandy reaches its highest point at the Signal d'Ecouves in the forest of the same name, north of Alençon—an undramatic 413m (1,355ft).

All this means that there is some great countryside suitable for a variety of outdoor pursuits. There are plenty of easy walks but the activity of choice in the Orne is riding. King of this country is undoubtedly the horse and distinguished among the Orne's numerous equestrian centres is oldest of France's national stud farms.

There are, as well, towns and other man-made monuments worth visiting. Alençon, Normandy's southern gateway, is a handsome market town known for its lace-making industry; Argentan has a cluster of buildings testifying to a royal heritage; and Sées has a magnificent Gothic cathedral. Among the innumerable noble houses littering the Orne, the two moated stately homes of Carrouges and Château d'O are outstanding.

As for food and drink, the Orne produces its share of highly rated ciders, perries and Calvados brandies but they are all overshadowed by its most famous export: Camembert, which originates from the village of the same name but has its showcase museum in the nearby town of Vimoutiers.

ALENÇON

Normandy's southern gateway is a handsome old market town and heart of a traditional lace-making industry. Alençon began life as a Gallo-Roman fortified town on the banks of the Sarthe river and it only began to grow and prosper in the 13th century when it became the seat of a dukedom that later passed into the hands of the French monarchy. In the 17th century royal laceworks were established here by Jean-Baptiste Colbert, Louis XIV's finance minister which at their peak employed more than 8,000 people. On 12 August 1944, the town was liberated from German occupation not by British or American troops like most of Normandy, but by a French army under General Leclerc.

A WALK ROUND TOWN

The natural place to start a walking tour of the town is in the tourist information office in the Maison d'Ozé, a 15th-century mansion. Through an arch and you are in the place de la Magdeleine, a market square beside the Flamboyant Gothic Église Notre-Dame whose interior is lit by 16th-century stained-glass windows. Go down the Grande rue and you come to Alençon's oldest building, the Café des Sept Colonnes, the half-timbered 15th-century former home of the municipal executioner. Rue du Chateau, as its name suggests, leads you past the ducal castle protected by two stout 14th-century towers.

There are two sights worth seeing in this part of town: the Halle au Blé, a corn exchange from the early 19th century built to a circular plan, and the Musée des Beaux Arts et de la Dentelle (tel 02 33 32 40 07; Jul, Aug daily 10–12, 2–6; Sep–end Jun Tue–Sun 10–12, 2–6), a museum of fine arts and lacework which is housed in an old Jesuit college. The best way to return to your starting point is down rue du Jeudi which has several fine old houses on it dating from different centuries.

INFORMATION

www.paysdalencontourisme.com

⊞ 220 J9 ⚑ Maison d'Ozé, place de la Magdeleine, 61000 Alençon ☎ 02 33 80 66 33 ⏲ Jul, Aug Mon–Sat 9.30–7, Sun, public holidays 10–12.30, 2.30–5; Sep–end Jun Mon–Sat 9.30–12.30, 1.30–6 ☐ Alençon

Opposite *Lace-making is a traditional craft in Alençon*
Below *The 15th-century Maison d'Ozé*

ARGENTAN

www.argentan.fr

This historic town on the banks of the river Orne has a royal and industrial heritage and makes a good base for touring the Suisse Normande area. Argentan was home to Eleanor of Aquitaine (c1122–1204), wife of both King Louis VII of France and then King Henry II of England, and was visited by her son Richard the Lionheart. Negotiations were held here in an attempt to reconcile Henry II with Archbishop Thomas Becket, but the talks failed and the king's knights departed from the town on their murderous mission to Canterbury Cathedral in 1170.

Between 1134 and 1618, the city was ringed by two walls with 20 turrets dominating the skyline; of these, today's visitors can still see the 12th-century keep and the Tour Marguerite. The 14th-century château now houses law courts, and the castle's Chapelle St-Nicolas is used as the tourist office. In the 18th century, the town was an administrative headquarters for the region and a home to nobility. After the French Revolution

Below The 16th-century brick-built gatehouse at the Château de Carrouges, with decorative geometric patterns

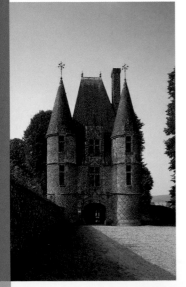

Argentan was able to maintain its influence, as its riverside location and the advent of the railways made it a key industrial centre during the 19th and 20th centuries.

The Mémorial de Montorel-Coudehard (Apr daily 10–5, May–Sep daily 9.30–6pm, Oct–Mar Wed, Sat and Sun 10–5), northeast of Alençon, is a museum commemorating the last, bloody battle in Normandy in 1944 as Allied troops encircled the remants of the German 5th and 7th armies

✚ 220 J8 ℹ 6 place du Marché, Chapelle St-Nicolas, 61205 Argentan ☎ 02 33 67 12 48 ◷ Jul, Aug Mon 9–1, 2–6.30, Tue–Sat 9–6.30; Sep–end Jun Mon–Fri 9.30–12.30, 2–6, Sat 9.30–12.30, 1.30–5.30 🚆 Argentan

CHÂTEAU DE CARROUGES

www.monum.fr

This moated château, with its beautiful grounds, is the principal lure to Carrouges. For five centuries, the red-brick, granite and slate edifice was home of the Le Veneur family, until it was purchased by the State in 1936. Today's château evolved from the 14th to the 17th centuries. It is a testament to the age of gracious living, with furnishings dating from the Renaissance to Restoration periods. The Le Veneur family were lavish hosts—the 1473 guest list included King Louis XI of France. No less interesting to visitors is life below stairs; don't miss the impressive battery of copper pans and mixing bowls in the kitchens.

The well-maintained gardens and estate are set between the two forests of Écouves and Andaines, themselves containing some of the most dramatic landscapes in the area and forming part of the Normandy-Maine Natural Regional Park (▷ 73). The château's immaculately restored outbuildings house the park's offices and information centre. Of particular note in the grounds is the renovated miniature château, its conical towers serving as a flamboyant gatehouse to the estate.

Some claim that Carrouges castle is named for Karl le Rouge, whose blemished face bore witness to a confrontation between his jealous mother, unfaithful father (the lord of the manor) and a fairy temptress. A more likely origin of the name is a corruption of the word *carrefour*, meaning 'crossroads'.

Don't miss the 11th-century church of Ste-Marguerite de Carrouges in the village.

✚ 219 J9 ✉ 61320 Carrouges ☎ 02 33 27 20 32 ◷ Mid-Jun to end Aug daily 9.30–12, 2–6.30; Sep, Apr to mid-Jun daily 10–12, 2–6; Oct–end Mar daily 10–12, 2–5. Closed public holidays ❓ Access for visitors with disabilities 🚆 From Alençon, follow the D112 and N12 towards Domfront, then take the D909 to Carrouges

CHÂTEAU DE SASSY

A sturdy red-brick castle, with tall chimneys and neat formal gardens, stands by the hamlet of St-Christophe-le-Jajolet in farming country outside Argentan (▷ this page). The hilltop house was built in 1760, and in 1850 the estate became home to the dukes of Audriffet-Pasquier. Gaston d'Audiffret, ex-mayor of St-Christophe-le-Jajolet and destined to become President of the French Senate, married the niece and heir of the Duc Pasquier, *préfet* (chief admininstrative officer) of the Paris police, uniting the two families. Their descendants still live here today.

On display in the house are some fine tapestries and a lock of hair cut from the head of King Louis XVI before he went to the guillotine in 1792. This was presented to a member of the Pasquier family who had acted as the monarch's defence counsel during his trial. In 1925, the family commissioned garden restorer Achille Duchêne to design and build a classical terraced garden to replace the original vegetable garden in front of the château.

✚ 220 J8 ✉ 61570 St-Christophe-le-Jajolet ☎ 02 33 35 32 66 ◷ Mid-Jun to mid-Sep daily 10.30–12.30, 2–6; mid-Sep to end Sep, mid-Mar to mid-Jun Sat–Sun, public holidays 3–6 🚆 From Alençon

CHÂTEAU D'O

Home to a family that included some canny royal courtiers, this Gothic castle was built in 1484 on the site of an 11th-century fort for Jean d'O, chamberlain to France's King Charles VII. Jean's descendant François d'O (c1551–94) was something of a political chameleon, managing to stay in favour with each of the ever-changing powerhouses of the period. Among his useful political appointments, he was finance adviser to King Henri III and, later, counsellor to King Henri IV. François's fickle alliances during the Wars of Religion led to accusations that he was siphoning off royal funds to pay for the château's west wing, added in 1590.

The château's pale gold and grey stone façade, decorated with red and black brick patterns, is reflected in the still waters of the moat. Carved on the south wing is the O family emblem, the ermine. The old gatehouse is adorned with elaborate carvings and François's west wing has an arcade and windows with ornate grilles. Although the castle is a private residence, the interior is open to the public. Its rooms are furnished in 18th-century style; highlights include a series of trompe l'oeil paintings of the Greek god Apollo and the nine muses, who are depicted as eagles in flight. These frescoes were discovered during renovation works.

IN THE GARDEN

The grounds may be upstaged by the majesty of the château itself, but they are stunning in their own right. Close to the house, a walkway across the moat leads to a tranquil courtyard and simple gardens give way to woodland. These walks from the main house lead past a chapel and an orangery, which often hosts temporary exhibitions.

The wealth of the gardens does not lie in its lovely old rose bushes, but rather in its classic potager. Here are fruit trees and herb beds, as well as an impressive range of traditional vegetables, including almost 200 varieties of marrows, cucumbers and gourds. Visitors can dine in the former farm buildings, once home to estate workers and now housing a restaurant.

INFORMATION

✚ 220 J8 ✉ 61570 Mortrée ☎ 02 33 28 88 71 🕔 12 Jul–30 Aug 🍴 La Ferme du Château 🚊 Surdon (6km/4 miles) 🚌 From Caen, follow the N158 towards Sées until you reach Mortrée ❓ Access for visitors with disabilities restricted to grounds only

Above *Reflected in the moat, the Château d'O is built around three sides of a north-facing courtyard*

Above *Percheron horses at an open-day display at Haras National du Pin*
Right *The church of Notre-Dame-sur-l'Eau in Domfront*

DOMFRONT

www.domfront.com

Unrivalled views over the landscape of Lower Normandy make pretty Domfront an essential stop on a clear day. Dominated by the remnants of an 11th-century fortress perched high on the hilltop overlooking the Varenne river, the town has clusters of typical stone and timber houses lining its cobbled streets.

At the foot of the hill stands the church of Notre-Dame-sur-l'Eau, where Archbishop of Canterbury Thomas Becket is said to have celebrated Mass in 1166.

In spring and summer, brick-bordered flowerbeds, pots and hanging baskets justify Domfront's reputation as one of Normandy's Villes Fleuries (Flower Towns). The town is equally renowned for its produce—it lies in the heart of Camembert country, and also makes the brandy Calvados Domfrontais (from apples and pears), Pommeau (a fortified apple drink) and Poiré (perry). In spring, the white blossom of the pear orchards outside Domfront provides an unforgettable sight and scent.

In early August the town stages a medieval fair, with music, markets and feasting.
🕂 219 G8 🛈 12 place de la Roirie, 61700 Domfront ☎ 02 33 38 53 97 🕒 Tue–Sat 10–12.30, 2–6 🚄 Flers (23km/14 miles), then bus to Domfront

HARAS NATIONAL DU PIN

Known as the Versailles of the Horse, the Haras National du Pin is the oldest of 23 national stud farms, having been commissioned by King Louis XIV and built between 1715 and 1730. A palatial estate comprising 1,100ha (2,718 acres) of landscaped grounds adorned with imposing buildings is home to 10 breeds of thoroughbreds. Some 60 stallions live on the estate from July to February, with 20 in residence year-round.

The best day to visit is a Thursday between June and September, when each afternoon the stallions and horse-drawn carriages are seen in the main courtyard during the musical parade. Also on Thursday and during school holidays, the château opens its galleries of tapestries, paintings and period furniture. Stable, tack-room and forge tours include displays of traditional skills and crafts, while the Bergerie racecourse sees meetings in September and October and a three-day event in spring.

Not all local legends involve heroes with four legs. Alphonsine Plessis, on whose life the heroines of Alexandre Dumas's *La Dame aux Camélias* and Giuseppe Verdi's *La Traviata* were based, was born at Nonant-le-Pin nearby in 1824. At Gacé, meanwhile, you can visit a permanent exhibition celebrating legendary stars, from Greta Garbo to Maria Callas, who have played the role of Alphonsine.
🕂 220 K8 🖂 61310 Le Pin-au-Haras ☎ 02 33 36 68 68 🕒 Apr to mid-Sep daily 10–6; mid-Sep to end Mar daily 2–5 💷 Adult €3, student €3, child €2 ❓ Access to the stud for visitors with disabilities 🚌 From Argentan, take the N26 to Nonant-le-Pin and then Le Haras du Pin

MORTAGNE-AU-PERCHE

www.cdc-mortagne-au-perche.com

This slumbering hilltop town of sausages and sundials was once a regional capital. But since the province of Perche, established in 1114, was abolished after the French Revolution, Mortagne has had little need for civil servants. Instead, this fortified town now spends its energies on gastronomy, particularly on producing *boudin*. Up to 5km (3 miles) of the black sausage are consumed at the annual Festival du Boudin Noir held in March, attended by the world's leading pork butchers, when new members are inducted into the Brotherhood of the Knights of the Black Sausage. The Saturday morning farmers' market is the best place to find *boudin* and local ciders.

Mortagne's streets are lined with 18th-century townhouses, including several elegant hotels along the rue St-Croix. Look out for the palatial home of the local tax collector. The first floor of the Maison des Comtes du Perche, on rue de la Porte St-

Denis, is a museum (tel 02 33 25 25 87; Tue, Thu, Fri 2–6, Wed 9.30–12, 1.30–6, Sat 10–12, 2–5) devoted to the philosopher Alain (1868–1951).

The peaceful cloisters of the 16th-century hospital and the 13th-century crypt of St. André have been restored. The town also has two dozen sundials. In the public gardens behind the town hall is a reminder that this is a region of fine bloodstock. The equestrian statue here is of a local Percheron horse.

On the first weekend of September, Mortagne holds an annual horse fair. The August donkey festival is biennial.
➕ 220 L9 ℹ️ La Halle au Grains, 61400 Mortagne-au-Perche ☎️ 02 33 85 11 18 🕐 Mid-May to end Sep Tue–Sat 9.30–12.30, 2.30–6; mid-Jun to mid-Sep Mon 10–12.30, 2.30–6, Sun 10–12.30; Oct to mid-May Tue–Sat 10–12.30, 3–6 🚌 Alençon

PARC NATUREL RÉGIONAL NORMANDIE-MAINE
www.parc-naturel-normandie-maine.fr
This vast natural park has hiking, climbing and canoeing opportunities galore, picturesque villages to explore and gastronomic treats.

The huge Normandy-Maine Regional Natural Park is one of 32 such parks that preserve 10 per cent of France's countryside. Straddling two regions, Normandy and the western Loire, the 134,000ha (331,000-acre) protected zone is home to 160,000 people as well as animals and birds. The Écouves, Andaines, Perseigne and Sillé forests, covering 60,000ha (148,000 acres), shelter deer and boar.

Tributaries of the Orne river flow north through the park towards the Channel, while the waters of the Sarthe, Mayenne, Egrenne and Varenne head west to the Atlantic. In places these seem little more than brooks; elsewhere, such as at Villiers, the gorges are dramatic.

The Mancelles Alps include the loftiest point in western France, Mont des Avaloirs (417m/1,368ft). On lower ground is the Passais country, lush farmland covered with apple and pear orchards. Forest rangers take groups on rambles, mushroom hunts and deerstalking expeditions, and anglers have rivers and streams to discover.

With several of Normandy's 10 listed gourmet products hailing from Domfront, there is every reason to make a detour to the pretty hilltop town (▷ 72). The Maison de la Pomme et de la Poire (tel: 02 33 59 56 22; Jul–Aug daily 10–12.30, 2–6; Apr–end Jun, Sep to mid-Oct 10–12, 2–6), a museum and orchard in Barenton, west of Domfront, promotes the history of local fruits and demonstrates techniques of making cider and the less common poiré. The spa towns of Bagnoles-de-l'Orne and Belle Époque Tessé-la-Madeleine both make excellent bases for exploring the park, as do Alençon (▷ 68–69), Sées (▷ this page), Carrouges (▷ 70), La Ferté-Macé and Domfront (▷ 72).
➕ 219 G8 220 J9 ℹ️ Maison du Parc, 61320 Carrouges ☎️ 02 33 81 13 33 🕐 Jun–end Sep Tue–Sun 10.30–6.30; Oct–end May Tue–Fri 10–12, 2–5

ROCHE D'OËTRE
The high point of a drive through Suisse Normande, the Roche d'Oëtre is a 118m (387ft) rock face with unrivalled views over the Orne valley and the Rouvre gorge. From the road, take a signposted track to the cliff top. An observation point indicates the landmarks to be seen. There is no barrier, so keep well back from the edge. Stop off at nearby Pont d'Ouilly to visit St. Roch chapel, scene of the St. Roch pardon ceremonies in August. The church is decorated with frescoes of the saint's life.
➕ 203 S7

SÉES
A major religious centre on the banks of the river Orne, Sées is famous for its magnificent Gothic cathedral (daily 9–7). In AD400, St. Latuin became the first Bishop of Sées, although the cathedral that stands today, a blend of both Norman and Île-de-France Gothic styles, was constructed in the 13th and 14th centuries. With much of the original stained glass intact, the transept is bathed in light, which, along with its music, has been a hallmark of Sées. On Fridays and Saturdays in July and August, enjoy the celebrated son et lumière show. Musical entertainment is held on the Orne's riverbanks on Sundays in August.

The great religious heritage of Sées extends beyond the cathedral. Former 14th–18th-century canonical lodgings house the Musée Départementale d'Art Religieux (tel 02 33 28 59 73; Jul–end Sep Wed–Mon 10–6), with paintings, sculptures and religious regalia.
➕ 220 K8 ℹ️ Place du Général de Gaulle, 61500 Sées ☎️ 02 33 28 74 79 🕐 Jun–end Sep Mon–Sat 9.30–12.30, 2–6; Oct–end May Mon 2–6, Tue–Fri 9–12.30, 2–6, Sat 9–12.30 🚌 From Alençon

VIMOUTIERS
Vimoutiers hosts an apple fair on the third weekend in October, but for most of the year the fruit is eclipsed by Normandy's most celebrated cheese. The Musée du Camembert (opening hours as for the tourist office) is the most important attraction, and two statues pay homage to the dairy tradition. One depicts the Normande breed of cow, while the other commemorates Marie Harel (1761–1812), who lived in the village of Camembert 5km (3 miles) away. Marie sheltered a priest during the Revolution, and in return for her kindness he gave her the monastic recipe for Camembert cheese. While you are in town, admire the stained-glass windows of the Église Notre-Dame and visit the 16th-century Maison de Charlotte Corday (not open to the public), home of the woman who, on 13 July 1793, assassinated Revolutionary leader Jean-Paul Marat in his bath.
➕ 220 K7 ℹ️ 21 place de Mackau, 61120 Vimoutiers ☎️ 02 33 67 49 42 🕐 Apr–end Oct Mon 2–6, Tue–Sat 9.30–12.30, 2–6, Sun 10–12.30; Nov–end Mar Mon 2–5.30, Tue–Sat 10–12.30, 2–5.30 🚉 Lisieux (30km/19 miles)

DRIVE

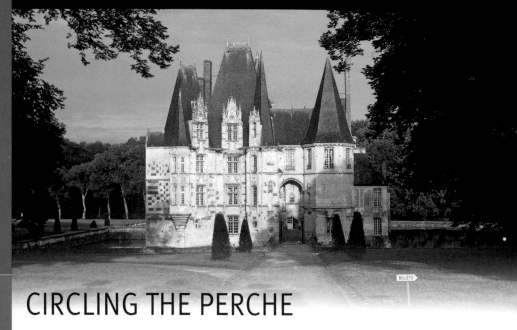

CIRCLING THE PERCHE

Although this tour passes through a handful of towns with fine churches, it is a discovery of Normandy at its most rural. Vast forests, rolling hills, meandering rivers and timbered manor houses are reminders that the Perche is the land of the horse and the hiker, and that motorists are mere visitors.

THE DRIVE
Distance: 221km (137 miles)
Allow: 1 day
Start/end: Alençon

HOW TO GET THERE
Alençon is reached from junctions 18 and 19 of the A28 *autoroute*.

★ Start your journey at the town of Alençon (▷ 69), the southern gateway to Normandy, which boasts several fine gabled timber houses. The town's tradition of lace-making is remembered with two museums (▷ 68–69), and the numerous gift shops are also testament to the craft, which makes a good souvenir.

Leaving town, ignore the signs towards the direct N138 road to Sées and instead take the scenic D26 route out into the Fôret d'Écouves, which forms part of the Parc Naturel Régional Normandie-Maine.

❶ Parc Naturel Régional Normandie-Maine (▷ 73) encompasses four forests, the largest of which is Écouves. The temptation here is to pull over and set off on a forest walk, but before you do so ensure you pick up a map from the information centre at Carrouges (▷ 70) and stick to marked trails. The park is home to deer as well as snakes and wild boar.

Drive along the D26, following road signs for the Rochers du Vignage.

❷ The Rochers du Vignage are granite rocks next to a stream a little way from the roadside. Walkers can hike from here to la Croix Madame to the west, with panoramic views, then take the GR36 hiking route to the Signal d'Écouves further north (see right).

This rural setting played a part in the Battle of Normandy. After

Général Leclerc liberated Alençon on 12 August 1944, Allied soldiers encountered German troops in the forest at Rochers du Vignage. On the left-hand side of the road here is a tiny war cemetery with 19 French graves, while a little further on, on the right, is a monument to Roger Remy, an 18-year-old soldier of the 2nd Armoured Division.

Continue on the D26 to the Croix de Médavy crossroads, easily seen thanks to the Sherman tank standing in tribute to the 2nd Armoured Division. Consider stopping at the crossroads to follow the walking trail up to the Signal d'Écouves, at 417m (1,368ft) the highest point in Normandy. Turn right at the crossroads onto the D226, following the road until you can bear right onto the D908 into Sées.

❸ Sées sits on the banks of the river Orne and is famous for its

Opposite *The pitched roofs of the Château d'O and its slender spires are echoed in the trees planted in the avenue before it*

magnificent cathedral (▷ 73), which is illuminated at night in summer. If you are passing through on a summer Sunday, take a break here to enjoy live music by the waterside.

From Sées, take the N158 to Mortrée, turning right onto the D26 to reach the Château d'O.

❹ The fairy-tale Château d'O is surrounded by water and imbued with political history (▷ 71). There are lovely gardens and a restaurant in one of the farm buildings on the estate.

Follow the D26 until it becomes the D16, then follow signs for Le Pin-au-Haras to reach the Haras National du Pin.

❺ The Haras National du Pin, known as the Versailles of the Horse, is a royal stud farm that was built by King Louis XIV. The elegant 17th-century buildings are worth breaking your journey to discover,

especially if you can visit during one of the musical displays of horsemanship (▷ 72).

Follow the N26 east beside the river Risle towards the country town of l'Aigle.

❻ L'Aigle has typical half-timbered buildings and a weekly livestock market, and is dominated by the clock tower of its 11th- to 15th-century Église St-Martin. Admire the stained glass in the church and visit the Musée Juin 1944, devoted to the Battle of Normandy.

Drive south on the D930 to the Abbaye de la Trappe.

❼ The Abbaye de la Trappe is set in beautiful, tranquil surroundings, which makes it worth stepping out of the car for even though the buildings themselves are not particularly impressive. It is easy to understand that it was here, in the 17th century, that the Abbot de Rance instigated the famous Trappist vow of silence and abstinence. Continue on the D930 to Mortagne-au-Perche.

❽ Mortagne-au-Perche is home to the region's most famous black pudding, the *boudin noir* (▷ 72–73), although it is equally proud of the area's celebrated Percheron horses—the breed is honoured with a statue in the public gardens. Don't miss the 13th-century crypt of St-André Church.

Head south on the D938 to Bellême. From here, you can take a detour around the manor houses that lie to the southeast: Taking the D920, D9, D277 and D7, loop around the manors of Courboyer, l'Angenardière and Les Feugerets, then return to Bellême to continue the drive.

Take the D955 west from Bellême to the D21. Follow this road through La Perrière, with its splendid view of the Butte de Montgaudry, a strategic hill in medieval times, and skirt the border between Normandy and Sarthe as you take the D311 from Mamers back to Alençon.

WHEN TO GO
Spring, summer and autumn are the times to see the forest at its best.

PLACES TO VISIT
MUSÉE JUIN 1944
✉ Place Fulbert de Beine, 61300 l'Aigle
☎ 02 33 24 19 44 **⊙** Spr–Oct Tue–Wed, Sat, Sun 2–6 **▥** Adult €4.50, child €2.50

ABBAYE DE LA TRAPPE
www.latrappe.fr
✉ 61380 Soligny-la-Trappe ☎ 02 33 84 17 00

WHERE TO EAT
ÎLE DE SÉES
www.ile-sees.fr
Between Sées and the Château d'O.
✉ 61500 Macé ☎ 02 33 27 98 65
⊙ Tue–Sat 12–1.45, 7.30–8.45, Sun 12–1.45. Closed Dec and Jan

LE GENTY-HOME
✉ 4 rue Notre-Dame, 61400 Mortagne-au-Perche ☎ 02 33 25 11 53 **⊙** Mon–Sat 12–2.30, 7–9, Sun 12–2.30

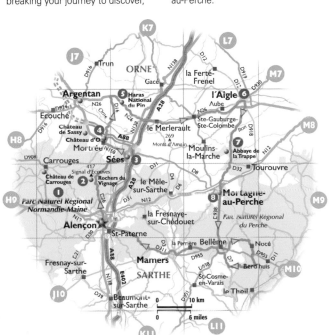

REGIONS ORNE • DRIVE

SUISSE NORMANDE AND THE ORNE VALLEY

This tour takes in some of the high points of the Suisse Normande, a pretty, hilly region south of Caen and bounded by the river Orne. The river runs beside the road for much of your drive. The roads are narrow, single track in places, always winding and sometimes steep, so high speeds are not advisable. The route takes in attractive towns and villages and some good viewpoints.

THE DRIVE

Distance: 110km (68 miles)
Allow: 1 day
Start/end: Caen

★ Caen (▷ 90–92) is the ancient capital of the Norman dukes and is full of interest. Sights include the castle, the Mémorial de Caen and the two abbeys—the Abbaye-aux-Hommes, built by William the Conqueror, and the Abbaye-aux-Dames, built by his wife, Mathilde.

Leave from below the castle, in the heart of town, and follow the 'Toutes Directions' signs, then signs for Rennes-Granville as far as the racecourse at La Prairie. From there, pick up the D8, signed for Évrecy and Aunay-sur-Odon, and follow this road to Évrecy.

❶ At Évrecy you will pass a small group of World War II memorials on the left. The countryside around Caen is full of memorials to the bitter fighting of 1944; this one is dedicated to the men of the 43rd (Welsh) Division. There is a Churchill tank and a monument to Hill 112, declaring 'Whoever holds Hill 112 holds all of Normandy'.

Turn left at the church in Évrecy onto the D41. At Amayé-sur-Orne, turn right at the outskirts of the village onto the D212, signed for Thury-Harcourt. Turn left at the hamlet of Le Hom, crossing the river and an old railway track into Thury-Harcourt.

❷ The town of Thury-Harcourt (▷ 102) is a market town and visitor base for the Suisse Normande and

the Vallée de l'Orne. It is a pretty and prosperous town with a ruined moated château and a park. Two gatehouses with beehive-shaped roofs, one wing and a bricked-up façade are all that can be seen of the château today. A plaque on the park wall pays tribute to British forces.

Follow the D562 along the river for 13km (8 miles) then, at a large roadside cross, take the D133A down into the middle of Clécy.

❸ Clécy (▷ 94) is set in one of the most attractive parts of the Orne valley, at a point where the river is overlooked by high cliffs, and is popular as a base for walking and touring. It's a good place to stop for lunch and a stroll—follow signs to the Pont du Vey, passing Clécy's miniature railway museum. Don't cross the bridge, but admire the watermill on the other side. There are fine views and walks along the Orne valley from the Pont du Vey. The best way to see the river is from the footpath or the road that runs alongside it, overlooking the riverside hotels, the canoeists and the climbers who scramble on the cliffs by the old viaduct.

Follow the main road, signed for Le Lande, round past a little art gallery on your right and several riverside cafés and restaurants on your left. Drive through Le Bô and Cossesseville, with their lovely churches. (These roads may be flooded in winter.) With the river on your right, continue along the D167 through Pont-d'Ouilly. At Le Bâteau, take the D18E towards the parking and picnic area by the viaduct. At the end of the viaduct turn sharp right under the arches on the D18A, signed St-Philbert, continuing to the top of the hill and the viewpoint at Roche d'Oëtre.

④ The Roche d'Oëtre viewpoint overlooks the river Rouvre. Be warned that this 118m (387ft) precipice has no barrier, so observe the warning signs, be extra careful on wet or windy days, and keep control of small children.

Return the way you came, under the viaduct. Turn right back onto the D18 through Le Mesnil-Villement. At the

T-junction turn left onto the D511, then right onto the D43. It's then a left turn onto the D241 to Tréprel. Continue on the D241 through farming country north to Bonnoeil and Angoville, then left onto the D6 to Meslay. Turn right onto the D23 to Bretteville-sur-Laize. Cross the river Laize and turn left onto the D132, following the Laize valley to the D562. Turn right here to return to Caen through small suburban towns.

WHEN TO GO
Some roads on this tour may be flooded in winter.

WHERE TO EAT
AU SITE NORMAND
www.ausitenormand.com
🏠 1 rue des Châtelets, 14570 Clécy
☎ 02 31 69 71 05 🕐 Closed early Dec–end Feb

Opposite *The tree-lined River Orne at Pont Ouilly*
Below left *Looking across the rural Suisse Normande*
Below *Boats below the La Lande Viaduct*

Above *The Casino de Lac in Bagnoles-de-l'Orne is reflected in the lakewater, with small craft moored alongside*

ALENÇON
LA LUCIOLE
www.laluciole.org
Whether you're into jungle jazz, hip-hop, heavy metal or accordion music, this is the venue to see contemporary bands and musicians. Events take place on the large or small stages or, during festivals, outside in the grounds.
✉ 171 route de Bretagne, 61000 Alençon
☎ 02 33 26 53 72 ⏰ Performances Sep–end Dec, Feb–end Jun. Box office from Sep Tue–Fri 2–7

SCÈNE NATIONALE 61
The national theatre of Alençon, Flers and Mortagne-au-Perche specializes in performance art, world music and puppetry. The box office here is open weekday afternoons and a full schedule can be found at tourist offices. There is also a venue at the Château Duhazé in Flers and at Mortagne-au-Perche (▷ 72).
✉ 2 avenue de Basingstoke, 61000 Alençon ☎ 02 33 29 16 96 ⏰ Box office: Mon–Fri 1–6.30; performance times vary
👋 Ticket prices vary with performances

BAGNOLES-DE-L'ORNE
CASINO DE LAC
The blackjack table, English roulette wheel and 100-plus slot machines attract the players, but there is also plenty for non-gamblers: Dancing to a live big band, weekend tea dances, cabaret revues and shows are all on the summer schedule.
✉ 6 avenue Robert Cousin, 61140 Bagnoles-de-l'Orne ☎ 02 33 37 84 00
⏰ Hours vary. Performances usually start at 9pm 👋 Admission free; €100 minimum to play the tables

HOTEL DU BERYL
Among the treatments offered here are seaweed and sea-salt baths for a mineral boost, and detox or 'frigi thalgo' chilling sessions to improve circulation. The sauna and steam room are included with all packages. Open to non-residents.
✉ Rue des Casinos, 61140 Bagnoles-de-l'Orne ☎ 02 33 38 44 44 ⏰ Daily 9–6
❓ Treatments by appointment

JEAN-CLAUDE LEBARON
Come here to discover the Orne's chocolate specialties, such as *étriers normands* and melt-in-the-mouth miniature swans. At the counter, choose from freshly made chocolates to create your own gift assortment in a neatly tied box, or try their *tarte normande* and glass of green tea in the tearoom.
✉ 14 rue des Casinos, 61140 Bagnoles-de-l'Orne ☎ 02 33 37 92 10 ⏰ Feb–end Oct Mon–Sat 7.15–1, 3–8, Sun 7.15–8; Nov–Jan closed Wed

CAMEMBERT
FERME PRESIDENT LE BOURG
www.fermepresident.com
In a renovated 18th-century farm, learn about the Pays d'Auge and its Camembert cheese. The museum tells the story of Marie Harel (▷ 73) with an audio-tour, demonstrates cheese-making methods and ends with a tasting session.
✉ Le Bourg, 61120 Camembert ☎ 02 33 36 06 60 ⏰ Jun–Aug daily 10–12, 2–6; Mar–end May, Sep–end Oct by appointment only 👋 Adult €5, child (11–16) €2

DOMFRONT
CHAIS DU VERGER NORMAND
Buy and taste cider, Pommeau, Calvados and the famed Domfront Poiré from the town's old cellars. Visitors can see an exhibition of agricultural and distilling equipment. Those taking the one-hour guided tour receive a special gift.

Rue du Mont-St-Michel, 61700 Domfront
02 33 38 53 96 Mon–Fri 9–12, 2–6,
Sat 9.30–noon

ESSAY
KARTING 61
www.karting61.com
A 1.6km (1-mile) karting track 10km
(6 miles) southeast of Sées that has
a self-draining surface guaranteeing
road-hugging performance in rain.
Circuit du Pays d'Essay, La Barre, 61500
Essay 06 15 90 15 52 Tue–Sun 2–6
€15 for 15 mins

FLERS
CAP FL'O
www.recrea.fr/flers/capflo
Indoor and outdoor swimming pools
for all the family, a big bubbling
whirlpool bath and, especially for the
kids, a huge waterslide for splashing
and squealing. There are an aqua-
gym and hydrotherapy centre.
Centre Aquatique du Pays de Flers, Les
Closet, 61100 Flers 02 33 98 49 49
Jul, Aug daily 10–6, 7 or 9; Sep–end Jun
daily but shorter hours. Closed one week in
Mar and one week in Sep for maintenance
Swimming pools: adult €5.30, child
(4–12) €4.20. Lockers: €1 coin

JOUÉ-DU-BOIS
LA POELERIE
www.le-brewery.com
This tiny brewery, 5km (3 miles)
east of the town of La Ferté-Macé,
has created Normandy beer in
apple country since 2001, after
storms damaged local orchards.
Traditional-style ales include Norman
Gold, a light bière blonde, and a
stronger, darker bière brune called
Le Conquérant. The beers can be
bought from the brewery, housed
in a traditional farm on the site of an
11th-century forge. Free tastings.
61320 Joué-du-Bois 02 33 37 77 26
Thu–Sun 10–8

MORTAGNE-AU-PERCHE
ART ET PASSIONS
www.artetpassions.com
Art et Passions is home to a picture
restorer and frame shop, and has
exhibitions of works by local artists.
This is a good place to pick up

FESTIVALS AND EVENTS

MARCH
FESTIVAL DU BOUDIN NOIR
The celebrated black pudding
sausage of the Perche (▷ 72) is
fêted with three days of feasting,
tasting and merrymaking.
There are markets and musical
entertainment.
Mortagne-au-Perche 02 33 85 11
18 Second or third weekend in Mar

JUNE–JULY
LES MUSICALES DE MORTAGNE
This music festival sees chamber
concerts, with local and national
musicians, staged across the
Perche region.
Mortagne-au-Perche 02 33 85 11
18 Last weekend in Jun and the first
two weekends in Jul

JULY
AUTOUR D'UN PIANO
Internationally acclaimed pianists
perform in the majestic setting of
the historic château (▷ 70).
Château de Carrouges, 61320

paintings by up-and-coming and
respected new talent. The shop also
sells pictures by acclaimed naive
artist Prune Bardoux.
33 place de la République, 61400
Mortagne-au-Perche 02 33 83 91 71
Tue–Thu 10.30–noon, Fri–Sat 10–12,
3–6

LE CARRÉ DU PERCHE
www.lecarreduperche.com
This bright, glass-fronted modern
building is part of the Scène
Nationale 61 theatre complex, based
in Alençon (▷ 69).
23 rue Ferdinand de Boyères, 61400
Mortagne-au-Perche 02 33 85 23 00
Times vary depending on performance
Ticket prices vary depending on
performance

COUASNON
This family jewellery business has
been serving the local community

Carrouges 02 33 31 90 90 Second
fortnight in Jul and first week in Aug

AUGUST–SEPTEMBER
SEPTEMBRE MUSICAL DE
L'ORNE
www.septembre-musical.com
This concert season makes use
of such diverse venues as the
Haras National du Pin royal stud
(▷ 72) and country churches, sites
that provide lovely backdrops to
evenings of jazz, baroque music,
opera and dance. Food tastings
usually feature too.
Across Orne 02 33 26 99 99
Late Aug–end-Sep

DECEMBER
FOIRE AUX DINDES
The annual turkey fair held just
outside town attracts chefs and
families arriving from miles around
to choose their Christmas bird.
Sées 02 33 28 74 79 Second
Sat in Dec

for 45 years. It specializes in smart
contemporary jewellery
2 rue Ste-Croix, 61400 Mortagne-au-
Perche 02 33 25 16 20 Tue–Sat
9.15–12, 2.15–6. Closed one week in Feb

ST-PIERRE-DU-REGARD
RAIL-BIKING
An unusual way to explore the
Suisse Normande region is to board
a rail-bike, seating up to four, and
then pedal along 6.5km (4 miles)
of disused railway track between
Pont-Erambourg and Berjou stations,
just east of the town of Condé-sur-
Noireau. Exhibitions in the station
buildings and rail carriages suggest
sights to look out for. Explanatory
panels line the route.
Gare du Pont-Erambourg, 61790
St-Pierre du Regard 02 31 69 39 30
Jul–Sep daily 10–6; Oct–end Jun
Sat–Sun 10–6, Mon–Fri 2–4 €15 per
four-seater bike

EATING

Above *The exterior of Au Bout de la Rue in Flers*

PRICES AND SYMBOLS

The restaurants are listed alphabetically (excluding Le, La and Les) by town. The prices given are the average for a two-course lunch (L) and a three-course dinner (D) for one person, without drinks. The wine price is for the least expensive bottle. All the restaurants listed accept credit cards unless otherwise stated.

For a key to the symbols, ▷ 2.

L'AIGLE
LE DAUPHIN

The arrival of Régis Ligot in this unpretentious family-run hotel restaurant revitalized the menu. His signature creation, *galettes de socca aux légumes et homard décortiqué* (chickpea galettes with vegetables and lobster), tempts gourmets.
✉ Place de la Halle, 61300 L'Aigle ☎ 02 33 84 18 00 🕐 Mon–Sat 12–1.30, 7.15–9.30, Sun 12–1.30 ✋ L €35, D €35, Wine €25

ALENÇON
LE BISTROT

This cozy venue has the blackboard menus and chequered tablecloths of a Parisian bistro. Honest, good-value food, such as marinated fresh anchovies and a hearty sausage dish, is waiting to be enjoyed at this warm, friendly eatery.
✉ 21 rue de Sarthe, 61000 Alençon ☎ 02 33 26 51 69 🕐 Tue–Sat 12–2, 7–9.30. Closed Aug ✋ L €12.50, D €15, Wine €11

ARGENTAN
HOSTELLERIE DE LA RENAISSANCE

www.hotel-larenaissance.com
Arnaud Viel is passionate about his cuisine. A particular Viel approach to the classics is the plate of *cuisses de grenouilles croûtées à la farine de pois chiche* (frog's legs cooked in a chickpea-flour crust). The dining room's black-and-white-tiled floor offsets the timber.
✉ 20 avenue de la 2e D.B., 61200 Argentan ☎ 02 33 36 14 20 🕐 Tue–Sat 12–2, 7–9.15, Sun 12–2pm. Closed early Aug, late Feb ✋ L €50, D €50, Wine €20

BAGNOLES-DE-L'ORNE
BOIS JOLI

www.hotelboisjoli.com
This 19th-century villa is now a hotel (▷ 81), and is an idyllic setting. Chef Loïc Malfilatre's *rosace de sole et langoustines aux pommes de terre écrasée* (sole and langoustine with crushed potato), has won praise.
✉ 12 avenue Philippe-du-Rozier, 61140 Bagnoles-de-l'Orne ☎ 02 33 37 92 77 🕐 Daily 12–2, 7–9.30. Closed mid-Feb to end Mar ✋ L €30, D €40, Wine €15 🅿 Private parking

FLERS
AU BOUT DE LA RUE

www.auboutdelarue.com
The retro design here includes old photos and an open dining room allowing you to see into the kitchen. Jacky Lebouleux suggests house specialties, including *agneau en croûte de pain d'épices* (gingerbread-wrapped lamb).
✉ 60 rue de la Gare, 61100 Flers ☎ 02 33 65 31 53 🕐 Mon–Tue, Thu–Fri 12–2, 7.30–9.30, Wed 12–2pm, Sat 7.30–9.30. Closed Aug ✋ L €25, D €30, Wine €20

ST-VICTOR-DE-RÉNO
AUBERGE DE BROCHARD

A young team has converted a country house into an intimate restaurant. The menu offers a good *terrine maison* (house terrine). A dessert highlight is the *tarte tatin*.
✉ Le Brochard, 61290 St-Victor-de-Réno ☎ 02 33 25 74 22 🕐 Tue–Sat 12–1.30, 7.30–9.15, Sun 12–1.30. Closed Mon, Tue eve, Sun eve and Nov ✋ L €25, D €35, Wine €15

STAYING

Above *Walking to the entrance of Le Manoir du Lys hotel in Bagnoles-de-l'Orne*

PRICES AND SYMBOLS
The prices are the lowest and highest for a double room for one night including breakfast, unless otherwise stated. All the hotels listed accept credit cards unless otherwise stated. Note that rates can vary widely throughout the year.

For a key to the symbols, ▷ 2.

BAGNOLES-DE-L'ORNE
BOIS JOLI
www.hotelboisjoli.com
The family-run Bois Joli manor house, hiding in a park, was built in the Anglo-Norman style. Relax in the gardens with an aperitif, then move indoors to the dining room (▷ 80) and pretty bedrooms.
✉ 12 avenue Philippe-du-Rozier, 61140 Bagnoles-de-l'Orne ☎ 02 33 37 92 77 🕐 Open all year 🍴 €72–€152, excluding breakfast (€11) 🛏 20

LE MANOIR DU LYS
www.manoir-du-lys.fr
The hotel stands on the edge of the Andaine forest. Bedrooms look out onto the orchard or gardens. Beside the main house are seven family-friendly cabins on stilts. There are bicycles for rent, and a restaurant).
✉ La Croix Gauthier, 61140 Bagnoles-de-

l'Orne ☎ 02 33 37 80 69 🕐 Closed Jan 🍴 €120–€205, excluding breakfast (€5) 🛏 25 rooms, 7 cabins 🏊 Outdoor heated

MACÉ
L'ÎLE DE SÉES
www.ile-sees.fr
This country-house hotel is surrounded by beautiful grounds. A dining room leads onto large terraces. The simple bedrooms are decorated in pastel colours, and the hotel is an ideal stopover for visitors.
✉ Vandel, 61500 Macé ☎ 02 33 27 98 65 🕐 Closed Jan 🍴 €65, excluding breakfast (€8) 🛏 16 🅿 50 cars

NONANT-LE-PIN
LE PLESSIS
This pretty half-timbered home offers bed-and-breakfast in large bedrooms. The excellent evening meal is shared with the family.
✉ 61240 Nonant-le-Pin ☎ 02 33 35 59 02 🕐 Year-round 🍴 €40, including breakfast. Evening meal €15, including drinks 🛏 3

RÂNES
HOTEL SAINT-PIERRE
www.hotelsaintpierreranes.com
This lovely stone-built mansion has a warm, friendly atmosphere. An elegant dining room serves local

dishes, and bedrooms are cozy.
✉ 6 rue de la Libération, 61150 Rânes ☎ 02 33 39 75 14 🕐 Year-round 🍴 €58–€78, excluding breakfast (€8.50) 🛏 12

SÉES
LE DAUPHIN
A former coaching inn, Le Dauphin is a Logis de France hotel, in a quiet area. Attractive bedrooms with four-poster beds are among its features. Dogs are welcome.
✉ 31 place des Anciennes Halles, 61500 Sées ☎ 02 33 80 80 70 🕐 Closed late Nov, mid–end Jan, Sun eve, Mon Oct–May except public holidays 🍴 €61–€87, excluding breakfast (€12) 🛏 7

SILLY-EN-GOUFFERN
LE PAVILLON DE GOUFFERN
www.pavillondegouffern.com
This former 16th-century hunting lodge is surrounded by a deer park. The furnishings are a blend of the classic and the contemporary. Vast windows make the main restaurant feel airy. A lake is filled by springs that meander through the forests.
✉ 61310 Silly-en-Gouffern ☎ 02 33 36 64 26 🕐 Closed Christmas 🍴 €75–€200, excluding breakfast (€12) 🛏 19 rooms, 1 suite

CN197859

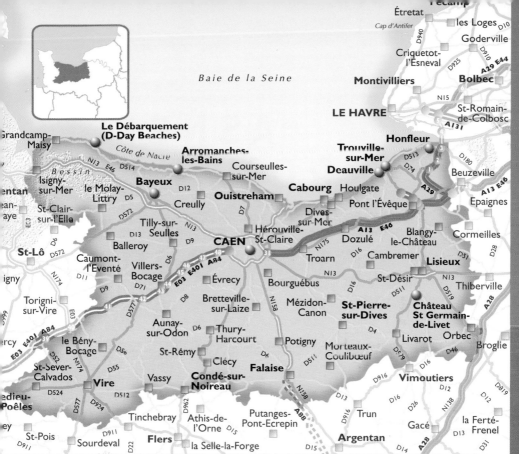

CALVADOS

The name of Calvados is synonymous with Normandy's famous apple brandy and if this hints at the good life, then this is certainly one aspect of what is arguably the most attractive *département* of Normandy. It is also the most interesting because it is inseparable from two defining moments of history. In the 11th century, this was the power base of William, baron of Normandy and conqueror of England. Nine centuries later, an invasion force sailed the other way and on 6 June 1944 the decisive battles of World War II were fought on the beaches of the Côte de Nacre (Mother of Pearl Coast). These two episodes have left a trail of impressive (and often sobering) heritage, beginning with the Bayeux Tapestry (recording William's version of the events of 1066) and ending with the Mémorial de Caen, in the departmental capital, a war museum whose real theme is peace.

In marked contrast to the towns and villages of the D-Day landing coast, with their innumerable cemeteries and memorials to eventful times, are the beaches of the Côte Fleurie (Flowery Coast) on the other side of the Orne river. Here, the resort of Deauville thrives as a fashionable playground for Parisian society, especially the idly rich and glamourous and Honfleur, at the mouth of the Seine, manages to be both a working port and an inspiration to artists. Behind the coast, the Pays d'Auge is a beautiful expanse of countryside of half-timbered villages and proud manor houses. Highlights here are Beuvron-en-Auge, one of the prettiest towns in France, and the pilgrimage centre of Lisieux. If, on the other hand, you like your landscapes more rugged you can always follow the Orne river inland from Caen into Suisse Normande (Swiss Normandy), an attractive area of hills and gorges.

ARROMANCHES-LES-BAINS

The countryside surrounding this peaceful holiday resort is still dominated by reminders of the 1944 D-Day landings. British Prime Minister Winston Churchill and US President Franklin Roosevelt had been planning Operation Overlord, the Allied invasion of Normandy, for a year before D-Day itself and Arromanches was its hub. While this stretch of coast was not as well fortified as the most likely invasion point near Calais to the north, Gold Beach lacked a port large enough for the equipment required. So, the Allies created portable harbours, one for the Americans at Omaha Beach, the other, Mulberry Harbour, to be installed overnight at Arromanches.

After dark on 5 June 1944, some 2,000 landing craft set sail from England, the fleet towing the harbours in small sections across the Channel. These temporary jetties were set up at right angles to the beach. From the cliff tops above the beach, visitors can see the remains of the harbour's vast arc, one of the most vivid images of the battle still in existence. Over a period of three months 2.5 million troops and 4 million tonnes of equipment landed here.

MUSÉE DU DÉBARQUEMENT

www.normandy1944.com

The official D-Day Landing Museum, on the beach site of the harbour itself, uses a bombardment of images to evoke the events of D-Day to forceful effect. It displays a model of the scene in 1944 and has a collection of personal memorabilia donated by soldiers who took part in the invasion. Photographs and film clips may also be seen.

✉ Place du 6 Juin, 14117 Arromanches les-Bains ☎ 02 31 22 34 31 ⏲ May–end Aug daily 9–7; Sep daily 9–6; Oct, Mar daily 9.30–12.30, 1.30–5.30; Nov, Dec, Feb daily 10–12.30, 1.30–5; Apr daily 9–12.30, 1.30–6. Closed 24, 25 and 31 Dec, Jan ⛟ Adult €6.50, child €4.50

ARROMANCHES 360

www.arromanches360.com

The circular cinema on the cliff top screens a powerful 20-minute, wordless, documentary, which is an excellent evocation of the day itself and a superb introduction to the story for older children. The experience helps them appreciate less animated exhibitions along the coast.

✉ Chemin du Calvaire, 14117 Arromanches-les-Bains ☎ 02 31 22 30 30 ⏲ Jun–end Aug daily 9.40–6.40; Sep, Oct, Apr, May daily 10.10–5.40; Nov, Mar daily 10.10–5.10; Dec, Feb daily 10.10–4.40. Closed Jan ⛟ Adult €4.20, child/senior €3.70, under 10/World War II veteran free

INFORMATION

www.arromanches.com

✚ 214 Q4 ⓘ 2 rue du Mal Joffre, 14117 Arromanches-les-Bains

☎ 02 31 22 36 45 ⏲ Jul, Aug Mon–Sat 9.30–6.30, Sun 9.30–12.30, 2–6.30; Sep–end Jun daily 9–12, 2–4 🚌 From Bayeux

TIP

» Don't be put off by the garish advertisements for the Arromanches 360, as the film is both powerful and effective.

CALVADOS • SIGHTS

REGIONS

Clockwise from opposite *Road signs to the D-Day beaches; a field gun at Arromanches; Mulberry Harbour site*

BAYEUX

INFORMATION

213 G5 Pont St-Jean, 14400
Bayeux ☎ 02 31 51 28 28 Jul–Aug
Mon–Sat 9–7, Sun 9–1, 2–6; Apr, May,
Jun, Sep, Oct daily 9.30–12.30, 2–6;
Nov–end Mar Mon–Sat 9.30–12.30,
2–5.30 From Caen From
Cherbourg and Caen

INTRODUCTION

The world's most famous piece of embroidery, the 11th-century tapestry
depicting the Battle of Hastings, lives in this medieval town. Clean streets,
timbered buildings and the gentle sound of watermills in the medieval quarter
make Bayeux a welcome diversion on the Battle of Normandy route.

The principal lure of Bayeux is, of course, its tapestry, but the place has
more recent historical significance, being the first town liberated from German
occupation after D-Day. The Musée Mémorial de la Bataille de Normandie (tel
02 31 51 46 90; mid-May to end Sep daily 9.30–6.30) focuses on the 1944
battle. Bayeux's less violent heritage is displayed in the beautifully timbered
and gabled Hôtel du Doyen (tel 02 31 92 14 21; Jul, Aug daily 10–12.30, 2–7;
Sep–Jun 10–12.30, 2–6), where you can see an ever-changing schedule of art,
porcelain and lace-making exhibitions.

WHAT TO SEE

BAYEUX TAPESTRY

The tapestry, measuring 70m (230ft) long but only 50cm (20in) high, now
housed in Bayeux's 17th-century former seminary. The tapestry, displayed in
the ground floor gallery, is a masterpiece of political propaganda and cartoon
storytelling and was commissioned by William the Conqueror's half-brother,
Odo, Bishop of Bayeux. Although popular legend has it that William's wife,
Queen Mathilde, was the creative force behind the work, it was in fact stitched
by English nuns over a period of 10 years, between 1070 and 1080. The frame-
by-frame drama of how William, Duke of Normandy, won the crown of England
in 1066 is punctuated by Latin captions, and by dramatic scenes of Halley's
comet, shipwrecks and banquets. The story is told in 58 chronological scenes
divided into three episodes: a visit by Harold, later claimant to the crown, to
Normandy in 1064–66 (scenes 1–23); the death of Edward the Confessor on
5 January 1066 causing a crisis over the succession and preparations for the

Above *A section of the Bayeux Tapestry*
Opposite *A medieval street parade and
fair outside the cathedral*

Norman invasion to be launched in the spring of 1066 (scenes 24–38); and as a climax the landing in England on 28 September 1066 leading to the Battle of Hastings on 14 October 1066 (scenes 39–58) in which William defeats Harold. Multilingual audio guides including a simplified version for children provide a running commentary and an exhibition explains the needlecraft. The first floor of the museum is devoted to an exhibition about William the Conqueror and the invasion of England which provides useful context and background for understanding the tapestry. Arrive early to see the tapestry, since coach parties tend to crowd the place out from mid-morning onwards and spoil the view ✉ Centre Guillaume le Conquérant, 13 bis rue de Nesmond ☎ 02 31 5125 50 🕐 May–end Aug daily 9–7; Sep, Oct, mid-Mar to end Apr daily 9–6.30; Nov to mid-Mar daily 9.30–12.30, 2–6; closed second week of Jan ✋ Adult €7.70, child (10–18) €3.80, under 10 free

TIP

» Your entry ticket to the tapestry also grants you free admission to the exhibitions at the Hôtel du Doyen.

NOTRE-DAME DE BAYEAUX

The 11th to 15th-century cathedral, with its predominantly 13th-century Gothic architecture, sports a carved fresco over the south entrance depicting the murder of Archbishop Thomas Becket in Canterbury in 1170 by soldiers of England's King Henry II. The cathedral was the original home to the Bayeux Tapestry, which is now housed in its own building nearby (see above). ✉ Rue du Bienvenu 🕐 Jul–end Sep daily 8.30–7, Oct–end Dec, Apr–end Jun daily 8.30–6, Jan–end Mar daily 8.30–5

BAYEUX
▷ 86–87.

BEUVRON-EN-AUGE
www.cambremer.com

Cited as one of the prettiest villages in France, Beuvron-en-Auge is probably Normandy's top photo opportunity. There are picturesque tableaux at every turn, the timbered houses brightened up with tubs of geraniums that crowd every window sill and spare inch of pavement. The floral abundance reaches its peak in early May, when crowds flock to the annual geranium festival.

Between the timbering, gables and wattle and daub of the artists' cottages and the steep-roofed covered market, you will catch a glimpse of a spire or two, one the dainty steeple of the 17th-century Église St-Martin and the other belonging to the medieval chapel St-Michel de Clermont. Little remains of the ancient seat of the château of the dukes of Harcourt, but the village's 15th-century manor house is an impressive example of typical Pays d'Auge architecture. Despite Beuvron's chocolate-box prettiness, the authentic character of the region may still be found here, as the village is on the official cider route. Some 20 cider-makers offer tastings and visits to apple presses within an easy drive of the village. With so many towns closer to the coast blighted by wartime bombing, Beuvron is an unscathed reminder of the beauty of Camembert

and Calvados country and of the traditional rural way of life.
🚹 215 J5 ℹ️ 14 Les Halles, 14430 Beuvron-en-Auge ☎ 02 31 39 59 14 🕓 Jul, Aug Wed–Sat 10.30–1, 2.30–7, Sun 10.30–1, 3–5.30; Apr–end Jun, Sep Fri 3–6, Sat 10–12.30, 2.30–6, Sun 10–12.30; Oct–end Mar Fri 3–5.30, Sat 10–12.30, 2.30–5.30. Out of season, contact the tourist office at rue Pasteur, 14340 Cambremer ☎ 02 31 63 08 87 🚌 From Lisieux

CABOURG
www.cabourg.net

Gamblers, golfers, philosophers and exhibitionists changed a fishing port from a backwater to a haunt of the rich and famous when Cabourg became a playground of Parisians in the 1850s. In 1853, lawyer Henri Durand-Morimbau, in partnership with local architect Paul Leroux, turned a sleepy harbour of sand dunes and fishing boats into the resort of Cabourg-les-Bains. Its original casino and Grand Hôtel (▷ 116) were joined by a second casino and 2,500-seat theatre, and by 1884 the railway line from Paris had been extended to Cabourg and neighbouring Dives (▷ 100) and Normandy's new seaside towns were linked by a waterfront tramway from Deauville (▷ 95).

In the early 20th century, new golf courses and luxury summer homes gave Cabourg a reputation for exclusivity. French President Raymond Poincaré (1860–1934) came here to unwind and automobile tycoon Louis Renault (1877–1944) found it a haven from the world of business. Most famously, novelist Marcel Proust (1871–1922) fictionalized the resort as Balbec in À la Recherche des Temps Perdu, where he compared watching the wealthy hotel guests dining in restaurant windows to an aquarium.

In World War II, the gentility of the grand buildings was shattered when the Nazis took over much of the town and established brothels for officers and soldiers. One former bordello became a girls' school after the Liberation. Post-war saw

the jet set returning in the 1950s and chanteuse Edith Piaf topping the bill at the casino's stage. In the following decade, the pioneering spirit saw France's first topless sunbathing. Today, Cabourg's casino still attracts high rollers, with movie buffs hitting town for the summer film festival.
🚹 214 J5 ℹ️ Jardins du Casino, 14390 Cabourg ☎ 02 31 06 20 00 🕓 Jul, Aug daily 9.30–7; school holidays Sep–end Jun Mon–Sat 9.30–12.30, 2–6, Sun 10–12, 2–6; school terms Sep–end Jun Mon–Sat 10–12.30, 2–5.30, Sun 10–12, 2–4. Closed Tue Nov–end Mar 🚌 From Caen 🚉 From Lisieux in peak season

CAEN
▷ 90–92.

CANAPVILLE
Nestling in an unlikely setting between the peaceful river Toques and a busy road is Canapville's Manoir des Evêques de Lisieux (tel 02 31 65 24 75; Jul, Aug Wed–Mon 2–7), once the country seat of the bishops of Lisieux's diocese (▷ 100). A smart timber-framed building dating back to the 13th century and decorated in the Pays d'Auge style during the 15th century, the manor house is notable for its tiled roof and some interesting woodcarvings, including a bishop's head on the gatepost. Inside, the ground-floor rooms are furnished in 18th-century style and there are displays of Chinese porcelain. Visitors can walk through the gardens, stopping off at the apple store and traditional cider press.
🚹 215 K5 ✉️ Place de la Mairie, 14804 Deauville ☎ 02 31 14 40 00 🕓 Jul–end Aug Mon–Sat 9–7, Sun 10–6; Sep–end Jun Mon–Sat 10–6, Sun 10–1, 2–5 🚌 From Lisieux

CHÂTEAU DE BALLEROY
www.chateau-balleroy.com

This elegant, symmetrical pink and grey château was built by the legendary architect François Mansart for Jean de Choisy in 1636. Standing at the end of a long avenue of trees, it provides a spectacular backdrop to the hot-air balloon meetings that are held here. The ballooning connection dates to the castle's acquisition in 1970 by American publishing magnate, senator and record-breaking balloonist Malcolm Forbes, who established the world's first balloon museum in a converted stable block here. The museum covers the history of the sport from the Montgolfier brothers' pioneering flight in 1783 to the first successful crossing of the Atlantic in 1978.

Forbes continued a tradition of high-profile masters of Balleroy displaying their passions at the château. Count Albert de Balleroy (1828–72) was an acclaimed artist, known for his studies of hunting hounds. He famously shared a Paris studio with the Impressionist Édouard Manet, and was a friend of the poet Charles Baudelaire and painter Camille Pissarro. Albert de Balleroy's paintings adorn the oak-panelled Salon Louis XIII at the château. In contrast, the Salon d'Honneur is graced by a selection of royal portraits by Charles de la Fosse, Claude Vignon and Juste d'Egmont. But the château's true treasure is its remarkable cantilevered stairway, designed by Mansart himself.

The remarkable two-floor 17th-century *colombier* (dovecote) was considered a status symbol in feudal Normandy.

✚ 213 F5 ✉ 14490 Balleroy ☎ 02 31 21 60 61 🕓 Jul, Aug daily 10–6; Sep to mid-Oct, mid-Mar to end Jun Wed–Mon 10–12, 2–6 ✋ Adult €8, child €6 🚌 From Bayeux

CHÂTEAU DE FONTAINE-HENRY
www.château-de-fontaine-henry.com
This splendid, privately owned château offers a glimpse of gracious living.

Magnificently emerging above the treetops in the unlikely setting of the Mue valley between Caen and the coast, the Château de Fontaine-Henry dominates its peaceful hamlet of stone houses. The original part of the castle was built for the influential Harcourt family at the end of the 15th century, and has carved Gothic stone walls. The later wing, added around 1550, is completely different in style. It's an extravagant palatial confection with an exaggerated soaring slate roof that overshadows even the pointed Renaissance spires. The neoclassical elements were added during the reign of France's King Henri II (1519–59).

Today, the château provides an imposing setting for many high-profile exhibitions, and its permanent art collection is an attraction in its own right. Furniture dating from the Louis XV period to the 19th century and a beautiful selection of porcelain gathered from across Europe and the Far East is testament to generations of collectors. Paintings span 300 years of fine artists, with canvases from the Renaissance to the 19th century, including a study of nymphs and satyrs by French painter Nicolas Poussin (1594–1665).

The oldest building on the estate is the late medieval chapel, dating from the mid-13th century. It has an elegant square tower and small narrow windows in the lancet style. The nave was adapted to suit the fashions of the 16th century. Of note inside are the stone choir stalls lining the walls.

Unlike many châteaux open to the public by day, Fontaine-Henry also allows a few visitors to stay the night, albeit in the stable block. The former saddlery has been converted into a *gîte* (holiday home), sleeping up to four people.

Musical tours of the castle, led by costumed guides, are held on Friday evenings in summer.

✚ 214 H5 ✉ 14610 Fontaine Henry ☎ 06 89 84 85 57 🕓 Mid-Jun to mid-Sep Wed–Mon 2.30–6.30; mid-Sep to 1 Oct, Easter to mid-Jun Sat–Sun 2.30–6.30. Closed Nov–Easter ✋ Adult €7, child (8–16) €5 🚌 From Caen

Clockwise from opposite *A colourful grocery shop sign; the ceiling of the study in Château de Balleroy is decorated with hot-air balloons; a tapestry in Château de Fontaine-Henry*

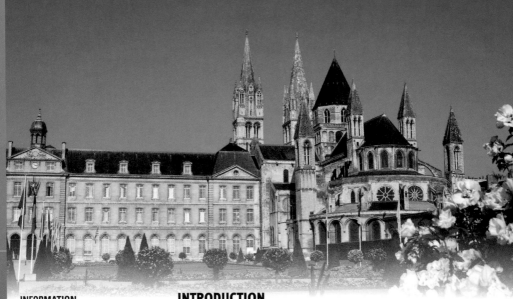

INFORMATION

www.caen.fr/tourisme
✚ 214 H5 ℹ Place St-Pierre, 14000
Caen ☎ 02 31 27 14 14 ◷ Jul, Aug
Mon–Sat 9–7, Sun 10–1, 2–5; Mar–end
Jun, Sep Mon–Sat 9.30–6.30, Sun 10–1;
Oct–end Feb Mon–Sat 9.30–1, 2–6, Sun
10–1 🚉 Caen

INTRODUCTION

William the Bastard, better known to history as William the Conqueror, was born in Falaise in 1027 but it was the more strategic city of Caen he chose as a base from which to expand his territories and his power. Around 1060, he built the palace-fortress complex which still presides over the centre and, with his cousin and wife, Mathilde, he also founded Caen's twin abbeys—one for men; one for women—in a bid to gain readmission to the church after the couple had been excommunicated for a marriage which was declared incestuous.

When William left to conquer England in 1066, he appointed Mathilde as regent of the duchy of Normandy and she governed from Caen in his stead while he established his new kingdom across the Channel. She was buried in her favoured city in 1068 and William followed suit in 1087.

Over subsequent centuries, Caen's wealth grew from manufacturing and trade and its most astute and industrious citizens prospered. One visible sign of this is the Hotel d'Escoville, on place St-Pierre in the heart of town, now the tourist information office, a beautiful mansion built in 16th century by the merchant Nicholas le Valois d'Escoville.

In June 1944, Caen was one of the principal objectives of the invasion of Normandy, although it didn't fall to the Allies until a month after the D-Day landings. By that time, heavy bombing had destroyed many of its old buildings and after the war it had to be rebuilt. Inevitably, it has its share of drab post-war architecture but there are enough surviving monuments to make a visit here a highlight of a trip to Normandy. The purpose-built peace museum in the suburbs, the Memorial de Caen, could justify a trip here in by itself.

WHAT TO SEE

MÉMORIAL DE CAEN

The museum displays start with the post-World War I peace pledges of 1919, and then move through newsreels and scenes of daily life to the horrors of the Holocaust and Nazi occupation during World War II. Multi-screen special effects recount the Battle of Normandy, and a harrowing film, *Espérance*

Above *Abbaye St-Étienne is also known as the Abbaye des Hommes*

(Hope), hammers home the empty truth of post-World War II peace, with painful images of conflicts in Europe, Africa and the Middle East. Sections of the Berlin Wall mark out a huge new Cold War exhibit, and an observatory reveals current locations of global disorder and suffering.

🚼 92 off map at A1 ✉ Esplanade Eisenhower, 14000 Caen ☎ 02 31 06 06 45 🕐 Jul, Aug daily 9–8; Sep, Oct, Feb–end Jun daily 9–7; Nov–end Jan 9–6. Closes some weeks in Jan 🚌 Town bus 2

MUSÉE DES BEAUX-ARTS

The restored ramparts of the 11th-century ducal castle, founded by William the Conqueror in 1060, provide a pleasant walk and enclose the Musée des Beaux-Arts, a splendid collection of works by Dutch, Italian and French artists incuding a street scene by Pieter Bruegel the Younger (1564–1638) and the 16th-century *Madonna and Child* triptych by Cima da Conegliano (*c*1459–1517).

🚼 92 B2 ✉ Le Château, 14000 Caen ☎ 02 31 30 47 70 🕐 Wed–Mon 9.30–6 🚌 Town bus 2, 8, 9; tramway A, B to St-Pierre or Université

MUSÉE DE NORMANDIE

Also in the château is the Museum of Normandy, which fills in many of the gaps in the region's history between the better known dates of 1066 and 1944.

🚼 92 B2 ✉ Le Château, 14000 Caen ☎ 02 31 30 47 60 🕐 Jun–end Sep daily 9.30–6; Oct–end May Wed–Mon 9.30–6. Closed 1 Jan, Easter Sunday, 1 May, 11 Nov, 25 Dec 🚌 Town bus 2, 8, 9; and tramway A, B to St-Pierre or Université

ABBAYE ST-ÉTIENNE

The so-called Men's Abbey was constructed in 1066 and restored during the 18th century. Inside, limed oak-panelled rooms are adorned with paintings from the 17th–19th centuries. You can see William the Conqueror's tomb at the Renaissance-Gothic abbey church of St-Étienne, although only his thigh bone remains after a raid by Huguenots in the 16th century. The abbey itself is now Caen's Hôtel de Ville (Town Hall).

🚼 92 A2 ✉ Esplanade Jean-Marie Louvel, 14000 Caen ☎ 02 31 30 42 81 🕐 Daily 8.15–12, 2–7.30 ✋ Adult €2.20, under 18 free, student/senior €1.10 Mon–Sat, Sun free 🚌 Town bus 1, 2, 3, 4, 5, 8, 11, 14 and 18 ☛ Guided tours 9.30, 11, 2.30, 4

ABBAYE DE LA TRINITÉ

Today, the Women's Abbey also serves as a public building—it is now home to the Conseil Regional de Basse-Normandy (Lower Normandy Regional Council). The severe Romanesque architecture remains typically Norman in design, and

TIPS

» If you are pressed for time when touring Normandy, but do not want to miss out on the Mémorial de Caen, stay on the city's Périphérique ring road and follow signs for the museum rather than going into the centre itself.

» The 24-hour city bus pass is great value at €3.30 per person and it's sold on buses and trams.

Below *D-Day landmark: Pegasus bridge in the Bassin St-Pierre*

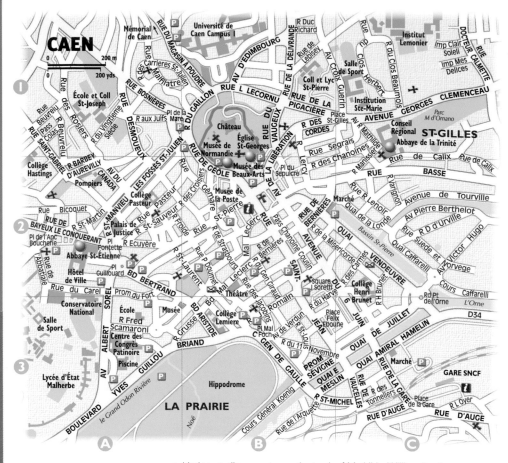

guided tours allow you to see the tomb of Mathilde, William the Conqueror's queen (1032–83), the grand staircase and the cloister. In good weather, the abbey grounds provide a memorable stroll. The Parc Michel d'Ornano is an elegant 18th-century garden adjoining the abbey, with the dainty flowerbeds, avenues of lime trees, a sprawling cedar and a maze.

✚ 92 C1 ✉ Place Reine Mathilde, 14000 Caen ☎ 02 31 06 98 98 🕓 Daily 2.30–4. Closed 1 Jan, 1 May, 25 Dec 🚌 Town bus 4

MORE TO SEE

LE PLAN DE ROME

The glory that was Rome—at a scale of 1:400! This plaster model of the city of Rome at the time of Emperor Constantine (cAD280–337) measures 70sq m (750sq ft) and was built by architect Paul Bigot. A *son et lumière* presentation (€2.50) should appeal to the more theatrical historian.

✉ Campus 1, Université de Caen, Esplanade de la Paix, 14032 Caen ☎ 02 31 56 62 00 🕓 Sep–end Jun appointment only ✋ Adult €2.50, student €1.80

COLLINE AUX OISEAUX

The 50th anniversary of D-Day in 1994 saw the municipal rubbish tip near the Mémorial de Caen reinvented as a glorious floral park, dedicated to peace. The site has terraced flower beds, a rose garden and paths accessible to wheelchair-users. Other gardens nearby honour the US, the UK and Canada.

✉ Avenue Mountbatten

Below The cloisters in the Abbaye aux Dames (Abbaye de la Trinité), which is now also a public building

CHÂTEAU ST-GERMAIN-DE-LIVET

Find the beauty of the Loire's châteaux in Normandy. This castle is a treasure trove of paintings and furniture. Just 7km (4 miles) from the town of Lisieux (▷ 100) in the heart of the Pays d'Auge is the Château de St-Germain-de-Livet, a veritable fairy-tale palace of round towers and colourful brick and stone walls reflected in the waters of a hidden tributary of the river Toques. With peacocks strutting on the lawns and ducks quacking in the river that wraps itself around the base of the towers, St-Germain-de-Livet is part pleasure palace, part fortress. The castle dates from the 15th century, its two remaining wings meeting at a turreted gatehouse. The earliest section is a traditional Norman half-timbered manor house, which connects with a romantic 16th-century patchwork of chequered white stone, green-glazed tiles and red bricks. Superbly renovated by Julien Pillaut in the 1950s, the building is the property of Lisieux town.

The first room you come to is the grand Salle des Gardes, which is in the oldest part of the castle and is dominated by an enormous fireplace. The Louis XIII and Louis XIV chairs here are among the earliest items of the furniture collection, but the main attraction in this first room are the frescoes depicting chivalric tableaux, slightly damaged, but redolent of the room's history.

ARTISTIC COUSINS

You will see furniture from the Louis XV and Louis XVI periods and an 18th-century sedan chair as you walk through the château. On the first floor are reminders of St-Germain-de-Livet's association with the arts: Caricatures and a painted screen here are signed by the poster artist Leonetto Cappielo (1875–1942). Tiled salons lead to the castle's famous Chambre Delacroix, furnished with items bequeathed by the artist Eugène Delacroix (1798–1863) to his cousin Léon Reisener, the castle's owner in the 19th century.

INFORMATION

www.ville-lisieux.fr

✠ 215 K6 ✉ 14100 St-Germain-de-Livet ☎ 02 31 31 00 03 🕐 Daily 11–6. Closed Dec, Jan, 1–15 Oct, 1 May 💰 Adult €6.45, under 18 free 🚌 From Lisieux

TIPS

» It is forbidden to take pictures inside the château.

» Lisieux and other towns often hold exhibitions of art by Delacroix and Reisener, the last Romantics before the age of the Impressionists.

Below *Looking like something from a fairy-tale, the Château St-Germain-de-Livet appears to float on the water*

CHÂTEAU DE VENDEUVRE

www.vendeuvre.com

A museum of miscellany provides an insight into the intimacies of 18th-century Norman aristocratic life.

Vendeuvre lies on the river Dives between the Pays d'Auge and Suisse Normande. Building started on the château in 1750, when architect Jacques-François Blondel was commissioned to create a summer house for Alexandre de Vendeuvre. Today, this home is a cabinet of curiosities and provides a rare glimpse into the life of the Norman nobility of the 18th century. Listed as an historic monument, the airy house provides a backdrop for displays of the minutiae of country living. Visitors buy tickets allowing admission to as many of the attractions in the château and its grounds as they wish.

In the state bedroom, there are wig-stands, powders and potions as the room is set for a lady's preparation for an evening's entertainment. Across in the smoking room, you'll find the paraphernalia of tobacco and snuff, along with a pipe-smoking automaton. The Salon de Compagnie, meanwhile, is where ladies would play cards as their lap dogs reclined in elegant kennels.

Accommodation for four-legged companions is a specialty of the house. One of the most popular attractions is a miniature bed, complete with authentic hangings, made for the pet cat of King Louis XV's daughter. Dog kennels are a theme of mini-exhibitions, which display a large collection of royal and aristocratic dwellings and carrying cases for pampered pets.

The Musée du Mobilier Miniature (Museum of Furniture Miniatures), in the castle's orangery, showcases exquisite masterpieces, minuscule scale-model desks, chairs and even staircases. These tiny works of art were made by master craftsmen during their apprenticeships as cabinet makers and carpenters. The stone vaulted kitchens have an animated cook.

✚ 219 J6 ✉ 14170 Vendeuvre ☎ 02 31 40 93 83 🌐 May–end Sep daily 11–6; Apr, Oct, Sun and public holidays 2–6. Closed Nov–end Mar ♿ Adult €6.90–€8.90, child €5.30–€6.90 (price depends on number of sights visited) ☕ Tearoom

CLÉCY

www.suisse-normande.com

Clécy sits on the banks of the river Orne and is an easy drive from the edge of Caen (▷ 90–92). For visitors on a photo-opportunity tour through the improbably pretty Suisse Normande, this is a great spot to stop for lunch and then stroll off its effects. Waterfront restaurants, *buvette* (refreshment) bars and picnic spots line the riverbanks near the Pont de Vay, with its fast mill race and houseboats, while high up in the town traditional inns are sheltered by storybook gables. Even the 19th-century church looks like an marriage between a dovecote and a collection of cuckoo clocks.

The Ecomuseé de l'Abeille, or Museum of Beekeeping (Jul, Aug Tue–Sun 3–6), provides the opportunity to taste honey flavoured by the local flora, while on the edge of town is the Musée du Chemin de Fer Miniature (Model Railway Museum, tel 02 31 69 07 13; Jul, Aug daily 10–12, 2–6.30; Jun, 1–15 Sep Tue–Sun 10–12, 2–6; mid-Sep to end Sep Tue–Sun 2–6; Oct, Mar Sun 2–5.30; Apr, May daily 10–12, 2–6. Closed Nov–end Feb), complete with a miniature Suisse Normande landscape through which the tiny trains travel. Discover paintings of the local area by Impressionist André Hardy (1897–1986) at the Musée Hardy (tel 02 31 69 79 95; Jul, Aug Mon–Sat 10–12.30, 2.30–6.30, Sun 10–12.30; mid-Sep to end Sep, Apr Tue–Fri 10–12.30, Sat 10–12.30, 2.30–5; May to mid-Sep Tue–Sat 10–12.30, 2.30–6.30, Sun 10–12.30). To experience these very views, hike through the hills on well-marked paths to such popular lookouts as the Pain de Sucre, with its vistas across the Orne valley.

✚ 219 H7 ℹ Place du Tripot, 14570 Clécy

☎ 02 31 69 79 95 🌐 Jul, Aug Mon–Sat 10–12.30, 2.30–6.30, Sun 10–12.30; early to mid-Sep, May, Jun Tue–Sat 10–12.30, 2.30–6.30, Sun 10–12.30; mid-Sep to Apr Tue–Fri 10–12.30, Sat 10–12.30, 2.30–5, Sun 10–12.30

CRÈVECOEUR-EN-AUGE

www.château-de-crevecoeur.com

Like Beuvron (▷ 88), the village of Crèvecoeur is an essential element of any exploration of the beautiful Pays d'Auge hinterland of the Côte Fleurie. At the moated 15th-century Château de Crèvecoeur manor house (tel 02 31 63 02 45; Jul, Aug daily 11–7; Sep, Apr–end Jun daily 11–6; Oct Sun 2–6. Closed Nov–end Mar), you can see the remains of the original 11th-century keep, plus the 16th-century gatehouse and the 12th-century chapel, which in more recent times has been used as a farm building. Such a complete ensemble of seigniorial buildings is unique in the region. Also make sure you see the timbered dovecote. During the summer season, the château stages exhibitions and re-enactments of scenes of medieval life, when visitors can dine with costumed characters from the past.

An unlikely additional exhibition, displayed next to the historic presentations, is centred on the oil industry and the work of the Schlumberger Foundation in sponsoring science education. The Schlumberger brothers, both involved in the petrochemical industry in the first half of the 20th century, financed the restoration of the château's original timber-framed and stone buildings.

The 18th-century Chateau de Canon, southwest of Crevecoeur has delightful gardens to stroll around in which French and English influences are combined. If you want to stay overnight, there is a treehouse available for rent as a *chambre d'hôte*.

✚ 215 J6 ℹ 11 rue d'Alençon, 14100 Lisieux ☎ 02 31 48 18 10 🌐 Mid-Jun to end Sep Mon–Sat 8.30–6.30, Sun 10–12.30, 2–5; Oct to mid-Jun Mon–Sat 8.30–12, 1.30–6 ✉ Lisieux during school term

DEAUVILLE

The fashionable summer playground of the rich and famous is the setting of an exclusive film festival. This famous resort on Normandy's north coast is characterised by huge mock-Norman hotels and the weekend homes of rich Parisians. Popular pastimes here include looking stylish on the seafront, betting on the races, gambling at the casino and taking in a cabaret show. If it is all very artificial, then that is the point—the resort is essentially an upmarket beach party.

It is hard to imagine that glittering Deauville is something of a newcomer to the holiday business. Until 1910, neighbouring Trouville (▷ 103) was the glamorous watering hole of choice for Parisians, then Eugène Conuché built a rival casino and racecourse at Deauville. Suddenly, Deauville became the chic place to play and to stay. It was here in 1916 that the former musical hall artiste and companion to an English aristocrat, Gabrielle 'Coco' Chanel, reinvented herself as a couturière. She created her first trademark jersey dress from traditional Normandy fishermen's sweaters.

THE SEASON

Deauville comes alive in July and August, when the season begins with the 'Swing In' jazz festival and continues with a summer of horse racing. The season ends with the American Film Festival in September, which—as those in the know will tell you—is far more glamorous than Cannes, since the stars wander around town and there are far fewer bodyguards and velvet ropes to keep ordinary people at bay. Don't visit too far out of season, since without bright sunshine and glittering glamour the place can feel very empty.

In summer, regular holidaymakers are offered a glimpse of the luxury lifestyle enjoyed by the wealthy greats of the past. The Villa Strassburger (tours Jul, Aug Tue and Wed 3pm, 4pm), originally built for the Rothschild family, was bought in the 1920s by an American millionaire. The Ancien Presbytere and Vieille École (both 1730), next to the church at the top of the town, are also fine buildings, and are used as occasional exhibition venues by the tourist office. Beach huts on Deauville's boardwalk are inscribed with the names of Hollywood legends who have graced its promenade.

INFORMATION

www.deauville.org
✚ 215 K5 🚹 Place de la Mairie, 14804 Deauville ☎ 02 31 14 40 00 🕐 Jul–end Aug Mon–Sat 9–7, Sun 10–6; Sep–end Jun Mon–Sat 10–6, Sun 10–1, 2–5 🚌 From Caen and Le Havre 🚃 From Lisieux in season

TIPS

» Deauville is very much a summer resort; out of season, there is little to do.
» Bring smart clothes with you, as the casino and race track are places to dress up and be seen.

Above *Seats and beach huts on Deauville's promenade carry the names of Hollywood stars*

D-DAY BEACHES

INFOMATION

www.calvados-tourisme.com
www.normandiememoire.com
www.6juin1944.com
🚗 212 E3–214 H5 🛈 Place St-Pierre,
14000 Caen ☎ 02 31 27 14 14 🕐 Jul,
Aug Mon–Sat 9–7, Sun 10–1, 2–5;
Mar–end Jun, Sep Mon–Sat 9.30–6.30,
Sun 10–1; Oct–end Feb Mon–Sat 9.30–1,
2–6, Sun 10–1 🚗 By far the best way
to get around the battle sites, memorials,
cemeteries and museums is by car, as
not all of them are accessible by public
transport ❓ Several companies offer
tours of the battlefields including
D-Day Battle Tours (www.ddaybattletours.
com) and Holts Tours (www.holts.co.uk).
The Normandie Pass entitles the bearer
to reduced admission to some sights. See
www.normandiememoire.com

ROUTES

Eight routes signposted 'Normandie
Terre–Liberté' guide the visitor
chronologically through the Battle of
Normandy in Calvados, Manche and Orne:
» Overlord–The Assault
» D-Day–The Onslaught
» Objective–A Port
» Cobra–The Breakout
» The Counter Attack
» The Confrontation
» The Encirclement
» The Outcome

Below *A monument on Utah Beach
commemorates the US landings*

INTRODUCTION

From the moment the US entered World War II in 1942, an Allied attempted
invasion of Occupied Europe became an inevitability. The German army, dug
in behind the 'Atlantic Wall'—a line of defences built from the Netherlands to
Brittany, expected the attack to come at the shortest sea crossing between
Britain and France, the Pas de Calais. The Allies, however, selected five
beaches on the Côte de Nacre in Normandy for the landings and General
Dwight D. Eisenhower was put in supreme command.

A moonlit night followed by a low tide at daybreak (to expose obstacles
on the beach) were essential requirements and this meant that few days
each month were favourable. The invasion had to be postponed for 24-hours
because of bad weather. In the early hours of 6 June 1944, Operation Overlord
commenced with airborne troops securing key objectives during the night.
Meanwhile, a fleet of 5,000 ships loaded with men and vehicles crossed the
English Channel. Astonishingly, preparations for the landings had been kept
secret from the Germans. Even so, the success of the landings was never
guaranteed. At dawn, 135,000 men and 20,000 vehicles began to come ashore
under heavy fire. The beaches are still known by the codenames they were
given for the invasion.

Both the invaders and the defenders knew that the success of the invasion
depended on events during the first 24 hours. German commanders, however,
were slow to realize the scale of invasion and the counter attack came too late
to prevent the Allies consolidating their gains. Throughout the rest of June and
July, the Allied armies fought their way west and south through Normandy,
taking key objectives including Cherbourg and Caen. By mid-August, the
remnants of the German 7th Army had been forced into an eastward retreat
through the 'Falaise pocket' (between Falaise and Argentan), a gap which
was gradually reduced to a narrow escape route between between Chambois,
St-Lambert, Trun and Tournai-sur-Dives which has become known as 'the
corridor of death' for the ease in which Allied planes were able to bomb them.
The Battle of Normandy ended on the morning of 22 August with the surrender
of the last troops of the 5th and 7th German Army. Except for lingering pockets
of resistance, such as Le Havre, western France was effectively liberated and
the advancing troops had a clear road to Paris.

WHAT TO SEE

UTAH

Utah, on the east coast of the Cotentin peninsula, was assigned to the US
army. Because of an error in navigation the first troops landed almost 2km (1.5
miles) south of their intended position at a point which was weakly defended.
Losses, as a result, were comparatively light: 200 killed, missing or wounded
out of 20,000 men successfully landed. One of the officers on the beach was
Brigadier General Theodore Roosevelt Jr eldest son of the former president
of the same name. During the night American paratroops had suffered heavy
losses in taking the town of Ste-Mère-Eglise, inland from Utah beach.

OMAHA

Omaha between Vierville-sur-Mer and Colleville-sur-Mer, also a US objective,
has become infamously known as 'Bloody Omaha'. The beach was easier than
the others to defend and naval and aerial bombardments prior to the infantry
assault had largely proved ineffectual. The landing at Omaha nearly failed and
a bridgehead only established in the face of horrendous casualties. An officer,
George A. Taylor, is said to have encouraged men who were reluctant to move

forward with the words: 'There are two kinds of people who are staying on this beach: Those who are dead and those who are going to die.'

GOLD

Gold, the central beach of the invasion, between La Rivière and Le Hamel, was given to the British Corps. They landed almost an hour after the Americans because of differences in the time of the tides. The day's objectives were largely achieved with troops breaking out of the beach through marshes after 'flail' tanks had cleared a way through the minefield. By the evening, the British had taken Arromanches and sent patrols into the suburbs of Bayeux. They had also managed to join up with the Canadians from Juno but not with the Americans from Omaha because of the heavy losses there which had delayed progress.

JUNO

Between the villages of Graye-sur-Mer and St-Aubin-sur-Mer, Juno was the only Canadian beach. Because of rough seas and offshore reefs, the landings here took place slightly later than planned; the tide had started to come in and 25 per cent of the landing craft were destroyed by submerged obstacles. The incoming tide and the narrow streets of the villages above the beach caused congestion problems as more men and vehicles were landed. Nevertheless, the Canadians managed to reach 8km (5 miles) inland before nightfall, only just short of their objectives: the Caen–Bayeux road and Carpiquet airfield.

SWORD

Sword between Lion-sur-Mer and Ouistreham, also a British beach, marked the eastern flank of the landings. The strategic Pegasus bridge (the pont de Bénouville, over the Caen canal), behind Sword beach, had been captured during the night by glider borne troops and nearby Ranville had become the first French village officially liberated. The Merville gun battery overlooking Sword had also been taken during the night, against overwhelming odds and at the cost of many casualties. The objective of the troops landing on Sword was to take Caen but the city only fell a month after D-Day.

LEGACIES OF WAR

The German occupation and the events of June–August 1944 are kept fresh in the memory of Normandy by numerous museums, memorials and cemeteries (for both Allied and German dead). Inevitably, these are concentrated along the Calvados coast used for the D-Day landings (▷ 106–109) but there are others in the Manche and Orne. There are particularly interesting museums at Arromanches (▷ 84–85), Bayeux (▷ 86–87), Caen (▷ 90–91), Falaise (▷ 100) and at Montmorel.

CEMETERIES

Some of the bodies of soldiers killed in the Battle of Normandy were repatriated but most are buried in 27 cemeteries:
» 16 British. The largest is at Bayeux where there are 4,868 graves.
» 2 Canadian.
» 2 American. The largest, at Colleville sur Mer, where there are 9,387 graves, has a visitors' centre (www.abmc.gov).
» 1 Polish.
» 1 French (des Gateys necropolis).
» 5 German. The largest of them, at Huisnes sur Mer, near Mont-St-Michel has 11,956 graves.

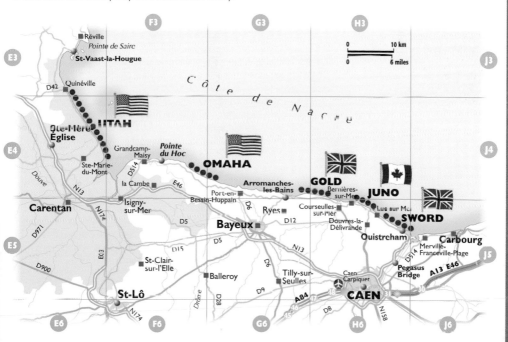

HONFLEUR

INFORMATION

www.ot-honfleur.fr
⊞ 214 K4 ℹ Quai Lepaulmier, 14602
Honfleur ☎ 02 31 89 23 30 ⓒ Jul, Aug
Mon–Sat 9.30–7, Sun 10–5; Easter–end
Jun, Sep Mon–Sat 9.30–12.30, 2–6.30,
Sun 10–12.30, 2–5; Oct–Easter Mon–Sat
9.30–12.30, 2–6, Sun 10–1 (school hols
only) 🚌 From Pont-l'Évêque

INTRODUCTION

This picturesque fishing town at the mouth of the Seine has given two gifts
to the world: Canada and the Impressionist movement. It was from this port
that Jean Denis set off to discover the St. Lawrence river estuary in 1506, and
Samuel de Champlain departed a century later to found Canada. It was also
under these Normandy skies that the 19th-century local painter Eugène Boudin
(1824–98), following in the steps of earlier artists, notably J. M. W. Turner
(1775–1851), experimented with painting weather conditions, passing on his
ideas to Claude Monet and the Impressionists.

However, Honfleur's wealth was actually built on salt. For generations,
fishing had been a local affair. However, as fishermen explored territories
further afield, they needed a method of keeping fish fresh on the return trip
to France. From the 16th century, salt preserved the massive hauls of cod
brought back from Newfoundland and the St. Lawrence estuary. It became a
precious commodity and the basis of Honfleur's prosperity.

Today, the town combines its principal industry with its artistic heritage. It
continues to attract painters, as well as visitors in search of a seafood supper.
If you arrive by car, follow signs to one of the larger car parks and prepared
to explore the improbably picturesque narrow streets and lively quaysides on
foot. Temptation awaits at each corner, and the lures of the port and town,
the antiques and art shops, the delicious fresh food and the ever-changing
exhibitions make nonsense of any prepared itinerary.

WHAT TO SEE
MUSÉE EUGÈNE BOUDIN

Here, works by French Impressionist and local painter Eugène Boudin
(1824–98) hang alongside pieces by Jean Baptiste Corot, Raoul Dufy

Above *A couple sit on the harbour looking
across at yachts and the town of Honfleur*

and one of Boudin's students, Claude Monet.
✉ Place Erik Satie, 14602 Honfleur ☎ 02 31 89 54 00 ⏰ Mid-Mar to end Sep Wed–Mon 10–12, 2–6; Oct–end Dec, mid-Feb to mid-Mar Mon, Wed–Fri 2.30–5, Sat–Sun 10–12, 2.30–5. Closed Jan to mid-Feb 👜 Adult €5.20, child/student €3.70

MAISONS SATIE
This modern museum experience is less conventional than the Musée Eugène Boudin (see above), but it is highly stimulating. It celebrates the life and work of another son of Honfleur, the eccentric composer and artist Erik Satie (1866–1925). Art and music join forces as you walk past surreal images while listening to Satie's music playing through headphones.
✉ Boulevard Charles V, 14602 Honfleur ☎ 02 31 89 11 11 ⏰ May–end Sep Wed–Mon 10–7; Oct–end Dec, mid-Feb to end Apr Wed–Mon 11–6. Closed Jan to mid-Feb 👜 Adult €5.40, child/student €3.90, under 10 free

VIEUX BASSIN
Jean-Baptiste Colbert (1619–83), King Louis XIV's finance minister, commissioned the Vieux Bassin (Old Dock) in 1681, ordering the demolition of part of the ramparts to open Honfleur out to its harbour and so realise its full trading potential. The only remnant of those original town walls is the 16th-century Lieutenance, a quirky-looking building at the entrance to the harbour, adapted from the former Caen gateway of the medieval fortress. The building's name dates from its original role as the home of the king's lieutenant. The arms of Honfleur are carved on the watch turrets and a statue of Our Lady of the Harbour perches in a niche. To prevent boats going in or out of the Vieux Bassin at night in order to avoid paying taxes, a chain was strung between the Lieutenance and a tower that once stood opposite the present bridge.

Tall, slate-fronted, oak-tiled and timber-framed buildings dating from the 16th to 18th centuries surround the Vieux Bassin. They may look alike but each is unique in size and shape. What they have in common is the strange fact that each has two ground floors, one opening onto the quayside (today usually housing ship's chandlers, art galleries or restaurants), and a second, half-way up the house, opening onto a street on the hill behind the port. Thus each building boasts two different householders.

The 15th-century church of Ste-Catherine, constructed by shipbuilders, has an 18th-century bell tower across the square as a precaution against fire. Buskers and craft stalls inhabit the pedestrian-only streets nearby.

The town's famous salt warehouses, in the rue de la Ville, were among the greatest salt stores of the region. Built in 1670 under the authority of Colbert, they had walls of stone taken from the ramparts and were topped with remarkable oak roofs. Originally, Honfleur had three stores that could hold 10,000 tonnes of salt, but one was destroyed by fire in 1892. The remaining two warehouses are listed buildings owned by the town and are now used as venues for concerts and exhibitions, when visitors have the opportunity to admire their magnificent oak beams.

MORE TO SEE
CHAPELLE DE NORE-DAME DE GRÂCE
The original Romanesque chapel here was built around 1023 by Richard II, Duke of Normandy, but was destroyed in a landslide in 1575; townsfolk erected the present chapel in the eraly 17th century. Hilltop Notre-Dame is worth visiting for the scores of votive offerings, p;laques, paintings and model ships donated by sailors and pilgrims. Among the worshippers who have stopped her to pray are Napoleon I, King Louis XII, Thérèse of Lisieux (▷ 100) and explorer Samuel de Champlain. At Whitsun the sailors of Honfleur return here for their annual pilgrimage.
✉ Côte de Grâce, 14602 Honfleur ⏰ Apr–end Oct daily 8.30–7; Nov–end Mar daily 8.30–6

TIP
» Unless you can visit out of season, arrive early to avoid the crowds of day-trippers.

REGIONS CALVADOS • SIGHTS

Above *For French Impressionism visit the Musée Eugene Boudin*
Below *Enjoy the sights from a café*

Above *Detail of a courtyard craft in the antiques centre of Dives-sur-Mer, where regular markets are held*

DIVES-SUR-MER

www.dives-sur-mer.com

William the Conqueror is celebrated in this one-time river port, from which he set sail in 1066 for England. He endowed the town with a church, Notre-Dame, which was expanded over the next 400 years, and was known locally as the Église St-Sauveur, thanks to the story told in one of its stained-glass windows about a statue of Christ the Saviour found in the sea. Halles, the wooden market hall, was constructed by monks in order to claim rents from traders; a typical local market is held here every Saturday morning, with an extra midweek market taking place on Tuesdays in July and August.

From July to mid-September, guided tours leave the market halls at 5pm to visit other historic sites around Dives-sur-Mer. Among these is the Hostellerie Guillaume le Conquérant, a post house that was once favoured by a visit from French writer Madame de Sévigné (1626–98), and the 16th- and 17th-century Manoir du Bois Hibout. Bicycles may also be rented to explore the countryside outside the town, while less energetic visitors may prefer to visit the various craft shops and restaurants near the marina, known as the Village Guillaume le Conquérant.

✠ 214 J5 🛈 Rue du Général de Gaulle, 14160 Dives-sur-Mer ☎ 02 31 91 24 66 🕐 Mid-Jun to mid-Sep Mon–Sat 10–12, 2–6

FALAISE

www.otsifalaise.com

www.château-guillaume-leconquerant.fr

The town of Falaise was largely destroyed during World War II, but the Château Guillaume le Conquérant remains, a crucial site in the history of Normandy and England (tel 02 31 41 61 44; Jul, Aug daily 10–7; Sep–end Dec, Feb–end Jun 10–6. Closed Jan). It was here that Duke Robert of Normandy had an assignation with Arlette, daughter of a local tanner, which resulted in the birth of his illegitimate son William the Conqueror in c1027. A history of controversy continues into the modern era. Today's debate rages over Bruno Decaris's contemporary restoration of the 12th-century keep and chapel and the 13th-century Tour Talbot in concrete and steel. The works incorporate a glass floor through which the foundations of the original castle may be seen, and a walk on the ramparts gives views of the Ante valley. Elsewhere in town, stop by the Hôtel Dieu hospital and old Fontaine d'Arlette.

The Musée Août 1944 (tel 02 31 90 37 19; Apr to mid-Nov 10–12, 2–6) tells the story of the World War II fighting that took place around Falaise and has a model of Canadian soldiers liberating the town. A less sombre diversion is found at Musées des Automates on the boulevard de la Libération (tel 02 31 90 02 43; Apr–end Sep daily 10–6; Oct–end Mar Sat, Sun, public holidays, school holidays 2–6. Closed 2nd week of Jan, 1st week of Feb). Children will enjoy the collection of clockwork figures and caricatures at this museum of animated department store window displays dating from the 1920s to the 1950s. Included here are mechanical tableaux of Christmas scenes, the Tour de France and fairylands that once graced the shop fronts of such Parisian institutions as the Galeries Lafayettes.

✠ 219 J7 🛈 Boulevard de la Libération, 14700 Falaise ☎ 02 31 90 17 26 🕐 May–end Sep Mon–Sat 9.30–12.30,

1.30–6.30, Sun (from 22 Jun onwards), public holidays 10.30–12.30, 2–4; Oct–1 May Mon–Sat 9.30–12.30, 1.30–5.30

LISIEUX

www.lisieux-tourisme.com

Pilgrims flock here in summer to pay homage to St. Thérèse of Lisieux, whose touching autobiography proved particularly popular during the hard days of World War I. Born Thérèse Martin in 1873, she moved with her family to Lisieux at the age of four. Throughout her childhood she begged her father to allow her to enter the Carmelite convent; aged only 15, Thérèse received papal dispensation to do so.

Always a frail young woman, Thérèse developed tuberculosis in the draughty convent. She died in 1897, aged just 24, shortly after completing her memoirs, *History of a Soul*. She was canonized in 1925 and her relics are displayed in the Carmelite chapel. In summer, a mini-train shuttles visitors between the chapel, Thérèse's family home at Les Buissonnets, and the domed basilica of Ste-Thérèse.

Also in Lisieux is the Gothic cathedral of St-Pierre, which contains the tomb of Bishop Cauchon, who executed Joan of Arc in 1431; it is also said to be where Eleanor of Aquitaine married England's King Henry II in 1152. The town itself provides a pause for reflection during a drive through the surrounding countryside, which is divided by old hedgerows and dotted with timbered farms and venerable manor houses.

On Saturday mornings (and Wednesday afternoons in summer) you can buy delicious cheeses and cider at the market.

✠ 215 K6 🛈 11 rue d'Alençon, 14100 Lisieux ☎ 02 31 48 18 10 🕐 Mid-Jun to end Sep Mon–Sat 8.30–6.30, Sun 10–12.30, 2–5; Oct to mid-Jun Mon–Sat 8.30–12, 1.30–6 🚌 From Rouen 🚉 From Rouen and Évreux

Opposite *The Allies landed at Sword beach in Ouistreham to be met by gun emplacements built by the German army*

ORBEC

www.mairie-orbec.fr

The fast-flowing river Orbiquet runs through Orbec in the valleys of the Pays d'Auge. The town, with its grand mansions and timber-fronted houses, owes its earliest wealth to the river, although the watermills gave way to textile mills in the 19th century. The later industries of cider- and cheese making continue, and the town is home to the Lanquetot cheese-makers.

In rue Grande the 16th-century Vieux Manoir is now a municipal museum with paintings, ceramics and Pays d'Auge artefacts (tel 02 31 32 58 89). The town's Église Notre-Dame (daily) was originally built in the 13th century and reconstructed in the 14th century after it was set ablaze by the English. A tower was added in the 15th century and a century later the building was remodelled in Renaissance style. In the 19th century, the church had a Gothic Revival makeover.

Orbec stages pottery classes for children in school holidays (call the tourist office).

➕ 215 L6 ℹ️ 6 rue Grande, 14290 Orbec ☎ 02 31 32 56 68 🌐 Jul, Aug Mon–Sat 9.30–12.30, 2–7, Sun 10–1; May, Jun, Sep Mon–Fri 9.30–12.30, 2–6, Sat 10–12.30, 3–6; Oct–end Apr Mon–Fri 9.30–12.30, 2–5.30, Sat 10–12.30, 3–5.30 🚌 From Lisieux

OUISTREHAM

www.ville-ouistreham.fr

Best known as Caen's ferry port, Ouistreham also boasts the traditional lures of a seaside town: The beach resort of Riva Bella has a casino and marina. Ouistreham was the site of D-Day's Sword Beach and is an obvious starting point for D-Day driving tours (▷ 106–109). The Musée de Débarquement no. 4 Commando, opposite the casino, contains many military exhibits (tel 02 31 96 63 10; Mar–end Oct daily 10.30–6), while the Musée du Mur de l'Atlantique is housed in a German bunker (tel 02 31 97 28 69; Apr–end Sep daily 9–7; Oct 4 Jan, 2 Feb–end Mar daily 10–6. Closed 4 Jan–2 Feb).

One survivor of the Battle of Normandy is the 11th-century Église St-Samson (daily 8.30–7). The church was built by Norman lords and served not only as a religious sanctuary but also as an army lookout post.

Ouistreham's lighthouse (Jul, Aug Sat, Sun 2–5.30) is another vantage point.

➕ 214 H5 ℹ️ Jardins du Casino, 14150 Ouistreham ☎ 02 31 97 18 63 🌐 Jul, Aug daily 10–1, 2–7; Sep, Apr–end Jun daily 10–12.30, 2–6.30; Oct–end Mar Mon–Sat 10–12.30, 2.30–6, Sun 10–12.30 🚌 From Caen

POINTE DU HOC

This 30m (100ft) cliff symbolizes D-Day's challenge. High above the American landing point at Omaha Beach, the German lookout point, its five artillery guns defended by the 352nd Infantry Division, was bombarded to allow US Rangers to climb the steep rocks of the Cotentin headland. The legacy of the Battle of Normandy is to be found in craters and chunks of concrete, now reclaimed by the landscape itself. From the viewing station and memorial, the vast theatre of the Omaha and Utah beach campaigns may be seen.

The story of the assault and of how the Rangers held out against the odds is retold at the Musée des Rangers, 5km (3 miles) west of the Pointe du Hoc at Grandcamp-Maisy (tel 02 31 92 33 51; daily 9.30–1, 2.30–6.30; closed Mon morning and Nov–end Jan).

➕ 213 F4 ℹ️ 118 rue A. Briand, 14450 Grandcamp-Maisy ☎ 02 31 22 62 44 🌐 Mon–Sat 9.30–1, 2.30–6.30, Sun 9.30–1

PONT-L'ÉVÊQUE

www.pontleveque.com

The town named after a bishop's bridge is famous for its creamy cheese, first produced here in the 12th century. Locally made Calvados brandy is another source of income for the town.

Its timber-framed buildings typify the Pays d'Auge; the 17th-century Hôtel Montpensier, with its painted frontage (now a library), and the brick and stone Hôtel de Brilly, today's town hall, are outstanding examples.

At the Musée du Calvados et des Métiers Anciens (tel 02 31 64 30 31; Apr–end Nov daily 10–12.30, 2–6.30, Dec–end Mar Mon–Fri 9.30–12.30, 1.30–5.30), visitors can learn about distilling. The Pont-l'Évêque's flamboyant Église St-Michel houses Franco-Prussian war memorials. May is the best time to visit, when there is a vintage car rally and a national cheese fair.

A farmer's market is held on Sundays June to October.

➕ 215 K5 ℹ️ 16 bis, rue St-Michel, 14130 Pont-l'Évêque ☎ 02 31 64 12 77 🌐 Jul, Aug Mon–Thu, Sat 10–6.30, Fri 10–7, Sun 10–1; May, Jun, Sep Mon–Thu, Sat 10–12.30, 2–6.30, Fri 10–12.30, 2–7, Sun 10–1; Oct–end Apr Mon–Sat 10–12.30, 2–6 🚌 Lisieux

ST-PIERRE-SUR-DIVES

www.mairie-saint-pierre-sur-dives.fr

Gastronomic tradition is as much a part of this typical country town as the stones of its abbey church, and never more so than on Monday mornings when the rafters of Les Halles, the market hall, echo to the sounds of poultry and traders vying for attention. This beamed barn of a market building is the very hub of the community and traders sell their chickens and ducks, cheese and *pains d'épices* (gingerbread cakes) until lunchtime. The present market is a reconstruction of the 13th-century building, which was bombed during World War II. The renovations relied on traditional methods, not one nail was used; instead, the cavernous temple to consumerism and community is held together with 290,000 wooden dowels. The market hall is open to visitors daily, and on the first Sunday of each month throughout the year it hosts an antiques market.

Jardin Conservatoire des Fleurs et des Légumes du Pays d'Auge, is a 600sq m (6,500sq ft) garden preserving flowers and vegetables traditionally grown throughout the Pays d'Auge. While the plants and shrubs from the windowboxes of the region might be more photogenic, the diversity of greenery here is nothing short of impressive.

St-Pierre's Benedictine abbey is one of the best-preserved ensembles of monastic buildings in Normandy. The abbey church dates from the 11th, 13th and 18th centuries, and has a meridian line carved across its nave that indicates the position of the sun at noon. In the tourist office, which is part of the abbey complex, an exhibition of cheese-making is open to visitors (same hours as thourist office).

➕ 219 J6 ℹ️ Rue St-Benoist, 14170 St-Pierre-sur-Dives ☎ 02 31 20 97 90 🕐 Mid-Apr to mid-Oct, Mon–Fri 9.30–12.30, 1.30–6, Sat 10.30–12.30, 2.30–5 (Jul, Aug Mon 9.30–6); mid-Oct to mid-Apr Mon–Fri 9.30–12.30, 1.30–5.30

THURY-HARCOURT

www.suisse-normande.com

Thury-Harcourt, the gateway to the Suisse Normande region, has the ruined, moated Château d'Harcourt, built in the 18th century and set in a large park (tel 02 32 46 29 70; mid-Jun to mid-Sep daily 10.30–6.30; Mar–mid-Jun, mid-Sep to mid-Nov Wed–Mon 2–6). Two gatehouses with strange beehive-shaped roofs, one wing and a bricked-up façade are all that remain of the building, although a ruined chapel in the grounds may also be visited. The single reminder that this is modern Normandy, rather than some central European utopia, is the plaque on the park wall paying tribute to the British forces who fought in the area during World War II. In the town is the Romanesque Église St-Sauveur, with a 12th-century door and 15th-century nave.

➕ 219 H6 ℹ️ 2 place St-Sauveur, 14220 Thury-Harcourt ☎ 02 31 79 70 45 🕐 Jul, Aug Mon–Sat 10–12.30, 2.30–6.30, Sun 10–12.30; Sep, May, Jun Tue–Sat 10–12.30, 2.30–6.30, Sun 10–12.30; Oct–end Apr Mon 2.30–5, Tue–Fri 10–12.30, 2.30–5, Sat 10–12.30 🚌 From Caen

VIRE

www.vire-tourisme.com

Vire is a traffic bottleneck on a busy through road, but if you walk around town you will find a few treasures that survived the war. The most important of these old buildings is the Porte-Horloge clock tower on the place du 6 Juin. The original 13th-century fortified gateway to the town was capped by its belfry and turret in the 15th century and adorned with a clock in 1840. The building hosts summer exhibitions.

Not much remains of Vire's original fortifications, most of which were destroyed well before the Battle of Normandy. The town castle played an important role in the Hundred Years War between France and England (1337–1453). In 1630, Cardinal Richelieu, chief minister to King Louis XIII, ordered the fortress to be razed to the ground; the sole surviving relic was the Norman keep, two sides of which still stand on the place du Château.

Notre-Dame church is an amalgam of styles, its Romanesque chapel having been reinterpreted in the Gothic style in the 13th century. In 1948, the church was restored following the damage of D-Day.

The 18th-century Hôtel-Dieu hospital on place Ste-Anne is now a museum of art and local traditions, including displays of Norman costume and crafts (tel 02 31 68 10 49). At nearby Vassy, a command post of the Knights Templar of Courval dates from 1140. You can view the privately owned manor house from the outside.

➕ 218 F7 ℹ️ Square de la Résistance, 14500 Vire ☎ 02 31 66 28 50 🕐 Jul, Aug Mon–Sat 9.30–1, 1.30–6; Sep–end Jun Mon–Sat 9.30–12.15, 1.45–6 (timetables may vary throughout the year) 🚌 From Caen 🚆 From Granville and Argentan

Below *Attractive flowers in the gardens at the ruined Château d'Harcourt*

TROUVILLE-SUR-MER

The classic 19th-century French seaside resort still offers beachfront fun, shopping and donkey races. Well before Deauville became the haunt of the Parisian party set (▷ 95), it was Trouville, just across the estuary of the Touques river, that lured the well-to-do to the Côte Fleurie as seaside holidays first came into fashion. Landscape artist Charles Mozin 'discovered' the resort in 1825, and his works, exhibited in Paris, soon drew painters Claude Monet and Jean Baptiste Corot, and writers Alexandre Dumas and Gustave Flaubert, to the coast in search of artistic and literary inspiration. By the heyday of the Second Empire (1852–70), the promise of casinos and the seaside proved a magnet to the fashionable Paris set. Consequently, Trouville established itself as very much the destination of choice in those heady days and was dubbed the Reine des Plages (Queen of Beaches).

CONTEMPORARY LIFE

The Villa Montebello, one of many private houses of the period, is today home to a municipal museum housing art treasures of this golden age (tel 02 31 88 16 26; Apr–end Sep Wed–Mon 11–1, 2–6). Many similar 19th century seafront villas near the wooden promenade still claim prime position alongside the casino, aquarium and seafood restaurants.

If Trouville seems a little less glamorous than today's glitzier neighbour Deauville, it nonetheless has a year-round life, with its own community thriving even outside the peak tourist season. There is a working fishing port, and behind the livelier resort you will find attractive shopping streets; these two worlds collide at the daily fish market next to the port, itself a listed building. On Wednesday and Sunday mornings a bustling quayside market sells a range of regional foods. In May, the town sees older traditions celebrated at the annual Fête de la Mer (Festival of the Sea), testament to Trouville's origins as a quiet fishing port.

INFORMATION

www.trouvillesurmer.org

🕇 215 K4 🛈 32 quai Fernand Moureaux, 14360 Trouville-sur-Mer
☎ 02 31 14 60 70 🕓 Jul, Aug Mon–Sat 9.30–7, Sun 10–4; Sep, Oct, Apr–end Jun Mon–Sat 9.30–12, 2–6.30, Sun 10–1; Nov–end Mar Mon–Sat 9.30–12, 1.30–6, Sun 10–1 🚌 From Lisieux and Caen
🚆 From Lisieux

TIP

▶▶ Come in August for donkey races on the beach.

Above *Colourful tents on the beach at Trouville*

HISTORIC CAEN

This trek through the oldest parts of the city follows in the footsteps of William the Conqueror, crossing from the King's Abbaye-aux-Hommes to Queen Mathilde's Abbaye-aux-Dames via a regal château and attractive cobbled streets.

THE WALK

Distance: 5km (3 miles)
Allow: 2 hours excluding visits to sights
Start: Esplanade de l'Hôtel de Ville
End: Place Courtonne

HOW TO GET THERE

From the Périphérique ring road, follow signs for 'centre ville' then 'Hôtel de Ville'. Park on place Louis Guillouard. To return to the car park after the walk, take bus 10 from place Courtonne to Hôtel de Ville.

★ Start the walk at the esplanade de l'Hôtel de Ville.

❶ The Abbaye St-Étienne (▷ 91) is also known as the Abbaye-aux-Hommes (Men's Abbey). This is the final resting place of William the Conqueror (died 1087), although a thigh bone is all that remains of the King's body after his grave was looted by Huguenots.

Return along the landscaped esplanade Jean Marie Louvel to place Fontette, home to the law courts with their imposing classical columns. Cross the square and walk through place St-Sauveur, past rows of dignified and well-proportioned townhouses, towards the war-damaged Église Vieux St-Sauveur. To the right of the church, follow rue St-Sauveur, turning right into rue Froide and then left onto bustling rue St-Pierre to reach the Église St-Sauveur.

❷ Lively rue St-Pierre is a good place for a mid-walk sugar boost, as *crêperies* and *chocolatières* number among its shops. At No. 52 is the Musée de la Poste, whose exterior alone is worth a photograph since the 16th-century timbered building is one of the best preserved in town. Inside you'll find a wonderful slice of nostalgia, courtesy of France's

la Poste, with its simple, old-fashioned celebration of the history of Normandy's postal and telephone service, with informative displays.

Continue to the end of the street and cross rue St-Jean to reach the Église St-Pierre.

❸ The Église St-Pierre's 72m (236ft) spire is a comforting town centre landmark should you ever get lost in Caen. Step inside the church to admire some unexpected carvings on the columns of the north side of the nave, including depictions of Arthurian legends.

From rue Montoir outside the church, follow signs to the entrance to the château.

❹ The château was founded by William the Conqueror and now houses two museums, the Musée

Opposite Shrubs and flower borders in the courtyard of the convent at the Abbaye-aux-Dames (Abbaye de la Trinité)

des Beaux Arts and Musée de Normandie (▷ 91). The original keep was destroyed during the French Revolution and more damage was inflicted on the castle during World War II. Despite this, the ramparts make a fine diversion on a sunny day.

Leave the Château by the meandering drawbridge pathway to reach rue Vaugeux, which twists as it crosses the avenue de la Libération below the castle walls. Take your time on rue Vaugeux to read the mouthwatering menus displayed in the restaurant windows and plan your evening meal. As you cross rue Poissonnière, the road becomes rue Buquet. Turn right onto rue Basse, then take the second turning on your left, rue Manissier, continuing up to place de la Reine Mathilde and the Abbaye de la Trinité.

⑤ At the Abbaye de la Trinité (▷ 92), also called Abbaye-aux-Dames (Women's Convent), round off your homage to William and Mathilde by paying your respects at the Queen's black marble tomb.

From the abbey and its gardens, retrace your steps along rue Manissier, turning right to regain rue Basse. Take the next left down into rue Samuel Bochard to arrive at place Courtonne.

⑥ Place Courtonne is a large open square linking Caen's waterways to the city centre. At one end is a pleasure port where yachts are moored, while opposite is the Tour Guillaume-le-Roy, situated on a busy traffic island. There are plenty of cafés and restaurants on place Courtonne with outdoor tables where you can take a well-earned rest.

PLACE TO VISIT
MUSÉE DE LA POSTE
✉ 52 rue St-Pierre, 14000 Caen ☎ 02 31 50 12 20 🕐 Mid-Jun to mid-Sep Tue–Sat 10–12, 2–6; mid-Sep to mid-Jun Tue–Sat 1.30–5.30 💷 Adult €2.50, child €1

WHEN TO GO
This is a year-round walk but Caen is at its best from spring to autumn, outside August.

WHERE TO EAT
AU BUREAU
Traditional fare.
✉ 21 place St-Sauveur, 14000 Caen ☎ 02 31 85 74 34 🕐 Mon–Sat 12–12

BRASSERIE MARTIN
▷ 114.

There are several crêperies and cafés on the walk for snacks.

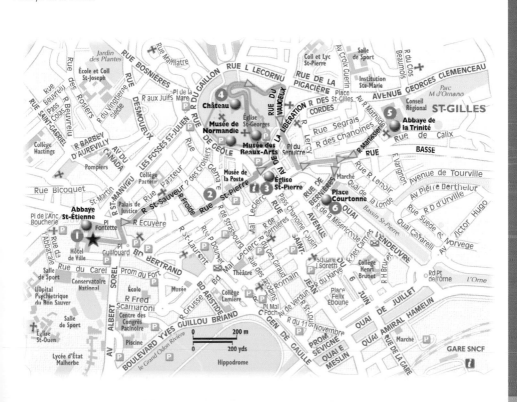

ALONG THE D-DAY COAST

This evocative drive through many of the key sites associated with D-Day begins at the first piece of French soil liberated in the Battle of Normandy and continues along the beaches and villages of the départements of Calvados and La Manche. Dozens of museums and cemeteries large and small line the route, and cafés, restaurants and shops along the coast have their own personal memories of 5 and 6 June 1944.

THE DRIVE

Distance: 160km (100 miles)
Allow: 1–2 days
Start: Ranville–Bénouville
End: Quinéville

HOW TO GET THERE

The drive begins at Pegasus Bridge, 10km (6 miles) northeast of Caen on the D515, between Ranville and Bénouville.

★ Pegasus Bridge was the landing site of Captain John Howard and his gliders, the first Allied arrivals on D-Day. The wartime bridge, seized and held by the British troops, was dismantled in 1993 owing to heavy traffic and a larger replica now crosses the Caen canal. The original bridge can be visited a few

metres away in the grounds of the Mémorial Pegasus, an inspiring museum of the 6th Airborne Division that has strong relationships with veterans and is the perfect starting point for a D-Day tour. Across the bridge, the Café Gondrée was the first place in France to be liberated by Allied troops. Still open as a café in summer, it is adorned with memorabilia.

Follow the D514 and well-signposted D84 to Ouistreham.

❶ At Ouistreham, visit the Musée du Mur de l'Atlantique (▷ 101) and the Musée du Débarquement no. 4 Commando (▷ 101) to learn the story of the first dawn landings on Sword Beach.

Continue on the D514 out of Ouistreham and along Sword Beach, passing small resorts. At Luc-sur-Mer, turn left onto the D83 for Douvres-la-Délivrande.

❷ Douvres-la-Délivrande is the site of a former German station with twin bunkers and is now home to the Musée Radar, which looks at the history of radar.

Take the D7 back towards the sea and turn left onto the D514 coast road towards Courseulles at Bernières-sur-Mer.

❸ In Courseulles, at the very spot where Canadian soldiers came ashore on 6 June 1944, is the Centre Juno Beach, which showcases

Canada's role in World War II and the country's contemporary culture.

Continue along the D514 via Ver-sur-Mer (where the Musée America Gold Beach is worth a visit) to reach Arromanches-les-Bains.

❹ Arromanches-les-Bains affords panoramic views over the Mulberry Harbour and has two very different museums telling the story of the prefabricated port and the D-Day landings (▷ 96–97). This is a good point on the drive to stretch your legs and take a breath of bracing sea air.

Head south from Arromanches on the D87 to Ryes, stopping at the British and Commonwealth Cemetery, with its 4,868 graves and memorial to 1,837 missing servicemen. Follow signs to Bayeux, taking the D12 into the centre of the town.

❺ Bayeux may attract busloads of visitors to see its tapestry, but its other claim to fame is as the first town in occupied France to be liberated in 1944. The Musée Mémorial de la Bataille de Normandie (▷ 86) has films and displays recalling the events. A lesser-known museum in the town is devoted to General de Gaulle.

Drive north out of town on the D6 to reach the coast at Port-en-Bessin-Hüppain, where you can visit the Musée des Épaves Sous-Marines du Débarquement, a museum devoted to 15 years of underwater diving expeditions to rescue items from D-Day wrecks sunk off the coast. Continue along the D514 parallel to Omaha Beach.

❻ Omaha Beach is the site of several D-Day reminders, the most poignant of which is the American Cemetery, with 9,386 neat white crosses, at Colleville-sur-Mer. The Musée Omaha—6 Juin 1944, just metres from the beach itself at St-Laurent-sur-Mer, displays uniforms,

weapons and other items from the battlefield. A little further along the coast at Vierville-sur-Mer is the Musée D-Day Omaha, which looks at the technological advancements made during the war that still affect daily life today.

Continue to Pointe du Hoc.

❼ Pointe du Hoc is the very symbol of the courage of Colonel Rudder's young American Rangers, who stormed its steep cliff face on D-Day (▷ 101). Stop here first before driving a further 5km (3 miles) to the Musée des Rangers at Grandcamp-Maisy, where you can learn the full story (▷ 101).

From Grandcamp-Maisy, take the D199 south, turning left onto the D113 and left again onto the D613 to reach La Cambe, where black crosses mark 21,500 graves in the German Cemetery. Continue on the D613 to join the N13, heading towards Cherbourg. Follow this for 29km (18 miles) before turning onto the D67 to Ste-Mère-Église.

❽ Ste-Mère-Église is still dominated by two images of D-Day: the mannequin of an American parachutist hanging from its church tower and the parachute-shaped Musée des Troupes Aéroportées, housing a Douglas C-47 aircraft (▷ 52) which dropped paratroopers.

Opposite *Crosses in the tree-lined American Military Cemetery at Colleville-sur-Mer*
Below *Maison Gondrée was the first house to be liberated in France during World War II*

Take the D523 out of town for 0.5km (0.3 miles), then turn left onto the D423 and left again on the D70 to reach Ste-Marie-du-Mont and the Musée du Débarquement d'Utah Beach. The beach is signposted from the D319. The trail of memorial milestones that mark the path of liberation stretches from here to Belgium. You can continue driving along the beach road until you reach Quinéville and its little Musée de la Liberté, depicting scenes from daily life in occupied France.

PLACES TO VISIT
MÉMORIAL PEGASUS
✉ Avenue de Major Howard, 14860 Ranville ☎ 02 31 78 19 44 🕐 May–end Sep daily 9.30–6.30; Oct to mid-Dec, Feb–end Apr daily 10–1, 2–5.30. Closed mid-Dec to end Jan ✋ Adult €5.50, child (8–25) €4.40

Below A monument at Omaha Beach: Defences withstood bombings and 2,400 US soldiers died within hours of landing

MUSÉE RADAR
Enquiries through Caen Memorial Museum (www.memorial-caen.fr) ✉ Route de Basly, 14440 Douvres-la-Délivrande ☎ 02 31 06 06 45 🕐 Mid-Jul to mid-Sep Tue–Sun 10–6

CENTRE JUNO BEACH
✉ Voie des Français Libres, B.P. 104, 14470 Courseulles-sur-Mer ☎ 02 31 37 32 17 🕐 Apr–end Sep daily 9.30–7; Mar, Oct daily 10–6; Feb, Nov–end Dec daily 10–1, 2–5 ✋ Adult €6.50, child (8–18) €5

MUSÉE AMERICA GOLD BEACH
✉ 2 place Admiral Byrd, 14114 Ver-sur-Mer ☎ 02 31 22 58 58 🕐 Jul, Aug daily 10.30–5.30. Closed Tue Sep–end Jun ✋ Adult €4, child (5–21) €2.40

MÉMORIAL DU GÉNÉRAL DE GAULLE
✉ 10 rue Bourbesnour, 14400 Bayeux ☎ 02 31 92 45 55 🕐 Jun–Aug daily 9.30–12.30, 2–6.30; Sep–end Nov, Mar–end May daily 10–12.30, 2–6. Closed Dec–end Feb ✋ Adult €3.50, child (5–21) €2.50

MUSÉE DES ÉPAVES SOUS-MARINES DU DÉBARQUEMENT
✉ Route de Bayeux, Commines, 14520 Port-en-Bessin ☎ 02 31 21 17 06 🕐 Jun–end Sep daily 10–12, 2–6 ✋ Adult €6, child (7–16) €3

MUSÉE OMAHA—6 JUIN 1944
✉ Avenue de la Libération, 14710 St-Laurent-sur-Mer ☎ 02 31 21 97 44 🕐 Jul, Aug daily 9.30–7.30; early to mid-Sep, mid-May to end Jun daily 9.30–7; mid-Sep to mid-Nov, mid-Mar to mid-May daily 9.30–6.30; mid-Feb to mid-Mar daily 10–12.30, 2.30–6. Closed mid-Nov to mid-Feb ✋ Adult €5.80, child (7–15) €3.30

MUSÉE D-DAY OMAHA
✉ Route de Grandchamp, 14710 Vierville-sur-Mer ☎ 02 31 21 71 80 🕐 Easter–end Sep daily 9.30–7.30; Oct–Easter daily 10–12.30, 2–6 ✋ Adult €5.30, child (2–25) €3

MUSÉE DU DÉBARQUEMENT D'UTAH BEACH
✉ 50480 Ste-Marie-du-Mont ☎ 02 33

71 53 35  Jun–end Sep daily 9.30–7;
Apr, May, Oct daily 10–6; Nov, Dec Sat–Sun
10–12.30, 2–5.30; Feb–end Mar daily
10–12.30, 2–5.30. Closed Jan 👆 Adult
€5.50, child €2

MUSÉE DE LA LIBERTÉ RETROUVÉE
✉ Avenue de la Plage, 50310 Quinéville
☎ 02 33 95 95 95 🕐 22 Mar–11 Nov
daily 10–7 👆 Adult €6, child €4

WHEN TO GO
Spring onwards is the best time
for this drive, since many of the
museums close during the winter.

WHERE TO EAT
LE LION D'OR
▷ 114.

LE BISTROT D'À CÔTÉ
✉ 10–12 rue Michel-Lefournier, 14520
Port-en-Bessin ☎ 02 31 51 79 12
🕐 Thu–Mon 12–1.30, 7–9.15. Closed Jan
to mid-Feb

Above *A World War II relic outside the
history centre at Utah Beach*

WHAT TO DO

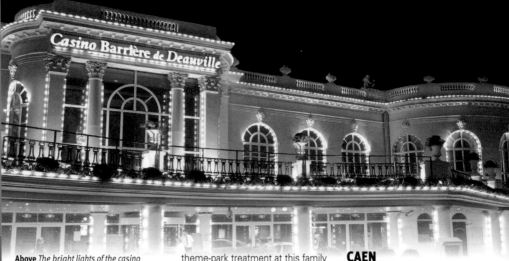

Above *The bright lights of the casino at Deauville*

BAYEUX

BAYEUX BRODERIE

www.bayeux-broderie.com

Chantal James demonstrates the techniques of the famous Bayeux stitch and sells tapestry kits. She is happy to help amateur needleworkers with tricky stitches.

✉ 39 rue du Bienvenu, 14400 Bayeux ☎ 02 31 51 05 81 ⏱ Mid-Apr to mid-Oct Tue–Fri 11–6.30, Sat 2–6.30. One day courses Sep–Apr (Mon by appointment)

BLONVILLE-SUR-MER

LES PLANCHES

www.lesplanches.com

This nightclub, at a small resort near Deauville, has an outdoor swimming pool. There are two dance floors, one playing current trends and the other reliving the sounds of the past.

✉ Les Longs Champs, 14910 Blonville-sur-Mer ☎ 02 31 87 58 09 ⏱ Jul, Aug daily 11pm–5am; Sep–Jun Fri–Sat 10pm–4am 🖐 €20

BRETTEVILLE-SUR-ODON

PARC FESTYLAND

www.festyland.com

Normandy's heritage gets the theme-park treatment at this family playground on the outskirts of Caen, where rides and attractions are divided into zones designed around historical periods. There is a choice of dining, from crêpes to sit-down restaurants.

✉ B.P. 50, 14760 Bretteville-sur-Odon ☎ 02 31 75 04 04 ⏱ Jul, Aug daily 10.30–7; Sep, late Mar–end Jun selected days 10–6 (phone for details) 🖐 Adult €13 (Jul–Aug €14), under 12 €9.50 (Jul–Aug €12) 🍴 ⊟ 🚻 🅿 Follow signs from Caen's Périphérique

LE BREUIL-EN-AUGE

CALVADOS CHÂTEAU DU BREUIL

www.château-breuil.fr

Not many distilleries have such an elegant setting. This one is in a 17th-century château south of Pont-l'Évêque, where apples are turned into the region's most famous export, the apple brandy Calvados. Take a guided tour and choose from various Calvados vintages or try Pommeau (Calvados and apple juice) or Coeur du Breuil (a Calvados-based liqueur).

✉ Les Jourdains, 14130 Le Breuil-en-Auge ☎ 02 31 65 60 00 ⏱ Jul–end Sep daily 9–6; Oct–end Jun 9–12, 2–6. Guided tours 9–11, 2–5 🖐 Adults €3, under-18s free

CAEN

6X

This narrow café-bar in Caen's main commercial street is a firm favourite with locals weighed down with shopping bags seeking mid-afternoon refreshment. On Sundays, the shopping crowd makes way for students enjoying the last late night of the weekend. The back room is rather pokey, so find a table near the door or outside on the terrace.

✉ 7 rue St-Sauveur, 14000 Caen ☎ 02 31 86 36 98 ⏱ Mon–Fri noon–1am, Sat 2pm–1am, Sun 4pm–1am 🚊 Tram to St-Pierre

LE CARRÉ NEW CLUB

In Caen's riverside district, this club is a hit with 30-somethings. The music policy is a canny blend of retro and the latest sounds. Before the main club opens its doors, the French Bar upstairs offers a welcome from 5pm. Karaoke on Tuesday and Wednesday.

✉ 32 quai Vendeuvre, 14000 Caen ☎ 02 31 38 90 90 ⏱ Tue–Sun from 10.30pm. Over 27 only 🖐 Tue–Wed often free, Thu–Sat €13 🚊 Tram to Résistance

CHARLOTTE CORDAY

This city-centre confectioner's

may be named after a notorious murderess, but the chocolates on sale are sheer heaven. The delicacies, made from pure cocoa butter, include the local speciality *rochers du château*.

✉ 114 rue St-Jean, 14000 Caen ☎ 02 31 86 33 25 🕐 Tue–Sat 9.30–12.30, 2.30–7 🚊 Tram to Résistance

LE CHIC
The dance floor is always packed at this nightclub, which despite its ever-changing programme of theme nights has an irresistible feel of the 1980s. The mixed crowds here include local students, holidaymakers and metropolitan weekenders from Paris.

✉ Place Courtonne, 14000 Caen ☎ 02 31 94 48 72 🕐 Tue–Sun 10.30pm–5am 🚻 €15; women admitted free before midnight at weekends 🚊 Tram to Bernières

L'ORIENT-EXPRESS
Despite the garish pink awning over its entrance, this bar near the fashionable banks of the Orne is the essential late-night pre- and post-club rendezvous for students and locals. It is also an excellent choice for meeting up in the late afternoon to make restaurant plans for the evening ahead.

✉ 24 rue du 11 Novembre, 14000 Caen ☎ 02 31 72 81 64 🕐 Daily 2.30–4 🚊 Tram to quai de Juillet

SOUTERROSCOPE DES ARDOISIÈRES
www.souterroscope.com
Seemingly endless underground passages and four vast subterranean chambers are waiting to be discovered in the former slate quarries under the *bocage* landscape of Caumont-l'Éventé. The guided tour (in either English or French) explains the mineral treasures and passes underground waterways and even rainbows. Warm clothing is advisable as the average year-round temperature stays below 12°C (54°F).

✉ Route de St-Lô, 14240 Caumont-l'Éventé ☎ 02 31 71 15 15 🕐 Jul, Aug daily 10–6; Sep, May, Jun Mon–Sat 10–5, Sun

10–6; Oct to mid-Dec, mid-Feb to end Apr Tue–Sat 10–5 🚻 Adult €9.45, child (4–12) €4.50 🍴 ❓ Accessible to visitors with disabilities

ZÉNITH DE CAEN
www.zenith-caen.fr
The auditorium here can seat up to 7,000 for the comedy, ballet, classical music concerts and other performances that are staged here.

✉ Rue Joseph Philippon, 14000 Caen 🕐 Performances usually start at 8.30pm 🚻 Ticket prices depend on the performance and can be purchased only at the venue on the night of the performance unless booked beforehand through a ticket agency

COURSEULLES-SUR-MER
AUX TROIS MATELOTS
You are as likely to meet a poet as a sailor in this wine bar around the corner from the quai des Allies in the port town of Courseulles-sur-Mer, 15km (9 miles) east of Arromanches-les-Bains. Have a rendezvous with the arts over a decent bottle of wine and a platter of cheese or *charcuterie*. Regular exhibitions of work by local painters, occasional poetry recitals from contemporary Norman writers and a reputation for good live music mark out this place as more than the usual bar or restaurant.

✉ 20 rue de la Marine, 14470 Courseulles-sur-Mer ☎ 02 31 97 53 13 🕐 Restaurant: Tue–Sat 12.30–1.45, 7.30–9, Sun 12.30–1.45

CREULLY
PARAPLUIES H2O
www.h2oparapluies.fr
The ultimate rainy-day diversion: Buy a hand-made umbrella and watch craftsmen at work in this shop, 9km (6 miles) southeast of Arromanches-les-Bains. These are the ultimate in brollies, with prices upwards of €60. Some are personally embroidered; others double as hardwood walking sticks. Special models keep the rain away yet allow the wind to blow through the material.

✉ Hameau de Creullet, 14480 Creully ☎ 02 31 80 31 35 🕐 Mon–Sat 9–12, 2–7 (Jul, Aug guided tour Wed at 11)

DEAUVILLE
CASINO DE DEAUVILLE
www.lucienbarriere.com
This casino and club is in a beautiful Belle Époque building on the seafront. There are slot machines, gaming tables, two bars, three restaurants and a nightclub, and the dress code is formal.

✉ Rue Edmond Blanc, 14802 Deauville ☎ 02 31 14 31 14 🕐 Slot machines: Mon–Thu 11am–2am, Fri 11am–3am, Sat 10am–4am, Sun 10am–3am 🚻 Free entrance needed but €10 needed

GOLF BARRIÈRE DE DEAUVILLE
www.lucienbarriere.com
You'll get beautiful views of the sea and the countryside from this 18-hole golf course on top of Mont Canisy, which offers fast greens and tough rough. After your round of golf, have a drink in the clubhouse or browse in the shop.

✉ Mont Canisy St-Arnoult, 14803 Deauville ☎ 02 31 14 24 24 🕐 Daily 9–6 🚻 Green fee from €50

DOUVRES-LA-DÉLIVRANDE
PÂTISSERIE DE LA BASILIQUE
You'll find this small village a stone's throw from the local beaches north of Caen, and the pâtisserie itself in a pretty half-timbered house. For three generations, the Jung family have been making Normandy specials such as *brasillés* (bread made with the local salted butter) and biscuits similar to Scottish shortbread.

✉ 3 place de la Basilique, 14440 Douvres-la-Délivrande ☎ 02 31 37 29 74 🕐 Wed–Sat 7.45–12.45, 2.15–7.45, Sun 7.45–7.45; Jul–Aug daily, same hours

HÉROUVILLE-ST-CLAIR
BEAUREGARD AVENTURE
www.beauregard-aventure.com
This obstacle course is suspended from the trees in the grounds of the beautiful Château de Beauregard. It has 98 challenges—ladders, slides, bridges and so on made out of ropes and logs—organized into eight routes graded by colour according to difficulty.

✉ Parc du Château de Beauregard, 14200 Hérouville-St-Clair ☎ 06 07 63 01 31

Normally schools hols 2–8 but times change through the year ⓌAdult €3–€22, child from €6

CAFÉ DES IMAGES
www.cafedesimages.fr
A state-of-the-art cinema complex and rendezvous for movie buffs, where English and American films are shown in their original language and there are plenty of themed seasons. There are also comfortable seats, low prices and a friendly café (with discounts for filmgoers), all easily reached by tram from central Caen (the last tram back to the city is at 11.50pm).
✉ 4 square du Théâtre, 14202 Hérouville-St-Clair ☎ 02 31 45 34 35 ⏰ Call for film times. Café: Mon–Fri 11.30am–10.15pm, Sat 3.30–10.15 Ⓦ €3.60–€7.50 🚃 Tramway B to Café des Images 🅿 ❓ Access for visitors with disabilities

HONFLEUR
ANTIC-DÉCO-ART
www.antic-deco-art-normandie.com
In a change from the heavy, dark furniture so typical of Normandy antiques shops, here you will find knick-knacks (bibelots), ivories, cameos, paintings and chandeliers against light walls, on polished tables and on the neatly tiled floor. It's just the place to buy a special gift or the finishing touch for your favourite room at home.
✉ 4 rue Brûlée, 14600 Honfleur ☎ 02 31 89 42 74 ⏰ Fri–Mon 10–1, 2.30–7, other days according to owner's whim

LES ARTS DE L'ENCLOS
www.galeriedaniellebourdette.com
The Danielle Bourdette-Gorzkowski art gallery on the quayside of Honfleur has constantly changing temporary exhibitions and is the place to buy works by such distinguished Norman painters as Yvonne Guégan and André Lemaitre.
✉ Quai St-Etienne, 14600 Honfleur ☎ 02 31 89 19 13 ⏰ Daily 10–12.30, 2.30–7

MARCHÉ TRADITIONNEL
This traditional market takes place on a pretty square presided over by a 15th-century church and lined with half-timbered buildings now housing cafés. Treat yourself to the locally caught fish and farm produce on sale here, including fruit, vegetables and dairy products such as the Normandy cheeses Camembert and Livarot. In season, craft stalls often line the streets leading up to the main market.
✉ Place de l'Église Ste-Catherine, 14600 Honfleur ⏰ Sat 9.30–12.30

L'HÔTELLERIE
BROCANTE BEAU GEST
www.beau-gest.com
On the main road from Évreux to Caen, this treasure trove of a sale-yard has everything from farm tools to furniture, paintings, old clocks and kitchenware. It's well worth a rummage if you are looking for authentic souvenirs. No credit cards.
✉ Route Nationale 13–Le Bourg, 14100 l'Hôtellerie ☎ 02 31 63 18 16 ⏰ Daily 9–6

ISIGNY-SUR-MER
COOPÉRATIVE LAITIÈRE D'ISIGNY-STE-MÈRE
www.isigny-ste-mere.com
The produce from this dairy co-operative is famous the world over, and since 1986 use of its name has been controlled, just as with champagne. The dairy is known for its crème fraîche, but it also produces a butter with a particularly distinctive taste, as well as cheeses (Camembert, Mimolette, Pont-l'Évêque), some of which are made from unpasteurised milk. Book in advance if you want to take a guided tour between September and June.
✉ 2 rue du Docteur Boutrois, 14230 Isigny-sur-Mer ☎ 02 31 51 33 88 ⏰ Guided tours Jul–Aug Mon–Sat at 10, 11, 2, 3, 4 Ⓦ Guided tours: adult €3, child €2

LISEUX
BOWLING DE LISIEUX
www.bowlinglisieux.com
The high spot—literally above the town—of Lisieux by night is its ten-pin bowling alley, the social hub after the local bars close at 1am.
✉ 69 rue de Paris, 14100 Lisieux ☎ 02 31 62 19 30 ⏰ School holidays

Mon–Thu 3pm–2am, Fri–Sat 3pm–4am, Sun 8pm–2am. At other times Mon, Tue, Thu 8pm–2am, Sun, Wed 3pm–2am, Fri–Sat 3pm–4am Ⓦ €5.50 per game, €2 shoe hire

LE GRILLON
A favourite with the student crowd for its reasonable prices and contemporary music policy, this bar comes into its own in summer when tables spill out from behind the smoked-glass windows onto the pavement terrace. There are also occasional live music performances.
✉ 80 rue Henry Chéron, 14100 Lisieux ☎ 02 31 62 14 50 ⏰ Mon–Thu 8am–10pm, Fri–Sat 8am–1pm

LE WEB CAFÉ
With bright blue awnings and colourful tables and chairs set outside in a corner of Lisieux's central square, this cybercafé is as much a place to surf the real thoroughfares as the information superhighway. They have Karaoke nights too.
✉ 6 place de la République, 14100 Liseux ☎ 02 31 62 07 62 ⏰ Mon–Sat 8–8

LIVAROT
LE VILLAGE FROMAGER
www.graindorge.fr
Learn why the Normans call Livarot cheese 'Le Colonel', discover which red wines are best served with Pont-l'Évêque cheese, and watch commercial cheese-making in action during a free tour of this prettily timbered and flower-bedecked dairy some 20km (12 miles) southwest of Lisieux. There are also occasional Pays d'Auge art exhibitions held here.
✉ 42 rue du Général-Leclerc, 14140 Livarot ☎ 02 31 48 20 00 ⏰ Mon–Fri 9.30–12, 1.30–5, Sat 9.30–noon. Open Sun Jul, Aug Ⓦ Tours: free

OUISTREHAM
THALAZUR
www.thalazur.fr
This is a thalassotherapy seawater health spa, with hydrotherapy, seaweed treatments, a heated salt-water swimming pool, a Jacuzzi, a

sauna and a gym. Health and beauty treatments are offered à la carte or on a residential basis, and there are special weeks for singles.

✉ Avenue de Cdt-Kieffer, 14150 Ouistreham ☎ 02 31 96 40 40 ◔ Mon–Sat 8.30–8, Sun 8.30–6. Reservations (essential) taken 9–6. Closed Dec ✋ Choice of two treatments €64 (€68 Sat, Sun)

PONT-L'ÉVÊQUE
LES TONNEAUX DU PÈRE MAGLOIRE
www.les-tonneaux-du-pere-magloire.com
Fun for the family, this themed restaurant serves dinner inside huge Calvados barrels from the Père Magloire cellars. Telephone for information on special evenings celebrating Norman heritage, when diners can learn to churn their own butter and join in folk songs and traditional games. You can also take the Père Magloire Calvados cellar tour nearby (tel 02 31 64 30 31).

✉ Route de Trouville, 14130 Pont-l'Évêque ☎ 02 31 64 65 20 ◔ Restaurant: daily noon–2.30, 7–9.30. Cellar tour: May–end Sep 10.30, 11.30, 2.30, 3.30, 4.30, 5.30; Oct, Apr 11, 2.30, 3.30, 4.30. Shop: Nov–Mar Mon–Fri ✋ Cellar tour: adult €2.50, child free

PONT-D'OUILLY
ROCK 'N' ROLL ADVENTURES
www.rocknrolladventures.com
Explore the miles of mountain bike trails in Suisse Normande with English-speaking guides. Rental bikes are available and the operator, based in a farmhouse on the river Orne, offers other activities including motocross riding, power boating, paintball, go-karts, rock climbing, kayaking, kite surfing, waterskiing and horseback-riding. Packages are inclusive of food, activities and accommodation.

✉ Le Relais des Amis, rue de la Liberation, 14690 Pont d'Ouilly ☎ 02 31 69 83 34 ◔ All year ✋ Weekend full board from £199 per person, including three activities

VIRE
GUY DEGRENNE
www.guydegrenne.com
Guy Degrenne's fame stems from

MAY
FÊTE DES MARINS
Across town, this traditional festival blends religious services with folk celebrations. Fishing boats, colourfully decorated for the occasion, sail from the old port to be blessed by the priest, and there is a procession of sailors up to the chapel of Notre-Dame de Grace.

✉ Honfleur ☎ 02 31 89 23 30 ◔ Whitsun weekend

JUNE
MARATHON DE LA LIBERTÉ
This mass jog along the 'Freedom' coastline is a commemoration of the Battle of Normandy.

✉ D-Day beaches ☎ 02 31 27 90 30 ◔ Weekend closest to 6 Jun

LES JOURNÉES ROMANTIQUES
Films with a feel-good factor are shown on the big screen as the resort spends a week celebrating full-length and short romantic movies on the theme of love.

✉ Cabourg ☎ 02 31 91 20 00 ◔ One week in Jun

JULY
FÊTE MÉDIÉVALES
Troubadors, jesters and jugglers take to the streets around the cathedral as the town re-enacts a traditional medieval fair.

✉ Bayeux ☎ 02 31 51 28 28 ◔ First weekend in Jul

FESTIVAL SWING'IN DEAUVILLE
The big-band sound comes to the fashionable resort, with concerts in the casino theatre and events around town.

✉ Deauville ☎ 02 31 14 40 00 ◔ One week in Jul

FÊTE DU FROMAGE
AOC (appellation d'origine contrôlée) cheese from Normandy and France, together with some excllent wines, are celebrated with a market. Gastronomy turns to greed with Sunday's Livarot cheese-eating contest.

✉ Livarot ☎ 02 31 63 47 39 ◔ Late Jul

JULY–AUGUST
FÊTE DE LA MER
Sea-shanties and boat trips characterize the Festival of the Sea, when the port celebrates its fishing tradition with a party on Saturday and a Mass on Sunday.

✉ Trouville-sur-Mer ☎ 02 31 14 60 70 ◔ Late Jul or late Aug

SEPTEMBER
FESTIVAL DU CINÉMA AMÉRICAIN
Hollywood's stars arrive for the American Film Festival, one of Europe's most accessible yet prestigious film festivals.

✉ Deauville ☎ 02 31 14 40 00 ◔ First half of Sep

its original range of steel cutlery, and the company's stylish tableware, from glass bowls to children's crockery, is now sold in France's smartest stores. Take a guided tour of the workshops where the famous knives and forks are manufactured, then shop at the factory outlet store on avenue de Bischwiller.

✉ Route d'Aunay, 14500 Vire ☎ 02 31 66 44 44 ◔ Tours (75 mins): Tue, Thu by appointment only. Closed Aug ✋ Tours: adult €3.50, child (under 18) €1.20

LE TIFFANY
www.le-tiffany.com
This is two clubs in one, with one room playing the latest techno and house and another dance floor for more retro partygoers. The garden is a great place for chilling out.

✉ Route de Champ-du-Boult, 14500 Vire ☎ 02 31 68 62 27 ◔ Sat and eve of national hols 11pm–5am ✋ €10 (Includes first drink)

EATING

Above *Sample Normandy's seafood dishes*

PRICES AND SYMBOLS

The restaurants are listed alphabetically (excluding Le, La and Les) by town. The prices given are the average for a two-course lunch (L) and a three-course dinner (D) for one person, without drinks. The wine price is for the least expensive bottle. All the restaurants listed accept credit cards unless otherwise stated.

For a key to the symbols, ▷ 2.

AUDRIEU

CHÂTEAU D'AUDRIEU
www.château-audrieu.com
Three adjoining dining rooms grace this château (▷ 116). Fresh flowers enhance fireplaces, wood panelling and chandeliers. The food, prepared by Cyril Haberland, is presented on fine china bearing the crest of the château. His signature dishes marry contemporary panache with Norman flavour, as in such main course delicacies as *pigeon en cocotte* (pigeon casserole) with apples. To accompany your meal, choose from some superb vintage wines.
✉ 14250 Audrieu ☎ 02 31 80 21 52
🕐 Tue–Fri 7–9.30, Sat–Sun 12–2, 7–9.30. Closed mid-Dec to end Jan 🍴 L €55, D €95, Wine €25

BAYEUX

LE LION D'OR
www.liondor-bayeux.fr
This former coach house, dating back to the 18th century, provides a lovely setting for a meal. Chef Patrick Mouilleau cooks reliable regional dishes—try his rabbit confit with sage and a *mille-feuille* of carrots, or the salmon steak pansautéed in olive oil and thyme.
✉ 71 rue St-Jean, 14400 Bayeux ☎ 02 31 92 06 90 🕐 Tue–Fri, Sun 12–2.30, 7.30–10, Sat, Mon 7.30–10. Closed mid-Dec to mid-Jan 🍴 L €25, D €55, Wine €16

LE PAVÉ D'AUGE
The restaurant is in the marketplace and original markethall features have been retained. One old favourite on the menu is escalope of warm salt cod, which is served with a home-made chutney.
✉ Place du Village, 14430 Beuvron-en-Auge ☎ 02 31 79 26 71 🕐 Jul, Aug Tue–Sun 12–1.45, 7.30–9.30; Sep–end Jun Wed–Sun 12–1.45, 7.30–9.30; closed Mon 24 Nov–26 Dec, 1–8 Jul 🍴 L €35, D €35, Wine €30

CAEN

BRASSERIE MARTIN
www.brasserie-restaurant-martin.com
The city's most famous dish, *tripes à la mode de Caen* (Caen-style tripe), and other regional specialties are on the menu at this lively venue. The legendary restaurant has been given a facelift. Happily, the food policy is unmodernized, and reliable fare—some say the best in town—keeps the place busy.
✉ 1 place Courtonne, 14000 Caen ☎ 02 31 44 18 06 🕐 Daily 12–2, 7–10 🍴 L €20, D €20, Wine €7.50

LE PRÉSSOIR
Yvan Vautier has taken over as chef at this reputable eatery, which is popular among local businessmen. It is close to Caen's Périphérique making it accessible to travellers going to Cotentin or the Pays d'Auge. Dishes include the house specialty *le ris de veau au homard et huile truffée* (veal sweetbreads with lobster and truffle oil).
✉ 3 avenue Henry-Chéron, 14000 Caen ☎ 02 31 73 32 71 🕐 Tue–Fri 12.30–1.30, 7.30–9.30, Sat 7.30–9.30, Sun 12.30–1.30. Closed Aug 🍴 L €44, D €66, Wine €30
🅿 Private parking

CAMBREMER

CHÂTEAU LES BRUYÈRES
www.châteaulesbruyeres.com
Dine on the veranda, where the chef will invite you to sample some

of his original recipes based on traditional regional cuisine, including an interesting plate of scallops with foie gras. Among the desserts is a dramatic flambée of strawberries in Pays d'Auge Calvados. The château has accommodation (▷ 117).

✉ Route du Cadran, 14340 Cambremer ☎ 02 31 32 22 45 🕐 Tue–Sun 12–1.30, 7.30–9. Closed Jan ✋ L €60, D €60, Wine €20

CRÉPON
FERME DE LA RANÇONNIÈRE
www.ranconniere.com
The dining room in this 18th-century farmhouse hotel (▷ 116–117), has a rustic authenticity. Relax under beamed ceilings, as you settle down to a platter of fresh seafood served at linen-draped tables.

✉ Route d'Arromanches, 14480 Crépon ☎ 02 31 22 21 73 🕐 Daily 12–1.30, 7–9. Closed Jan ✋ L €30, D €40, Wine €15

CRESSERONS
LA VALISE GOURMANDE
www.lavalisegourmande-caen.com
This 18th-century priory, with its courtyard, luxurious gardens and pristine dining room, sets the scene for an intimate dîner à deux. The food is classic Norman fare, such as poitrine de cochon braisée au cidre fermier (pork braised in farmhouse cider). The restaurant is only a few minutes from the coast.

✉ 7 rue de Lion-sur-Mer, 14440 Cresserons ☎ 02 31 37 39 10 🕐 Wed–Sat 12–2, 7.30–9, Sun 12–2, Tue 7.30–9. Closed early Mar, mid Sep to end Oct ✋ L €30, D €40, Wine €24

CREULLY
HOSTELLERIE ST-MARTIN
www.hostelleriesaintmartin.com
This restaurant lies beneath the vaulted ceilings of Creully's original 16th-century market. Monsieur Legrand, the owner and chef, is justifiably proud of the regional country fare he produces as well as his more complex speciality dishes. The house foie gras with apples, or a duck steak with honey sauce, will stimulate the palate of any gourmet. These dishes are at their

best when accompanied by wine from Monsieur Legrand's extensive cellars.

✉ Place E. Paillaud, 14480 Creully ☎ 02 31 80 10 11 🕐 Daily 12–2, 7–9.30. Closed end Dec to mid-Jan ✋ L €14, D €20, Wine €12.50

DEAUVILLE
AUGUSTO
www.restaurant-augusto.com
At Augusto, a chic bistro, the staff claim to be the 'kings of lobster'. The house special is lobster served with fresh pasta, while other incarnations of the crustacean include lobster mousse and broth. There are also fish and meat dishes. Eat outside or in a marine-inspired dining room. Choose from prix fixe menus or eat à la carte.

✉ 27 rue Désiré le Hoc, 14800 Deauville ☎ 02 31 88 34 49 🕐 Thu–Mon 12–2.30, 7–10.30, open daily Jul, Aug until midnight ✋ L €22, D €50, Wine €23

DIVES-SUR-MER
CHEZ LE BOUGNAT
www.chezlebougnat.fr
Traditional family favourites are the secret of this restaurant's success. French comfort food, including the classic winter warmer pot au feu, appeal to young and old alike. Locals like this unpretentious seaside eatery for its reliable food and ambience. Dogs are welcome at the restaurant.

✉ 27 rue Gaston-Manneville, 14160 Dives-sur-Mer ☎ 02 31 91 06 13 🕐 Daily 12–2, Thu–Sat 7–10, Sun–Wed 7–10. Closed Jan ✋ L €19, D €25, Wine €14

FALAISE
L'ATTACHE
Housed in an old coaching inn, this small restaurant has an excellent wine list—nurturing the cellar is the passion of the patron, Alain Hastain. Service in the dining room is attentive and friendly. The use of local fish, fresh herbs and spices makes the menu interesting.

✉ Rond-point Nord de l'Attache, 14700 Falaise ☎ 02 31 90 05 30 🕐 Thu–Mon 12–2, 7–9, Tue 12–2. Closed late Sep–early Oct ✋ L €20, D €20, Wine €15

GOUPILLIÈRES
AUBERGE DU PONT DE BRIE
www.pontdebrie.com
Frédérique and Thierry Cottarel's auberge has an enchanting dining room with a stone fireplace, and has much to offer with its seasonal fare. For a typical taste of Normandy, consider the pork cooked in cider.

✉ Halte de Grimbosq, 14210 Goupillières ☎ 02 31 79 37 84 🕐 Wed–Sun 12.15–1.30, 7.15–9. Closed mid-Nov to early Jan, late Feb–early Mar ✋ L €20, D €30, Wine €16

HONFLEUR
FERME ST-SIMÉON
www.fermesaintsimeon.fr
Produce from the kitchen garden adds to the flavours when you lunch in the dining room with its vaulted ceiling, or on the terrace. This hotel restaurant has earned a reputation as one of the finest in Normandy. Try homard façon Tourville (Tourville-style lobster) or opt for langoustines sur gelée de crustacés (langoustines in a shellfish aspic).

✉ Rue Adolphe Marais, 14600 Honfleur ☎ 02 31 81 78 00 🕐 Daily 12.30–2, 7–9, Tue 7–9 ✋ L €130, D €130, Wine €30

HOULGATE
HÔTEL RESTAURANT 1900
www.hotel-1900.fr
Dine in style at the restaurant of Houlgate's small Hôtel 1900. Its signature dish a turbot fillet served à la Houlgataise with baby vegetables infused with fragrant rosemary.

✉ 17 rue des Bains, 14510 Houlgate ☎ 02 31 28 77 77 🕐 Daily 12–2.30, 6.30–10 ✋ L €18.50, D €30, Wine €17

THURY-HARCOURT
LE RELAIS DE LA POSTE
This old post house has an old-fashioned dining room with a beamed ceiling. Its fine wine cellar, complements the classic dishes. Try the terrine of foie gras, which is partnered with apple chutney.

✉ 7 rue de Caen, 14220 Thury-Harcourt ☎ 02 31 79 72 12 🕐 Jun–Sep daily 12–2, 7–9. Closed Fri, Sat L, Sun D Oct–end May, mid-Dec to end Jan ✋ L €18, D €27, Wine €16

STAYING

Above *The exterior of the elegant Château d'Audrieu in Audrieu*

PRICES AND SYMBOLS

The prices are the lowest and highest for a double room for one night including breakfast, unless otherwise stated. All the hotels listed accept credit cards unless otherwise stated. Note that rates can vary widely throughout the year.

For a key to the symbols, ▷ 2.

AUDRIEU
CHÂTEAU D'AUDRIEU

www.châteaudaudrieu.com
In the middle of a park sits this 18th-century château. Rooms range from attic apartments to standard family rooms. The lavish Louis XV and art deco suites are superior options, and there are salons, drawing rooms and a classy restaurant (▷ 114). In the gardens is a heated pool.
✉ 14250 Audrieu ☎ 02 31 80 21 52 ◑ Closed mid-Dec to early Jan ✋ €134–€441, excluding breakfast (€18) ⓘ 25 rooms, 4 suites ⌧ Outdoor heated

BAYEUX
CHÂTEAU DE BELLEFONTAINE

www.hotel-bellefontaine.com
This family-run hotel is near the centre of Bayeux yet surrounded by water and set in beautiful grounds.

The high-ceilinged rooms are spacious and tastefully furnished. Enjoy coffee and croissants in the vaulted breakfast room or on the veranda. In addition, there are facilities for guests with disabilities. This makes a good base for those visiting the Bayeux Tapestry as well as the D-Day landing beaches.
✉ 49 rue de Bellefontaine, 14400 Bayeux ☎ 02 31 22 00 10 ◑ Closed Jan ✋ €80–€140, excluding breakfast (€12) ⓘ 14 rooms, 6 suites ⓟ Private parking

CABOURG
GRAND HÔTEL

www.mercure.com
As you walk through this magnificent building, where novelist Marcel Proust holidayed up until World War I, you will feel transported back into the Belle Époque. The renovated, bright and sunny bedrooms have either sea or garden views, and sports and leisure activities are available. The hotel is popular for exhibitions, seminars and concerts.
✉ Promenade Marcel Proust, 14390 Cabourg ☎ 02 31 91 01 79 ◑ Year-round ✋ €225–€305, excluding breakfast (€19) ⓘ 70 ⌧ Indoor

CAEN
LE DAUPHIN

www.le-dauphin-normandie.com
A former priory in the centre of Caen, this refurbished building has interconnecting family rooms of a good standard. Traditional Norman specialties are served in the restaurant.
✉ 29 rue Gémare, 14000 Caen ☎ 02 31 86 22 26 ◑ Closed mid-Feb–early Mar, late Oct–early Nov ✋ €85–€190, excluding breakfast (€14) ⓘ 32 rooms (12 non-smoking), 5 suites (3 non-smoking) ⌧ Indoor ♨ Sauna ⓟ Private parking ⌷ Tram to St-Pierre

HÔTEL DU HAVRE

www.hotelduhavre.com
It is great to find simple budget accommodation in the centre of the city. The basic rooms here have ensuite bathrooms.
✉ 11 rue du Havre, 14000 Caen ☎ 02 31 86 19 80 ◑ Year-round ✋ €45–€58, excluding breakfast €6) ⓘ 19 ⓟ Private parking ⌷ Tram to Résistance

CAMBREMER
CHÂTEAU LES BRUYÈRES

www.châteaulesbruyeres.com
Follow the tree-lined drive to this

magnificent château, an inspiration to many famous writers. Each room is beautifully personalized, with ornate furnishings. Savour the delights of the restaurant, which uses garden-grown food (▷ 114–115). Themed weekends are available, including cider tasting.

✉ Route du Cadran, 14340 Cambremer ☎ 02 31 32 22 45 ◎ Open all year ✋ €105–€195, excluding breakfast (€12) ⓘ 23, 1 suite 🏊 Outdoor

CRÉPON
FERME DE LA RANÇONNIÈRE
www.ranconniere.fr
This hotel is in a fortified 13th-century building, which forms part of a quiet village near Bayeux and Arromanches and not far from the sea. Rooms are comfortable, with beamed ceilings and exposed stone walls, and decorated in rustic-style with antiques. The restaurant serves regional cuisine.

✉ Route de Creull Arromanches, 14480 Crépon ☎ 02 31 22 21 73 ◎ Restaurant closed Jan ✋ €191, excluding breakfast (€11) ⓘ 35

DEAUVILLE
L'AUGEVAL
www.augeval.com
In the centre of Deauville, this lovely gabled house is perfect for a seaside break. Enjoy food of the region in the elegant dining room, on the terrace or by the swimming pool. Among the extra facilities are a gym and outdoor table tennis, and horseback-riding can be arranged.

✉ 15 avenue Hocquart de Turtot, 14800 Deauville ☎ 02 31 81 13 18 ◎ Year-round ✋ €60–€142, excluding breakfast (€12) ⓘ 42 🏊 Outdoor 🌊

HOSTELLERIE DE TOURGÉVILLE
www.hostellerie-de-tourgeville.fr
Originally built as a country estate by film director Claude Lelouch, this complex of country houses is full of character. You have a choice of rooms or split-level apartments fit for any Hollywood diva. Facilities and sports available include tennis, golf, swimming and horse-riding.

✉ Chemin de l'Orgueil Tourgéville, 14800

Deauville ☎ 02 31 14 48 68 ◎ Closed mid-Feb to early Mar ✋ €130–€250, excluding breakfast (€16) ⓘ 25 rooms, 19 apartments 🏊 Outdoor 🌊 Sauna

HONFLEUR
FERME ST-SIMÉON
www.fermesaintsimeon.fr
This was practically a clubhouse for the artists of the Honfleur school: the guest list has included Jean Baptiste Corot, Claude Monet, Eugène Boudin and Alfred Sisley. Today, the cider press has been converted into a spa. Follow in the footsteps of the Impressionists and stay in one of the softly furnished bedrooms. Terraces, where you can try regional cuisine, overlook the sea. Among the organized tours is a trip to Étretat.

✉ Rue Adolphe Marais, 14600 Honfleur ☎ 02 31 81 78 00 ◎ Year-round ✋ €220–€450, excluding breakfast (€22–€27) ⓘ 38 rooms and apartments 🏊 Indoor 🌊 Spa

LES MAISONS DE LÉA
www.lesmaisonsdelea.com
Nestling in the old part of Honfleur, this former salt warehouse has been turned into a unique hotel and cottage. The antiques and colourful fabrics add to the other-wordly atmosphere. You can relax by the fireside in the library, or unwind in the privacy of your bedroom, appreciating the hotel's tranquillity.

✉ Place Ste-Catherine, 14600 Honfleur ☎ 02 31 14 49 49 ◎ Year-round ✋ €120–€200, excluding breakfast (€15) ⓘ 24 rooms, 4 suites, 1 apartment

LISIEUX
HÔTEL DE LA COUPE D'OR
www.la-coupe-d-or.com
This budget hotel in the heart of Lisieux has bedrooms that, although not large, are pleasantly decorated in a country style. The restaurant's vast, rustic dining room serves regional dishes. This is a good place to recover after a long drive.

✉ 49 rue Pont Mortain, 14100 Lisieux ☎ 02 31 31 16 84 ◎ Year-round ✋ €55–€60, excluding breakfast (€7.50) ⓘ 16

NOTRE-DAME-D'ESTRÉES
AU REPOS DES CHINEURS
www.au-repos-des-chineurs.com
In the 17th century, this hotel and tea room was a coaching inn, and it retains its beamed ceilings. *Chineurs* means 'antiques hunters', which is appropriate as everything here is for sale, from the furniture to the fine china cups. The rooms (some with whirlpool tubs) look out across meadows.

✉ Chemin de l'Église, 14340 Notre-Dame-d'Estrées ☎ 02 31 63 72 51 ◎ Open all year ✋ €51–€150, excluding breakfast (€12) ⓘ 10

PORT-EN-BESSIN
LA CHENEVIÈRE
www.lacheneviere.com
This 18th-century château has rooms decorated in classical style but with modern amenities such as TV and a mini-bar. Additional facilities include a laundry service, babysitting and Internet access. You can even order fresh flowers for your bedroom. The restaurant, serving seasonal foods, is run by chef Claude Esprabens.

✉ Escures-Commes, 14520 Port-en-Bessin ☎ 02 31 51 25 25 ◎ Closed Dec–end Apr ✋ €240–€370, excluding breakfast (€21) ⓘ 29

VIEUX FUMÉ
CHATEAU DU MESNIL D'O
www.lemesnildo.com
A charming bed and breakfast in a château built in the 18th century and renovated in the 1980s. It is surrounded by a beautiful park. There are only four guest bedrooms, all lovingly decorated with period furniture and with views over the extensive grounds.

✉ Château du Mesnil d'O, 14270 Vieux Fumé ☎ 02 31 20 01 47 ◎ Open all year ✋ €110 ⓘ 4

EURE

The Eure river forms the frontier between Normandy and the Île de France as it flows north to meet the Seine. If anything characterizes the *département* named after it, it is freshwater in all its forms—not only rivers and streams but also canals, ponds and wetlands—and every kind of man-made structure associated with it—mills, weirs, wash-houses and bridges, ancient and modern.

Everywhere you travel you come to towns with street plans adapted to the rivers that run through them: the capital city of Évreux built around a Gothic cathedral and clocktower; pretty Pont-Audemer, known as the Little Venice of Normandy because of the channels and canals running through it; and Louviers, which even has a monastic cloister striding nonchalantly from one river bank to the other. At Vernon, the town's most distinctive building balances picturesquely over the water on stone stilts and Verneuil-sur-Avre offers its surviving outer defensive moats for an interesting walk. The Eure's most popular attraction by far focuses upon that lily pond at Giverny which inspired the artist Claude Monet. And the Château de Broglie has a splendid water garden.

Away from the waterside, the Eure varies between woodlands such as the Forêt de Lyons in the north to plains and farmland south of Évreux. Dotted around the landscape are the medieval abbeys of Le Bec-Hellouin (the most outstanding), Bernay, Fontaine-Guerard and Montemer and handsome stately homes including Beumesnil, Champ-de-Bataille and Fleury-la-Forêt (housing a doll and toy museum). Other châteaux were built in earlier times not as luxurious country residences but as structures of defence in the wars between the English and French: Brionne, Gisors and, most magnificently, Richard the Lionheart's Château Gaillard, which stands guard proudly over a loop of the Seine at Les Andelys.

ABBAYE DU BEC-HELLOUIN

This working abbey provides a haven of quiet reflection. It has been an historic seat of learning for 1,000 years. The walled Abbey of Bec-Hellouin has the air of a venerable centre of learning, one whose history has been intertwined with that of England for a millennium. Some come for guided tours, others for academic research in the library, and the resident monks welcome travellers seeking a religious retreat. But even an hour spent in the tranquil grounds, with birdsong the only sound to be heard, is revitalizing.

POLITICAL INFLUENCE

The abbey was founded in the Middle Ages as a place of learning, but it soon established itself as a major influence on politics. Lanfranc (c1005–89), an adviser to William the Conqueror and later Archbishop of Canterbury, taught here. The abbey continued to maintain strong links with England through the turbulent years surrounding the murder of Archbishop of Canterbury Thomas Becket in 1170, and even beyond King Henry VIII's break with Rome in the 16th century.

During the French Revolution, the monks were expelled, books and tapestries were looted and the 13th-century church and chapter house were demolished. Even the bells were melted down. In 1948, the State acquired the abbey, and monks returned the following year.

Today, a smart village street leads to the abbey grounds. The tall Tour St-Nicolas, the only surviving medieval building, is separate from the rest of the abbey, which sits in the Risle valley 45km (28 miles) southwest of Rouen. The original church no longer exists, and today's services are held in the newer 17th- and 18th-century buildings (visitors welcome; Matins 7am). The central cloisters, dating from the 17th century, remain a particularly spiritual place, while the waterside Cour de France garden is another location for reflection. Since the abbey remains a place of learning, the library is open to visitors only by prior arrangement with the abbey librarian (tel 02 32 43 72 64).

INSPIRED CREATIVITY

Unlike the cheeses and alcoholic drinks produced by other religious communities, the monks' workshop at Le Bec is famous for its stylish tableware. The plates, bowls and vases are on sale in the abbey shop. The workshop itself, Les Ateliers du Bec, is open to visitors (▷ 138).

INFORMATION

www.abbayedubec.com

✚ 222 M5 ✉ 27800 Le Bec-Hellouin ☎ 02 32 43 72 60 Ⓖ Guided tours of interior: Jun–Sep Mon–Sat 10.30, 3, 4, 5, Sun 12, 3, 4; Oct–May Mon–Sat 10.30, 3, 4, Sun 12, 3, 4. Grounds only: daily 8am–9pm. Les Ateliers du Bec: Mon–Sat 11–11.45, 2.45–5.45, Sun 12–1, 2.30–7 ♿ Adult €5, child €3.50, under 12 free 🚌 Brionne (7km/4.5 miles) 🍴 Restaurants in the village ❓ Access for visitors with disabilities: grounds accessible, one or two low steps to each of the buildings, toilets not wheelchair-friendly 🅿 Free parking in village centre

TIPS

» Check out times of religious services before you visit—the shop is manned entirely by members of the monastic community, so it closes during prayers.
» When a coach party arrives, stay away from the buildings. The grounds are large enough to allow you to find tranquillity away from the crowds.
» The pretty village of Le Bec-Hellouin is worth a stroll.

Opposite *Half-timbered houses line the street leading to Tour St-Nicolas*
Below *The remains of Abbaye du Bec-Hellouin*

LES ANDELYS

INFORMATION

www.ville-andelys.fr

✚ 223 P5 ℹ Rue Philippe Auguste,
27702 Les Andelys ☎ 02 32 54 41 93
🕲 Jun–end Sep Mon–Sat 10–12, 2–6,
Sun 10–12, 2–5; Apr, May Mon–Sat
10–12, 2–6, Sun 10–1; Oct Mon–Fri 2–6,
Sat 10–12, 2–5; Nov–end Feb Mon–Fri
2–6, Sat 10–1; Mar Mon–Fri 2–6, Sat
10–1, 2–5 🚌 From Évreux (marked
'Les Andelys') 🚊 Gaillon Aubevoye
(12km/7.5 miles)

Above *The Seine runs through
Les Andelys*

INTRODUCTION

It may now be ruined but Château Gaillard, the starkly silhouetted fortress that
Richard the Lionheart ordered to be built on a cliff at a strategic point above the
Seine, has lost none of its awe and majesty over the centuries.

Les Andelys on the river bank below, midway between Paris and Rouen and
once a bordertown between France and England, is intimately linked to the
château and has a rich artistic and industrial heritage. Andely le Jeune, today
dubbed Petit Andely, flourished from modest modest beginnings as a fishing
port on the Seine.

In the 13th century, as the château was being constructed, so the church
and hospital became popular halts for pilgrims trekking from northern to
southern Europe. The castle's fortunes fluctuated until Henry IV (1553–1610)
and then Cardinal Richelieu (1585–1642) decided on its partial demolition.
Civic life flourished outside the city walls. The suburb La Madelaine became a
centre of weaving, while watermills and vineyards added to the prosperity.

The wool trade gained a fine reputation with clothmaker Louis Flavigny
holding a royal warrant. Silkworks were established to widen the range of
textiles. By the 19th century, wine merchants joined middle-class mill owners.
In the mid-19th century, as the town was being discovered by a generation of
writers and artists including Victor Hugo and Nicolas Poussin, the usually canny
business community made its biggest mistake by rejecting the offer to have a
railway station. Thus, Les Andelys did not get the crucial rail links that boosted
trade in rival towns.

WHAT TO SEE

CHÂTEAU GAILLARD

High on a chalky hilltop overlooking a loop of the river Seine, the ruins of
the Château Gaillard were the heart of Anglo-French politics in the Middle
Ages. This once-majestic fortress was built in 1196 by Richard the Lionheart
(1157–99), King of England and Duke of Normandy, to defend Rouen from the

French King Philippe Auguste (1165–1223). The castle took 12 months to build, leading Richard to refer to it as 'My beautiful one-year-old'. French troops seized the fortress in 1204 (▷ 21). Today, one tower, several walls and a keep remain but you can still get a good idea of the layout of the fortress. It was vulnerable to one side only and this was protected by a triangular-shaded outwork with five towers and a moat around it. The tall inner wall is made up of 19 arcs rather than a smooth surface; this was an innovation for 12th-century military architecture and made the castle harder to attack.

✉ 27702 Les Andelys ☎ 02 32 54 41 93 🕐 Mid-Mar to mid-Nov, Wed–Mon 10–1, 2–6
👆 Adult €3, child (10–16) €2.50, under 10 free

TIP
» Visit during the four horse-racing days in spring and summer, when traditional trotting events are staged on an old race track below the château.

LES ANDELYS

Below Château Gaillard is Les Andelys, once two separate settlements, Petit Andely and Grand Andely. Petit Andely, on the banks of the river and once a small fishing village, has historic stone and timber houses and shops. On its cobbled square stands the 12th-century church of St-Sauveur, used by pilgrims going to Santiago de Compostela in Spain.

Grand Andely, once called Andely-Le-Vieux, was a royal favourite in Gallo-Roman times. Notre-Dame church, with its lovely stained glass, is built on the site of a convent founded by Clothilde (cAD474–545), wife of Clovis I, King of the Franks. St. Clothilde is credited with a miracle: According to local legend, exhausted workmen constructing the church called on her for help, and her prayers turned the waters of the nearby fountain into a fortifying wine. Pilgrims later came to drink the miraculous waters for their strength-giving powers.

THE A-LIST

The waterside position of Les Andelys strengthened its wool trade and for many years it was a leading textile town. Eventually, farming boosted the local economy and its role in the grain trade led to the building of several grand hotels. Novelist Victor Hugo (1802–85) was among the literary guests to stay at the Hôtel le Grand Cerf. He wrote the line 'The wide fireplace with its proud shield devours an entire oak tree to heat us' in the visitor book. Another visitor was the playwright Pierre Corneille (1606–84), who was married in the town.

Many buildings dating from the 16th to 19th centuries were ruined in World War II, but one, near the fountain, is now the Musée Nicolas Poussin (tel 02 32 54 31 78), which pays homage to the eponymous 17th-century artist, the town's most famous son. Musée Normandie-Niémen tells the story of the Normandie-Niémen air squadron, which was created by Charles de Gaulle in 1942 (tel 02 32 54 49 76).

Below left *Château Gaillard glows in the early-morning light*
Below *A statue of St. Saveur*

BEAUMONT-LE-ROGER

www.cc-beaumont-le-roger.com

The gleaming white ruins of the Prieuré de la Ste-Trinité greet visitors to this town on the outskirts of the Beaumont forest. To discover the town of Beaumont-le-Roger is to discover Roger de Beaumont, who turned a simple settlement into a powerful town.

Originally it was a peaceful Roman village in the green Risle valley, land that came to be owned by Norman dukes. In 1017, Judith, wife of Duke Richard II, established an abbey at nearby Bernay (▷ right), and the estate passed into the hands of Onfroy de Vieilles. His son was Roger de Vieilles, later known as Roger de Beaumont (c1022–94), who became a powerful adviser to William the Conqueror. It was Roger who acted as counsellor to Queen Mathilde, helping her govern Normandy while her husband was invading England. After the success of the Norman Conquest, Roger built a château, fortified the village and founded the church of St-Nicolas and the priory. The estate later passed into the hands of Robert d'Artois (1287–1343), adviser to England's King Edward III.

The priory was built by Roger in 1070, but the remains visible today date from the 13th century. After the French Revolution, the priory was abandoned and its relics moved to the Église St-Nicolas. The flying buttresses of the priory line the roadside as you climb to the nave.

Today's Beaumont is a pleasant country town, a good base for visiting nearby châteaux and hiking in the forest. The church of St-Nicolas is still standing, albeit with 17th-century additions, and has some excellent 16th-century stained-glass windows. Its clock tower sports an animated Roman soldier who chimes the hours.

✚ 222 M6 ℹ 1 rue de Belgique, 27170 Beaumont-le-Roger ☎ 02 32 44 05 79 🕐 Tue 9.30–12, 2.30–5.30, Wed 10–12, 2.30–5.30, Thu 10–12, 2.30–5, Fri 9.30–12, 2.30–5.30, Sat 9.30–12, 2–5.30 🚌 Évreux–Louviers 🚉 From Évreux

BERNAY

www.bernay27.fr

Bernay is best known for its abbey, which was founded in the 11th century by Judith of Brittany, wife of Richard II, Duke of Normandy. Springtime pilgrims still make their way to Bernay for the Whit Monday services at the Basilique Notre-Dame de la Couture (Our Lady of the Fields). The oldest part of today's church dates back to the 13th century, when the 11th-century building was expanded for the seasonal visitors. In the 16th and 19th centuries it was enlarged again. The only remaining part of the original sanctuary is the crypt, but there are carved capitals in the choir in the Romanesque part of the church. Stained glass, from the 15th to 19th centuries, fills the naves with dappled light.

Construction work started on Bernay's other church, the Église Ste-Croix, in 1374 and was completed at the end of the 19th century. Its interior owes much to the former abbey church of Bec-Hellouin (▷ 120–121), and it harbours a 17th-century nativity scene and 16 statues of the Apostles and Evangelists that were carved in the 14th century. The church organ, restored in 1998, is often played in concerts.

The Musée des Beaux-Arts (tel 02 32 46 63 23; open mid-Jun to mid-Sep Tue–Sun 10–12, 2–7; mid-Sep to mid-Jun Tue–Sun 2–5.30), in an old abbey building on the place Guillaume de Volpiano, contains examples of ceramics and tableware from the 16th to the 19th centuries, concentrating on the blue-and-white faïence of Rouen (▷ 160–164).

✚ 222 L6 ℹ 29 rue Thiers, 27300 Bernay ☎ 02 32 43 32 08 🕐 May to mid-Sep Mon–Sat 9.30–12, 2–6.30, Sun 10–1; mid-Sep to end Apr Mon–Sat 9.30–12, 2–5.30 🚌 From Pont-Audemer 🚉 From Lisieux and Évreux

BRIONNE

The remains of a square-sided keep perch high above the lovely town of Brionne and the trout-rich river Risle. The climb to the top is worth it, if only for the impressive views over the waterway and its valley. The fortress harks back to the days when Brionne was annexed by William, Duke of Normandy, in 1050 after a three-year siege, which wrested control of the area from the dukes of Burgundy. Much of the 11th-century fort was dismantled in the 18th century, but several broad

stone walls remain as a symbol of William's power.

Such signs of machismo and military might are not the only image of Brionne. Visitors can enjoy a collection of vintage toys at Au Pays de la Poupée, a doll museum (tel 02 32 45 76 24; May–end Sep daily on request); wander around the 15th-century Église St-Martin, with its slate steeple; and enjoy the local delicacy, *truite fumée* (smoked trout), in traditional taverns.

✚ 222 M5 🛈 1 rue du Général de Gaulle, 27800 Brionne ☎ 02 32 45 70 51 🕐 Easter–end Oct Mon–Sat 9.30–12.30, 1.30–5.30, Sun 10.30–12.30; Nov–Easter Mon–Sat 9.30–12.30, 1.30–5.30 🚌 From Évreux 🚉 Brionne

BROGLIE

www.bernay27.fr

Among the beech groves of the Charentonne valley, the Château de Broglie dominates this small town. A private residence, the château is said to have been built on the site of a Roman fort by William the Conqueror in the 11th century. John Lackland, England's King John (c1167–1216), stayed here several times. During the Hundred Years War (1337–1453), the château was taken from the English by Jean d'Orléans, companion of Joan of Arc. Although the château is not open to the public, the town's 11th-century church, which has Romanesque and Renaissance styles, may be visited (daily 9–6).

Behind the church, the 15th-century Maison de la Léproserie (Leprosarium), on whose wood beams grotesque faces are carved, is a fine photo opportunity. Also near the church, find the birthplace of celebrated civil engineer Auguste Fresnel (1788–1827); in front of the house is a bronze bust of the scientist, by David d'Angers (c1788–1856). Fresnel designed lenses to magnify the power of lighthouses and was elected to the Académie des Sciences in 1823. Even more famous was his cousin, Prosper Merimée (1803–1970), the author of *Carmen*, whose work to preserve national monuments saved many great treasures.

Broglie's water garden, the Jardin Aquatique (tel 02 32 44 60 58), has lawns and marshlands along its canal banks. Bamboo and willow trees flourish among the water-loving grasses, with ornamental rhubarbs and lobelia adding colour.

✚ 222 L6 🛈 place des 3 Maréchaux, 27270 Broglie ☎ 02 32 46 27 52 🕐 Mid-Apr to mid-Sep Tue–Fri 2.30–5.30, Sat 10.30–12.30, 2.30–5.30, Sun 9.30–12.30 🚉 Bernay

CHÂTEAU DE BEAUMESNIL

www.châteaubeaumesnil.com

The splendid 17th-century Château de Beaumesnil, known as Le Mesnil Royal, stands in 80ha (200 acres) of woodland and flamboyantly landscaped gardens. These grounds, dating from the 17th century, were laid out in the fashion of the royal gardener André le Nôtre by his protégé La Quintinie, and host an antiques fair on August's first weekend. During the summer months, when the house and grounds are open to the public, children are drawn to the challenge of the maze, while others explore the Louis XIII castle itself.

Beaumesnil village, surrounded by the Pays d'Ouche, has castles, manor houses, grand estates and cider presses nearby. At St-Pierre-de-Mesnil, a moated castle, the Château du Blanc Buisson (1290), is open year-round. Also worth seeing are the red-brick dovecote at the 16th-century Manoir de Val and the 15th-century Tour de Thevray.

✚ 222 M6 ✉ 27400 Beaumesnil ☎ 02 32 44 40 09 🕐 Jul, Aug daily 11–6; Easter–end Jun Fri–Mon 2–6; Sep Wed–Mon 2–6 🎟 Adult €7, child (12–21) €3.50, under 12 free 🚉 Bernay

CHÂTEAU DU CHAMP-DE-BATAILLE

www.duchampdebataille.com

Noted for its remarkable gardens, this wonderful brick-and-stone residence dates from the 17th century. Recent owners have lavished design, research and

Above *The Château de Beaumesnil*
Opposite *The view from the fortress at Brionne*

generous budgets on the building to ensure that it is once again worthy of its grounds.

Originally constructed by Alexandre de Créqui, the château was home to the influential Harcourt family until just before the French Revolution. Its most recent history saw it serving as a prisoner of war camp and women's prison before being repurchased by the Duke of Harcourt after World War II. The Duke began a restoration project that was completed by France's leading contemporary designer, Jacques Garcia, who bought the estate in 1992. The library, salons and bedrooms are furnished with taste and respect for tradition, while original 16th- and 17th-century furnishings, clocks, porcelain and fabrics make each room a glimpse of a lost world. It is remarkable that such a recent private collection can give so authentic a view of the past, from the splendour of the salons down to the kitchens.

The courtyards and grounds are equally unmissable. While the full tour is expensive, it does make visitors feel like privileged guests.

✚ 222 M6 ✉ 27110 Le Neubourg ☎ 02 32 34 84 34 🕐 Gardens: Jul, Aug daily 10–6; May, Jun, Sep daily 2–6; Easter–end Oct Sat, Sun, public hols 2–6. Chateau: Jul, Aug daily 3.30–5.30; Easter–end Oct Sat, Sun, public hols 3.30–5.30. Admission all year to pre-booked groups 🚌 From Évreux

CONCHES-EN-OUCHE

www.conches-en-ouche.fr

The town of Conches, in the Pays d'Ouche, is between the forest of Conches and the Rouloir valley. Originally a Celtic settlement that was later seized by the Romans, it became Norman in 1034 when the lords of Tosny inherited the fiefdom of Châtillon. During this golden age of pilgrimage, the Tosny nobility would join the long march to the shrine of Santiago de Compostela in Spain. On their return from one journey, they stopped at Conques-en-Rouergue in southwest France, where they witnessed the cult of St. Foy, martyr of Agen. Roger de Tosny moved St. Foy's relics to Châtillon, where he built a church dedicated to the martyr, and Châtillon became known as the Conques (later Conches) of the Pays d'Ouche.

The present Gothic Église Ste-Foy dates from the 15th century. Its 56m (184ft) spire dominates the town, although this is a copy of the original, which collapsed during a storm in 1842. The tomb of 11th-century theologian and philosopher Guillaume de Conches is housed in the church, which is noted for its stained-glass windows, among the best examples of 16th-century Norman glasswork in existence. A description of the windows may be obtained from the tourist office.

Glasswork is one of Conches' great claims to fame. The Musée du Verre et de la Pierre (tel 02 32 30 90 41; Jun to mid-Sep Wed–Sat 10–12, 2–5, Sun 2–5; Mar–May, Oct, Nov Wed–Sat 2–5.30), on the route de Ste-Marguerite, has three stunning windows by François Décorchemont (1880–1971), a local artist who is credited with reviving the medieval style of glasswork.

On rue Paul Guilbaud, everyday Norman life through the ages is celebrated at the Musée du Terroir Normand (tel 02 32 37 92 16; Jun to mid-Sep Wed–Sat 10–12, 2–5.30, Sun 2–6).

The most vivid image of Conches is the ruined 12th-century fort built by the Tosny family. Photogenic ivy-covered towers and a circular keep dominate the neat gardens.

✚ 222 M7 🛈 Place A. Briand, 27190 Conches-en-Ouche ☎ 02 32 30 76 42 🕒 Jul–end Aug Tue–Sat 10–12.30, 2–5.30 and Sun 10–12.30 🚌 From Évreux 🚆 From Évreux

ÉCOUIS

A royal passion for hunting may be the reason for the unexpected appearance of the magnificent church of Écouis (tel 02 32 69 43 08 to organize a visit) in such an undistinguished setting.

At the time, Écouis was a prosperous market town. Its position close to the royal hunting grounds of the Forêt de Lyons (▷ 132) and the fact that its parish church of St-Aubin came under the authority of Bec-Hellouin Abbey (▷ 120–121) led to its fortunes being favoured by the court. King Philippe IV's finance minister, Enguerrand of Marigny (1260–1315), commissioned the town's hospital and won royal and papal permission to upgrade St-Aubin to a grander institution.

In September 1313, the new church was consecrated in the presence of the papal legate. This was the crowning moment of Enguerrand's career; just 18 months later he was hanged for sorcery. King Louis XI and Louis XII both visited the church, and its most famous canon, St. Vincent de Paul (1581–1660), is remembered on a bronze medal in the choir. After the French Revolution, Enguerrand's tomb was destroyed and the church looted; few of the 52 statues commissioned by him remain. From 1996 to 1999, stained-glass windows were created in the period style by Sylvie Gaudin.

✚ 223 P5 ✉ 4 rue du Général de Gaulle, 27140 Gisors ☎ 02 32 27 60 63 🕒 Apr–end Sep daily 10–12, 2–6; Oct–end Mar Mon–Fri 9–12, 2–6 🚌 From Évreux

GISORS

Gisors is the capital of the Vexin Normand region and crowns a rare hill in an otherwise flat landscape. This is the crossroads of the historic Plantagenet, Vexin and seaward trails, and the junction of three provinces: Picardy, Normandy and Île-de-France.

In the Plantagenet era (1154–1399), the fort and town passed from English to French hands, so that Gisors became a prized possession of England's King Henry II (1133–89) then King Philippe Auguste of France (1165–1223). The resulting French and English military architecture is an interesting hybrid. The Tour du Prisonnier was the town gaol in the 16th century; graffiti scratched by prisoners can be seen on the walls.

St-Gervais-et-St-Protrais, the imposing parish church of Gisors, dates from the 12th–16th centuries and includes Renaissance features.

✚ 223 Q5 🛈 4 rue du Général de Gaulle, 27140 Gisors ☎ 02 32 27 60 63 🕒 Apr–end Sep daily 10–12, 2–6; Oct–end Mar Mon–Fri 9–12, 2–6 🚌 From Évreux

Left *Castle ruins with Gisors beyond*
Opposite *Stained glass detail, Église St-Foy, Conches-en-Ouche*

ÉVREUX

INFORMATION

www.ot-pays-Évreux.fr

✚ 223 N6 🛈 Place du Général de Gaulle, 27000 Évreux ☎ 02 32 24 04 43 🕓 Jun–end Sep Mon–Sat 9.30–6.15, Sun 10–12.30 🚊 Évreux

Above *A café with the Cathédrale Notre-Dame as a backdrop*

INTRODUCTION

The capital of the Eure departement, Évreux is now a modest-sized town of 54,000 people and you wouldn't guess at its eventful history. Founded as a Gallo-Roman settlement it was sacked and burnt, first by the Vandals, then the Vikings, then the English and French. In June 1940 it was bombed by the Germans as they closed in on Paris and bombed again by the Allies in 1944 as they liberated Normandy. It's hardly surprising, therefore, that there's not much left of the old Évreux but there are enough scattered monuments left to make a visit rewarding. Allow time, in particular, to visit the municipal museum.

WHAT TO SEE

PLACE DU GÉNÉRAL DE GAULLE

Évreux's spacious main square centres on a fountain representing the river Eure and its tributaries.It is dominated by the 43.9m (144ft) high Beffroi, the last remnant of Évreux's medieval fortifications and a unique example of a Norman belfry. It was built in Flamboyant Gothic style between 1490 and 1497. At the top is a bell called Louyse which cast in 1406.

Across the square from the tower are the Hotel de Ville (town hall), a late 19th century neoclassical building on the site of the castle of the counts of Évreux, and the theatre, built in 1903 in Italian style, with scenes from Moliere and Shakespeare painted inside. From the square you can walk beside a branch of the river Iton to reach the cathedral and museum.

CATHÉDRALE NOTRE-DAME

The town's cathedral was consecrated in 1076 but there is little left of the original structure. The fact that it is still a magnificent, mainly Flamboyant Gothic, building is testament to the town's stoic rebuilding plans after successives fires in its early history. It escaped remarkably unscathed from the bombs of World War II although it needed some rebuilding. The inside is lit by stained glass windows dating from the 13th to 16th centuries.

MUSEE DE ÉVREUX

Built in 1499, the bishop's palace adjacent to the cathedral contains a delightful provincial museums. The first rooms on the ground floor contain an eclectic mix of historical objects and paintings and upstairs on the first floor there are two rooms full of 17th and 18th century furniture.

The highlight of the museum, however, is the basement, a spacious modern hall dedicated to local archeology. One side of it is formed by a surviving stretch of the town's third century AD ramparts and a section of Roman road. ☎ 02 32 31 81 90 🕐 Tue–Sun 10–12, 2–6

EGLISE ST-TAURIN

To the west of the city centre is this former abbey church dedicated to St Taurinus (died 412), the first bishop of Évreux, whose relics are contained in a 13th-century gold-plated and enameled silver chest. It is in a range of styles including Romanesque, Gothic and baroque.

TIPS

» Hear stories of the town from private taxi drivers, who offer commentated tours of the city (from €40 for six people; book in the tourist office).

» One Saturday each month, the tourist office organizes a heritage walking tour.

Left *Statues and the bell tower in the main place du Général de Gaulle*

GIVERNY

INFORMATION

www.giverny.org

⊞ 223 P6 ⓘ 36 rue Carnot, 27201 Vernon ☎ 02 32 51 39 60 ⓒ May–end Aug Tue–Sat 9.30– 12.15, 2.15–6.30; Sep–end Apr Tue–Sat 10–12, 2–5 🚌 From Évreux 🚃 Vernon, then taxi or bicycle the 5km (3 miles) to Giverny

INTRODUCTION

Thousands of visitors leave Normandy's main sightseeing trail to visit this modest village near Vernon in the Seine valley which has become a shrine to its most famous inhabitant, Claude Monet (1840–1926). Ironically, there are no original works by Monet in the pretty pink and green house where he lived until his death, although plenty of prints and copies adorn the rooms. The crowds are lured by the garden, the lily pond and its famous Japanese bridge, which are kept as close as possible to the way they were in Monet's day.

Although it was undoubtedly art that put Giverny on the map, the village existed quietly long before Monet arrived. Not far from the church is a megalithic monument known as 'the grave of St Radegonde', suggesting that the site was inhabited in Neolithic times. More probably, the village dates from Gallo-Roman times—in 1838, Gallo-Roman graves were discovered here, and as the churchyard was being restored in 1860, workmen discovered plaster coffins dating to the earliest centuries of the Christian era. While today's visitors recognize Giverny for its irises and waterlilies, the area was once celebrated for its grapes rather than its flowers. Back in the heyday of St. Wandrille Abbey (▷ 150), the monks owned several vineyards in the area.

If Monet adopted Giverny because it was a peaceful rural retreat where he could enjoy nature and explore the use of light and colour in his work, his presence transformed it as other artists came looking for the same inspiration, followed by sightseers curious to see what all the fuss was about. In 1992 the industrialist and art collector Daniel J. Terra, consolidated Giverny's reputation on the European coach tour route by founding the Museum of American Art.

WHAT TO SEE

MAISON DE CLAUDE MONET

www.fondation-monet.com

Monet bought this house, with a vegetable garden and an orchard, in 1895,

Above *You've seen the bridge over the lily pond in art galleries, now cross the real thing in Monet's garden*

having rented it as a family home since 1883 for himself, his two sons, and Alice Hoschedé and her six children. The story goes that the artist first saw Giverny through a train window in 1833 and fell in love with it, although the railway line has since closed. Monet painted the irises and lily pond scenes that were his final obsessions here.

The interior of the house is laid out as it was in Monet's day, but there is no time to linger: Tour guides are not allowed to talk to their groups inside the building and visitors are hustled through to avoid gridlock. Once outside, you can take time to explore the walled garden—Le Clos Normand, in front of the house—and the lily pond across the road. The Clos Normand contains 100,000 plants that are replaced each year and another 100,000 perennials, while the famous lily pond was created by the artist by diverting a branch of the river Epte into his garden. A main road divides the gardens, but an underpass takes visitors to the pond. Wonderful though the gardens are, the crowds mean they are not a place for contemplation. The art trail spills over onto the nearby streets; rue Claude Monet is filled with artists' workshops and galleries.
✉ Fondation Claude Monet, rue Claude Monet, 27620 Giverny ☎ 02 32 51 28 21 ⏰ Apr–end Oct Tue–Sun 9.30–5.30 ♿ Adult €5.50, child €3, under 7 free

MUSÉE D'ART AMÉRICAIN

www.maag.org

Once Monet began exhibiting his work in Paris, Giverny became a popular subject for aspiring artists. Four years after his arrival in 1883, a stream of painters descended on the village. Willard Metcalf, Louis Ritter and Theodore Wendel were among the first Americans to arrive, and they were soon followed by a succession of lesser-known artists, who took rooms at the town's Hôtel Baudy (see below). Monet himself, while welcoming some of the initial arrivals, soon distanced himself from the others and did not encourage a salon or Giverny movement. The museum today houses a collection of around 100 works by these visitors, as well as both permanent and temporary exhibitions of paintings of other parts of France by American artists.
✉ 99 rue Claude Monet, 27620 Giverny ☎ 02 32 51 94 65 ⏰ Apr–end Oct Tue–Sun 10–6 ♿ Adult €5.50, child (12–18) €3, under 12 free

RESTAURANT BAUDY

Once known as the Hôtel Baudy, this former boarding house and bar is where Monet met up with Auguste Renoir, Alfred Sisley, Camille Pissarro and Auguste Rodin. Now a restaurant and café, the place preserves its 19th-century style. Stop here for a drink, snack or meal, and then explore the bar where the artists gathered, the rose garden and Giverny's first artists' studio.
✉ 81 rue Claude Monet, 27620 Giverny ☎ 02 32 21 10 03 ⏰ Apr–end Oct Tue–Sat 10–11.30, Sun 10–7

TIPS

» Arrive early to see the lily pond without the crowds.
» Visit in early summer to see the gardens at their very best.
» Wheelchair-users can cross the main road between the gardens as an alternative to the underpass.
» The neighbouring town of Vernon (▷ 133) is well worth a visit, as it is the closest place to find actual work by Monet.

Above left *People enjoy the paintings and objects displayed in Monet's former studio, now a museum*
Above right *Colourful flowers in the gardens*

www.lyons.tourisme.free.fr
✚ 223 P5 🛈 20 rue de l'Hôtel-de-Ville,
27480 Lyons-la-Forêt ☎ 02 32 49 31
65 🕐 Tue–Sun 10–12, 2–5 🚉 Gisors
(30km/19km)

LYONS-LA-FORÊT

Surrounded by the Forêt de Lyons, with its acres of tall beech trees, the village of Lyons-la-Forêt is a lovely cluster of 17th-century timber-framed houses set around a 13th-century wooden market hall. Lyons was built on the site of a 12th-century fortress and grew up along the perimeter of the feudal moat. Its church, Église St-Denis, also dates from the 12th century. The tourist office is on the ground floor of the Hôtel de Ville, with its splendid 18th-century décor. The area is famed for its farmhouse meats, with some farms open to visitors.

As well as being a popular base for rural holidays, Lyons is where Maurice Ravel (1875–1937) composed *Le Tombeau de Couperin* in 1917. The house where he stayed is marked with a plaque. If the Lyons area seems strangely familiar, that is probably because of its popularity with French film directors; Jean Renoir (son of Impressionist painter Auguste), in 1932, and Claude Chabrol, in 1990, chose the village as a backdrop for their film versions of Flaubert's novel *Madame Bovary*.

LAND OF ABBEYS AND CASTLES

The 10,600ha (26,200-acre) Forêt de Lyons, once a royal hunting ground, is the setting for an abbey, a convent and two castles. The ruined Cistercian Abbaye de Mortemer (tel 02 32 49 54 34) dates from the 12th to the 13th centuries, and over the years the beauty of its buildings has attracted many distinguished visitors, among them King Richard the Lionheart (1157–99). The abbey contains a museum of monastic life that also includes displays on ghost stories and folk legends of the region. In season, visitors can tour the abbey grounds in a little train. Some 11km (7 miles) southwest of Lyons-la-Forêt is the 12th-century Cistercian Abbaye Notre-Dame de Fontaine-Guérard (tel 02 32 49 03 82), a convent with a medicinal garden.

The Château de Fleury-la-Forêt (tel 02 32 49 63 91), an easy drive from Lyons-la-Forêt, has a toy and doll museum and an animal ark in its grounds. Visitors can stay overnight and breakfast in the old kitchens. Nearby, on the edge of the forest, is the 16th to 17th-century Château de Vascoeuil (tel 02 35 23 62 35), which hosts modern art exhibitions. There is a 17th-century dovecote in the grounds.

Above *A row of half-timbered houses alongside trim lawns in Lyons-la-Forêt*
Opposite *The town of Vernon has a collection of original works by Monet*

PONT-AUDEMER

Known as the Little Venice of Normandy, as it is wrapped and lapped by two branches of the river Risle, Pont-Audemer was once a town of tanners. The trade flourished by the waterside, and any trip through the narrow alleyways and canals of the old centre passes former tanneries where animal skins were hung out to dry. Today, the town's timbered and gabled buildings are adorned with hanging baskets and antique cast-iron and copper lanterns. Small wooden bridges and unexpected waterways, with floral displays, have gained Pont-Audemer recognition as one of the prettiest detours in France.

Sights include the church of St-Ouen, where austere Romanesque and extravagant Renaissance styles sit side by side. Inside, the light is filtered through stained glass dating from the 16th and 20th centuries. On Monday, a market offers a good range of food and crafts.

🔒 222 L5 🅸 Place Maubert, 27500 Pont-Audemer ☎ 02 32 41 08 21 🌐 Jun–end Sep Mon–Sat 9–12.30, 2–6, Sun 10–12; Oct–end May Mon–Sat 9–12.30, 2–5.30 🚆 Pont-Audemer

VERNEUIL-SUR-AVRE

Another fortified stronghold guarding the border between France and Normandy, Verneuil was once a strategic military settlement ringed by ramparts and moats. The town was founded in 1120 by King Henry I of England (1068–1135). Today, many of the fortified walls remain and the surviving outer moats provide an interesting walk. A severe and brooding tower, the Tour Grise, was built as a keep or dungeon by King Philippe Auguste (1165–1223) when the town was taken by the French in 1204. The Hundred Years War saw Verneuil in the firing line again as France fought England.

Verneuil has a religious as well as a military heritage. An ornate yet rather chunky 15th-century Gothic tower stands on top of the 12th-century Église de la Madeleine. Inside, bright colours mark out the vaulting and are mirrored in the stained-glass windows and statuary. The church is surrounded by 15th- and 16th-century stone and half-timbered houses. Notre-Dame church dates from the 12th century. Also worth a visit is the chapel in the 17th-century former Benedictine Abbaye de St-Nicolas.

🔒 221 M8 🅸 129 Place de la Madeleine, 27130 Verneuil-sur-Avre ☎ 02 32 32 17 17 🌐 Jun–end Sep Mon 2–6, Tue, Fri 10–12, 2–6, Sat 10–12, 2.30–6, Sun 10.30–12, 3–6 (in winter it closes Sat afternoon and Sun all day) 🚆 From Évreux

VERNON

Although neighbouring Giverny (▷ 130–131) has long been overtaken by the crush of tourism, the town of Vernon, unsaddled by the brand of a famous artist, has retained its own identity. But while most tourists ignore it in favour of Giverny, Vernon's Musée Alphonse-Georges Poulain (tel 02 32 21 28 09, Apr–end Sep Tue–Fri 10.30–12.30, 2–6, Sat–Sun 2–6; Oct–end Mar Tue–Sun 2–5.30) actually owns works by Impressionist Claude Monet (1840–1926), whereas none may be seen in the artist's home town. Housed in a stone and timber building with carved exterior beams, the museum was established to display a collection of stuffed birds. However, thanks to the generosity of Monet and his family, the gallery is now home to a circular study of water lilies by the master, as well as a view of the cliffs of Pourvill.

Many typical Norman buildings in the town survived the air raids of World War II. The lovely Maison du Temps Jadis, the oldest building in town, now houses the tourist office. Walking through the town, look out for faces carved into the timbers of the old houses. Vernon also has some interesting fortifications, built to protect it in its role as a border town between the kingdom of France and the duchy of Normandy. Included among these is a circular keep, all that remains of a 12th-century building; it is not open to the public. Another fortification that may be admired from the outside only is the medieval Château des Tourelles, built by King Philippe Auguste of France (1165–1223). Three of its original towers have survived, while the fourth has been restored after World War II bomb damage. The château can be seen from the outside, but it is not open.

Visit Vernon's church of Notre-Dame to see its abstract stained glass, and stop by the 18th-century Château de Bizy, 4km (2.5 miles) outside town, to see its tapestries. Visitors who come to see Monet's paintings are surprised by the entertainment and dining on offer.

The timbered Vieux Moulin, a remnant of an old bridge, balances above the river on stone stilts.

🔒 223 P6 🅸 36 rue Carnot, 27201 Vernon ☎ 02 32 51 39 60 🌐 May–end Sep Tue–Sat 9–12.30, 2–6, Sun 10–12; Oct–end Apr Tue–Sat 10–12, 2–5, Sun 9–12.30, 2–5.30

GIVERNY

The lovely riverside village of Giverny (▷ 130–131), spread across a hillside near Vernon, is the most visited place in Normandy. Crowds of art- and garden-lovers flock to see the home of Claude Monet and the world's most famous lily pond, immortalized in some of the artist's best-known paintings.

THE WALK

Distance: 9km (5.5 miles)
Allow: 2.5 hours
Start/end: Maison de Claude Monet

HOW TO GET THERE

Giverny is near Vernon, off the D5, west of Paris (and possible as a day-trip from the capital).

★ Start outside the Maison de Claude Monet. In 1883 the artist moved into this pastel-pink house with grass-green shutters, where he had worked with Auguste Renoir, Alfred Sisley and Édouard Manet for a number of years. He designed the gardens himself and created his famous water garden with its lilies and Japanese bridge. The main garden, with its 12 resident gardeners, still keeps to Monet's design and is a palette of changing hues from spring to autumn. Near the house, Monet's enormous studio is filled with huge copies of his works.

Head along rue Claude Monet, towards the Musée d'Art Américain. Take the lane to the right, called chemin Blanche-Hoschéde, then go right again almost immediately up the narrow rue Hélène-Pillon, which curves left before becoming a dirt track. Follow this path along the backs of houses, running parallel to rue Claude Monet below, until you reach the end of the village. Turn left (signposted GR2 and marked with red and white paint markers) up a steep path, then turn right at the first intersection. The path snakes across open meadowland towards the woods, with sweeping views over the Epte valley below.

At the next crossing of footpaths, go left and climb up through oak woods. At this point you leave the GR2 and the path is now marked in yellow. At the next crossroads, go right. At the edge of the woods, take the grassy path on the left, passing alongside pastureland then more woodland. As you reach the woods, turn right towards a small road. Turn left onto the road, which runs steeply downhill. After 50m (55yd), bear right, then right again along a track bordering the woods of La Réserve on the right, and flanked by fields on the left. When you come to a crossroads level with a small yellow house on the left, continue straight, then go left along the fringe of the Garenne woods.

Turn to the right in the woods, once again following the red and white signs of GR2. Soon you will come to a promontory marked by a large cross, with a magnificent view of the Seine.

Continue down a steep, narrow path leading to the hamlet of Manitaux; it comes out on a small lane bordered by cottages. Turn left, following the course of a former railway track until you reach the edge of Giverny. Go along the grassy path behind the first houses in the village, until the path joins the Sente des Grosses Eaux and, soon afterwards, rue Claude Monet.

Back on the main street of the village, proceed past the church, where Monet lies buried, to the Restaurant Baudy.

❶ The Restaurant Baudy was once a boarding house and the rendezvous of various painter friends of Monet, including Auguste Rodin, Alfred Sisley, Auguste Renoir, Paul Cézanne, Camille Pissarro and various visiting American artists. It was also the site of the first studio and the first art exhibitions in the village.

Continue along the main street to the Musée d'Art Américain.

❷ The Musée d'Art Américain houses a permanent collection of works by Monet's American contemporaries in France, as well as temporary exhibitions.

Continue along rue Claude Monet, filled with galleries and artists'

workshops, before returning to Monet's house and garden at the far end of the village.

PLACES TO VISIT
MAISON DE CLAUDE MONET
▷ 130–131.

MUSÉE D'ART AMÉRICAIN
▷ 131

RESTAURANT BAUDY
▷ 131.

WHEN TO GO
Monet's house and gardens are closed on Mondays and from November to April.

WHERE TO EAT
MOULIN DE FOURGES
▷ 142–143.

Clockwise from opposite *The creeper-covered veranda of Maison de Claude Monet; a bust of Monet in his gardens; a visitor stands on the Japanese bridge over the lily pond*

DRIVE

ALONG THE VALLEY OF THE EURE

The river after which the Eure *département* is named forms a gentle open valley to the east of Évreux. This drive explores its lower length from the ruins of a historic château to Pont de l'Arche which stands close to the river's confluence with the Seine.

THE DRIVE
Distance: 123 km (76 miles)
Allow: 1 day
Start and finish: Évreux

HOW TO GET THERE
Évreux (▷ 128–129) is 20km (12 miles) west of the A13 Paris–Rouen motorway.

★ From Évreux, take the N13 towards Paris. Beyond the outskirts, turn off right on to the D67 for Le Vieil-Évreux.

❶ Gisacum, just outside Le Vieil-Évreux ('Old Évreux'), is the excavated remains of a large religious complex dating from the second century AD. It has now been turned into an 'archaeological garden': a combination of park, reconstruction and stark modern additions. Even if the visitor centre is closed you can still see most of the site in a 20-minute walk.

Continue on the D67 through Boisset-les-Prevanches (which has

a small 17th-century château with grounds that can be visited) and across rich farmland to Epieds. Turn off right here on to the D163 to la Coutoure-Boussey.

❷ La Coutoure-Boussey has a museum of wind instruments in celebration of its traditional local craft industry with items on display ranging from the 18th century to the present day.

A short way along the D833 brings you to Ivry-la-Bataille

❸ There's not much left of the ruined 10th-century castle of Ivry-la-Bataille that stands on the top of a wooded hill immediately above the town but it makes for a pleasant walk. Start behind the church by going through the metal gate beside the brick tower marked 'Arsenal'.

Turn left on to the D836 and at Garennes, cross the river and continue on the D836 to Pacy-sur-Eure.

❹ The busy town of Pacy-sur-Eure is the departure point for an old-fashioned railway (▷ 140). When the trains are not running you can still see vintage rolling stock parked in the sidings of the station.

Resume the D836 heading north from Pacy through Menilles.

❺ Beside a chapel above the village of Cocherel is the tomb of Aristide Briand (1862–1932), several times prime minister of France and winner of the Nobel Prize for peace. After World War I he dedicated his energies to trying to get the governments of the world to agree to a pact making war illegal.

After 18km (12 miles) on the D836, turn left, over the river Eure, into Acquigny.

❻ The grounds of the Château d'Acquigny, beside the Eure, are open to visitors. The gardens are classically-inspired drawing on influence of the Mediterranean.

Recross the bridge, turn left back on to the D836 and go through Pinterville. Turn left into Louviers.

Above *The Château d'Acquigny*
Opposite *A white-and-red Eure valley tourist train at Pacy*

❼ A modest town whose fortunes were built on cloth manufacture, Louviers is crossed by 12 branches of the river Eure. Its most singular monument is the Cloître des Penitents, the cloister of a former monastery which unusually straddles the river. Also worth seeing are the church, the tourist information office (a red-striped, timber-framed building) and two streets of old half-timbered houses, the rue Ternaux and the rue des Grands Careaux.

From Louviers take the N15 to Pont-de-l'Arche.

❽ Pont-de-l'Arche is a harmnious town of half-timbered houses gathered around the church of Notre Dame des Arts. One of the stained glass windows in the church shows boats being towed on the river. Outside the town, heading for the motorway, is the Abbaye de Bonport, a Cistercian abbey founded by Richard the Lionheart.

The fastest route to return to Évreux is on the D6015, then N154/A154 motorway

PLACES TO VISIT
GISACUM
✉ 8 rue des Thermes, 27930 Le Vieil-Évreux ☎ 02 32 31 94 78 ⏰ Mar to mid-Nov daily 10–6 (except Sat 2–6pm) ✋ Free

MUSÉE DES INSTRUMENTS À VENT
✉ La Couture-Boussey ☎ 02 32 36 28 80 ⏰ Tue–Sun 2–6; closed 20 Dec–10 Jan

CHÂTEAU D'ACQUIGNY
www.château-acquigny.com
✉ 1 rue Aristide-Briand, 27400 Acquigny
☎ 02 32 50 23 31 ⏰ Apr–end Oct Sat, Sun and public hols 2–6, Jul–end Aug daily 2–7 ✋ Adult €6.50, child (over 8) €4

ABBAYE DE BONPORT
✉ Pont de l'Arche ☎ 02 35 02 19 42 ⏰ Apr–end Sep Sun and public hols 2–6.30, Jul, Aug Sun–Fri 2–6.30

WHEN TO GO
This route can be driven at any time of year.

WHERE TO EAT
LA TABLE DU BEARNAIS
Gourmet cuisine with strong influences from the chefs origins in southwest France.
✉ 40 rue A. Briand, 27400 Acquigny
☎ 02 32 40 37 73

LA FERME DE COCHEREL
www.lafermedecocherel.fr
Family-run hotel and restaurant in a restored old farm on the bank of the Eure.
✉ 8 rue Aristide Briand, Cocherel
☎ 02 32 36 68 27 ⏰ Closed Tue, Wed

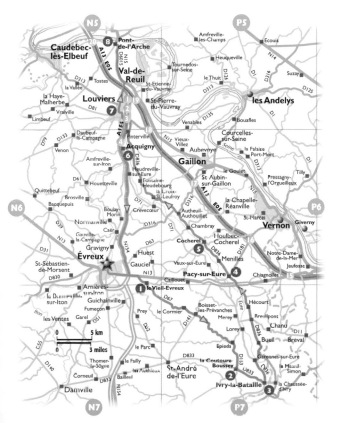

Above Decorative tea caddies holding loose tea for sale on a market stall

AIZIER
VIKING AVENTURE
www.vikingadventure.com
This is a forest adventure park 10km (6 miles) northeast of Pont-Audemer. Take the tree-top trail, swinging from high branches, or perhaps enjoy a morning's paintballing.
✉ 27500 Aizier ☎ 02 32 57 24 46 🕐 Apr–Sep daily 10–7 ✋ Tree-top trail: €11–€23. Paintball: €23 for 200 balls (from age 16 with an adult) 🚗 Take the D89 from Bourneville towards Quillebeuf-sur-Seine; after 3 km (2 miles) turn right and follow signs to 'Viking Aventure'

LES ANDELYS
HÔTEL DES VENTES
There is nothing quite like a French provincial auction house. If your command of the language is not up to it, stay very still; if you are confident enough to bid, you could go home with a bargain. In Les Andelys, auctioneer Jacqueline Cousin is in charge as locals sell the family silver. Themed sales of objets d'art, jewellery and haute couture are held year-round. Summer, mid- winter and Easter

see the best items go under the hammer.
✉ 15 rue Sadi Carnot, 27700 Les Andelys ☎ 02 32 54 30 04 🕐 Sales: Sun 2.30. Viewing: Sat 3.30–6, Sun 10.30–noon

RACE TRACK
Race day in Les Andelys is an old tradition, when eight trotting races are held over a 1,450m (1,586yds) grass course beneath the Château Gaillard (▷ 122–123). Grandstands are erected and hundreds of spectators make a day of it.
✉ Route de Louviers, Tosny, 27700 Les Andelys ☎ 02 32 69 54 26 🕐 Four Suns a year (Apr, May, Jul, Sep) 2.30

LE BEC-HELLOUIN
LES ATELIERS DU BEC
Originally established in 1034, the Abbey of Bec-Hellouin has been home to a community of Benedictine monks since 1948 (▷ 121). The brothers run a workshop manufacturing fine ceramics (tableware, dishes, vases and candlesticks), which incorporate antique designs.
✉ Abbaye du Bec-Hellouin, 27800 Le Bec-Hellouin ☎ 02 32 43 72 60 🕐 Workshops: Mon–Sat 11–11.45, 2.45–5.45. Boutique: daily 2.45–5.45

BOISEMONT
LE PRESSOIR D'OR
www.pressoir.com
The picturesque setting of a 17th-century farmhouse and its gardens, 6km (4 miles) from Écouis, provides a perfect backdrop to cider buying. The gingham cloth-covered tables in the reception room are stacked with apple *compotes*, cider vinegars and even breakfast preserves created by the award-winning farm.
✉ St-Jean-de-Frenelles, 27150 Boisemont ☎ 02 32 69 41 25 🕐 Mon, Tue, Thu, Fri 9.30–12, 2–6, Sat, Wed 2–6. Closed Sun

CORMEILLES
DISTILLERIE BUSNEL
www.distillerie-busnel.com
Normandy's biggest Calvados manufacturer makes a contrast to the region's homely family-run cider farms. The distillery, 20km (12.5 miles) southwest of Pont-Audemer, was built in 1910 and is also home to the Maison du Pays d'Auge, so the guided visit not only takes the visitor through the stages of production, but also celebrates local heritage. It's worth a visit, but don't miss out on seeing the farmhouse alternatives.
✉ Route de Lisieux, 27260 Cormeilles

☎ 02 32 57 80 08 ◉ Apr–end Oct
10–12.30, 2.30–7 ⊌ Adult €2, under 12 free

LA COUTURE-BOUSSEY
BRASSERIE HOTTETERRE
www.brasseriehotteterre.com
This pleasantly surprising farm
visit, 4km (2.5 miles) west of
Ivry-la-Bataille, promises shopping,
drinking, entertainment and even
a bed for the night. During the
afternoon, guided tours of the
brewery provide an opportunity
to learn about the local Hotteterre
beers, which can then be bought
in the shop. On certain evenings
(phone for the schedule) the place
becomes a live-music venue for jazz
and blues concerts.

The brasserie also has some
lovely *chambre d'hôte* (bed-
and-breakfast) rooms within the
farmhouse for overnight stays.
✉ 12 rue Hotteterre, 27750 La Couture-
Boussey ☎ 02 32 36 76 06 ◉ Brewery
tours (by appointment) ⊌ Concerts.
€5 €10. Accommodation: from €60–€70
per night

DAMVILLE
CHOCOLATRIUM CLUIZEL
www.cluizel.com
Master *chocolatier* Michel Cluizel
has been creating truffles in
Normandy since the 1940s and his
products are sold around the world.
The family's Damville chocolate
factory, half-way between Évreux
and Verneuil-sur-Avre, employs
200 people and has a museum and
visitor centre. Tour before you buy.
✉ Avenue de Conches, 27240 Damville
☎ 02 32 35 20 75 ◉ Museum: Tue–Sat
10–6. Shop: Mon–Sat 10–6 ⊌ Adult €5,
child (6–18) €4, under 6 free

ÉVREUX
AU JARDIN DE POMONE
www.au-jardin-de-pomone.com
Whether you are shopping for
a family picnic or for gifts, this
high-quality grocery shop is worth
browsing. Good wine cellars,
an excellent cheese counter
and mouthwatering hampers of
traditional Normandy delicacies are
all to be found in one place.

✉ 15 rue Edouard Féray, 27000 Évreux
☎ 02 32 39 65 37 ◉ Tue–Fri 8.30–12.30,
2.30–7.30, Sat 8.30–7.30, Sun 8.30–12.30

CHOCOLATIER PÂTISSIER AUZOU
When faced with sumptuous
chocolates such as *zouzous
d'Auzou, pommes Normandes
au Calvados* and other irresistible
delicacies at this popular pastry shop
you'll be tempted to stop counting
calories. It's pure heaven for the
sweet-toothed.
✉ 34 rue Chartraine, 2700 Évreux ☎ 02
32 33 28 05 ◉ Tue–Sun 9.30–12.15, 2–7

FORUM ESPACE CULTURE
A small cultural shopping centre
selling a wide range of books and
CDs for the car. And, if you require
it, they also have a photocopier here.
✉ 18 rue de la Harpe, 27000 Évreux
☎ 02 32 31 20 59 ◉ Mon 2–7, Tue–Sun
10–7 ⊌ Internet access: €1 per 15 minutes

LE MATAHARI
The essential hip haunt of Évreux is
a former locksmith's. Bright and cool
during the day, it is the ideal place to
settle down and linger over the local
papers and a coffee. In the evenings,
DJs play rock sounds into the night.
The waterside terrace is a favourite
weekend hangout for students.
✉ 15 rue de la Petite Cité, 27000 Évreux
☎ 02 32 38 49 88 ◉ Mon–Sat
10am–1am, Sun 10am–8pm

LE NEW WORLD
www.lenewworld.com
Always packed, even during the
week, this popular club has regular
theme nights. The main dance floor
tends towards techno sounds, while
a smaller disco revives the sounds
of the 1980s and 1990s.
✉ 15 boulevard de Normandie, 27000
Évreux ☎ 02 32 62 36 43 ◉ Thu, Sun
10.30pm–4am, Fri, Sat 10.30pm–5am
⊌ Thu free before midnight, €5–€8 after
midnight; Fri women free before midnight;
after midnight women €5–€8, men €11; Sat
and hols women €11, men €13

LE PARVIS BOWLING
This ten-pin bowling alley has eight
lanes with electronic scoreboards,

plus a pool hall and restaurant.
Advance booking is advisable on
weekends.
✉ 2 rue Franklin D. Roosevelt, 27000
Évreux ☎ 02 32 62 42 33 ◉ Mon 7.30pm–
midnight, Tue–Thu 2pm–2am, Fri–Sat and
eve of public hols 2pm–4am, Sun and public
hols 2.30–midnight. Restaurant closed
Sun–Mon ⊌ Dinner and bowling package:
€27.50 and €34. Adult afternoon: €5, evening
€6 and €1.40 for shoe hire

PUB MACLÉOD
Unlike most Continental Irish pubs,
this is more a meeting place for the
locals than an expat hangout. At the
weekend it becomes a tapas bar,
and in summer live bands play in
the garden once or twice a month
as customers tuck into a barbecue.
Known in Évreux as Le Mac, it plays
Celtic music and serves a variety
of beers.
✉ 47 rue Jean Jaurès, 27000 Évreux
☎ 02 32 33 00 09 ◉ Tue–Sat 11am–1am

JOUY-SUR-EURE
LA GUINGUETTE
Come to Jouy-sur-Eure, 15km
(9 miles) east of Évreux, for a
traditional Sunday afternoon
guinguette country tea dance.
Favourite waltzes and ballads are
played on the accordion as couples
of all ages take to the dance floor.
There's no need to dress in your
Sunday finery, just don't wear
jeans or trainers. If you come on a
Saturday evening, however, put on
your smartest clothes and phone
ahead to book for dinner.
✉ 49 rue de l'Ancienne Abbaye, 27120
Jouy-sur-Eure ☎ 02 32 36 18 99 ◉ Fri,
Sun 3–7; Fri, Sat 9.30 ⊌ €10 without drinks

LÉRY
BASE RÉGIONAL DE PLEIN AIR ET
DE LOISIRES DE LÉRY-POSES
Some 16km (10 miles) north of
Louviers between Léry and Poses
are two fabulous lakes between the
rivers Seine and Eure. From April to
October, two beaches on the Lac
des Deux Amants are supervised,
and by the lakeside you will find
golf courses, volleyball sets and
a hire shop. The Lac de Mesnil is

busier year-round, with windsurfing, canoeing, rock climbing, caving and rowing on offer.

✉ 27690 Léry ☎ 02 32 59 13 13
🕐 Daily 10–7 🅿 €4–€6 per car

LOUVIERS
LA GARE AUX MUSIQUES
In the year 2000, Louviers converted its former railway station into a music venue. A full line-up of concerts is matched by the station's role as a music maker in its own right, with workshops and recording studios giving the place a soul.

✉ Place des Anciens d'Indochine, B.P. 621, 27406 Louviers ☎ 02 32 25 78 00
🕐 Mon–Fri 2–midnight, Sat 2–8 ✋ Prices vary with performance; on first and last Fri of month during school term from €6 per hour

GRAIN DE CAFÉ
Despite a choice of a dozen excellent coffees, this address is a firm favourite with lovers of fine teas. Around 70 varieties of tea are always on the menu at this tiny café, which has a few seats on the street and is popular with Louviers' chattering classes.

✉ 39 rue du Matrey, 27400 Louviers
☎ 02 32 40 29 22 🕐 Tue–Sat 9.30–7
✋ Cup of tea: €2

LE MOULIN
This 18th-century mill has a long and distinguished history. Twice destroyed by fire in the 19th century, bomb-damaged in World War II and finally bought by the town in 1980, Le Moulin reopened as an arts centre in 2000. The venue has two theatres, a café and a bar.

✉ Rue des Anciens Combattants Afrique du Nord, 27406 Louviers ☎ 02 32 40 22 39
🕐 Times vary with performance ✋ Ticket prices depend on programme 🖥 🎭

MISEREY
LA PASSÉE D'AOÛT
Blackberries and figs make excellent jams, but at Miserey, 8km (5 miles) east of Évreux, you can taste not only the fruits you might normally expect to find, but also carrot, prune and rhubarb. The owner, Vivianne, makes and sells her home-made

preserves from her parents' fruit farm. You can pop by to pick up a jar of jam or stay the night in one of the simple *chambre d'hôte* bedrooms and taste a selection over breakfast.

✉ 1 rue du Stade, 27930 Miserey ☎ 02 32 67 06 24 🕐 Mon–Sat ✋ Double room: €48 per night

MONTFORT-SUR-RISLE
VAL DE RISLE
www.ckvalderisle.fr.st
Make your way down the fast-flowing waters of the river Risle in a two-man canoe. You could attempt the 8km (5-mile) journey from Montfort- sur-Risle (15km/9 miles southwest of Pont-Audemer) to Corneville alone, take a guide with you for the half-day 9km (5.5-mile) expedition from upstream Pont-Authou to Montfort, or make a day of it and battle 17km (10.5 miles) of waters with your guide from Pont-Authou all the way to Corneville. A reservation is essential.

✉ 27290 Montfort-sur-Risle ☎ 02 32 56 37 14 🕐 Tue–Sun 9–12, 2–5 ✋ Half-day: €15 per person. Full day: €25 per person. Guide: €35 per half-day

LE NEUBOURG
MUSÉE DE L'ECORCHÉ D'ANATOMIE
Little boys will love this eccentric medical museum, dedicated to the work of Dr. Auzoux, who in the early 19th century came up with a technique of making anatomical models from paper and cardboard. Astonishingly realistic re-creations of human bodies, revealing muscles, veins and bones, along with a generous array of internal organs and body parts ranging from eyes to limbs, are on display, some dating back 150 years or more.

✉ Espace Culturel, 54 avenue de la Liberation, 27110 Le Neubourg ☎ 02 32 35 93 95 🕐 Wed–Sat 2–6 ✋ Adult €4.50, child €3.50

PACY-SUR-EURE
CHEMIN DE FER DE LA VALLÉE D'EURE
www.cfve.org
With three scenic routes to choose

from, a trip on this vintage train, departing from Pacy, east of Évreux, is the ideal way to discover the Eure valley. The century-old Pacy station was completely renovated in 2003 and is the start point for trips to Breuilpont, Chambray and Cocherel. Throughout the year, an imaginative programme of events ranges from dinners aboard the train to country markets on the platforms at Pacy. The train can also be hired for private parties.

✉ Place de la Gare, 27120 Pacy-sur-Eure
☎ 02 32 36 04 63 🕐 Train services: Jul Sun 11.30, 2.50, Wed 2.30, national hols 3pm; Aug Sun 11.30, 2.50, 4.30, Wed 2.30, national hols 3 pm; Jun, Sep Sun 2.50 ✋ Adult from €8, under 16 from €6. Private rental from €320

STE-OPPORTUNE-LA-MARE
MARCHÉ AUX POMMES
Apples, ciders and Calvados from the orchards of the Eure are the principal lure to this monthly farmers' market, 8km (5 miles) north of Pont-Audemer. You will also find foie gras, sausages, cheeses and honeys from local hives.

✉ 27680 Ste-Opportune-la-Mare
🕐 Oct–end Apr first Sun morning of the month

VASCOEUIL
PARC DU CHÂTEAU
www.château-vascoeuil.com
A relaxing afternoon walk through the grounds of the castle at Vascoeuil, 10km (6 miles) from Rouen, is worth a detour, even if you don't visit the museum, with its works by painter Fernand Léger (1881–1955) and film director Jean Cocteau (1889–1963). The river Crevon runs through the 5ha (12-acre) garden, which contains more than 50 contemporary sculptures; here, you can see works by Salvador Dalí (1904–89) and Georges Braque (1882–1963) among the trees and plants.

✉ Château de Vascoeuil, 8 rue Jules Michelet, 27910 Vascoeuil ☎ 02 35 23 62 35 🕐 Easter to mid-Nov, Jul, Aug daily 11–6; Mar–end Jun, Sep–end Oct Tue–Sun, and Mon on national hols 2.30–6

🐾 Gardens, museum and exhibitions: Adult €7.50, child (10–18)/student €5.50

VERNEUIL-SUR-AVRE
LE BOIS DES AIGLES
www.leboisdesaigles.com
Watch displays of falconry at this 5ha (12-acre) park 5km (3 miles) east of Verneuil-sur-Avre, home to more than 100 birds of prey. Outside showtime, you can see the birds at home in 35 tree-filled aviaries.
✉ Route Nationale 12, Bâlines, 27130 Verneuil-sur-Avre ☎ 02 32 32 14 75
🕐 End March–early Nov daily 10–6 during French school hols; at other times Tue–Sun 10–6 🐾 Adult €10, child €7

FONDERIE D'ART CLAUDE ALEXANDRE
www.alexandrefigurines.com
Visit the Les Barils foundry, 8km (5 miles) west of Verneuil-sur-Avre, to see Claude Alexandre at work casting and painting France's well-known model soldiers. Alexandre's detailed pewter and lead figurines are the star attraction of his museum, with such scenes from French history as the storming of the Bastille and the Battle of Waterloo. At the museum shop you can buy model soldiers and chess sets to take home.
✉ 3 rue de Gournay, Les Barils, 27130 Verneuil-sur-Avre ☎ 02 32 37 64 70
🕐 Foundry visits: Jul, Aug daily 11–12.30 2.30–6; Sep–end Jun phone to book an appointment. Museum and shop: Jul, Aug daily 11–12.30, 2.30–6; Sep–end Jun by appointment 🐾 Museum: adult €4, child €3.10. Museum and workshop: adult €5.50, child €4.50 🚻 🅿 Free ❓ Access for visitors with disabilities

VERNON
LE CAFÉ DE FRANCE
This is a useful address, especially at weekends, for visitors adding Vernon to their Giverny itinerary. Open far longer hours than most bars in the heart of town, the Café de France serves coffee early in the morning before the crowds head off on the Monet trail, and a late-night beer or glass of wine at the end of an exhausting day's sightseeing.

FESTIVALS AND EVENTS

MAY
FÊTE DE L'ÉTAMPAGE
The annual branding of the cattle at Marais-Vernier, 12km (7.5 miles) northwest of Pont-Audemer, brings a whiff of cowboy culture to Normandy. The event is marked with entertainment and plenty of food.
✉ Marais-Vernier ☎ 02 35 37 23 16
🕐 Beginning of May

JUNE
JOURNÉES MEDIÉVAL
The streets around the château are transformed as the town dresses up for its old-style markets, merrymaking and *son et lumière* show.
✉ Les Andelys ☎ 02 32 58 28 74
🕐 Last weekend in Jun

LE ROCK DANS TOUS SES ÉTATS
Three days of live music erupt across town as Évreux stages its annual rock festival.
✉ Évreux ☎ 02 32 24 04 43 🕐 Last weekend in Jun

JUNE–JULY
LES MASCARETS
This three-week summer entertainment festival brings together established performers and street musicians in a programme ranging from concerts to impromptu sets on street corners by buskers from across Europe.
✉ Pont-Audemer ☎ 02 32 41 08 21
🕐 late Jun to mid-Jul

JULY
FESTIVAL DE LA MARIONNETTE EN PAYS RISLE-CHARENTONNE
Puppeteers from far and wide gather for the official festival programme and for fringe events held in the streets away from the main stages.
✉ Bernay 🕐 Four days in early Jul

VIÈVRE, TERRE DES MYSTÈRES
A spectacular *son et lumière* show 18km (11 miles) south of Pont-Audemer, blending local history with folk tales and legends, begins at sunset.
✉ Épreville-en-Lieuvin ☎ 02 32 42 09 16
🕐 Selected evenings throughout Jul

NOVEMBER
FÊTE DE LA POMME, DU FROMAGE ET DU CIDRE
Great Normandy produce is celebrated with a festival of apples, cheeses and ciders. There are tastings and a chance to buy the best from local farmers.
✉ Évreux ☎ 02 32 24 04 43 🕐 First Sun after All Saints' Day (1 Nov)

You can also eat well for under €15 here, and there is a pleasant pavement (sidewalk) terrace for watching the town revive after the working day.
✉ 59 rue d'Albuféra, 27200 Vernon ☎ 02 32 51 16 69 🕐 Thu–Sat 6.30am–11.30pm; Sun–Wed noon–9.30 (can vary)

ESPACE PHILIPPE AUGUSTE
Vernon's theatre stages a variety of entertainments, from dance to classic theatre, experimental performance and children's shows. It also hosts a spring book fair.

This independent arts centre flourishes despite Vernon's proximity to Paris and Rouen. Time a visit so that you arrive for a concert.
✉ 12 avenue Victor Hugo, 27200 Vernon ☎ 02 32 64 53 16 🕐 Oct and May performance times vary 🐾 Variable

EATING

PRICES AND SYMBOLS
The restaurants are listed alphabetically (excluding Le, La and Les) by town. The prices given are the average for a two-course lunch (L) and a three-course dinner (D) for one person, without drinks. The wine price is for the least expensive bottle. All the restaurants listed accept credit cards unless otherwise stated.

For a key to the symbols, ▷ 2

BEUZEVILLE
LE RELAIS DE POSTE
www.le-relais-de-poste.com
This 19th-century coaching inn in a large garden is now a hotel and restaurant with a friendly atmosphere. It serves imaginative local cuisine with dishes. There is a private car park. Beuzeville is a short way off the A13 mortoway, west of Pont-Audemer and southwest of Honfleur.
✉ 60 rue Constant Fouché, 27210 Beuzeville ☎ 02 32 20 32 32 🕐 Closed Sun eve, Mon, Tue eve 🖐 L €20, D €35, Wine €12

CAMPIGNY
LE PETIT COQ AUX CHAMPS
www.lepetitcoqauxchamps.fr
Located in a beautiful thatched

building a short way southwest of Pont-Audemer, this restaurant and small hotel serves mainly traditional cooking with a choice of fixed menus available. The foie gras is a specialty but the fish and seafood, veal and lamb are all good choices as well.
✉ La Pommeraie Sud 27500 Campigny ☎ 02 32 41 04 19 🕐 Apr–Oct daily; Nov–Mar closed Sun eve 🖐 L €45, D €50, wine included

CONCHES-EN-OUCHE
RESTAURANT ET HÔTEL DU CYGNE
Tucked away in a cottage that was once a coach house, this dining room has a tiled floor and beamed ceiling. The menu changes seasonally, but always reflects good, local produce. Foie gras is usually an option.
✉ 2 rue Paul Guilbaud, 27190 Conches-en-Ouche ☎ 02 32 30 20 60 🕐 Tue–Sat 12–2.30, 7.30–9.30, Sun 12–2.30. Closed Oct 🖐 L €18, D €28, Wine €15

LES DAMPS
AUBERGE DE LA POMME
Here you can choose from interesting fish dishes, all served up in russet-toned surroundings.

Occasional events are organized on the terrace and gardens.
✉ 44 rue de l'Eure, 27340 Les Damps ☎ 02 35 23 00 46 🕐 Mon, Thu–Sat 12–2, 7–9, Tue, Sun noon–2. Closed Aug 🖐 L €30, D €42, Wine €27 🅿 Good parking facilities available

ÉVREUX
LA GAZETTE
This lovely bistro has much to offer. Chef Xavier Buzieux creates some unexpected flavours; for example, a red mullet fillet is served with the southern salt-cod specialty *brandade de morue* and a pistachio vinaigrette. Round off the meal with the powerfully refreshing eucalyptus sorbet.
✉ 7 rue St-Sauveur, 27000 Évreux ☎ 02 32 33 43 40 🕐 Mon–Fri 12–2, 7–9.30, Sat 7–9.30. Closed Aug 🖐 L €20, D €39, Wine €17

FOURGES
MOULIN DE FOURGES
www.moulin-de-fourges.com
This beautiful mill stands just a couple of miles from Giverny but it is a relaxing sanctuary away from the crowds on the Monet trail. The food makes innovative use of local produce. You can stay the night here.

Opposite *Make a point of enjoying oysters along Normandy's coast*
Below *Chefs plate up*

✉ 38 rue du Moulin, 27630 Fourges
☎ 02 32 52 12 12 🕐 Tue–Sat 12–2.30, 7.30–10, Sun 12–2.30 ♿ L €35, D €40, Wine €21

GISORS
LE CHASSE MAREE
www.chassemar.com
The pleasant restaurant of the Hotel de Dieppe concentrates on 'the sea and the season'. One of their rich and special dishes combines sole and salmon with leeks and white wine.
✉ 1 Avenue de la Gare, 27140 Gisors
☎ 02 32 55 25 54 🕐 Closed Thu, Fri lunch and Sun eve ♿ L €28, D €30, Wine €12

IGOVILLE
AUBERGE DU PRESSOIR
www.auberge-du-pressoir.com
This restaurant, in a pretty 18th-century stone building on the road between Louviers and Rouen, is decorated in warm colours. The menu concentrates on traditional cuisine with some creative flourishes and careful presentation. Specialties include oysters and the *foie gras de canard au porto*.
✉ RN 15, Lieu dit Le Fort, 27460 Igoville
☎ 02 35 23 27 77 🕐 Tue, Thu 12–2, 7–9.15, Fri, Sat 12–2, 7–10.15, Wed, Sun noon–2. Closed Wed eve, Sun eve and Mon all day ♿ L €20, D €38, Wine €15

NOTRE DAME DU HAMEL
LE MOULIN DE LA MARIGOTIERE
www.moulin-marigotiere.com
This gourmet restaurant in a renovated mill in a quiet corner of countryside in the southwest corner of the Eure has views over the Charentonne river and a pleasant terrace for summer lunches. The chef takes pride in his seasonal cuisine prepared using mainly regional products. There is a very good selection of wines.
✉ Le Village, 27390 Notre Dame du Hamel
☎ 02 32 44 50 11 🕐 Closed Sun eve, Mon eve, Tue eve, Wed eve ♿ L €40, D €75, Wine €21

PONT-AUDEMER
BELLE-ISLE SUR RISLE
www.bellile.com
Chef Pascal Larouche produces such specialties as the famous *magret du canard du pays aux figues frêches* (local duck with fresh figs). The menu also features other meat and fish dishes, and local cheeses. A blend of business lunchers and hedonists sets this manor house (▷ 145) apart.
✉ 112 route de Rouen, 27500 Pont-Audemer ☎ 02 32 56 96 22 🕐 Daily 7.15–9.30, Thu–Sun 12–2. Closed mid-Nov to mid-Mar ♿ L €30, D €60, Wine €23

PONT-ST-PIERRE
L'HOSTELLERIE LA BONNE MARMITE
www.la-bonne-marmite.com
The dining room in this former coaching inn (▷ 145), has a romantic atmosphere. Dishes celebrate the local turbot, lobster and duck. Angelique Hain and Alexandre Da Silva manage the restaurant. The wine list has 850 vintages dating back as far as 1858.
✉ 10 rue René Raban, 27360 Pont-St-Pierre
☎ 02 32 49 70 24 🕐 Wed–Sat 12–2.15, 7–9.15, Sun 12–2.15. Closed late Feb–late Mar, late Jul to mid-Aug ♿ L €25, D €35, Wine €13

VERNEUIL-SUR-AVRE
HOSTELLERIE LE CLOS
www.hostellerieduclos.fr
Set in a 12th-century village, this fairy-tale manor house nestles in parkland. The grand dining room, with trompe l'oeil decoration, leads onto a sunny terrace. The chef prepares seasonal dishes, which can be accompanied by wines from a mature list that includes some fine Calvados.
✉ 98 rue de la Ferté-Vidame, 27133 Verneuil-sur-Avre ☎ 02 32 32 21 81
🕐 Daily 12–2, 7.30–9. Closed mid Dec to late Jan ♿ L €45, D €78, Wine €25

VERNON
LES FLEURS
In this half-timbered house in the heart of Vernon, Bernard Lefebvre creates evolving menus that will enchant any palate. When asparagus comes into season, regular diners adore the arrival of Graux's delicious blend of the vegetable with lightly pan-fried scallops. The restaurant's attention to detail in the kitchen is matched by the service and presentation.
✉ 71 rue Carnot, 27200 Vernon ☎ 02 32 51 16 80 🕐 Tue–Sat 12–2, 7.30–9.15, Sun 12–2. Closed early Mar, early Aug ♿ L €37, D €40, Wine €21

PRICES AND SYMBOLS

The prices are the lowest and highest for a double room for one night including breakfast, unless otherwise stated. All the hotels listed accept credit cards unless otherwise stated. Note that rates can vary widely throughout the year.

For a key to the symbols, ▷ 2.

LES ANDELYS
LA CHAINE D'OR

www.hotel-de-charme-gastronomie.hotel-lachainedor.com

La Chaine d'Or has kept the original name it used when it was a coaching inn where tolls were collected in the 18th century. But the décor is more stylish at this *auberge* today. In the summer, enjoy your breakfast on the terrace. Dishes at the restaurant, overlooking the river Seine, are prepared from local, seasonal produce.

✉ 27 rue Grande, le Petit Andely, 27700 Les Andelys ☎ 02 32 54 00 31 🕐 Closed Jan 🖐 €78–€132, excluding breakfast (€12) 🚻 11

BRAY ET LU
HOTEL LES JARDINS D'EPICURE

www.lesjardinsdepicure.com

A hotel and restaurant complex which, starting with its names, promises pleasures corporal, culinary and cultural. The accommodation, which includes some suites and one room equipped for disabled guests, is in three different buildings: the Castel Napoleon III (the main house), the Villa Florentine) and the renovated stable block. Facilities include a swimming pool, sauna, hammam and Jacuzzi.

Although this is just outside Normandy itself, the hotel is well placed for sightseeing.

✉ 16 Grande Rue, 95710 Bray et Lu ☎ 01 34 67 75 87 🖐 €140 🚻 18

CAHAIGNES
CHÂTEAU DE REQUIÉCOURT

www.châteauderequiecourt.com

A beautifully restored 19th-century château standing in its own large park which includes a pond visited by wild ducks. It has bright and spacious bedrooms. Breakfast can be eaten in the pretty winter garden which has views over the grounds. Extras on offer include a shiatsu massage or an hour's tour in a vintage car.

✉ 5 rue de la Chartreuse, 27420 Cahaignes ☎ 02 32 55 37 02 🖐 €80–€120 🚻 5

CONNELLES
LE MOULIN DE CONNELLES

www.giverny.org/hotels/connelle

A beautiful 19th-century half-timbered house standing in its own grounds on the bank of the Seine between Les Andelys and Louviers. Most of the rooms look over the river. There are two swimming pools (one for summer, one for winter) and a sauna.

The hotel's restaurant is open daily in summer but closes on Sunday and Tuesday evenings, and all day Monday at other times.

✉ 40 route Amfreville sous les Monts, 27430 Connelles ☎ 02 32 59 53 33 🖐 €140, excluding breakfast (€13) 🚻 13 (6 are suites)

EMALLEVILLE
CHÂTEAU D'EMALLEVILLE

www.châteaudemalleville.com

A renovated Norman stately home in its own parkland offering quiet and a sense or aristocratic living. Some of the bedrooms are in the château itself; others in the outbuildings. For more privacy you might want to stay in the charmingly converted pigeonnier (dovecote) or rent the gardener's house (*maison du jardinier*), which sleeps four people.

All the rooms are hung with original works of art.

✉ 17 rue de l'Église, 27930 Emalleville ☎ 02 32 34 01 87 💶 €140 ℹ 11 plus the *masion du jardinier*

ÉVREUX
NORMANDY HOTEL
www.normandyhotel.eu
As well as being the most charming place to stay in the heart of the city, this is also a gourmet restaurant with home-made foie gras, lobster and whole pigeon on the menu. It has a private car park.

✉ 37 rue Édouard Feray, 27000 Évreux ☎ 02 32 33 14 40 💶 €78–€112 ℹ 20

GAILLON
CHÂTEAU CORNEILLE
www.château-corneille.fr
This 18th-century château is set in beautiful grounds, and its original barn houses a convivial restaurant. Bedrooms, meanwhile, have been modernized and furnished to suit current tastes. Summer guests enjoy relaxing on the veranda.

✉ 17 rue de l'Église, Vieux Villez, 27600 Gaillon ☎ 02 32 77 44 77 🕐 Year-round 💶 €103–€124, excluding breakfast (€11) ℹ 19

LOUVIERS
HOTEL DE LA HAYE LE COMTE
www.manoir-louviers.com
A renovated 16th-century manor house just outside Louviers in which the rooms are decorated with antiques. It has various facilities for games and sports includling a golf practice range and tennis court. Dinner in the restaurant in winter is by candlelight in front of a wood fire.

✉ 4 route de La Haye Le Comte, 27400 Louviers ☎ 02 32 40 00 40 💶 €100 ℹ 14

LYONS-LA-FORÊT
CHÂTEAU DE FLEURY LA FORÊT
www.château-fleury-la-foret.com
This magnificent château, at the end of a drive flanked by lime trees, is one of the area's main attractions. It

is also a *chambre d'hôtes* (bed and breakfast) offering two comfortable rooms and a suite.

✉ 27480 Lyons-La-Forêt ☎ 02 32 49 63 91 💶 €72–€115 ℹ 3

LA LICORNE
www.licorne-hotel-restaurant.com
Surrounded by Europe's largest beech forest, this 17th-century inn stands in a pretty village. Behind a half-timbered façade are tastefully decorated guest rooms furnished with antiques. The inviting dining room serves regional specialities.

✉ La Licorne, B.P. 4, 27480 Lyons-la-Forêt ☎ 02 32 48 24 24 🕐 Closed late Dec to mid-Jan 💶 €99–€180, excluding breakfast (€12) ℹ 20

LES LIONS DE BEAUCLERC
www.lionsdebeauclerc.com
Very much a *maison bourgeoise*, the Lions de Beauclerc offers an antiques shop within the hotel itself. All bedrooms have antique furnishings. Nearby you will find tennis, swimming and horseback-riding.

✉ 7 rue de l'Hôtel de Ville, 27480 Lyons-la-Forêt ☎ 02 32 49 18 90 🕐 Year-round 💶 €59–€72, excluding breakfast (€9) ℹ 6

NASSANDRES
LE SOLEIL D'OR
www.domainedusoleildor.com
The exterior of this building is typical of the local architecture, so prepare for a surprise—the bedrooms are uncompromisingly modern. The hotel has a café with themed musical evenings and the lovely village is close to the river Risle.

✉ 1 chausée de Roy, La Rivière Thibouville, 27550 Nassandres ☎ 02 32 45 00 08 🕐 Year-round 💶 €55–€90, excluding breakfast (€10) ℹ 12 rooms, 2 apartments

PONT-AUDEMER
BELLE-ISLE SUR RISLE
www.bellile.com
This 19th-century mansion is in a landscaped, rose-filled park. Each bedroom is individually decorated and named. Some have balconies overlooking a garden. Not only is

there an indoor seawater pool, but also an outdoor pool. Other activities include rowing, canoeing, golf and riding. There is a good restaurant (▷ 143).

✉ 112 route de Rouen, 27500 Pont-Audemer ☎ 02 32 56 96 22 🕐 Closed mid-Nov to mid-Mar 💶 €125–€242, excluding breakfast (€15) ℹ 20 🏊 Outdoor and indoor 🚭

PONT-ST-PIERRE
L'HOSTELLERIE LA BONNE MARMITE
www.la-bonne-marmite.com
Tucked in a pretty village, this one-time coaching inn is now an inviting hotel that combines plenty of character with modern comforts. Wine and dine by candlelight, then retire to a bedroom lavishly furnished in the Louis XVI style with canopy beds.

✉ 10 rue René Raban, 27360 Pont-St-Pierre ☎ 02 32 49 70 24 🕐 Closed late Feb–late Mar, late Jul to mid-Aug 💶 €70–€99, excluding breakfast (€9) ℹ 9

ST PIERRE DE VAUDRAY
HOSTELLERIE SAINT PIERRE
www.hotel-saintpierre.com
An elegant, turretted manor house hotel with a restaurant and bar in a beautiful spot facing the Île du Bac, an islet in the river Seine not far from Louviers. Many of the rooms have windows looking on to the water so that you can watch the boats go by.

✉ 6 chemin de la Dique, 27430 St Pierre de Vaudray ☎ 02 32 59 93 29 💶 €90–€185 ℹ 11

VERNEUIL-SUR-AVRE
CHÂTEAU DE LA PUISAYE
www.châteaudelapuisaye.com
Guests are invited to fish in the carp pond in the grounds of this Napoleon III château which has guest rooms in the east wing and an independent *gîte* (the old hunting lodge) for eight people. Breakfast is generous and an evening meal using home-grown seasonal fruit and vegetables is also served.

✉ La Puisaye, 27130 Verneuil sur Avre ☎ 02 32 58 65 35 💶 €110 ℹ 5

SEINE-MARITIME

As the name suggests, Normandy's northernmost *département* combines two elements: the Seine and the sea. This triangle of territory is bordered by France's most famous river to the south and to the northwest by the coast of the English Channel. In between the two is the wedge-shaped chalk plateau of the Pays de Caux while, further inland, to the northeast, are the pleasant pasturelands and orchards of the Pays de Bray—but sights are sparse in these two rural areas which probably won't make much claim on your attention.

Two historic but contrasting port cities on the Seine dominate the *département*—Rouen and Le Havre. The former, up river and far inland, the capital of the Haute-Normandie region, is a handsome cluster of old houses around a magnificent cathedral spire. It is haunted by two French heroines: Joan of Arc, who was executed here, and Flaubert's ficticious *Madame Bovary*. Le Havre is all the opposite: A place that has had to look forward rather than back. Flattened by bombs in World War II, it had to be entirely rebuilt and its amalgam of uncompromisingly contemporary has made it is a listed World Heritage Site which is surprisingly interesting to visit.

On its way between these cities, the Seine describes exaggerated meanders and passes three great early medieval abbeys where a sense of peace and spirituality lingers from earlier times: St-Martin-de-Boscherville, Jumieges (the finest of them) and Wandrille.

The seashore of the *département* is called the Côte d'Albâtre (Alabaster Coast) and you only have to visit Étretat to appreciate why. Either side of this charming resort are enormous bright white cliffs which have inspired and continue to inspire countless artists. Other places on the coast worth visiting are the royal town of Eu, the port-cum-resort of Dieppe and Fécamp where Benedtine liqueur is made.

ABBAYE DE JUMIÈGES

The abbey that can be regarded as the blueprint for the great Norman churches of France and England. Let your imagination fill in the gaps between the stones when you visit the impressive ruins of the Abbey of Jumièges within their park. Although much of the buildings were destroyed in the 18th century, you can still sense their majesty. The roofless ruins of the 11th-century church of Notre-Dame and its earlier 10th-century neighbour, the Église St-Pierre, are the perfect backdrop to a romantic stroll.

Founded in AD654 by St. Philibert, then burned down by the Vikings, the Benedictine abbey rose to its first period of greatness under the dukes of Normandy with the construction of the Église St-Pierre around AD940. Jumièges grew until the Hundred Years War, when it began to decline; by 1792, just seven monks remained and the abbey was looted. In 1852, the Lepel-Cointet family began restoration work and Jumièges became a state-owned national monument in 1947.

Today, the imposing bone-white abbey ruins, standing among centuries-old trees, still dominate the village of Jumièges. Although open to the skies, the Notre-Dame church buildings remain stunning examples of Norman church architecture, the lack of vaulting seeming to illuminate the detail of the stone and woodwork of the walls, arcades and towers. While the west of the church is well preserved, smaller chapels have long gone; beyond the transept some 13th-century Gothic restorations of older Romanesque features hint at what might once have been. The west wall of the lantern tower survives and the south transept leads to the Passage Charles VII between Notre-Dame and the Église St-Pierre. Some painted decorations remain in the older church, while the choir is decorated with *culots* (carvings).

MYTHS AND MISTRESSES

Hear about the abbey's myths and legends on the guided tour. One of these concerns the lime-tree avenue in the gardens between the abbey and 17th-century house of Abbot François de Harlay. Allegedly, the avenue is named after Agnès Sorel, mistress of Charles VII (1403–61), who used it as a trysting place to meet the king.

INFORMATION

www.jumieges.fr
www.monum.fr
🔲 222 M4 ✉ 24 rue Guillaume-le-Conquérant, 76480 Jumièges ☎ 02 35 37 24 02 🕐 Apr–end Sep daily 9–6.30; Oct–end Mar daily 9.30–1, 2.30–5.30 ♿ Adult €5. Guided tours included in admission price (in French only) 🚆 Rouen (28km/17.5 miles) 🚫 No café on site 🏬 Shop with an excellent range of monastic and regional gifts, as well as a good selection of reference books in French and English ❓ Shop has wide aisles for wheelchair-users; the park offers a strenuous wheelchair ride; toilets in the shop (at the main entrance) are well equipped for visitors with a disability

TIPS

» Wear comfortable shoes, for a visit to the abbey is essentially a country walk.
» Bring a blanket and sweater with you when attending concerts.
» Admire the illuminated white stone buildings against the midnight sky during evening nocturnes (May–Sep, selected Sats).

Opposite and below They abbey's main church, Notre-Dame, was consecrated in the presence of William the Conqueror

Clockwise from left to right *Abbaye de St-Wandrille; a wallaby in the Parc Zoologique at Clères; Château de Miromesnil*

ABBAYE DE ST-WANDRILLE

www.st-wandrille.com
Behind a grand gateway copied
from that at the royal Château of
Fontainebleau near Paris, today's
Abbaye de St-Wandrille is a
bewildering architectural cluster.
Founded in AD649 by Count
Wandrille as a study centre, the
abbey's original buildings were
destroyed by the Vikings. Rebuilt
in the 13th to 16th centuries, the
abbey passed into secular hands
after the French Revolution,
becoming first a working mill and
then a private home. In 1931, it
began its latest religious incarnation
as a Benedictine monastery.

This confusing history explains
the juxtaposition of styles of the
surviving buildings: The 17th-century
library and Louis XIV staircase, for
example, are a luxurious contrast
to the simple ruins of the older
cloister. Be sure to see the restored
refectory and former bookbinding
workshop.

The 20th century has also left its
architectural legacy: The Chapel le
Notre-Dame, which was built by the
monks between 1952 and 1968 and
consecrated in 1977 (the previous
chapel was bombed in 1944). The
modern abbey church, rebuilt in
1967–69, was converted from a tithe
barn that was transported here from
Neuville-du-Bosc. The monks sell
their home-made jam at the abbey
shop, and religious services held
here are noted for their evocative

Gregorian chants at morning Mass
and vespers.
✚ 214 M4 ✉ 76490 St-Wandrille-Rançon
☎ 02 35 96 23 11 ⏰ Ruins open daily
6.15–1, 2–7.15. Guided tour of interior and
cloister: Easter–1 Nov daily 3.30 ✋ Free
🚉 Yvetot (16km/10 miles)

ARQUES-LA-BATAILLE

The Battle of Arques may have
been fought and won more than
400 years ago, but the brooding
grey-stone ruins of the château loom
above the town as a reminder of the
conflict that gave the place its name.
Where the river Varenne meets the
Béthune, so on 21 September 1589
did the Catholic Duke of Mayenne
come to meet Protestant King
Henri IV in battle over the King's
succession at the royal castle
(▷ 22), which was said to be able
to withstand any cannonball. At the
end of the day, the strong walls and
weather brought victory to the King.

The main part of the castle
was built during the 11th and 12th
centuries and was added to until
the 16th century. Atop a rocky hill,
and with a rigged square keep,
the château is reached via a steep
meandering road from the *mairie*
(town hall) in the main square below.
Splendid views of the countryside
can be had from its walls, and the
last of the three doors leading
into the castle has a carved image
of the Battle of Arques. Another
homage to Henri IV and the battle
can be found in the contemporary

woodwork of a chapel within the
16th-century church of Notre-Dame
de l'Assomption.
✚ 217 N2 ℹ Pont d'Ango, 76204 Dieppe
☎ 02 32 14 40 60 ⏰ Jul–end Aug daily
9–7; Oct–end Apr Mon–Sat 9–12, 2–6; May,
Jun, Sep Mon–Sat 9–1, 2–7, Sun 10–1, 3–6
🚌 From Rouen 🚉 Arques-la-Bataille

CAUDEBEC-EN-CAUX

www.caudebec-en-caux.com
The southern part of the Pays de
Caux region borders the river Seine,
and among the attractive resorts
on this pretty stretch of the river is
Caudebec-en-Caux, which has held a
lively Saturday market in the square
for more than 600 years. The scene
is dominated by the exquisite late-
Gothic church of Notre-Dame, with
its fine stained-glass rose window.
A century in the building, the church
was completed in 1539, when it
was hailed by King Henri IV as the
most beautiful in his kingdom.
Note the main western doorway,
which is carved with more than 300
figures. The church and a handful of
neighbouring houses survived a fire
in 1940, which destroyed much of
the historic core of Caudebec.

There is plenty more to see in
town, including the 14th-century
ramparts with their integral prison
and the Musée Briochet-Brechot
(tel 02 35 96 95 91), a local history
museum housed in the Maison
des Templars. Here, alongside
reminders of the turbulent days of
the 16th-century Wars of Religion,

are images of natural threats to the town, including devastation by fire and flooding from tidal surges, or bores, washing up the Seine, which once made sightseeing along the river a dangerous occupation. Today, safe and attractive views of the Seine can be enjoyed from waterfront terraces. Along the river is Villequier, where, in 1842, a treacherous tidal bore claimed the lives of the daughter and son-in-law of writer Victor Hugo. The Musée Départemental Victor Hugo (tel 02 35 56 78 31), housed in the family home of Charles Vacquerie, Hugo's son-in-law, details the author's life.

216 M4 Place du Général de Gaulle, 76490 Caudebec-en-Caux 02 32 70 46 32 Apr–end Sep daily 9.30–6.15 From Rouen

CHÂTEAU DE MARTAINVILLE

The 15th-century Château de Martainville is home to a heritage centre that preserves regional traditions. Called the Musée des Traditions et Arts Normands, the centre is perfectly suited to the style of the château, which has many original features, with Gothic brick chimneystacks outside and imposing fireplaces within. Some 400 years of domestic furnishings, tableware and artefacts are displayed in the grand reception rooms, with old Rouen and Pays de Caux chairs and buffets, and plenty of blue and white crockery and copper pans. In the grounds is a very photogenic 18th-century cart shed with traditional timbering and a dovecote dating from the 16th century.

223 P4 76116 Martainville-Épreville 02 35 23 44 70 Apr–end Sep Mon, Wed–Sat 10–12.30, 2–6, Sun 2–6.30; Oct–end Mar Mon–Sat 10–12.30, 2–5, Sun 2–5.30 Adult €3, under 18 free

CHÂTEAU DE MIROMESNIL

www.chateaumiromesnil.com

The home of the third Marquis de Miromesnil (1723–96), chancellor to King Louis XVI, is more famous as the birthplace of a literary lodger. The author Guy de Maupassant was born in this 16th-century red brick

and stone château, south of Dieppe, on 5 August 1850. Maupassant's parents rented the castle from 1849 to 1853, and the works of the great short-storywriter now have pride of place in the library.

Today, the château attracts many visitors to its well-tended grounds (Jul–end Aug 10–1, 2–6, €4), which are dominated by a sprawling cedar tree. The park itself is an excellent example of 18th-century landscaping, walls of Varengeville brick and white stone marking out each distinct area. Of particular note are the kitchen gardens, a traditional French *potager* with rows of vegetables separated by lines of blue delphiniums.

Little remains of an earlier house, built some way from the present site, except for the chapel of St-Antoine, which was once linked with Fécamp Abbey. The chapel was renovated in the 16th and 18th centuries and in 1950 received three new stained-glass windows, designed by Guy de Vogüé. The current owner of the estate is the Comte de Vogüé, who may often be seen guiding summer visitors around the house and its park.

217 N2 76550 Tourville-sur-Arques 02 35 85 02 80 Apr–end Sep daily 2–6 Adult €6.30, child (10–17) €4, under 7 free Arques-la-Bataille (5km/ 3 miles)

CLÈRES

www.ot-cleres.fr

For a century, Clères' appeal has not been its 15th-century château but the Parc Zoologique de Clères Jean Delacour (tel 02 35 33 23 08; Apr–end Sep daily 10–7; Oct daily 9–12, 1.30–5; closed Nov–Mar) that lies in the grounds. On neat lawns and around well-tended lakes lives an incongruous community of antelopes, kangaroos, gibbons, deer, flamingoes and peacocks, which roam in semi-liberty through the park as imagined by the zoo's creator, naturalist Jean Delacour.

217 N3 59 avenue du Parc, 76690 Clères 02 35 33 38 64 Apr–late Sep Mon 2–5, Tue–Fri 10–12, 2–5.30, Sat–Sun,

public hols 2–6; late Sep–end Mar Mon 2–5, Tue–Fri 10–12, 2–5.30 From Rouen

CÔTE D'ALBÂTRE

The Alabaster Coast consists of 120km (75 miles) of cliffs, coves, peaks and green valleys between Le Tréport and Le Havre. Named for the alabaster hues of the rock faces, the white-chalk and grey-flint headlands and crags have been steadily eroded by the wind and waves. The original limits of the Normandy shore now stand as pillars in the sea at such spots as Étretat (▷ 154), and the combination of fast-changing skies, white cliffs and verdant plateaux led to this spot becoming the cradle of Impressionism. The advent of the railways brought artists Eugène Boudin, Camille Pissarro and Alfred Sisley to the coast, while the light and natural forms at Étretat and Le Havre inspired Monet. The Alabaster Coast's villages are charming, the towns of Étretat, Eu (▷ 155) and Fécamp (▷ 155) are distinctive, and the coastline rewards walkers. Some coves are inaccessible by land and others reached by ladders. Dieppe is the biggest draw (▷ 152–153), but Le Tréport is the prettiest diversion (▷ 165).

216 K2–M2 Pont d'Ango, 76204 Dieppe 02 32 14 40 60; Jul–end Aug Mon–Sat 9–1, 2–7; May, Jun, Sep Mon–Sat 9–1, 2–7, Sun 10–1, 3–6; Oct–end Apr Mon–Sat 9–12, 2–6 Dieppe, Fécamp, Le Tréport, Le Havre

DIEPPE

INFORMATION

www.dieppetourisme.com
☩ 217 N2 ℹ Pont d'Ango, 76204
Dieppe ☎ 02 32 14 40 60 ✆ Jul–end
Aug Mon–Sat 9–1, 2–7; May, Jun,
Sep Mon–Sat 9–1, 2–7, Sun 10–1,
3–6; Oct–end Apr Mon–Sat 9–12, 2–6
🚌 From Rouen ⛴ From Newhaven

INTRODUCTION

There's something cheerily authentic about Dieppe, which has always had its gaze more fixed across the English Channel than towards the rest of France.

The town grew in importance after William the Conqueror embarked from here on his second voyage to England in 1067. From the 15th to the 17th centuries it prospered from both mercantilism and piracy. King Francois I's shipbuilder, Jean Ango, organized expeditions from Dieppe to capture Portuguese ships and their cargoes. Subsequently the port became the hub of the African ivory trade.

In the mid-19th century its beach became a fashionable place to bathe and the port began its long-standing ferry link with Newhaven. Distinguished visitors over the next decades included Renoir, Monet, Pissarro, Gaugin and Whistler; and this was where a humbled Oscar Wilde stepped into exile after being released from prison in 1897.

In World War II, Dieppe was the setting for the controversial Operation Jubilee in 1942 in which a force of 6,000 Allied troops, mostly Canadians, attempted a landing. They were unable to overcome German defences and suffered heavy casualties. Whether the episode was an avoidable disaster or a way of learning lessons vital to the success of D-Day is still subject to debate.

Part fishing port, part ferry terminal, part spa and part low-key holiday resort, modern Dieppe takes all this history in its stride and while its past glamour is now somewhat faded it makes up for this in the life in its waterfront cafés. Bounded by two roads, the boulevard Maréchal Foch is a promenade running the length of this shingle beach seafront, parallel to the Grande Rue, a pedestrianized shopping street.

Above *Dieppe has retained an attractive working harbour*

WHAT TO SEE

HARBOUR AND SEAFRONT

Dieppe's main sights can be found by the waterfront. The Avant Port is packed with working boats and pleasure craft, and is reached via the twin Pont d'Ango and Pont Colbert bridges, designed by Gustave Eiffel (1822–1923). Between the pleasure ports and modern ferry terminal is the historic seafarers' district of Le Pollet.

Parallel to the main seafront promenade is the boulevard de Verdun, which runs southwest to the 15th-century Les Tourelles, the last remaining gate from the town's original fortifications. Further inland, along Grande Rue, find the place du Puits Salé, whose original salt-water well was replaced by a fountain. Artists Claude Monet, Auguste Renoir and Raoul Dufy shopped for their art supplies in the square.

CHÂTEAU MUSÉE

www.mairie-dieppe.fr
The round-turreted 15th-century château is now a museum displaying paintings by Auguste Renoir, Eugène Boudin and Camille Pissarro, as well as a noted ivory collection—a reminder of Dieppe's 17th-century ivory-carving industry and the town's strong links with Africa. In addition to the painting and seafaring legacies of the town, the museum also celebrates Dieppe's musical heritage with a gallery devoted to the composer Camille Saint-Saëns (1835–1921).
✉ Rue de Chastes, 76200 Dieppe ☎ 02 35 06 61 99 🕐 Jun–end Sep daily 10–12, 2–6; Oct–end May Wed–Mon 10–12, 2–5. Closed 1 May, 1 Nov, 25 Dec ✋ Adult €3.50, child €2, under 12 free

NOTRE-DAME DE BON SECOURS

This cliff-top church, which was constructed in 1876 in memory of victims of the sea, watches over maritime traffic entering the port on one side and the shingle beaches of the Alabaster Coast on the other.
✉ Chemin de Falaise, 76200 Dieppe 🕐 Daily 10–6

CITÉ DE LA MER

At this maritime museum and aquarium in the heart of the fishing quarter, history meets ecology in displays on the English Channel.
✉ 37 rue de l'Asile Thomas, 76200 Dieppe ☎ 02 35 06 93 20 🕐 Daily 10–12, 2–6 ✋ Adult €5, child (4–16) €3.50, under 4 free

TIPS

» A tour of Dieppe's memorials takes in Abraham Duquesne, scourge of pirates (place National), the founders of Québec, Canadian war heroes and the inventor of the coffee filter (square du Canada).
» The old fishermen's houses along the quai du Hâble make great photographic subjects.
» Seafood restaurants can be found along qual Henri IV.
» Dieppe's centre is easily managed on foot with a map from the tourist office.

Below left *A gull perched on a beam with the harbour in the background*
Below *Cité de la Mer*

INFORMATION

www.Étretat.net

✚ 215 K3 ℹ Place Maurice Guillard,
76790 Étretat ☎ 02 35 27 05 21

🌐 Mid-Jun to mid-Sep daily 9–7;
mid-Sep to mid-Jun daily 10–12, 2–6

🚌 From Bréauté at weekends and from
Le Havre 🚆 Bréauté (19km/12 miles)

TIPS

» Take the cliff walk at sunset, when
the chalk changes colour with the
fading light. At nightfall, the cliffs
shine dramatically thanks to dazzling
illuminations that reflect their stark white
grandeur above the dark sea.

» Check weather reports before taking
the cliff walk off-season (▷ 166–167).

» Hardy visitors can join locals for the
New Year's Day swim!

» Pack your golf clubs; one of France's
most spectacular golf courses is on the
cliff top.

ÉTRETAT

Dramatic blue-grey cliffs have been spectacularly moulded by the elements at
the jewel of the Alabaster Coast. Étretat is best enjoyed out of season, when
its bay is deserted and the arches of the magnificent chalk headlands seem
to straddle the ocean. The effect of the cliffs here is that of a grand cathedral
carved out of France itself, its flying buttresses arching into the sea. At low
tide a vast cave in the cliff face appears on the pebbled beach. On the Falaise
d'Amont cliff, visitors stop by the sailor's chapel of Notre-Dame de la Garde
(closed to the public) to admire views across the bay to the Falaise d'Aval
and its adjacent 70m-high (230ft) rock stack, known as the Aiguille d'Étretat
(Étretat Needle).

In town, visit the place du Maréchal Foch, with a reconstructed wooden
covered market (built in 1926) amid a cluster of attractive 16th-century
townhouses. Étretat's church of Notre-Dame dates back as far as the 11th
century and has been listed as an historic monument since the mid-19th
century.

ARTISTIC EXPOSURE

A modest fishing village for most of its life, Étretat nestled in obscurity until
the mid-19th century, when writers Guy de Maupassant and Alexandre Dumas
discovered the charms of its cliff-enveloped pebble beach. Chic visitors arrived
from Paris, lured by the paintings of Jean Baptiste Corot, Eugène Boudin,
Eugène Delacroix and Claude Monet. The composer Jacques Offenbach
(1819–80) bought a house here, which he dubbed Villa Orphée in honour
of his greatest musical triumph and whose 10 rooms he named after his
compositions.

Étretat remembers its heroes as well as its artists. A plaque in the main
square recalls a World War I hospital and liberation by Scottish troops in World
War II. High on the eastern cliffs next to Notre-Dame de la Garde, a monument
honours the aviators Charles Nungesser and François Coli, whose plane
l'Oiseau Blanc was last seen crossing these cliffs in 1927 on its ill-fated bid
to fly from Paris to New York. Their bodies were never recovered, presumed
drowned in the Atlantic.

At the Manoir de Cateuil on the Le Havre road, is the dairy farm of Le
Valeine (tel 02 35 27 14 02; guided visits only Jul–end Aug Sat–Wed 11. Shop
Mar–end Nov daily 9–12.30, 2–7), which demonstrates local crafts. You can see
how farmers make cheeses, ice cream and cider, and enjoy a tasting or two.

Below *The chalk cliffs close to Étretat offer
excellent views over the sea and town*

Above *Copper stills, used to brew Bénédictine liqueur in the Palais Bénédictine in Fécamp*

FU

www.ville-eu.fr

Of all the varied diversions on the Alabaster Coast, Eu has the most regal history. It was here in 1050 that the notorious nuptials between William, Duke of Normandy and future King of England, and his cousin Mathilde of Flanders took place, a marriage that had a profound effect on Norman history. As penance for the incestuous marriage, William and Mathilde founded Abbaye St Étienne (▷ 91) and Abbaye de la Trinité (▷ 92–93) in Caen.

The town's association with royalty continued in the 19th century, when King Louis-Philippe (1773–1850) entertained England's Queen Victoria (1819–1901) here during the state visit of 1843. Louis-Philippe was very fond of Eu's château, a building dating from 1578 and built on the site of William's original castle. In the late 19th century, France's leading architect, Viollet-le-Duc, remodelled the castle as a family home for Louis-Philippe's grandson, the Comte de Paris. Now a municipal building, the castle houses the Musée Louis-Philippe (tel 02 35 86 44 00; mid-Mar to early Nov Sat–Mon, Wed–Thu 10–12, 2–6, Fri 2–6), which showcases the stunning regal apartments and suites, including the bedroom used by Queen Victoria and Prince Albert.

Eu was the birthplace of François and Michel Anguier, France's great 17th-century baroque sculptors. The brothers went on to work on the Palais du Louvre in Paris.

🕇 217 P1 🛈 41 rue Paul Bignon, 76260 Eu ☎ 02 35 86 04 68 🕐 May to mid-Nov Mon–Sat 9.30–12.30, 2–6.30, Sun 10–1; mid-Nov to end Apr Mon–Sat 9.30–12, 2–5.30 (closed Sun, public hols)
🚃 Eu

FÉCAMP

www.fecamptourisme.com

On the Alabaster Coast is the flamboyant Palais Bénédictine (tel 02 35 10 26 10, mid-Jul to end Aug daily 10–7, Mar to mid-Jul, Sep to mid-Oct 10–1, 2–6.30; mid-Oct to end Feb 10.30–12.45, 2–6), where the liqueur Bénédictine is made (not, contrary to myth, by monks).

Alexandre le Grand obtained the 16th-century elixir's recipe from a Venetian monastery and started a distillery in 1863, commissioning Camille Albert to create the neo-Gothic and neo-Renaissance palace.

The project was shrewd marketing rather than an eccentric folly. Artworks perpetuated the myth of a monastic drink as well as keeping a tradition of religious art in the town. In the Gothic Room are treasures from Fécamp's abbey; other rooms contain the works of Flemish, French and Italian masters. Before leaving, visit the Espace Contemporain, famous for its modern art exhibitions.

The 12th-century Église de la Trinité was part of Fécamp's abbey and harbours a relic said to be the blood of Christ. Also inside the church is the Angel's Footprint. According to legend, as bishops met in AD943 to discuss which saint should be patron of the new church, an angel appeared and commanded that it be dedicated to the Holy Trinity. Before leaving, he left his footprint on a stone.

Fécamp is also a major fishing port. Some of the tales from 400 years of cod fishing are retold in the Musée des Terre Neuvas (tel 02 35 28 31 99; Jul, Aug daily 10–7; Sep–end Jun Wed–Mon 10–noon, 2–5.30). The museum has a splendid reconstruction of a shipwreck, and displays on the sea, its beaches and cliffs; it also has an excellent section devoted to shipbuilding.

Hear the story of chocolate through the ages, with product tasting, at the Musée Découverte du Chocolat (tel 02 35 27 62 02; Jul, Aug daily 9–12, 2–6.30, Sep–end Jun closed Sun).

🕇 216 L3 🛈 113 rue Alexandre le Grand, 76403 Fécamp ☎ 02 35 28 51 01 🕐 Jul, Aug daily 9–6.30; Sep–end Mar Mon–Fri 9–6, Sat 9.30–12.30, 2–6, Sun 9.30–12.30; Apr–end Jun Mon–Fri 9–6, Sat–Sun, public hols 10–6 🛈 Point d'Informations Maison du Patrimoine, Auberge du Gran Cert, 10 rue des Forts ☎ 02 35 28 51 01 🕐 Daily Mon–Fri 8–12, 1.30–5.30
🚃 Fécamp

LA
HEVE

LE HAVRE

INTRODUCTION

Only the most imaginative passenger arriving in Le Havre on the ferry could conceive that such a modern concrete conurbation of housing blocks, goods yards and oil refineries could ever have inspired one of the most influential art movements of the past 150 years. Of course, it was not today's industrial port of Le Havre, bounded by the Channel and Seine estuary, that seduced painter Claude Monet (1840–1926) and his followers. However, their essential inspiration—the light—is still there. Monet grew up in what was then a more picturesque seaside town, and his sunrise painting of the boats here, entitled *Impression–Soleil Levant* on its (c1873), gave Impressionism its name.

This great seaport has a heritage that predates Monet. King Francois I (1495–1547) created the town in 1517, when the harbour of Harfleur (as featured in the lines of Shakespeare's *Henry V*, 'Once more into the breach') silted up. Harfleur is now hidden in industrial quarter of greater Le Havre.

The new port, named Havre de Grâce, was built on estuary marshland which benefited from long high tides. The royal naval shipyard developed into a commercial port, its transatlantic trade supplying goods to rebels at America's War of Independence and receiving tobacco and coffee in return. From the 1850s, Le Havre was Europe's gateway to New York, the sailing vessels and steamships eventually giving way to the great ocean liners.

In November 1944, 80 per cent of the town was destroyed by bombing, and architect Auguste Perret (1875–1954) was commissioned to create a new city. The 160ha (370-acre) site of his bold redesign—the largest post-war building budget in France—attempts to make use of the light that influenced the Impressionists. On grey and rainy days, the weather is less than kind to the harsh, modern materials of Perret's brave new city, but when the sun shines or the evening's artificial lighting kicks in, Le Havre has a definite contemporary style. In 2005 it was made a UNESCO World Heritage Site, the first 20th-century urban settlement in Europe to join the list.

INFORMATION
www.lehavretourisme.com
🚻 215 K4 ℹ️ 186 boulevard Clémenceau, 76059 Le Havre ☎ 02 32 74 04 04 🕐 Easter–end Oct Mon–Sat 9–7, Sun, public hols 10–12.30, 2.30–6; Nov–Easter Mon–Sat 9–6.30, Sun, public hols 10–1 🚌 From Lisieux, Caen and Caudebec-en-Caux (connection with Rouen) 🚉 Le Havre (trains from Rouen)

Opposite *St-Adresse lighthouse*
Left *Le Havre's harbour*
Below *The curves of Le Volcan, the cultural centre*

WHAT TO SEE

SEAFRONT

Some 2km (1.25 miles) of seafront within an easy walk of the city centre provide all the facilities of a modern resort, with gardens, sand and pebble beaches, playgrounds, hot showers, changing rooms and even bicycle paths. The Blue Flag beach has a safety zone, manned by lifeguards from mid-June until mid-September, as well as special floating beach wheelchairs to provide easy access to the sea for visitors with disabilities. Sailing is another option, available from the city's marina. Between the beach and the city is Perret's new district, with a spacious main square in front of the town hall and a tree-lined boulevard, avenue Foch, which is best explored on sunny afternoons.

MUSÉE DES BEAUX-ARTS ANDRÉ MALRAUX

The cultural lighthouse of Le Havre is undoubtedly the finest art gallery in Normandy. Named after a celebrated art critic, this showpiece glass building is as close as an indoor space can get to bathing in the natural light that launched a whole artistic movement. If you spend a long afternoon here in autumn, the changing colours of the sky affect the mood of the museum. The two local heroes are, of course, Le Havre's own home-grown Fauvist, Raoul Dufy (1877–1953), and Honfleur's most famous son, Eugène Boudin (1824–98). Choose to start your visit with a walk by the works of this pair, or take the more conventional route, passing paintings by 17th- to 20th-century masters and stopping along the way to admire Jean-Honoré Fragonard's *Tête de Jeune Homme* (c1760–80) and one of Claude Monet's celebrated water lilies studies alongside canvases by Alfred Sisley and Auguste Renoir.

✚ 159 A3 ✉ 2 boulevard Clemenceau, 76600 Le Havre ☎ 02 35 19 62 62 🕐 Mon, Wed–Fri 11–6, Sat–Sun 11–7. Closed public hols ✋ Adult €5, under 18 free

ÉGLISE ST-JOSEPH

The most successful of Perret's innovations, with a 106m (348ft) tower made from 13,000 shards of stained glass, this concrete building was completed in 1957. It is best enjoyed within, the coloured glass making kaleidoscopic patterns on the walls and floor.

✚ 159 A2 ✉ 76600 Le Havre ☎ 02 32 74 04 04 🕐 Daily 10–6, exept during services

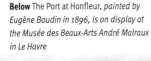

Below The Port at Honfleur, *painted by Eugène Boudin in 1896, is on display at the Musée des Beaux-Arts André Malraux in Le Havre*

LE VOLCAN

www.levolcan.com

Le Havre's dramatic cultural centre, created by Oscar Niemeyer, the designer

of Brasilia, is the focal point of the commercial docks in the modern town, its sweeping concrete curves offering a liberating contrast to the more rectangular buildings that lie between the port and beach. The building itself houses a national theatre and concert halls, as well as a cinema. The varied schedule of events is published on the venue's website.

✚ 159 B2 ✉ Espace Oscar Niemeyer, 76063 Le Havre ☎ 02 35 19 10 20

CATHÉDRALE NOTRE-DAME
A 16th- and 17th-century confection of Gothic and Renaissance styles, Le Havre's cathedral sports reptilian gargoyles and flying buttresses. There is a rose window above the north entrance, which is known as the Ave Maria door after the inscription on the façade. The coat of arms of Cardinal Richelieu (1585–1642), chief minister to King Louis XIII, adorn an organ donated by the *éminence grise* in 1637.

✚ 159 B3 ✉ Rue de Paris, 76600 Le Havre ☎ 02 32 74 04 05 🕐 Daily during daytime

MUSÉE DE PRIEURÉ
Displayed within this old inn is the story of Harfleur, the forgotten precursor to Le Havre. Moving from prehistoric and Roman remains to images of the town in its medieval heyday, the displays allow visitors to imagine the past and see exhibitions by contemporary artists.

✚ 159 off map at C2 ✉ Rue de l'Abbaye, 76600 Le Havre ☎ 02 35 24 51 00 🕐 Fri–Tue 11–6, Wed 2–6, Sat–Sun 11–6 ✋ Adult €2, under 18 free

Above *Le Havre's cultural centre, Le Volcan, at dusk*

ROUEN

INTRODUCTION

Rouen rises on the horizon as a blur of steeples—most notably those above the grandly Gothic Notre-Dame Cathedral and nearby Abbey of St-Ouen—making for a memorable first view, especially if you are lucky enough to arrive at dawn or dusk. Don't be put off by the sprawling modern perimeter as you approach: The historic core of cobbled streets lined with tall, half-timbered houses is a treat to explore.

The Romans established a settlement on the site of today's Rouen in the first century AD, calling it Rotomagus. In the Middle Ages, Rouen became the seat of the Dukes of Normandy, who won the English throne in 1066. Later, it was at the heart of the Hundred Years War between the French and the English. One of the most defining—not to say traumatic—events in French history took place here during the war. On 30 May 1431 Joan of Arc was burned at the stake as a heretic in what is now the place du Vieux Marché. Much later, in the 19th century, Gustave Flaubert immortalized the city of his birth by setting the scandalously realistic novel *Madame Bovary* in and around it.

Today, Rouen has one of the largest ports in France, despite being so far inland. The city lies on the Seine, 86km (53 miles) from the estuary at Le Havre. The contrast between the working docks along the river and the Gothic spires and quaint old streets of the city heart is striking.

Any tour of the heart of the city should begin with a visit to the tourist office (opposite the cathedral) which occupies Rouen's oldest Renaissance building, the former tax collector's office, dating from 1509. This is just one of many buildings deriving from the merchant trade that was the engine of Rouen's development over the centuries. Later buildings, including 19th-century stores, art deco shop fronts and post-World War II blocks, run down to the port. The city was heavily bombed during World War II and many historic buildings are the result of meticulous renovation.

INFORMATION

www.rouentourisme.com

⊕ 223 N4 ℹ 25 place de la Cathédrale, 76000 Rouen ☎ 02 32 08 32 40 🕐 Mon–Sat 9–12.30–1.30 6

🚊 Rouen (good connections to Paris)

SEINE-MARITIME • SIGHTS

REGIONS

Opposite *Looking down a street to the Gros Horloge*
Below *Timber-framed houses near the Cathédrale de Notre-Dame*

TIPS

» If you are visiting at a weekend, take advantage of the 'Beaux Weekend' promotion, offering two nights' hotel accommodation for the price of one. There are similar deals at Rouen's museums.

» Visit Rouen during the last week in May to take part in the Fêtes Jeanne d'Arc (Joan of Arc festivities), which usually coincide with the city's main cultural festival. On the Sunday closest to 30 May, local children throw flowers into the Seine from the Boïeldieu Bridge, the spot where Joan's ashes were scattered on the water.

» A good time to experience the Abbey of St-Ouen is during one of the many concerts held there. The organ is one of the most famous in France.

» Every five years (make a date for 2013), the world's greatest sailing ships gather along the quays for L'Armada, eight days of celebrations in June or July.

WHAT TO SEE

CATHÉDRALE DE NOTRE-DAME

Rouen Cathedral is one of the great churches of France, known across the world thanks to Impressionist painter Claude Monet's *Cathédrales de Rouen* series (1892–93). Monet worked on the paintings from the second floor of what is now the tourist office.

The cathedral's Gothic architecture spans 400 years, from the mid-12th to early 16th centuries. The dark, shadowy interior is offset by flashes of bright blue light through the stained-glass windows, which date from the 13th century. The choir contains tombs of many dukes of Normandy, while the crypt holds the heart of King Richard I (the Lionheart) of England. The 151m (495ft) spire, the tallest in France, was built in the 19th century. In summer months a spectacular light show projects images, inspired by the paintings of Monet, onto the cathedral façade.

✠ 162 B3 ✉ Place de la Cathédrale, 76000 Rouen ◷ Apr–end Oct daily 8–12, 2–6; Nov–Mar Mon 2–6, Tue–Sat 7.45–12, 2–6, Sun 8–6

AÎTRE ST-MACLOU

A short walk from the Gothic Église St-Maclou (mid-Mar to end Oct Mon–Sun 10–12, 2–6; Nov to mid-Mar 10–12, 2–5) in place Barthélemy is its unusual annexe, the Aître St-Maclou. This pretty courtyard of timbered buildings is now home to the city's School of Fine Arts.

A more macabre history is hinted at by the skulls that adorn the woodwork. This was a plague cemetery, built to house the remains of the victims of

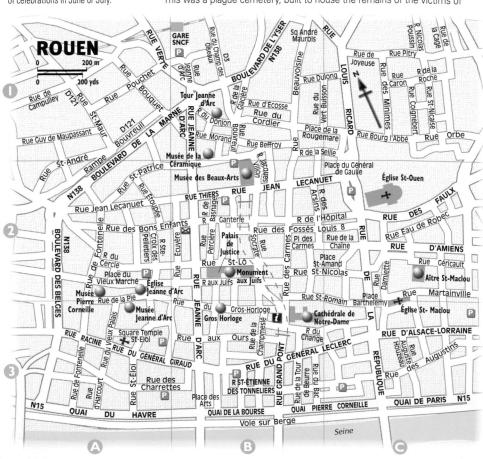

the Great Plague of 1348, which claimed the lives of 75 per cent of Rouen's population.

🕇 162 C2 ✉ Rue Martainville, 76000 Rouen ⊕ Courtyard:Jun–end Oct daily 8–8; Nov–end May daily 8–7 ✋ Free 🚇 Palais de Justice 🚋 3, 13

GROS HORLOGE

No visit to Rouen is complete without a stroll under the 14th-century Gros Horloge, a huge, one-handed, ornamental clock mounted on a sumptuously carved Renaissance arch straddling the road of the same name. Once part of a nearby belfry, the remarkable timepiece was moved to its present position in the 16th century, after locals complained that it was impossible to see the clock face in the old town's narrow streets.

🕇 162 B3 ✉ Rue du Gros-Horloge

JOAN OF ARC

This is the city of Joan of Arc (Jeanne d'Arc in French), and the tales surrounding France's greatest folk heroine would alone be lure enough for visitors. On the place du Vieux Marché, a short stroll from the Gros Horloge (see above), a large cross marks the spot where Joan of Arc was executed. The nearby Église Jeanne-d'Arc (1981) is a stunning combination of modern slate and copper work on the outside, with light from Renaissance stained-glass windows within. The windows were salvaged from the earlier church of St-Vincent, destroyed during World War II. The wonderful contemporary sculpture was inspired by the saint's martyr's pyre.

The remains of the two towers in which Joan was imprisoned from Christmas 1430 until her execution in 1431 can be seen on rue du Donjon. These vestiges of King Philippe Auguste's castle, built in 1204 and scene of Joan of Arc's trial, incorporate the Tour Jeanne d'Arc and traces of the Tour de la Pucelle. You can learn more about the medieval heroine at the Musée Jeanne d'Arc, on place du Vieux Marché (tel 02 35 88 02 70; mid-Apr to mid-Sep daily 9.30–7; mid-Sep to mid-Apr 10–12, 2–6).

Above *A stained-glass window in the cathedral*
Below *The spire of the cathedral seen through the ruined windows of the old Bishops' Palace*

Above *The Gros Horloge*
Below *Detail of a statue on a building opposite the medical laboratory in Rouen*

LITERARY CONNECTIONS

There is the chance to pay homage to Rouen's literary heritage at museums dedicated to *Madame Bovary* author Gustave Flaubert (1821–80) and playwright Pierre Corneille (1606–84). The Musée Flaubert et d'Histoire de la Médecine is in the house where Flaubert was born, at 51 rue de Lecat (tel 02 35 15 59 95; Tue 10–6, Wed–Sat 10–12, 2–6). Flaubert's father was a surgeon and the museum contains not only displays about the novelist's life but also medical implements from the 19th century. The Musée Pierre Corneille is in the eponymous playwright's birthplace, at 4 rue de la Pie (tel 02 35 71 63 92; Wed–Thu 2–6; Sat–Sun 2–6 in school holidays).

MUSÉE DES BEAUX-ARTS

This gallery has an impressive collection of paintings, drawings, sculptures and objets d'art dating from the 16th century to the present day. Highlights include Michelangelo da Caravaggio's *Flagellation of Christ* (c1606–7) and works by Auguste Renoir and Claude Monet.

✚ 162 B2 ✉ Esplanade Marcel-Duchamp, 76000 Rouen ☎ 02 35 71 28 40 ⏰ Wed–Sun 10–6 ✋ Adult €3, child (under 18) free

MUSÉE DE LA CÉRAMIQUE

Learn more about the distinctive blue-patterned Rouen ware (faïence), which rose to popularity in the 17th and 18th centuries. If you want to buy some, you'll also find it in the antiques quarter of the old town.

✚ 162 B1 ✉ 1 rue Faucon, 76000 Rouen ☎ 02 35 07 31 74 ⏰ Wed–Mon 10–1, 2–6; closed public hols ✋ Adult €2.30, under 18 free

MONUMENT AUX JUIFS

The Jewish Monument, in the courtyard of the 16th-century Palais de Justice, is in fact the remains of the oldest-surviving Jewish building in France. Believed to date from the 12th century, the site is the last remaining vestige of the city's ghetto, destroyed after the expulsion of the Jews in 1306. Although it was originally thought to have been a synagogue, experts now believe it was a *yeshiva*, or religious school. Note that you can't enter the courtyard, but you can see the monument from outside.

✚ 162 B2 ✉ Rue aux Juifs

ST-MARTIN-DE-BOSCHERVILLE

www.abbaye-saint-georges.com
The 12th-century abbey church of St-Georges (tel 02 35 32 10 82; Apr–end Oct daily 9–6.30; Nov–end Mar daily 2–5), which dominates the village square of St-Martin-de-Boscherville, is among the best-preserved Romanesque churches in Upper Normandy. In 1114, Guillaume de Tancarville commissioned an abbey to be built on a former pagan site of worship. A religious community had already been established in the grounds of Boscherville manor by an earlier Tancarville, Raoul, who had once been tutor to the young William the Conqueror and later fought alongside him at the Battle of Hastings. Under William's patronage, the estate eventually settled on the religious community.

St-Georges' stark façade is typical of the string of pearly white churches that once adorned the Normandy landscape. Inside, the airy interior has surprisingly secular capitals displaying medieval jousting scenes. Visitors can tour the cloisters and chapter house, as well as gardens that follow the original 17th-century plans. The orchard, kitchen garden and herb gardens are open to the public, and the estate has impressive panoramic views across the abbey lands and the Seine valley.

🕇 222 N4 🛈 25 place de la Cathédrale, 76000 Rouen 🕿 02 32 08 32 40 🕔 Mon–Sat 9–12.30–1.30–6 🚆 Rouen (12km/7.5 miles), then bus 🚌 Rouen

LE TRÉPORT

www.ville-le-treport.fr
From springtime, Le Tréport has a lively weekend buzz as Parisians let their hair down at the fishing port on the river Bresle, where Normandy meets Picardy. Just as in summer months, the bustling harbourside and shingle beaches below the Alabaster Coast cliffs are a magnet for holidaymakers who have discovered this modest alternative to Dieppe, along the coast (▷ 152–153).

The attraction of the resort is obvious. Old houses huddle together along the picturesque streets of Le Cordiers Cordant fishermen's quarter, while the steep 378-step climb to the Calvaire des Terrasses offers views across the slate roofs of the town and along the coast.

🕇 217 P1 🛈 Quai Sadi Carnot, 76470 Le Tréport 🕿 02 35 86 05 69 🕔 Jul, Aug daily 8.30–7; Sep–end Jun Mon–Sat 10–12, 2–6, Sun 9.30–1 🚆 Le Tréport 🚌 From Dieppe

VALMONT

Valmont's château and abbey, a 11km (7-mile) drive inland from Fécamp, offer a glimpse into the age imaginatively invented by the faux-religious Palais Bénédictine (▷ 165). The vestiges of the Abbaye de Valmont (tel 02 35 27 34 92) are 16th- and 17th-century amendments to a 14th-century building. After the French Revolution the abbey became a private home to which the artist Eugène Delacroix (1798–1863) was a frequent visitor. Only the small Chapelle de la Vierge remains intact and its 15th-century stained-glass windows tell the story of the Virgin Mary.

🕇 216 L3 🛈 Quai Sadie Carnot, 76403 Fécamp 🕿 02 35 28 51 01 🕔 Jul, Aug daily 9–6.30; Sep–end Mar Mon–Fri 9–6, Sat 9.30–12.30, 2–6, Sun 9.30–12.30; Apr–end Jun Mon–Fri 9–6, Sat–Sun, public hols 10–6 🚆 Fécamp (12km/7.5 miles), then taxi

VARENGEVILLE-SUR-MER

Varengeville is less a town than a cluster of villages in the woods that line the coast road south of Dieppe, a pretty drive or bicycle ride from the port that is punctuated by plenty of distractions. The highlight is the extravagant and lavishly decorated Manoir d'Ango, built in 1530 by privateer and master of politics Jean Ango (▷ 152) as a summer residence. Ango commissioned the fashionable Italian artists of the day to create grand artworks from sculpture to (long gone) frescoes. In the Renaissance house he would entertain such influential guests as King François I. Nearer the sea is the Parc Floral du Bois des Moustiers (tel 02 35 85 10 02; mid-Mar to mid-Nov daily 10–8), which is best visited between Easter and June when the magnolias and rhododendrons are in flower. The gardens surround a lovely house built at the end of the 19th century by the great English architect Sir Edwin Lutyens. Both the church and Chapelle St-Dominique in Varengeville boast stained-glass windows by the Cubist Georges Braque, who, like artist Joan Miró and film director Jean Cocteau, discovered the resort in the early 20th century.

🕇 216 N2 🛈 Pont d'Ango, 76204 Dieppe 🕿 02 32 14 40 60 🕔 Jul–end Aug Mon–Sat 9–1, 2–7; May, Jun, Sep Mon–Sat 9–1, 2–7, Sun 10–1, 3–6; Oct–end Apr Mon–Sat 9–12, 2–6 🚌 From Dieppe

Below *The quayside at Le Tréport is abuzz with activity throughout the warmer months*

WALK

ÉTRETAT

The Côte d'Albâtre (Alabaster Coast) stretches 100km (62 miles) from Dieppe to Étretat and beyond. It is a formation of imposing white cliffs that seem to mirror the white cliffs of Dover across the Channel. At Étretat the seascape is at its most spectacular, with sheer cliffs pierced by massive arches and a solitary needle rock soaring to 70m (230ft) a little way offshore. This coastal walk can be rough in places (wear sturdy, non-slip shoes or walking boots), but the breathtaking panoramas make it worthwhile.

THE WALK

Distance: 6.5km (4 miles)
Allow: 2.5 hours
Start/end: Étretat

HOW TO GET THERE

Étretat is on the Côte d'Albâtre, between Le Havre and Fécamp.

★ Étretat (▷ 154–155) was a modest, obscure fishing village until the mid-19th century, when the writers Guy de Maupassant and Alexandre Dumas discovered its lovely pebbled beach enveloped by cliffs, and the great artists of the day began to paint the dramatic scenery. Fashionable visitors arrived from Paris and elsewhere, lured by the views reproduced by Eugène Boudin, Eugène Delacroix and Claude Monet. In town, visit place du Maréchal Foch, with its wooden covered market built in 1926 amid a cluster of 16th-century townhouses. For golfers, the 18-hole clifftop course is France's highest golf links, with views guaranteed to put you off your stroke.

Start on the promenade. Walk to the eastern end, then turn right, up a flight of 83 brick steps that opens out onto a grassy clifftop pathway. Continue past a children's theme park and up to the top of the Porte (or Falaise) d'Amont.

❶ Falaise d'Amont affords spectacular views of the western Falaise d'Aval across the bay, where a 70m (230ft) rock stack known as the Aiguille d'Étretat (Étretat Needle) stands in the sea beyond the cliffs. Stop at the Chapelle Notre-Dame de la Garde, a sailors' chapel, then turn inland to a carved monument commemorating the French aviators Charles Nungesser and François Coli, whose plane, *L'Oiseau Blanc*, was last seen crossing these cliffs in 1927 on its ill-fated bid to fly from Paris to New York. The aviators were presumed drowned in the Atlantic; their bodies were never recovered.

Continue along the cliff edge, past the chapel, and go down some steps leading to the arch of Amont. A steep, slippery and narrow pathway, cut into the chalky stack, offers wonderful views of the alabaster cliffs to the east. A wooden handrail and a ladder assist in the final descent to a small beach. Retrace your steps, past the chapel and back down the brick steps. Proceed along the promenade, an unbroken curve of café-lined concrete above the steep shingle beach. At the far end, another flight of steps, followed by a steep, well-trodden, flint-filled path, leads up beside a scenic golf course to Porte d'Aval. Bear right along the cliff edge, crossing a narrow bridge and onto the top of the cliff arch—not for those with a fear of heights!

❷ The cliff arch offers stunning vistas over Étretat's slate roofs and to the Porte d'Amont beyond. Legend has it that many centuries ago three beautiful sisters were imprisoned by an evil lord in a cave at the foot of these cliffs. Continue along the windswept cliff edge, admiring the wildflowers, yellow gorse and purple sea cabbage, and on to a second arch, La Manne-Porte, with breathtaking views stretching as far as the port of Le Havre-Antifer.

Just beyond the next headland, Pointe de la Courtine, follow a track inland (the GR21, marked with a red and white stripe). Branch left, where two paths meet, to Valaine. At the next intersection, leave the GR21 and head straight on down a narrow country lane, through the attractive brick and stone farm buildings of Ferme la Valaine.

❸ Ferme la Valaine is a lovely old farmhouse selling home-produced cider, Calvados and goat's cheese.

Follow the road as it winds gently downhill, past grazing goats, until you reach the D940. Turn left back

into the middle of Étretat and left again to return to the waterfront.

WHEN TO GO
Check weather reports before starting the cliff walk, as the wind may be strong and the steps slippery. Hardy visitors might like to join the locals for the traditional New Year's Day swim!

WHERE TO EAT
DORMY HOUSE
▷ 178.

Clockwise from opposite *Looking down to Étretat; monument to Nungesser and Coli; a section of the Falaise d'Aval near Étretat*

LOWER SEINE VALLEY

The Seine is at its most flamboyant as it pours out of the city of Rouen and rushes seawards. Taking in an exuberant serpentine swoop of the river that encompasses a landscape of pretty villages and grand abbeys, this drive leads its followers from the city out into the Pays de Caux.

THE DRIVE

Distance: 72km (45 miles)
Allow: at least an afternoon
Start: Rouen
End: Caudebec-en-Caux

HOW TO GET THERE

The drive starts in Rouen, capital of Normandy.

★ Rouen (▷ 160–164) is an inspirational place of martyrs and artists, of kings and of powerful bishops. The city centre has half-timbered buildings and magnificent churches, its sights including the cathedral, the Gros Horloge clock tower and a fine arts museum.

Leave the spires of Rouen behind you, taking the industrial quayside roads that become the D982, and following signs for St-Pierre-de-Mannerville and Route de l'Abbaye. Turn left onto the D267 to arrive at St-Martin-de-Boscherville.

❶ St-Martin-de-Boscherville's large central square is dominated by the stark white 12th-century abbey church of St-Georges, and it has plenty of parking spaces as well as a bar and an inn. The abbey gardens are open to the public, and contain a discovery trail and shop. The church itself is light and airy, with some interesting capitals inside that feature scenes of medieval jousting.

Return to the D982 and follow the road past the small but pretty riverside resort of Duclair, with its ferry crossing, tubs of flowers and waterfront restaurants. Here, or perhaps further along the route at Jumièges, you can take a ferry across to the opposite bank of the Seine. At Yainville, turn left onto the D143 towards Jumièges.

❷ The Abbaye de Jumièges (▷ 149) was largely destroyed in the 17th century, but its ruins are

still majestic and stand in well-maintained parkland. The roofless 11th-century abbey church and the neighbouring 10th-century Église St-Pierre in particular are perfect photographic subjects. If you fancy extending this gentle drive into a two-day event, try to stop off here for a summer evening's *son et lumière* entertainment.

Back on the D143, turn left onto the D982 and left again along the D22 to reach picturesque St-Wandrille-Rancon.

❸ The Abbaye de St-Wandrille (▷ 150) dominates the higgledy-piggledy houses and shops of the village. Its fortunes have taken it from a 13th–16th-century abbey to a mill and a private residence, then back again to a religious community, the result being a mixture of the palatial and the rustic. A church, in a converted barn, and the cloisters

are open to the public. Buy a jar of fruity home-made jam from the Benedictine monks in their shop or listen to their moving chants in the church.

Return to the D982, driving under the stark and imposing Pont de Brotonne before reaching Caudebec-en-Caux.

④ Caudebec-en-Caux is best visited in time for its bustling Saturday morning market, held beneath the beautiful late-Gothic church of Notre-Dame, with its fine stained-glass windows (▷ 150–151). However, you may have to park some way from the church on market day. Sitting on one of the prettiest stretches of the Seine, Caudebec is a three-star Ville Fleurie (Flower Town) with plenty of attractive picnic spots down by the water's edge.

Follow the river on the D81, passing through Villequier, where, in 1842, the treacherous tidal currents claimed the daughter and son-in-law of the writer Victor Hugo. The quayside family home of Charles Vacquerie, Hugo's son-in-law, is now a museum (▷ 151). Keep on the same road until you reach Norville. Here, take the D281 to the extravagant Gothic Château d'Etelan.

⑤ The private Château d'Etelan, a contemporary of Rouen's Palais de Justice (▷ 170), is a listed monument, principally for its beautiful Ste-Madeleine chapel, with Renaissance stained glass, frescoes and statuary. The 15th-century château was built for Louis Picard, chamberlain to King Louis XII (ruled 1498–1515). It was here that Catherine de Medici, as regent, famously proclaimed the succession of her son King Charles IX in 1560. Other illustrious guests at the castle have included King Henri IV and the writer and philosopher Voltaire, known to his parents as François-Marie Arouet.

Return to Caudebec-en-Caux via the D81 and D281.

PLACES TO VISIT
CHÂTEAU D'ETELAN
✉ 76330 St-Maurice-d'Etelan ☎ 02 35 39 91 27 🕐 Mid-Jun to end Sep Sat–Tue 11–1, 3–7. Easter–end Oct by appointment 🖐 Adult €4, under 10 free

WHEN TO GO
Late spring and summer is the best time, when the Pays de Caux is at its prettiest, the window boxes are blooming and you can dance by the river at Caudebec-en-Caux (▷ La Marine, below).

WHERE TO EAT
LE CHEVAL BLANC
www.lecheval-blanc.fr
Regional dishes.
✉ Place René Coty, 76490 Caudebec-en-Caux ☎ 02 35 96 21 66 🕐 Mon–Sat 12–1.30, 7.30–9, Sun 12–1.45. Closed 22–31 Dec

LA MARINE
Traditional country cooking on the banks of the Seine. There is dancing on the terrace on Sundays.
✉ 18 quai Guilbaud, 76490 Caudebec-en-Caux ☎ 02 35 96 20 11 🕐 Mon–Thu 12.30–2, 7.30–9, Fri–Sat 7.30–9, Sun 12–2

Opposite *The former abbey of St. Wandrille*
Above *Stone steps in the grounds of the ruined Abbaye de Jumièges*

ROUEN

This walk links the two major churches of Rouen and the key figures from the city's history, Joan of Arc and Claude Monet. It takes in much of the attractive gabled streets around the heart of the city and all sights are never more than a few minutes' stroll from the shops.

THE WALK
Distance: 2.5km (1.5 miles)
Allow: 2 hours
Start/end: Place du Vieux Marché

HOW TO GET THERE
Coming into town from the direction of Le Havre, follow the river bank to quai Gaston Boulet. Turn left here onto boulevard des Belges and right onto rue de Crosne, following this to reach place du Vieux Marché, where you can park.

★ The walk begins in place du Vieux Marché, Rouen's old market square, where a cross stands at the spot where Joan of Arc was burnt at the stake on 30 May 1431. The remains of the St-Sauveur church, where playwright Pierre Corneille was baptized, can be seen nearby on place St-Sauveur, while in the centre of place du Vieux Marché is the Église Jeanne-d'Arc, now a

quarter of a century old. The church incorporates stunning Renaissance stained glass salvaged from the bombed St-Vincent church.

Take the rue du Gros Horloge, passing beneath the clock itself.

❶ The Gros Horloge is Rouen's famous clock, with a Gothic belfry and Renaissance arch. Try to tell the time by the clock face's single hand, which passes imperceptibly between the hours (▷ 163).

Turn left into rue Touret, which leads to rue aux Juifs and the Palais de Justice.

❷ The Palais de Justice is the most beautiful medieval building in Rouen, and was once Normandy's parliament; today, it houses the city's law courts. Turn right, and the Monument aux Juifs (▷ 164) is

found on your left, the remnants of a Jewish school hidden under the courtyard of the courts.

Continue down the road until you reach rue des Carmes. Here, turn left and then take the third road on your right: rue de l'Hôpital. As the road becomes rue des Faulx, you will pass a cluster of tall, narrow, timber-framed houses on your right and the Église St-Ouen on your left.

❸ The Église St-Ouen is often mistaken for Rouen's cathedral itself, and was once the church of one of Normandy's most influential Benedictine abbeys. Imposing and majestic, St-Ouen's vaulted ceilings are some 33m (108ft) high, and its interior is dappled by the light of 80 stained-glass windows.

Turn right along little rue du Pont de l'Arquet, following it to the junction with rue Eau de Robec, where you will find the Musée National de l'Education.

④ At the Musée National de l'Education you can discover how children were taught in French schools from the 16th century onwards. On display are paintings, exercise books, school desks, toys and games.

Head back along picturesque rue Eau de Robec, then turn left at the junction with little rue des Boucheries St-Ouen. Cross rue d'Amiens (where you may notice some fine statuary on the façades of buildings) and continue to place St-Aubert. Walk down rue Damiette to place Barthélemy, where you can visit the Église St-Maclou.

⑤ The Église St-Maclou is a splendid example of the flamboyant Gothic style and also sports stunning Renaissance carved doors.

From the church, take rue Martainville, turning left into No. 186 for the Aître St-Maclou.

⑥ The Aître St-Maclou was originally a plague cemetery (▷ 162), a role belied by the pretty courtyard of timbered buildings until you spot the skulls hidden in the woodwork.

Retrace your steps to place Barthélemy, then cross rue de la République and walk along rue St-Romain. On your right is the Archevêché (Archbishop's Palace), where Joan of Arc was condemned to death in 1431 and then pardoned 25 years later. Opposite the palace is the impressive wrought-iron shopfront of Roussel. Continue walking along the street until it opens out into place de la Cathédrale.

⑦ The Cathédrale de Notre-Dame (▷ 162), as painted by Impressionist Claude Monet, is an iconic image of the city. Summer *son et lumière*

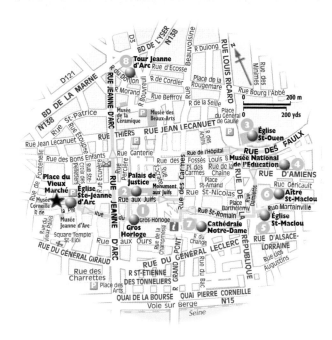

shows bring Monet's paintings to life, projecting them onto the façade of the cathedral itself. Stop at the tourist office in the square to pick up details of current events in the city, which you can read over a coffee or lunch.

Take rue du Gros Horloge once more—with occasional diversions through the pedestrianized shopping streets—then turn right onto rue Jeanne d'Arc. At the end of the road is the Tour Jeanne d'Arc.

⑧ Tour Jeanne d'Arc, a 13th-century tower, is all that remains of the castle where the folk heroine was tried and sentenced.

PLACES TO VISIT
ÉGLISE ST-OUEN
✉ Place Général de Gaulle, 76000 Rouen
🕐 Apr–end Oct Tue–Thu, Sat–Sun 10–noon, 2–6; Nov–end Mar Tue–Thu, Sat–Sun 10–12, 2–5.30. Closed mid-Dec to mid-Jan

MUSÉE NATIONAL DE L'EDUCATION
✉ 185 rue Eau de Robec, 76000 Rouen
☎ 02 35 07 66 61 🕐 Mon, Wed–Fri

10–12.30, 1.30–6, Sat–Sun 2–6. Closed Tue
🎟 Adult €3, child (under 16) free

ÉGLISE ST-MACLOU
✉ Place Barthélemy, 76000 Rouen
🕐 Mon–Sat 10–5, Sun 10.30–5.30. Closed public hols

TOUR JEANNE D'ARC
✉ Rue du Donjon, 76000 Rouen
🕐 Apr–end Sep Mon, Wed–Sat 10–12, 2–6, Sun 2–6; Oct–end Mar Mon, Wed–Sat 10–12, 2–5, Sun 2–5 🎟 €1.50 for everyone

WHEN TO GO
The walk can be enjoyed at any time of year. The sites associated with Joan of Arc are scenes of celebration on the Sunday closest to 30 May during the Fêtes Jeanne d'Arc.

WHERE TO EAT
LE P'TIT ZINC
▷ 177.

RESTAURANT DUFOUR
▷ 177.

Opposite *Timber-framed houses along rue des Faulx, near the Église St-Ouen*

AMFREVILLE-LES-CHAMPS
LA FERME AU FIL DES SAISONS
www.lafermeaufildessaisons.com
This is a farm visit with a difference:
There are donkey rides for the kids
and summertime tea parties, as
well as a year-round exhibition on
the local linen tradition. The farm
shop sells ciders, farmyard terrines,
honey, cheese and fruit juices.
✉ Route de Yémanville, 76560 Amfreville-
les-Champs ☎ 02 35 56 41 46 ⊕ Jul,
Aug daily 4–7; Sep–end Jun Wed 2–7,
Fri 2–7.30, Sat 9.30–12, 2–7 ✋ Free
🚗 Amfreville-les-Champs is 22km
(14 miles) south of the Alabaster Coast's
St-Valery-en-Caux via the D20

LES AUTHIEUX-RATIÉVILLE
FERME DES AUTHIEUX
CHAPEAU DE PAILLE
www.chapeaudepaille.fr
Possibly even more fun than a picnic
is the chance to pick your own fruit
and vegetables direct from the farm.
As well as collecting your salad
vegetables or fresh berries from the
fields here at Les Authieux-Ratiéville,
just east of Clères, you can buy
cold meats and pâtés from the
farm shop.
✉ 76690 Les Authieux-Ratiéville ☎ 02

35 33 56 30 ⊕ Mid-May to end Oct daily
9–12, 2–7; Nov to mid-May daily 9.30–12,
2–6

CRIQUELOT L'ESNEVAL
AQUABOWLING
www.aquabowling.free.fr
This lively leisure centre combines
a swimming pool and bowling
alley but also has a spa and gym
and offers other games including
billiards. There is a bar and
restaurant.
✉ 2 route de Mondeville, 76280 Criquelot
L'Esneval ☎ 02 35 27 02 69 ⊕ Swimming
pool: Mon–Fri noon–8, Sat noon–7, Sun
9–1, 2–6. School hols Mon–Fri 1–8, Sat
noon–7, Sun 9–1, 2–6. Bowling Mon 2–8,
Tue–Thu 2–8, Fri–Sat 2pm–2am, Sun 2–8.
School hols Mon 2–8, Tue–Sat 2–8, Sun
9–1, 2–8 ✋ Swimming pool €3.90, bowling
€4.70–€6.10

DIEPPE
ATELIER COLETTE
The traditional Dieppois maritime
craft of ivorywork, featuring
meticulously carved objets d'art,
is for sale in this workshop
commemorating a disappearing art.
Rest assured; these days bone and
synthetic ivories are used by today's

craftsmen. In the same street, at
No. 2, the neighbouring Atelier d'Art
Ragault (tel 02 35 82 10 50) is open
daily by appointment but charges
€5 admission.
✉ 3 rue Ango, 76200 Dieppe ☎ 02 76
37 04 05 ⊕ Mon–Sat 3–7 (but best to
phone first)

CASINO DE DIEPPE
www.casino-dieppe.fr
Play blackjack and roulette at the
gaming tables, or settle down with
a glass of champagne and some
Cole Porter in the Piano Bar. This
resort casino has a good restaurant
and live cabaret entertainment in
the summer season. Smart dress
is essential.
✉ Boulevard de Verdun, 76200 Dieppe
☎ 02 32 14 48 00 ⊕ Slot machines
daily 10am–3am. Gaming tables Mon–Sat
9pm–3am, Sun 4pm–3am. Jackpot Bar
Sun–Thu 10am–3am, Fri, Sat 10am–4am.
Piano Bar Mon–Fri from 6pm, Sat 7pm, Sun
3pm–7pm. Tea dance. Hotel open all year
✋ Free but ID necessary

DIEPPE SCÈNE NATIONALE
www.dsn.asso.fr
This modern auditorium, one of
France's national theatre stages,

Opposite Children learning to sail in a train of small sailboats off the coast of Le Havre

hosts a variety of performances, including plays, dance and concerts, and has a cinema showing independent films and classics. There are touring productions from other regional theatres and a year-round programme of festivals and events. The good English-language website posts advance information on performances.

✉ Quai Bérigny, 76374 Dieppe ☎ 02 35 82 04 43 🕐 Daily 2–10 🎟 Ticket prices depend on performance

GOLF CLUB DIEPPE-POURVILLE
www.golf-dieppe.com
The 18-hole course was landscaped in 1897 by Willie Park, Jr. and has spectacular views of the white cliffs of Dieppe, the English Channel and the Pourville valley—bring your camera for the unmissable photo-opportunities at holes 7 and 17. Billed as the closest course in France to England's Sussex Downs, the club is used to English-speaking visitors.

✉ 51 route de Pourville, 76200 Dieppe ☎ 02 35 84 25 05 🕐 Mon–Fri 8–7, Sat, Sun 8–7.30 💶 May–end Sep €50 weekdays (€60 weekends and national hols); Oct–end Apr Mon–Fri €33, Sat, Sun and national hols €41. It is advisable to book beforehand.

ÉTRETAT
LE CLOS ARSÈNE LUPIN
www.arsene-lupin.com
France's answer to A. J. Raffles, the fictional gentleman thief, is Arsène Lupin, created in 1905 by author Maurice Leblanc. Lupin, master of disguise, cat burglar and all-round decent chap, is one of the most popular characters in French fiction. The author's house has been transformed into the fictional home of Arsène Lupin, where visitors are escorted through the early 20th-century building by the hero's sidekick, Grognard, on an imaginary tour of his life and exploits.

✉ Maison Maurice Leblanc, 15 rue Guy de

Maupassant, 76790 Étretat ☎ 02 35 10 59 53 🕐 Apr–end Sep daily 10am–5.45; school hols daily 11–4.45. All other times Sat, Sun 11–4.45 💶 Adult €6.75, child (6–16) €4.25, over 60 €5.75

JOA CASINO ÉTRETAT
www.joa-casino.com
Étretat's casino enjoys a magnificent location facing the famous cliffs, and even if you aren't tempted by the gaming rooms you might want to take in the sea views from the windows of the casino's panoramic restaurant.

✉ 1 rue Adolphe Boissave BP 18, 76790 Étretat ☎ 02 35 27 00 54 🕐 Daily from 10pm

VILLAGE ÉQUESTRE D'ÉTRETAT
www.village-equestre.cjb.net
This equestrian venue, which welcomes beginners, is south of Étretat at Le Tilleul. It offers guided rides through the beautiful surrounding countryside of forest and sea cliffs. There's a maximum of eight per group.

✉ 248–50 rue de la Sauvagère, 76790 Le Tilleul ☎ 02 35 27 04 22 🕐 Fri–Wed 💶 €23 per hour

FORGES-LES-EAUX
AUX DEUX GOUTTES D'EAU
This shop sells excellent reproductions of the old-style blue-and-white Rouenware pottery, including plates, tureens, vases and lamps. Visit the workshops and see the kilns where traditional earthenware and glazing techniques have been resurrected and re-created by Alexandre Audel and his fellow potters.

✉ Place de l'Ancienne Gare Thermale, 76440 Forges-les-Eaux ☎ 02 35 09 61 53 🕐 Daily 10–12.30, 3–7.30

LE HAVRE
ART'SPORT CAFÉ
www.artsportcafe.com
A useful combination of sports centre, café and restaurant in the centre of Le Havre. It has six squash courts, three badminton courts, a golf practice range, a mini football field and various exercise facilities.

Evening activities include live concerts.

✉ 1 rue Marcel Toulouzan, 76600 Le Havre ☎ 02 35 26 38 66 🕐 Mon–Sat 9–11, Sun 9–5 💶 Any activity for one day €30

AZOU-CHOCOLAT
www.auzou-chocolat.fr
The 'temple of chocolate' in Le Havre is one of a chain of craft *chocolatiers* in Normandy who use authentic cocoa imported from Ecuador. Try their specialty macaroons or les *zozous d'azou*.

✉ 19 rue A. Andrt Huet Parvis Espace Coty, 76600 Le Havre ☎ 02 35 41 30 70 🕐 Mon–Sat 9.30–7.30

COMTESSE DE BARRY
www.comtessedubarry.com
One of a chain of exquisite delicatessens where you can buy foie gras, terrines, ready-made dishes, wine, champagne, desserts and many other French specialties. They also have outlets in Rouen, Louviers and Cherbourg.

✉ 61 avenue René Coty, 76600 Le Havre ☎ 02 35 42 13 46 🕐 Tue–Sat 9.30–12.30, 2.30–7

LA GALERNE
www.lagalerne.fr
More than just the biggest and best bookshop in town, with 100,000 books to choose from, La Galerne is a literary and artistic hangout. The café is a great place to eavesdrop or chat with fellow shoppers, and the various cultural spaces within the building have a packed schedule of talks, debates and performances.

✉ 148 rue Victor Hugo, 76600 Le Havre ☎ 02 35 43 22 52 🕐 Mon–Sat 10–7

LE LOUNGE BAR PASINO
www.pasino-lehavre.fr
The lounge bar of the Pasino entertainment complex which includes a hotel, a casino, a spa and three restaurants is a popular venue for live jazz and rock concerts. It has a DJ at weekends and karaoke evenings twice a month

✉ Place Jules Ferry, 76600 Le Havre ☎ 02 35 26 00 00 🕐 Tue–Thu 7.30pm–2am, Fri, Sat 7.30pm–4am

REGIONS • SEINE-MARITIME • WHAT TO DO

173

LE MUSIC BAR

It could be so easy just to walk past this tiniest of bars without noticing it, but the seductive sounds from within lure passersby inside. Crowds packed into the split-level venue enjoy the eclectic art collection on the walls of what looks like an elderly aunt's spare bedroom, and the music, which ranges from reggae to punk via karaoke.

✉ 28 rue François Arago, 76600 Le Havre
☎ 02 32 74 04 04 ⊗ Tue–Sun 4pm–2am

MASSY

ARTMAZIA

Just 5km (3 miles) from the cheese centre of Neufchâtel en Bray is the world's longest permanent natural hedge maze, with some 3,500 copper beech trees and 3.5km (2 miles) of pathways. This eccentric installation is also an art centre with works to be found amid the twists and turns of the labyrinth and a full summer schedule of art and crafts workshops and exhibitions.

✉ 25 route de Neufchâtel, 76270 Massy
☎ 02 35 93 17 12 ⊗ Jul, Aug daily 2.30–6.30 ✋ Adult €4, child €3

ROUEN

LE CHAKRA

A predominantly gay crowd packs itself into this newest incarnation of the former Traxx club in Rouen's port district. DJs play house and techno sounds until late, with a mellower music policy at the weekend 'afters club' that keeps the party mood swinging until breakfast time.

✉ 4 bis, boulevard Ferdinand de Lesseps, 76000 Rouen ☎ 02 32 10 12 02 ⊗ Fri–Sat and eve of public hols 11pm–4am. Sat and Sun afters club: 5am–9am ✋ Fri €8, Sat €10 (prices include first drink) 🅿 Free parking nearby

CYBERNÉT

Catch up with your emails in the heart of old Rouen. This cybercafé has 31 computers with flat screens and a warm welcome from the friendly team behind the counter.

✉ 47 place du Vieux-Marché, 76600 Rouen
☎ 02 35 07 33 02 ⊗ Daily 10–8 ✋ €4 per hour of surfing

Above *There is a range of music venues in the Seine-Maritime region*

EXO 7

www.ex07.net

On the opposite side of the Seine to central Rouen, in the residential district of Petit Quevilly, discover this popular club for live gigs, with a year-round line-up of local and national bands. There is also a good calendar of theme nights, plus a play list that includes lots of dance-floor-pulling 1970s and 1980s tracks.

✉ 13 place Chartreux, 76140 Petit Quevilly
☎ 02 35 03 32 30 ⊗ Fri–Sat 11pm–5am. Closed Aug ✋ €10 (includes first drink), free for students before midnight 🚇 Jean Jaures

GLOBO LOCO CLUB

Not a club, but a shop that is a major meeting point for Rouen youth. Pick up the coolest streetwear here (such as the Comète label), as well as accessories and skateboards.

✉ 59 rue Jeanne d'Arc, 76000 Rouen
☎ 02 35 15 00 58 ⊗ Mon 2–7, Tue–Sat 10–1.30, 2–7 🚇 Palais de Justice

LE KIOSQUE

This is not the biggest or flashest club in Normandy, but it is an essential late-night rendezvous for the over-25s once the central bars close their doors at 2am. Le Kiosque welcomes a mixed crowd of gays and straights, students and 30-somethings. The big plus is that it is within walking distance of the heart of town, which is unusual in France where most nightclubs seem to be designed solely for motorists.

✉ 43c boulevard de Verdun, 76000 Rouen
☎ 02 35 88 54 50 ⊗ Thu–Sat 11pm–5am
✋ €14 (includes first drink), student €9
🚇 Boulingrin

MARCHÉ DU PLACE ST-MARC

A splendid open-air market in the heart of old Rouen. Pick up vintage magazines, old jewellery and classic kitchenware at the flea-market stalls and stock up on country fare from the food stalls. There are lots of ciders and cheeses, but also some delicious loaves of bread and *pain d'épices*, a moist gingerbread-style cake. On Sunday mornings, the butcher shops and ethnic food stores in the streets around the marketplace are also open.

✉ Place St-Marc, 76000 Rouen ⊗ Tue, Fri–Sat 8–6.30, Sun 8–1.30

MONASTÈRE DES BÉNÉDICTINES

Come here for delicious cakes and biscuits, including light and fluffy madeleines, baked and sold by the Benedictine nuns who work in the little cake shop at the side of St-Ouen abbey church.

✉ 14 rue Bourg-l'Abbé, 76000 Rouen
☎ 02 35 71 92 60 ⊗ Daily 10.15–11.45, 2.15–5.15 🚇 Boulingrin

LE SAXO

A fine chill-out zone by the weekend marketplace, this haunt of musicians, students and the laidback is a great place to enjoy an inexpensive drink and regular live performances. The accent is on jazz and blues. Early evening or daytime, sit outside on the terrace; around midnight find a table inside and enjoy the mellow sounds.

✉ 11 place Saint Mark, 76000 Rouen ☎ 02 35 98 24 92 🕐 Mon–Sun 9pm–2am

ST-MARTIN-DE-BOSCHERVILLE
ESPACE NORMANDIE AVENTURE
www.espaceaventure.com

Try acrobranching (swinging from tree to tree) at this forest adventure centre. There is a choice of three kids' routes and one adult trail to suit various levels of skill and fitness.

✉ Val St-Lénard, 76840 St-Martin-de-Boscherville ☎ 06 71 17 36 03 🕐 Apr, May Wed, Sat, Sun 1.30–7; Jun Wed, Sat 1.30–7, Sun 11–7; Jul, Aug daily 10–7; Sep, Oct Sat, Sun 2–6 👋 Adult €21, child €11 (more than 1.40m/4ft 6in tall €17)

ST MARTIN-EN-CAMPAGNE
LUDI'BULLE
www.recrea.fr/ludibulle

This sports and leisure centre up the coast from Dieppe has a swimming pool with slide, skating rink, squash courts and gym. Concerts are occasionally organized. Timetables and prices vary according activities.

✉ Rue de l'ancienne Foire, 76370 St Martin-en-Campagne ☎ 02 35 85 84 84 👋 Skating rink €5, child €3

ST-MICHEL-D'HALESCOURT
DOMAINE FOUGERAY-DUCLOS
A typical 18th-century farm in the Pays de Bray making traditional ciders, Calvados and the fortified aperitif Pommeau. In the orchards around the farmhouse, various varieties of apple tree are cultivated in the time-honoured manner.

✉ 76440 St-Michel-d'Halescourt ☎ 09 75 66 33 22 🕐 Jul, Aug Mon–Fri 2–6, Sat 9.30–12.30, 2–6; Sep–end Jun 2–6 except Wed, Sun

SASSEVILLE
CHÈVRERIE DU VIEUX MANOIR
This organic farm shop, 13km (8 miles) inland from the Alabaster Coast's St-Valery-en-Caux, has a fine range of ciders, jams and apple juices, but best of all is its tasty cheese, made using milk

FESTIVALS AND EVENTS

MAY
FOIRE AUX MOULES
Seafood tastings and much merrymaking are to be had during this springtime mussel fair.

✉ Le Tréport ☎ 02 35 86 05 69 🕐 Whitsun weekend

FÊTES JEANNE D'ARC
A medieval market and commemorative ceremonies are held by the river and at sites associated with Joan of Arc.

✉ Rouen ☎ 02 32 08 13 90 🕐 Weekend closest to 30 May

JUNE
MARCHÉ DE TERROIR
A country market of traditional food, drink and local crafts.

✉ Yvetot ☎ 02 35 95 08 40 🕐 Date varies from May to Jun

SEPTEMBER
FÊTE DU CIDRE
The Pays de Caux cider festival coincides with the area's apple harvest. There are music performances, tastings and markets.

✉ Caudebec-en-Caux ☎ 02 35 95 90 10 🕐 Held every other year but could change

from the alpine goats raised on the farm. Children will love visiting in springtime, when the newborn kids are on the farm and the milk and cheese are at their sweetest. Arrive at 5pm to see the milking.

✉ 76450 Sasseville ☎ 02 35 57 29 62 🕐 Mar–end Dec daily 5pm–7pm

LE TRÉPORT
PERLERIE ENTRÉ EN MATIÈRE
Madame Piskadio makes striking costume jewellery from sticks of tinted glass beading worked with a blowtorch. Pick up some original pieces from the selection in her shop, or commission something special. You can watch the artist

LES PUCES ROUENNAISES
Rouen's autumn flea market and antiques fair is an opportunity for bargain-hunting in the old city.

✉ Rouen ☎ 02 35 18 28 28 🕐 Second weekend in Sep

OCTOBER
FÊTE DU VENTRE
A one-day food fair and produce market, with things to eat and drink from across the region.

✉ Rouen ☎ 02 35 18 28 28 🕐 Late Oct

FÊTE DU HARENG
The annual herring festival is a celebration of Étretat's seafaring past and present, with folk traditions and plenty of food to eat.

✉ Étretat ☎ 02 35 27 05 21 🕐 End of Oct

DECEMBER
MARCHÉ DE NOËL
In the weeks leading up to Christmas Eve, wooden chalets appear in the centre of town, selling warm, spicy mulled wine, savoury cakes and Christmas nativity scene figurines.

✉ Rouen ☎ 02 35 18 28 28 🕐 Most of Dec

at work in her studio.

✉ 5 quai Francois 1er, 76470 Le Tréport ☎ 06 70 89 04 31 🕐 Jul, Aug daily 10–12, 2–7; Sep–end Jun Wed–Sun 10–12, 2–7

VEULETTES-SUR-MER
CENTRE NAUTIQUE DE LA COTE D'ALBATRE
www.cote-albatre.fr/centre-nautique

This marina offers the opportunity to practise different water sports including sailing, canoeing and windsurfing. Prices vary according to the particular activity.

✉ 39 Digue Jean Corruble (seafront), 76450 Veulettes-sur-Mer ☎ 02 35 57 97 00

PRICES AND SYMBOLS

The restaurants are listed alphabetically (excluding Le, La and Les) by town. The prices given are the average for a two-course lunch (L) and a three-course dinner (D) for one person, without drinks. The wine price is for the least expensive bottle. All the restaurants listed accept credit cards unless otherwise stated.

For a key to the symbols, ▷ 2.

DIEPPE
BISTROT DU POLLET

This bistro in the old fishing quarter serves more locals than day-trippers from the ferry port. The cozy restaurant has a huge selection of locally caught fish, and although the cooking is simple without any sauces, it is exquisite in flavour. One of the dishes is whole sea bass served with fresh spinach and mashed potato with black olives. The service and atmosphere are good yet relaxed.

✉ 23 rue Tête-de-Boeuf, 76200 Dieppe ☎ 02 35 84 68 57 🕐 Tue–Sat 12–2, 7–9.30. Closed mid to end Aug ✋ L and D €35, inclusive of wine

RESTAURANT DE L'HÔTEL WINDSOR

www.hotelwindsor.fr

The restaurant at the Hôtel Windsor has panoramic sea views and serves local specialties, with an emphasis on seafood, to a loyal market of holidaymakers from both France and abroad. The fresh shellfish platter and the foie gras are both highly recommended.

✉ 18 boulevard de Verdun, 76200 Dieppe ☎ 02 35 84 15 23 🕐 Daily 12–2.30, 7.30–9.30 ✋ L €22, D €50, Wine €24

EU
RESTAURANT MAINE

Sitting in this family-run restaurant, you will be fascinated by the eccentric variety of items on display all around you. The chef, Vincent Lavaud, prepares an excellent roasted lobster and 'surf and turf' is also represented on the menu. Among the desserts is a delicious chocolate and strawberry *mille-feuille* pastry with a lip-smacking raspberry coulis. A good selection of Bordeaux and burgundy wines is offered.

✉ 20 avenue de la Gare, 76260 Eu ☎ 02 35 86 16 64 🕐 Daily 12–1.30, 7.30–9 ✋ L €25, D €25, Wine €20

FÉCAMP
AUBERGE DE LA ROUGE

Relax in the family atmosphere of this *auberge*. Chef Paul-Aymeric Durel has added his own touch to the menu since he took over the kitchens in 2003, a fact that is apparent on tasting his *pavé de gros turbot roti à la sariette* (roasted turbot cutlets). There are some inventive vegetarian dishes too. The service is attentive.

✉ Route du Havre, 76400 Fécamp ☎ 02 35 28 07 59 🕐 Tue–Sat 12–2, 7–9, Sun 12–2. Closed early Feb ✋ L €19, D €29, Wine €17

LA PLAISANCE

www.restaurant-la-plaisance-fecamp.com

This restaurant, with views over the port and the cliffs, specializes in freshly caught fish and seafood. There is a fixed-price buffet on Friday evenings where you can help yourself as long as your appetite lasts.

✉ 33 quai Vicomté, 76400 Fécamp
☎ 02 35 29 38 14 🕐 Daily 12–2, 7–9.30
✋ L €15, D €25, Wine €15.50

JUMIÈGES
AUBERGE DES RUINES
www.aubergedesruines.fr
Facing the ruins of the abbey across the street, this restaurant has elegant table settings to complement its equally lovely food. The chef has opted for lighter dishes, including *ris de veau rôti jaune d'oeuf cru* (roast veal sweetbreads with raw egg yolk) served in its smoked spicy jus, and uses the finest local ingredients, which is reflected in the à la carte prices. Since Jumièges is half an hour from Rouen, the *auberge* has proved popular with city-break weekenders.
✉ 17 place de la Mairie, 76480 Jumièges
☎ 02 35 37 24 05 🕐 Mon, Thu–Sat 12–2, 7–9, Tue, Sun 12–2. Closed late Aug–early Sep, mid-Dec to mid-Jan ✋ L €35, D €50, Wine €26

ROUEN
LE CATELIER
www.lecatelier-rouen.fr
Dine on local delicacies in this Norman house close to the botanical garden. The dining room is elegant yet convivial. Chef Marie-France Atinault specializes in seafood—try scallops from Dieppe, turbot in a white wine sauce or lobster salad with cider butter and fried apples. Her husband, Daniel, will help you choose the best wine to go with your meal. There are several fixed-price menus.
✉ 134 bis, avenue des Martyrs de la Résistance, 76100 Rouen ☎ 02 35 72 59 90 🕐 Tue–Sat 12–2, 7–9. Closed first 3 weeks of Aug ✋ L €20, D €50, glass of wine from €4

L'ÉCAILLE
This acclaimed fish restaurant is one of the finest in the area. The chef, Marc Tellier, who deals directly with local fishermen and selects only the best catches, is also a keen fisherman himself. As well as the classic choices, the menu features a fresh special such as a salad of whole lobster with a *vinaigrette* dressing. Service is friendly and the wine list is very good.
✉ 26 Rampe-Cauchoise, 76000 Rouen
☎ 02 35 70 95 52 🕐 Tue–Fri 12–2, 7–9.30, Sat 7–9.30 ✋ L €31, D €45, Wine €45

LA PÊCHERIE
www.lapecherie.fr
At this friendly brasserie staff serve generous platters of fish and shellfish (langoustines, prawns and scallops), as well as less common combinations such as lobster in a cider reduction. A couple of meat dishes and some memorable desserts, including a spicy pineapple *carpaccio* and an Earl Grey tea-scented *crème brulée*, finish the line-up. You can sit outside on the small terrace in good weather.
✉ 29 place de la Basse Vieille Tour, 76000 Rouen ☎ 02 35 88 71 00 🕐 Mon–Fri 12–2.30, 7.30–9.30, Sat 7.30–10 ✋ L €25, D €40, Wine €16

LE P'TIT ZINC
The restaurant is tiny and the service can be hurried, yet the atmosphere and the food here are great. It is difficult to imagine how dishes like *entrecôte à la moelle et son gâteau de champignons* (marrowbone steak with a mushroom cake) can be produced so beautifully from such a small kitchen. Alain, the patron, recommends appropriate wines from his exceptional wine list and he considers Le P'tit Zinc more a wine cellar than a restaurant.
✉ 20 place du Vieux Marché, 76000 Rouen
☎ 02 35 89 39 69 🕐 Mon–Fri 12–2, 8–10, Sat 12–2. Closed Christmas ✋ L €25, D €25, Wine €18

RESTAURANT DUFOUR
This is a typical Norman restaurant close to the cathedral. The menu has a traditional feel, and as the restaurant is popular with both local and tourists, advance booking is advised. A specialty is the famous *caneton à la Rouennaise*, pressed duckling served with a flourish at your table (▷ 15).
✉ 67 bis, rue St-Nicolas, 76000 Rouen
☎ 02 35 71 90 62 🕐 Tue–Sat 12–1.30, 7–9.30, Sun 12–1.30 ✋ L €20, D €28, Wine €12

LA VILLA DU HAVRE
One of the city's gastronomic institutions has been recently transformed into a trendy tapas bar. There is no formal set menu but a selection of tapas can make an evening meal, although note that the prices can add up.
✉ 66 boulevard Albert-1er, 76600 Le Havre
☎ 02 35 54 78 80 🕐 Thu–Sun evenings
✋ Prices vary according to dishes ordered

VEULES-LES-ROSES
LES GALETS
This restaurant, on the Côte d'Albâtre, has a conservatory-style room where locals and visitors explore a menu rich in fish. Chef Frédéric Cauchye has combined timeless classics with new ideas. For those with the budget and the appetite, the *menu découverte* is worth trying. Look out for the oysters served with a terrine of baby leeks. The wine list has a good selection available by the glass.
✉ 3 rue Victor-Hugo, 76980 Veules-les-Roses ☎ 02 35 97 61 33 🕐 Thu–Mon 12.30–2.30, 7.30–9. Closed Tue, Wed
✋ L €36, D €50, Wine €18

YVETOT
AUBERGE DU VAL AU CESNE
www.valaucesne.fr
This 17th-century farmhouse sits in the heart of the countryside. Within the half-timbered *auberge* (▷ 179), chef Jerome Carel attracts seekers of culinary perfection. Among his various specialties is sole stuffed with a langoustine mousse, which has become a local legend. The rustic dining room has an open fireplace, and the service is friendly. You can take a postprandial stroll.
✉ Croix Mare, 76190 Yvetot ☎ 02 35 56 63 06 🕐 Wed–Sun 12–2, 7–9. Closed 3 weeks Jan, 2 weeks Aug ✋ L €35, D €45, Wine €22

PRICES AND SYMBOLS

The prices are the lowest and highest for a double room for one night, including breakfast, unless otherwise stated. All the hotels listed accept credit cards unless otherwise stated. Note that rates can vary widely throughout the year.

For a key to the symbols, ▷ 2.

AUMALE

LA VILLA DES HOUX

www.villa-des-houx.com

Convenient for the beaches at Le Tréport, this country house was once a local *gendarmerie*. You will be greeted by Alain and Michelle Mauconduit. The conservatory-style dining room is light and airy, with views over the gardens. Breakfast can be served on the terrace. Bedrooms are attractively furnished and have satellite TV, and there is also a lift for guests with disabilities.

✉ 6 avenue du Général de Gaulle, 76390 Aumale ☎ 02 35 93 93 30 ⊕ Closed Jan; Oct–end Apr Sun eve ✋ €75–€120, excluding breakfast (€8) ⓘ 22

BEZANCOURT

CHÂTEAU DU LANDEL

www.château-du-landel.fr

In the peaceful Forêt de Lyons, this palatial retreat is ideal for a weekend break. The château was once a staging post on the pilgrim route to Santiago de Compostela. Until 1870 it was owned by the Guild of Glass-makers, which explains the ornate chandeliers. The dining room has brick walls bearing stag heads, and the hotel can cater for private family parties.

✉ 76220 Bezancourt ☎ 02 35 90 16 01 ⊕ Closed mid-Nov to mid-Mar ✋ €87–€183, excluding breakfast (€11) ⓘ 17 ⌷ Outdoor

DIEPPE

LES ARCADES DE LA BOURSE

www.lesarcades.fr

This historic building in the heart of town takes its name from its covered arcade. The guest rooms, all of which have TV, are simply furnished and some have balconies with views of the harbour. Facilities include internet access and a renowned seafood restaurant.

✉ 1–3 arcade de la Bourse, 76200 Dieppe ☎ 02 35 84 14 12 ⊕ Year-round ✋ €63–€79, excluding breakfast (€8) ⓘ 21 ⌷ Sauna

ÉTRETAT

LE DONJON

www.ledonjon-Étretat.fr

Le Donjon is dramatically set in a 19th-century Anglo-Norman-style château overlooking the village and cliffs of Étretat. Some rooms have a spa bath-tub and all have satellite TV, yet they retain individuality. There is an on-site restaurant.

✉ Chemin St-Clair, 76790 Étretat ☎ 02 35 27 08 23 ⊕ Year-round ✋ €90–€250, exluding breakfast (€14) ⓘ 21

DORMY HOUSE

www.dormy-house.com

Perched on top of the cliffs of Étretat, this mansion has panoramic views from several bedrooms. Some rooms mix period furniture with bright tones, while others are more country style, with floral bedspreads and wooden chests of drawers. The elegant restaurant has large bay windows overlooking the sea.

✉ B.P. 2, route du Havre, 76790 Étretat ☎ 02 35 27 07 88 ⊕ Year-round ✋ €99–€155, excluding breakfast (€15) ⓘ 61

FÉCAMP

HÔTEL NORMANDY

www.normandy-fecamp.com

This former post house has spacious, comfortable yet basic modern rooms, all with satellite TV, which is a bonus at these prices. The interior of the restaurant, La Brasserie Maupassant, evokes the early 19th century.

✉ 4 avenue Gambetta, 76400 Fécamp

☎ 02 35 29 55 11 ◐ Year-round
♨ €54–€62, excluding breakfast (€7)
ⓘ 30 (5 non-smoking) Ⓟ For hotel guests

LE HAVRE
VENT D'OUEST
www.ventdouest.fr
Vent d'Ouest is between the heart of the city and the sea. Several bedrooms have a nautical look, while others have rural themes. The hotel doesn't have a restaurant but there is a tearoom that serves snacks.
✉ 4 rue Caligny, 76600 Le Havre ☎ 02 35 42 50 69 ◐ Year-round ♨ €98–€128, excluding breakfast (€12) ⓘ 35 Ⓟ Private parking

JUMIÈGES
LE CLOS DES FONTAINES
www.leclosdesfontaines.com
Features of this village property facing the Abbey de Jumièges include an orchard and an impressive pool. It is within reach of Giverny (▷ 130–131). Breakfast can be had on a terrace. Guests with a disability have access.
✉ 191 rue des Fontaines, 76480 Jumièges ☎ 02 35 33 96 96 ◐ Closed Jan ♨ €90–€140, excluding breakfast (€15) ⓘ 19 ⊠ Outdoor

MONTIGNY
LE RELAIS DE MONTIGNY
www.relais-de-montigny.com
This modern hotel, a couple of miles outside Rouen, looks onto a pleasant garden. The bedrooms, all with satellite TV, are comfortable and some have terraces. Local dishes are served in the restaurant and you can dine outside.
✉ Rue du Lieutenant Aubert, 76380 Montigny ☎ 02 35 36 05 97 ◐ Closed end Dec–early Jan ♨ €70–€83, excluding breakfast (€9.50) ⓘ 22

ROUEN
HÔTEL DES CARMES
www.hoteldescarmes.com
Situated in the middle of this medieval city, famous for its 100 bell towers, the Hôtel des Carmes makes an ideal base. Vivid prints make these rooms very individual, and surprisingly, for the budget,

it also offers Internet access. Babysitting can be arranged. The hotel doesn't have a restaurant, but there are plenty in the city (▷ 177).
✉ 33 place des Carmes, 76000 Rouen ☎ 02 35 71 92 31 ◐ Year-round ♨ €49–€65, excluding breakfast (€7.30) ⓘ 12 Ⓟ Secure parking ◉ Palais de Justice

LE VIEUX CARRÉ
www.vieux-carre.fr
This is part of an 18th-century building, restored in 2000 to give it the feeling of a private residence. A restaurant opens out onto a lovely courtyard. Some of the rooms look down onto the courtyard; others overlook the gardens.
✉ 34 rue Ganterie, 76000 Rouen ☎ 02 35 71 67 70 ◐ Year-round ♨ €58–€62, excluding breakfast (€7) ⓘ 14 Ⓟ Nearby ◉ Palais de Justice

ST-VALÉRY-EN-CAUX
LES HÊTRES
www.leshetres.com
An authentic Norman house, dating back to 1627, that has much to offer if you love nature, golf, food and fishing. Interior design ranges from sharply modern to rustic, timbered hideaways. Dogs are welcome and some rooms have easy access for guests with disabilities.
✉ 24 rue des Fleurs, 76460 St-Valery-en-Caux ☎ 02 35 57 09 30 ◐ Closed Jan to mid-Feb ♨ €90–€160, excluding breakfast (€17) ⓘ 5

SASSETOT-LE-MAUCONDUIT
CHÂTEAU DE SASSETOT
www.château-de-sassetot.com
This magnificent 18th-century château was once the summer residence of the Austrian Empress Sissi (1837–98). It stands in the centre of a large private estate, allowing you to appreciate the architecture among tranquil surroundings. From the bedrooms through to the dining and reception rooms, you will experience the elegance of the period.
✉ 76540 Sassetot-le-Mauconduit ☎ 02 35 28 00 11 ◐ Closed early Jan to mid-Feb

♨ €75–€314, excluding breakfast (€14) ⓘ 25 rooms, 3 suites

LE RELAIS DES DALLES
www.relais-des-dalles.fr
The gardens at this enchanting inn are well maintained with an abundance of flowers in summer. Inside, soft fabrics blend with wooden floors, panelling and beams, with a roaring fire in winter adding to the cosiness. The bedrooms are spacious, with lovely furnishings, beamed ceilings, tiled floors and rugs. There is an on-site restaurant.
✉ 6 rue Elisabeth d'Autriche, 76540 Sassetot-le-Mauconduit ☎ 02 35 27 41 83 ◐ Closed early Jan, mid-Dec to mid-Jan ♨ €72–€138, excluding breakfast (€12) ⓘ 4

LE TRÉPORT
LE SAINT YVES
This friendly family-run hotel is perfect for a beach holiday – it is at the edge of the port 30m (33yds) from the sea. The comfortably furnished bedrooms all have satellite TV. It is also convenient for visiting the local crafts shops, the casino and the fishing port.
✉ Place Pierre Sémart, 76470 Le Tréport ☎ 02 35 86 34 66 ◐ Year-round, except Christmas period ♨ €58–€75, excluding breakfast (€7.50) ⓘ 20 rooms, 3 suites

YVETOT
L'AUBERGE DU VAL AU CESNE
www.valaucesne.fr
Val au Cesne is a typical Pays de Caux *auberge*. Waiting in the garden to welcome new arrivals is a party of hens, ducks and cats. Inside, the cottage-style bedrooms have floral furnishings and private terraces leading onto the grounds. A large brick fireplace dominates the restaurant (▷ 177). Close by, white cliffs tower over the tiny fishing villages strung along the coast.
✉ Croix-Mare, 76190 Yvetot ☎ 02 35 56 63 06 ◐ Closed early Jan–end Jan, mid-Aug to early Sep, late Nov–early Dec ♨ €90, excluding breakfast (€9) ⓘ 5

Opposite *The swimming pool at le Clos des Fontaines hotel, Jumièges*

PRACTICALITIES

Practicalities gives you all the important practical information you will need during your visit from money matters to emergency phone numbers.

WEATHER

CLIMATE

» Normandy has a generally mild, dampish climate tempered by sea breezes. Some sheltered areas, bathed by the Gulf Stream, enjoy a microclimate benign enough for vines and subtropical plants to flourish.

» Extremes of temperature are rare, but the weather is always unpredictable, and can change very quickly. Rain may occur at any time of year, but is most prevalent in autumn and winter. Short-lived bursts of frost and snow occasionally shock the flowering mimosa in winter, and gales assail the ocean coastline from time to time. Mist and fog periodically obscure winter views and threaten shipping off Finistère's reefstrewn shores.

» Summer temperatures average just over 20°C (68°F), and are highest in August. In Haute Normandie the climate is very similar to that in the south of England, while the Cotentin peninsula feels more like the Channel Islands. But the Channel coast receives just 1,700 hours of sunlight a year, compared with 2,200 hours in southern areas of neighbouring Brittany.

» The interior, whose gentle hills are high enough to puncture Atlantic rain clouds, is generally wetter than low-lying coastal zones, and has wider temperature variations.

» For up-to-date weather information and forecasts for Normandy, look up www.meteo.fr.

WHEN TO GO

» In July and August, the beaches and campsites of the popular coastal resorts overflow with French families taking their traditional summer break. Prices soar, and traffic clogs the roads. It can be difficult to find a bed for the night, or a restaurant table. But the resorts are at their liveliest, providing a seamless round of happenings—regattas and boat trips, open-air concerts, fireworks and son-et-lumière shows. The biggest festivals attract huge gatherings.

» The advice to go in spring or autumn is trite but true, though you may find many other visitors have had exactly the same idea. To miss the crowds, try to avoid school holidays (British or French), and check whether your destination plans any major festivals or events during your visit.

ROUEN
TEMPERATURE

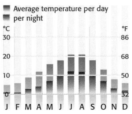

CHERBOURG
TEMPERATURE

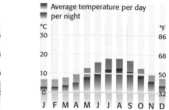

RAINFALL

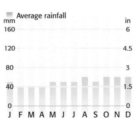

RAINFALL

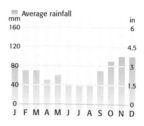

FRENCH EMBASSIES AND CONSULATES ABROAD		
COUNTRY	ADDRESS	WEBSITE
Australia	31 Market Street, St. Martin Tower, Level 26, Sydney, NSW 2000	www.ambafrance.au.org
	Tel (02) 92 68 24 00	
Canada	1501 McGill College, Bureau 1000, Montréal, Québec, H3A 3M8	www.consulfrance-montreal.org
	Tel 514 878-4385	
Ireland	36 Ailesbury Road, Ballsbridge, Dublin 4. Tel 312 77500	www.ambafrance.ie
New Zealand	34–42 Manners Street, Wellington, 12th floor, PO Box 11-343	www.ambafrance-nz.org
	Tel 644 384 25 55	
UK	58 Knightsbridge, London, SW1 7JT. Tel 020 7073 1000	www.frenchembassy.org.uk
US (Los Angeles)	10390 Santa Monica Blvd, Suite 410, Los Angeles, CA 90025	www.consulfrance-losangeles.org
	Tel 310/235-3200	
US (New York)	934 Fifth Avenue, New York, NY 10021. Tel 212/606-3600	www.consulfrance-newyork.org

TIME ZONES

CITY	TIME DIFFERENCE	TIME AT 12 NOON FRENCH TIME
Amsterdam	0	12 noon
Berlin	0	12 noon
Brussels	0	12 noon
Chicago	-7	5am
Dublin	-1	11am
Johannesburg	+1*	1pm
London	-1	11am
Madrid	0	12 noon
Montréal	-6	6am
New York	-6	6am
Perth, Australia	+7*	7pm
Rome	0	12 noon
San Francisco	-9	3am
Sydney	+9*	9pm
Tokyo	+8*	8pm

Clocks in France go forward one hour on the last Sunday in March, until the last Sunday in October.
* One hour less during Summer Time.

CUSTOMS

FROM ANOTHER EU COUNTRY

Below are the guidelines for the quantity of goods you can take in to France from another EU country, for personal use:

» 1kg of tobacco in any form, whether cigarette, cigars, cigarillos or smoking tobacco

» 110 litres of beer
» 10 litres of spirits
» 90 litres of wine (of which only 60 litres can be sparkling wine)
» 20 litres of fortified wine (such as port or sherry)

FROM A COUNTRY OUTSIDE THE EU

You are entitled to the allowances shown below only if you travel with the goods and do not plan to sell them.

» 200 cigarettes or
100 cigarillos or
50 cigars or
250gms of tobacco
» 60cc/ml of perfume
» 25ccl/ml of eau de toilette

» 2 litres of still table wine
» 1 litre of spirits or strong liqueurs over 22% volume;
or 2 litres of fortified wine, sparkling wine or other liqueurs
» Up to €175 of all other goods

» Spring is always lovely in Normandy, when the cider orchards froth into blossom, hillsides are ablaze with gorse, and local markets display cornucopias of top-quality early vegetables and Normandy's cattle make the most of fresh pasture. Autumn is a season of mellow fruitfulness, of apple-picking and mushroom-hunting. Late hydrangeas and geraniums still glow in gardens and window boxes. Huge equinoctial tides continually reshape coastal views, and migrant birds stream through the skies.
» Normandy has a longer and steadier holiday season than Brittany, boosted by short-break trade from Paris if there's good weekend weather.
» The enticing tropical appearance of Norman and Breton beaches can be deceptive. The shallow seas of Morbihan warm up a little by September, but in general sea temperatures stay cool all year.
» Many monuments and museums in France close on key national holidays (1 January, 1 May, 1 November, 11 November, 25 December), and bus and train services are much reduced.

WHAT TO TAKE

» A small rucksack or shoulder bag is useful for sightseeing. Bear in mind that these are attractive to pickpockets, so keep your money tucked away and an eye on your bag when you're in restaurants and other crowded places, especially in cities.
» A first-aid kit may be useful.
» If you wear glasses, take a spare pair and your prescription.
» Don't forget your camera!
» The strength of the sun can be masked by coastal breezes; take sunscreen and sunglasses during the holiday season.
» Much of your time may be spent outdoors, so take wet-weather gear, some warm, windproof clothing, and robust footwear. Save room in your suitcase for some of Brittany's stylish all-weather marine clothing and knitwear.
» In all but the swankiest places, smart casual clothing is perfectly acceptable for any occasion just about anywhere in Normandy. One or two dressier outfits may be appropriate for the evenings.
» When visiting churches or cathedrals, wear suitably modest clothing—beachwear and shorts

are not acceptable.
» Visitors from the UK and US will need adaptors for electrical equipment (▷ 188).
» There is a language guide on pages 205–209 of this book, but if you are keen to communicate in French you may find a separate phrasebook helpful.
» A lightweight pair of binoculars is worth packing, and possibly a bird or flower identification guide.
» You'll find English-language books and newspapers in the main towns, but it's cheaper to bring your own reading matter.

DOCUMENTS

» The key things to remember are travel and health insurance documents, money, credit cards and any medication you'll need. If you plan to drive in France, take your driving licence and, if using your own car, the vehicle registration and insurance certificates.
» Take the addresses and phone numbers of emergency contacts, including the numbers to call if your credit cards are stolen. Make photocopies of your passport, insurance documents and tickets, in

case of loss. Keep a separate note of your credit card numbers in case you need to report a theft to the police.

PASSPORTS/VISAS

» UK, US and Canadian visitors need a passport, but not a visa, for stays of up to three months. You should have at least six months' validity remaining on your passport. Citizens of EU countries that have National Identity cards need either a passport or National Identity card.

» For more information about visa and passport requirements, look up the French tourist office website (www.franceguide.com).

» Before you travel, check visa and passport regulations since these are subject to change.

» Take a photocopy of the relevant pages of your passport to carry around with you, so you can leave your actual passport in your hotel safe. Always keep a separate note of your passport number and a photocopy of the page that carries your details, in case of loss or theft.

Longer stays

» UK and other EU citizens who want to stay longer than three months should apply for a *carte de séjour* from the Préfecture de Police. US and Canadian visitors need a *carte de séjour* and a visa. For information call the Immigration Department of the French Consulate (▷ 182 chart).

TRAVEL INSURANCE

» Buy full health and travel insurance before you set off.

» EU citizens (plus nationals of Iceland, Liechtenstein, Norway and Switzerland) are entitled to receive reduced-cost emergency health care within any member state if they have the relevant documentation. For Britons, this is the European Health Insurance Card (EHIC), which was introduced in 2006 to replace the E111. Canadian nationals may use the French health system in the same way as EU residents, but comprehensive travel insurance is

still strongly advised for all visitors, whether from Europe or beyond.

» Check that your insurer has a 24-hour helpline.

MONEY

THE EURO

» The euro is the official currency of France. Notes are in denominations of €5, €10, €20, €50, €100, €200 and €500, and coins in denominations of €1 and €2, and 1, 2, 5, 10, 20 and 50 cents.

BEFORE YOU GO

» It is advisable to use a combination of cash, traveller's cheques and credit cards rather than relying on only one means of payment during your trip. Bear in mind that the number of banks and other outlets offering exchange facilities has plummeted since the introduction of the euro, so organize some euros in advance and take a credit card with you.

» Check with your credit and/or debit card company that your card can be used to withdraw cash from Automatic Teller Machines (ATMs) in France. It is also worth checking what fee will be charged for this and what number you should ring if your card is stolen.

TRAVELLER'S CHEQUES

» Traveller's cheques are a safer way of bringing in money as you can claim a refund if they are stolen— but commission can be high when you cash them.

ATMS

» Your card issuer will almost certainly charge you for withdrawing cash.

» ATMs are common in France, often with on-screen instructions in a choice of languages. Among the cards accepted are Visa, MasterCard and Diners Club. You'll need a four-digit PIN number.

» Some British credit cards are still not accepted in certain automatic machines in France because the 'smart' technology doesn't match. It is hoped that the new wave of

chip and pin cards will be more compatible.

BANKS

» Hours vary, but usual opening hours are Monday to Friday 8.30 or 9–12 and 2–5, although banks in cities may not close for lunch.

» In smaller towns and villages banks sometimes close on Mondays but open on Saturday mornings.

» Banks close during a national holiday. Only banks with *change* signs change traveller's cheques or foreign currency and you'll need your passport to do this.

BUREAUX DE CHANGE

» Bureaux de Change have longer opening hours than banks, but the exchange rates may not be so good. You'll find them at airports, ferry terminals, large railway stations and in major cities.

» Avoid changing large amounts of traveller's cheques at hotels as the rates may not be competitive.

CREDIT CARDS

» Most restaurants, shops and hotels accept credit cards, although some have a minimum spending limit.

TAXES

» Non-EU residents can claim a sales tax refund *(détaxe)* of around 12 per cent on certain purchases, although you must have spent more than €175 in one shop, at one time. Ask the store for the relevant forms, which the trader should complete and stamp. Give these forms to customs when you leave the country, along with the receipts, and they will be stamped. Post the forms back to the shop and they will either refund your credit card account or send you a cheque.

» Remember that you may have to show the goods to customs when you leave France, so keep them within easy reach.

» Exempt products include food and drink, medicine, tobacco, unset gems, works of art and antiques.

» The company Global Refund offers

PRICES OF EVERYDAY ITEMS

Takeout sandwich		€2.50–€3.50
Bottle of mineral water	(from a shop, 0.5 litre)	€0.50–€0.80
Cup of coffee	(from a café, espresso)	€1.50–€2
	(Crème, larger cup with milk)	€2.50–€3
Beer	(Un demi, half a litre)	€2.50–€3
Wine	Glass of house wine	€2.50–€3
Newspaper	French national newspaper	€1–€1.20
	International newspaper	€1.50–€2.30
Metro ticket	(single)	€1.50
	(per ticket, if you buy a carnet)	€1
20 cigarettes	(on average)	€7

TIPPING GUIDE

Restaurants (service included)	Change *
Hotels (service included)	Change *
Cafés (service included)	Change *
Taxis	10 per cent
Tour Guides	€1–€1.50
Porters	€1
Hairdressers	€1
Cloakroom attendants	30c
Lavatories	Change
Usherettes	30c

* Or more if you are impressed with the level of service

a reimbursement service (tel 01 41 61 51 51; www.globalrefund.com).

WIRING MONEY

» In an emergency, you can have money wired to you from your home country, but this can be expensive (as agents charge a fee for the service) and time-consuming.

» You can send and receive money via agents such as Western Union (www.westernunion.com) and Travelex (www.travelex.com.fr).

» Money can be wired from bank to bank, which takes up to two working days, or through Travelex and Western Union, which is normally faster.

CONCESSIONS

» If you are a student or teacher, apply to the International Student Travel Confederation (www.isic.org) in your own country for an International Student Identity Card (ISIC). This entitles you to various reductions during your visit.

» Seniors often get reduced-rate tickets on public transportation and on admission to museums and sights by showing a valid identity card or passport.

» Small children often have free entry to sights.

POST OFFICES

» Some larger post offices may provide ATMs.

» Cards accepted are listed on each dispenser and instructions are available in English.

» Money can be wired, through Western Union, via most post offices, and generally takes only a few minutes to receive

» International Money Orders can be sent from all post offices (for a fee).

» Some larger post offices offer exchange services in the following currencies: American, Australian and Canadian dollars, yen, British pounds sterling, Swiss francs and Swedish kronor, and Danish and Norwegian kroner.

TIPS

» Try to avoid using higher denomination notes when paying taxi drivers and when buying low-cost items in smaller shops.

» Never carry money or credit cards in back pockets. Watch out for thieves.

» Keep your spare money and traveller's cheques in your hotel safe (coffre fort) until you need them.

» Check the exchange rates for traveller's cheques and cash offered in post offices as well as in banks.

» In France, Mastercard is sometimes known as Eurocard and Visa is known as Carte Bleue.

» Some smaller hotels and inns don't accept credit cards, so find out before you check in.

HEALTH

BEFORE YOU GO

» EU citizens receive reduced-cost healthcare in France with the relevant documentation. For UK citizens, this is the European Health Insurance Card (EHIC), which must be stamped by the post office before you travel. Take a photocopy with you as well as the original, as this will be kept by the hospital or doctor if you need treatment. Full health insurance is still strongly advised. For all other countries full insurance is a must.

» Make sure you are up to date with anti-tetanus boosters. Bring any medication you need with you and pack a first-aid kit. In summer, always bring sun-protection cream.

IF YOU NEED TREATMENT

» The French national health system is complex. Any salaried French citizen who receives treatment by a doctor or public hospital can be reimbursed by up to 70 per cent. The same is true if you are an EU citizen and have a valid EHIC.

» If you are relying only on EHIC, rather than travel insurance, make sure the doctor you see is part of the French national health service (*a conventionné*), rather than the private system, otherwise you may face extra charges. In any case, you will have to pay up front for the consultation and treatment. To reclaim part of these costs, send the *feuille de soins* (a statement from the doctor) and the form supplied with your EHIC to the Caisse Primaire d'Assurance-Maladie (state health insurance office) before you leave the country. Call 0845 606 2030 (UK) to find the nearest office. You should also attach the labels of any medicine you have to buy.

» If you have to stay overnight in a public hospital, you will have to pay 25 per cent of the treatment costs, as well as a daily charge (*forfait journalier*). These are not refundable. It is far better to have full health insurance than to rely solely on the EHIC.

» Citizens of non-EU countries must

have full health insurance.

» If you are hospitalized and have insurance, ask to see the *assistante sociale* to arrange reimbursement of the costs directly through your insurers.

» In an emergency, dial 15 for Service d'Aide Médicale d'Urgence (SAMU) unit (ambulance). They work closely with hospital emergency units and are accompanied by trained medical personnel.

» If you are able to get yourself to a hospital, make sure it has a casualty or emergency department (*urgences*).

FINDING A DOCTOR

» In a medical emergency, your hotel should be able to help find a hospital or an English-speaking doctor. The number of the regional SOS Médecins (a duty-rota of doctors on call) is in the phonebook, also listed in local newspapers; otherwise call 15 for an ambulance. Main hospitals with casualty (emergency) units are located in all major cities—ask for the nearest *centre hospitalier* or *services des urgences*.

» Any pharmacy should be able

to direct you to a doctor (look for the green cross sign—if it is closed, a card in the window will tell you where the nearest one is). Pharmacists are trained to deal with minor medical problems and can provide first aid as well as over-the-counter medication.

FINDING A HOSPITAL

» Hospitals are listed in the phone book under *Hôpitaux*, and round-the-clock emergency services are called *urgences*.

» Private hospitals are a lot more expensive than public ones and treatment is not necessarily better. If you choose a private hospital, check that you are covered for the costs before receiving treatment.

USEFUL NUMBERS
Emergency medical aid/ambulance
15
General emergencies
112
Police
17
Fire (Pompiers)
18

DENTAL TREATMENT

» EU citizens can receive reduced-cost emergency dental treatment with their EHIC, although insurance is still advised. The reclaim procedure is the same as for general medical treatment.

» Visitors from countries outside the EU should check that their insurance covers dental treatment. It's a good idea to have a dental check-up before your trip.

PHARMACIES

» A pharmacy (pharmacie) will have an illuminated green cross outside. Most are open Mon–Sat 9–7 or 8, but when closed they usually post details on the door of another pharmacy that is open later (called the pharmacie de garde).

» Pharmacists are highly qualified and provide first aid, as well as supplying medication (some drugs are by prescription, or ordonnance, only). But they cannot dispense prescriptions written by doctors outside the French health system, so bring sufficient supplies of any prescribed drugs you need.

» Some pharmacists speak English and can direct you to local doctors or specialists.

» They also sell a range of health-related items, although it is less expensive to go to the supermarket for items such as soap, toothbrushes and razors.

» Some commonly used medicines sold in supermarkets at home (such as aspirins and cold remedies) can only be bought in pharmacies in France.

TAP WATER

» Tap water is safe to drink and restaurants will often bring a carafe of water to the table, although most French people opt instead for bottled water.

» In public places look for the sign eau potable (drinking water). Don't drink from anything marked eau non potable.

SUMMER HAZARDS

» The sun can be strong in

HEALTHY FLYING

» If you are visiting France from the US, Australia or New Zealand, you may be concerned about the effect of long-haul flights on your health. The most widely publicised concern is Deep Vein Thrombosis, or DVT. Misleadingly named economy class syndrome, DVT occurs when a blood clot forms in the body's deep veins, particularly in the legs. The clot can move around the bloodstream and could be fatal.

» Those most at risk include the elderly, pregnant women and those using the contraceptive pill, smokers and the overweight. If you are at increased risk of DVT see your doctor before departing. Flying increases the likelihood of DVT because passengers are often seated in a cramped position for long periods of time and may become dehydrated.

To minimize risk:

Drink water (not alcohol)
Don't stay immobile for hours at a time.
Stretch and exercise your legs periodically.
Do wear elastic flight socks, which support veins and reduce the chances of a clot forming.
A small dose of aspirin may be recommended; this thins the blood before the flight.

EXERCISES

1 Ankle Rotations	**2 Calf Stretches**	**3 Knee Lifts**
Lift feet off the floor. Draw a circle with the toes, moving one foot clockwise and the other counterclockwise.	Start with heel on the floor and point foot upward as high as you can. Then lift heels high keeping balls of feet on the floor.	Lift leg with knee bent while contracting your thigh muscle. Then staighten leg pressing foot flat to the floor.

Other health hazards for flyers are airborne diseases and bugs spread by the plane's air-conditioning system. These are largely unavoidable, but if you have a serious medical condition seek advice from a doctor before setting off.

OPTICIANS

It's always a good idea to pack a spare pair of glasses or contact lenses and your prescription, in case you lose or break your main pair.

NAME	WEBSITE
Opticiens Krys	www.krys.com
Lissac Opticien	www.lissac.com
Alain Afflelou	www.alainafflelou.com
Optical Center	www.optical-center.com
Optic 2000	www.optic2000.fr

Normandy between May and September, so pack a high-factor sun block.

» You may also like to take an insect repellent, although the insect bites you got in northwestern France are more likely to be irritating than dangerous.

» The likelihood of contracting food poisoning from shellfish is greater in the summer when ambient temperatures are higher. Toxic algal blooms (sudden proliferations of microscopic sea organisms) can sometimes affect fish—watch out for, and heed, local warnings.

ALTERNATIVE MEDICAL TREATMENT

» Alternative medicine, such as homeopathy, is generally available from most pharmacies.

» Alternative treatment is available, although chiropractics and reflexology are not widespread. Useful websites include www.chiropratique.org (the Association Française de Chiropratique), www.acupuncture-france.com (Association Française d'Acupuncture) and www.naturosante.com (listing alternative medical services and products).

BASICS

CAR RENTAL

» The absence of satisfactory public transport makes driving the only practical way to explore the rural villages and remote countryside of Normandy in depth, though it affords little pleasure in the larger cities. Congestion and parking can be a real headache in popular coastal areas in high season.

» It is often best to reserve a car in advance, making sure that full insurance is included in the package. You can also arrange car rental through some travel agents when you book your travel arrangements.

» See pages 30–31 for information on driving.

CHILDREN

» Look out for service stations (selling food and fuel, with play areas) or *aires* (scenic pull-ins with WCs and space to run around) on *autoroutes* and expressways, where restless children can stretch their legs.

» Most restaurants welcome children, although not many have highchairs and children's menus are not common outside family-friendly tourist resorts, so it's probably best to aim for family-style bistros where facilities are better and staff are more helpful.

» If you need special facilities in your hotel, such as a cot, or a child seat in your rented car, reserve them in advance.

» For baby-changing facilities while out and about, try the restrooms in department stores and the larger museums.

» Supermarkets and pharmacies sell nappies (diapers) and baby food, although they are often closed on a Sunday so make sure you stock up.

» Entrance to museums is often free to young children.

ELECTRICITY

» Voltage in France is 220 volts. Sockets take plugs with two round pins. UK electrical equipment will need an adaptor plug, which you can buy at airport and Eurostar terminals. American appliances using 110–120 volts will need an adaptor and a transformer. Equipment that is dual voltage should need only an adaptor.

LAUNDRY

» There are two options if you need a laundry service—a *laverie automatique* (laundrette) and a *pressing/nettoyage à sec* (dry-cleaners). Dry-cleaners are easier to find, but are more expensive. Some have an economy service, but this is not recommended for your best silk jacket.

LOCAL WAYS

» Greetings are often quite formal in France. Offer to shake hands when

you are introduced to someone, and use *vous* rather than *tu*. When speaking to people you don't know, it is polite to use *Monsieur* or *Madame*, or *Mademoiselle* for young women and girls.

» The continental kiss is a common form of greeting between friends, and the number of times friends kiss each other on the cheek varies from region to region.

» Address waiters and waitresses as *Monsieur, Madame* or *Mademoiselle* when you are trying to attract their attention. Never use *garçon*.

» Communicating in French is always the best option, even if you can manage only *bonjour, s'il vous plaît* and *merci* (hello, please and thank you). The French are protective of their language and your efforts to speak it will be appreciated. If your knowledge of French is limited, ask the fail-safe *Parlez-vous anglais?* and hope the answer is *oui*.

» Remember that it is traditional to say hello as you enter a shop, bar or café, particularly in small towns and villages, and that you are greeting your fellow customers as well as the proprietor. For a mixed audience, a *Bonjour Messieurs Dames* is the appropriate phrase. When it is your turn to be served, greet the server with *Bonjour Madame* or *Bonjour Monsieur*, then don't forget to say *merci* and *au revoir* or *bonne-journée* as you leave.

MEASUREMENTS

» France uses the metric system. Road distances are measured in kilometres, fuel is sold by the litre and food is weighed in grams and kilograms.

PLACES OF WORSHIP

» Some of France's greatest architectural treasures are the magnificent Gothic cathedrals of Normandy.

» They have become so popular as visitor attractions that it's easy to forget that they are still active places of worship. It's important to respect these churches and worshippers by dressing appropriately. Men should

INTERDIT SAUF G.I.G.-G.I.C.

wear long trousers rather than shorts and should avoid sleeveless shirts. Women should keep their knees and shoulders covered and men should remove hats on entering the building.

» Take photos only if it is permitted and don't forget to turn off your mobile phone.

SMOKING AREAS

» France has always had a laissez faire attitude to smoking but in recent years it has joined the European trend towards prohibiting smoking in public places by tightening the laws and enforcing them.

» Smoking is now banned in all museums, monuments, cinemas, theatres, offices, other workplaces, buses, trains, metros, bars, cafés, restaurants, nightclubs and casinos. Smokers, who account for around a quarter of the population, must now go outside if they wish to light up.

TOILETS

» Today's modern unisex public lavatories are a vast improvement on previous facilities. Coin-operated and self-cleaning, you can find them in most large cities.

» In smaller towns and villages, free public lavatories can normally be found by the market square or near

tourist offices, although cleanliness standards vary.

» Facilities in museums and other visitor attractions generally reach a good standard, so take advantage of them while you can. Restaurants and cafés provide WCs for their customers—at least buy a drink if you intend using them.

» Ask for *les toilettes* or WC (pronounced *vay, say*).

VISITORS WITH DISABILITIES

» France has made some headway in recent years in providing access and facilities for visitors with disabilities. All new buildings must take the needs of people with special requirements into account, and, where possible, existing buildings such as town halls, airports and train stations must be adapted with ramps and automatic doors. But the cobbled, hilly streets of many historic towns and villages in Brittany and Normandy can be a trial for wheelchair-users.

» Some visitor offices, museums and restaurants that are in old, protected buildings are still not fully accessible. A telephone call before going to a restaurant is a good idea to organize a more easily accessible table.

» For organizations that give further advice, ▷ 36.

FINDING HELP

Most visits to northwestern France are trouble-free, but make sure you have adequate insurance to cover any health emergencies, thefts or legal costs that may arise. If you do become a victim of crime, it is most likely to be at the hands of a pickpocket, so always keep your money and mobile phones safely tucked away.

PERSONAL SECURITY

» Take a note of your traveller's cheques numbers. Keep them separate from the cheques, as you will need them to make a claim in case of loss.

» Don't keep wallets, purses or mobile phones in the back pockets of trousers, or anywhere else that is easily accessible to thieves. Money belts and bags worn around the waist are targets, as thieves know you are likely to have valuables in them. Always keep an eye on your bags in restaurants, bars and on the metro, and hold shoulder bags close to you, fastener inwards, when you are walking in the streets.

» Thieves and pickpockets are especially fond of crowded places, such as rush-hour buses and trains, busy markets or popular festivals. Beware if someone bumps into you—it may be a ploy to distract you while someone else snatches your money.

» If you are the victim of theft, you must report it at the local police station *(commissariat)* if you want to claim on your insurance. Keep hold of the statement the police give you. You must also contact your credit card company as soon as possible to cancel stolen cards.

» Keep valuable items in your hotel safe *(coffre-fort)*.

» Theft of cars and theft from cars are significant problems in France. When you park your car, don't leave anything of value inside. It's even risky leaving anything at all in view that may attract the interest of a thief. Carry your belongings with you or leave them behind.

» On trains, try to keep your luggage where you can see it. Racks are usually at the ends of the carriages.

LOSS OF PASSPORT

» Always keep a separate note of your passport number and a photocopy of the page that carries your details, in case of loss or theft. You can also scan the relevant pages of your passport and then email them to yourself at an email account that you can access anywhere.

» If you do lose your passport or it is stolen, report it to the police and then contact your nearest embassy or consulate.

POLICE

» There are various types of police officer in France. The two main forces are the Police Nationale, who are under the control of the local mayor, and the Gendarmerie Nationale, who you often see at airports.

» You are likely to encounter the armed CRS riot police only at a demonstration or protest.

» In France, the police have wide powers of stop and search. It is wise to carry your passport in case a police officer stops you and requests your ID.

FIRE

» The French fire brigade deals with a number of emergencies in addition to actual fires. These range from stranded cats to road accidents and gas leaks. They are trained to give first aid.

HEALTH EMERGENCIES
▷ 186–187.

EMBASSIES AND CONSULATES IN PARIS

» Most national embassies are in the capital (see chart). There is no UK consular assistance anywhere in Normandy.

EMERGENCY NUMBERS	
General emergencies	112
Ambulance	15
Police	17
Fire	18
Directory enquiries (national)	118008

EMBASSIES AND CONSULATES IN PARIS		
COUNTRY	**ADDRESS**	**WEBSITE**
Australia	4 rue Jean-Rey, 75724; tel 01 40 59 33 00	www.france.embassy.gov.au
Canada	35 avenue Montaigne, 75008; tel 01 44 43 29 00	www.amb-canada.fr
Germany	13–15 avenue Franklin Roosevelt, 75008; tel 01 53 83 45 00	www.amb-allemagne.fr
Ireland	12 avenue Foch, 75116 tel 01 44 17 67 00	www.embassyofirelandparis.com
Italy	51 rue de Varenne, 75007; tel 01 49 54 03 00	www.amb-italie.fr
Spain	22 avenue Marceau, 75008; tel 01 44 43 18 00	www.amb-espagne.fr
UK	35 rue du Faubourg-St-Honoré, 75008; tel 01 44 51 31 00	www.amb-grandebretagne.fr
US	2 avenue Gabriel, 75008; tel 01 43 12 22 22	www.amb-usa.fr

COMMUNICATION

TELEPHONING

French numbers All numbers in France have 10 digits. The country is divided into five zones, indicated by the first two digits of the number (see chart). You must dial these two digits even if you are calling from within the zone. Numbers in Normandy begin with 02.

International calls To call France from the UK dial 00 33, then drop the first zero from the 10 digit number. To call the UK from France, dial 00 44, then drop the first zero from the area code.

Call charges Numbers beginning with 08 have special rates. 0800 or 0805 numbers are free. 0810 and 0811 numbers are charged at local rate. Other 08 numbers cost more than national calls; the prefixes 0893, 0898 and 0899 are particularly expensive.

PAYPHONES

» Nearly all payphones in France use a card *(télécarte)* rather than coins. You can buy these at post offices, *tabacs*, newsagents and France Telecom shops. Some phones also accept credit cards, although this may make the calls more expensive. You do not need to pay if you are calling an emergency number.

» The phone gives instructions in various languages. If the phone displays the blue bell sign, you can receive incoming calls.

» Phones in restaurants and cafés tend to be more expensive than public payphones. Also, check the rates for hotel phones.

MOBILE PHONES

» Contact your Customer Service department to find out if you have any restrictions on making calls from France and to check the charges.

» Check if you need an access code to listen to your voice mail.

GUIDE TO PRICES

» France Telecom Orange continues to be the default telephone carrier for most people but there are competitors which offer good rates

with no subscription necessary.

» One of the most popular companies is Telerabais (www.telerabais.com). Dial the 0811 number for the company in question and when you are connected enter the phone number (with the country code) you want to speak to followed by the hash-key (#). For the UK and Britain, the Telerabais access number is 0811 31 45 45. Calls are charged at the same rate as for a local call in France.

SENDING A LETTER

» You can buy stamps *(timbres)* for a letter *(lettre)* or a postcard *(carte postale)* at post offices and *tabacs*. Write *par avion* (by air) on the envelope or postcard.

» If you want registered post, ask for the letter to be sent *recommandé*. For a parcel *(colis)*, choose either *prioritaire* (priority) or the slower *économique*.

» Mailboxes are yellow. In larger cities, some have two sections, one for the local *département*, and another for national and international mail *(autres départements/étranger)*. Mail sent from France should take between two and five days to arrive, but can take longer.

POST OFFICES

» Post offices *(bureaux de poste)* are signposted. The postal service is known as La Poste.

» Opening hours are generally Monday to Friday 8–5 or 6, Saturday 8–12. Queues tend to be worst during lunch hours and in the late afternoon.

» Facilities usually include phone booths, photocopiers, fax *(télécopieur)* and access to the Minitel directory. *Poste Restante* services are available for a fee.

INTERNET ACCESS

» Most main towns have Internet cafés. Look for the Cyberposte sign in larger post offices, or see www.cyberposte.com. You buy a card at the counter, which can be recharged if you need more connection time. Certain hotels,

libraries (or *mediathèques*, as they are often called), supermarkets, bars and tourist offices also have internet terminals, many operated by France Telecom using a *télécarte*. Public internet access in France is relatively expensive compared with services in the UK or US.

LAPTOPS

» Most mid-range hotels and above now provide free WiFi internet access. You can connect to the Internet providing this service is supported by your ISP (Internet Service Provider). Remember that you may need a modem plug adaptor

» You may also need a currency convertor. Protect your machine against voltage surges.

COUNTRY CODES FROM FRANCE	
Australia	00 61
Belgium	00 32
Canada	00 1
Germany	00 49
Republic of Ireland	00 353
Italy	00 39
Monaco	00 377
Netherlands	00 31
New Zealand	00 64
Spain	00 34
Sweden	00 46
UK	00 44
US	00 1

PREFIXES	
00	International
01	Île-de-France (including Paris)
02	Northwest France
03	Northeast France
04	Southeast France
05	Southwest France
06	Mobile telephone numbers
0800/0805	Toll-free
08	Special-rate numbers

POSTAGE RATES FOR LETTERS	
Within France	€0.55
To Western Europe	€0.65
Rest of the world	€0.85

TOURIST INFORMATION

TICKETS

» Popular tourist towns, such as Rouen, may provide a reduced-rate pass for entry to the main sights and museums, or packages including free entry to some attractions and accommodation. Some schemes include low-cost transport, a free guided tour, a boat-trip or a *petit-train* ride. Ask the tourist office for details of any inclusive deals, but be realistic about how much use you are likely to make of them.

» Students with an International Student Identity Card (ISIC) and seniors get reduced-price entry at some museums.

» For information on show and concert tickets, see page 197.

TOURIST OFFICES

» France has a complex but generally very efficient tourist information system. At the top end of the scale is the centralised regional office known as Comité Régional de Tourisme. In Normandy, the head office is in Évreux, in Brittany it is in Rennes. These and their subordinate Comités Départemental (one in each *département*) mostly handle postal,

fax or telephone enquiries, some from overseas, rather than face-to-face.

» Visitors are much more likely to have direct contact with the *offices de tourisme* or *syndicats d'initiative* in individual towns and villages, where you can collect all sorts of maps, leaflets and brochures on the attractions of the local area. Just about everywhere you may want to visit in France has some kind of tourist office (often on the main square). If you can't see one, ask at the local *mairie* (town hall).

» A useful document is a *Guide Pratique*, an informative listing of more or less everything a town has to offer from dentists to DIY

shops. Accommodation brochures and public transport timetables are usually published separately, however. Make sure you get the current edition.

» Most promotional information is free, but you may have to pay for guidebooks, detailed touring maps or walks guides. Some brochures are available in English (though occasionally the translation can be more baffling than the *version originale*).

» Tourist offices can book accommodation for you, and sometimes sell tickets for excursions or events. Some have Internet points, or provide exchange facilities.

TOURIST INFORMATION IN NORMANDY		
TOWN/CITY	**TELEPHONE**	**WEBSITE**
Barfleur	02 33 54 02 48	www.ville-barfleur.fr
Bayeux	02 31 51 28 28	www.bayeux-tourisme.com
Caen	02 31 27 14 14	www.caen.fr/tourisme
Cherbourg	02 33 93 52 02	www.ot-cherbourg-cotentin.fr
Deauville	02 31 14 40 00	www.deauville.org
Dieppe	02 32 14 40 60	www.dieppetourisme.com
Giverny	02 32 24 04 48	www.ot-pays-evreux.fr
Honfleur	02 31 89 23 30	www.ot-honfleur.fr
Le Havre	02 32 74 04 04	www.lehavretourisme.com
Rouen	02 32 08 32 40	www.rouentourisme.com

» A sign with a letter 'i' ('information' logo) on it may simply denote a display board with a local map and other information such as hotel listings, rather than an office.

» If you arrive when a tourist office is closed, a local hotel may be able to provide a guide or map of the town, or information leaflets. These are sometimes available at museums or tourist attractions, and passers-by may be only too happy to tell you about their home town.

» Other kinds of tourist office include small seasonal *Points d'Information*, commercially operated *Maisons du Tourisme* and *Pays d'Acceuil Touristiques*, which provide excellent regional information by post or email but are not open to the public.

» If you are travelling through Paris, La Maison de la Bretagne, at 8 rue de l'Arrivée, Paris 75015 (Metro Montparnasse) can help organize your trip.

» The French government tourist offices overseas are generally called Maisons de la France. The UK office is at 178 Piccadilly, London, W1J 9AL (tel 020 7493 6594).

» Useful information in English can be found in the official tourist office site www.normandie-tourisme.fr.

» Increasingly, information for visitors overseas is provided online rather than in printed form (see Websites below).

OPENING TIMES

» Most museums in Normandy are closed on Monday in the off-season and some national museums close on Tuesday. In the high season they are generally open every day, sometimes without closing for lunch. If you are planning to visit a special museum, telephone in advance to check that it is open; sometimes public holidays, festivals or renovation may cause unexpected closures.

» Restaurants generally take at least

one day off a week (often Sunday or Monday), except in high season (July and August), when they stay open longer hours. Except in larger towns, many restaurants close completely from November to Easter. Lunch is generally served from 12–2 or 2.30 and dinner from 7.30–10 or 11. Brasseries may serve food all day.

» Most banks close at noon on the day before a national holiday, as well as on the holiday itself. Usual opening hours are 9–12 and 2–5 but may vary.

» Shops typically open 8am–6.30pm or 7.30pm. On Saturday and Sunday they may open mornings only.

USEFUL WEBSITES

www.aeroport.fr
Information on all of France's airports. (French)

www.fodors.com
A comprehensive travel-planning site that lets you research prices, reserve air tickets and put questions to fellow visitors. (English)

www.franceguide.com
Practical advice from the French Tourist Office on everything from arriving in France to buying a property. The site also has features on holidays and attractions. (French, English, German, Spanish, Italian, Dutch, Portuguese)

www.francetourism.com
The official US website of the French Government Tourist Office. (English)

www.lemonde.fr
Catch up on current events on the site of Le Monde newspaper. (French)

www.meteo.fr/meteonet
Weather forecasts for France. (French, English and Spanish)

www.monum.fr
Find out more about some of France's most historic monuments, on the site of the Centre des Monuments Nationaux. (French and English)

www.pagesjaunes.fr
France's Yellow Pages online. (French and English)

www.radio-france.fr
News, music and sport. (French)

www.theAA.com
The AA website contains a route planner, helpful if you are driving in France. You can also order maps of the country. (English)

www.tourist-office.org
Lists details of tourist information offices in France. (French)

Other websites are listed alongside the relevant sights and towns in the Regions section, and in the On the Move section.

Important ones include:

www.normandy-tourism.org

www.fncrt.com

www.tourisme.fr

www.fco.gov.uk

www.cdt-eure.fr

www.calvados-tourisme.com

www.manchetourisme.com

www.ornetourisme.com

www.seine-maritime-tourisme.com

www.abbayes-normandes.com

MEDIA

TELEVISION

» France has five non-cable television stations, the nationally owned and operated channels 2 and 3, the privately owned 1 and 6, and the Franco-German ARTE (channel 5). Almost all the shows are in French. There are commercials on all channels.

» TF1 has news, recent American and French films, soaps and shows.

» France 2 has news, recent French and foreign films, soaps, shows and documentaries.

» France 3, a regional and national channel, has regional and national news, regional shows, documentaries, mostly French films and, once a week, a film in its original language.

» ARTE is a Franco-German channel with shows in French and German. International films are shown in their original language and there are also cultural documentaries.

» M6 shows a lot of low-budget films and past American sitcoms and soaps. There are also some interesting documentaries.

» Digital television (TNT) has now taken off in France. More than 100 channels are on offer either through satellite or cable.

» If the TV listings mention VO (version originale), the show or film will be in the language in which it was made, with French subtitles (channel 3 usually screens a good VO film every Sunday at around midnight).

» Note that French television channels do not always keep exactly to schedule.

» Many hotels provide a basic cable service; this may include Sky or Eurosport, BBC World and CNN. Cable channels now offer multilingual versions of some shows. Ask at your hotel how to use this option. The commercial-free ARTE usually offers a choice between French and German for its cultural shows.

RADIO

» French radio stations are available mainly on FM wave lengths, with a few international stations on LW. All FM stations are in French. Stations (with their Paris frequencies) include:

» Chérie FM: 91.3 FM; French mainstream pop, news, reports.

» France Infos: 105.5 FM; news bulletins every 15 minutes.

» France Musique: 91.7 FM; classical and jazz music, concerts, operas, news.

» NRJ: 100.3 FM; French and international pop, techno, R'n'B.

» Radio Classique: 101.1 FM; classical music.

» Skyrock: 96 FM; rap, R'n'B.

» BBC Radio 4 198 kHz MW; news, current affairs, drama.

» BBC Five Live 909 kHz MW; news and sport, (reception is patchy in northwestern France).

» BBC World Service 648 kHz LW.

NEWSPAPERS

» In tourist areas and the major cities you can buy the main English dailies, sometimes a day old, at a price premium.

» The Economist, USA Today and The Wall Street Journal can be found at news-stands in cities, along with The European, which presents a pan-European perspective, and the International Herald Tribune, which reports news from a US standpoint.

» Most cities and regions have their own newspapers. In Brittany, you'll find the popular daily Ouest France and the Morlaix-based La Télégramme, plus regional periodicals. Normandy has its own regional paper, Paris-Normandie.

» Leading local newspapers play an active part in pressure politics in their area, though the issues of some may seem parochial to the outsider.

» One of the most widespread chain newsagents is Maison de la Presse, found in virtually every community of any size.

» If you want to find out what's happening in a French city, consult the 'what's on' supplements which are issued with some newspapers.

NEWSPAPERS

French daily newspapers have clear political leanings.

Le Monde
This stately paper, left-of-centre, refuses to run photos and uses illustrations

Libération
This lively youth-focused paper is more clearly leftist

L'Humanité
Left wing

Le Figaro
Mainstream conservative daily

Ouest France
A popular daily newspaper covering Brittany, Lower Normandy and Pays de la Loire

Journal du Dimanche
Sunday newspaper

CABLE TV

Depending on what cable option your hotel has, you may have some of the following channels:

BBC World	A global news service with magazine-style reports
Canal+	Shows recent films (some in the original language)
MTV	Contemporary music channel
MCM	The French version of MTV
Eurosport or Infosport	For major sporting events
Planète	Nature and science documentaries
RAI Uno	Italian
TVE 1	Spanish
Euronews	A European all-news channel
LCI	All news in French
Canal Jimmy	Shows some British and American shows like Friends and NYPD Blue in English or multilingual versions
Paris Première	A cultural channel with some films in English
Canal J	With children's shows until 8pm
Téva	A women's channel that runs English-language shows

» Listings magazines in Normandy include *Rouen's L'Agenda Rouennais* and *Le Cyber Noctambule*. You'll often see these distributed free of charge in tourist offices, music stores, cafés and hotels.

» Weekly news magazines include *Le Nouvel Observateur*, *Le Point* and *L'Express*.

» For TV listings the most popular magazine is *Télérama*.

FILMS AND BOOKS

FILMS

» Watching a French film is a good way to get the feel of the place before you visit.

» For a classic, try *Les Enfants du Paradis* (1945) directed by Marcel Carné. For *nouvelle vague* (new wave) cinema—often filmed with a hand-held camera—try *Jules et Jim* (1962), directed by François Truffaut and starring Jeanne Moreau, or *À Bout de Souffle* (1959), directed by Jean-Luc Godard. The surreal *Belle de Jour* (1967), starring Catherine Deneuve, caused a scandal at the time due to its erotic subject matter. The 1987 weepie *Au Revoir les Enfants* tells the story of a Jewish boy in occupied France in World War II.

» No reference to French movies would be complete without mentioning Gérard Depardieu, the actor who conquered France and then Hollywood. His best-known works include *Cyrano de Bergerac* (1990) and *Jean de Florette* (1986). The sequel to this, *Manon des Sources* (1986), stars a young Emmanuelle Béart, one of France's leading actresses.

» Jean-Pierre Jeunet's *Delicatessen* (1991) turns the controversial subject of cannibalism into a black comedy.

» Two French films of recent years which have enjoyed both critical and box office success are Jean-Pierre's Jeunet's *Amélie* (2001), starring Audrey Tatou, and *La Vie en Rose* (2007) directed by Olivier Dahan, about the life of Edith Piaf. The latter won its leading actress Marion Cotillard the first Oscar given for a performance in French.

Above *A bronze bust of the author Marcel Proust*

» Normandy's lush countryside has inspired many film-makers. *Les Parapluies de Cherbourg*, Jacques Demy's romantic 1964 comedy starring Catherine Deneuve, is an answer to *Singing in the Rain*, still fondly remembered by the umbrella-makers of the Cotentin.

» More familiar in the English-speaking world are Roman Polanski's *Tess*, filmed on location in Normandy and Brittany, *Un Homme et une Femme*, *Jules et Jim* and the unforgettable *Babette's Feast*.

» War-film fans hark back to *The Longest Day*, though Steven Spielberg's more recent take on D-Day, *Saving Private Ryan*, was not actually shot in Normandy due to high production costs.

BOOKS

» Normandy's writers, or adopted writers, read like a roll-call of France's literary giants. From the romantic poets of the Middle Ages such as Robert Wace (*The Romance of the Rose*), through Pierre Corneille (*Le Cid*), to Emile Zola, Guy de Maupassant, Stendhal, Victor Hugo—all have achieved fame.

» A lifelong resident of Rouen, Gustave Flaubert's lasting contribution was *Madame Bovary*, while Marcel Proust penned parts of *À la Recherche du Temps Perdu* in Cabourg.

» Jean-Paul Sartre (*Nausea*) and Simone de Beauvoir both taught at Rouen university.

» For some modern novels, try *Flaubert's Parrot*, by Julian Barnes, a wander by the Seine in Rouen, or *Odo's Hanging*, by Peter Benson, about the creation of the Bayeux Tapestry.

SHOPPING

Normandy is a great destination for modest self-indulgence. Comfort foods are local staples, while the cities and seaside resorts are home to boutiques that sell the top names in fashion to sophisticated holidaymakers.

FOOD AND DRINK

With agriculture ruling much of its countryside, Normandy produces classic fare that has inspired restaurant menus and family meals for centuries. The pastures of Basse-Normandie yield some of the best dairy produce in the world. Cheeses, such as Camembert, Pont-l'Évêque and Livarot, are found in shops across the region. At farm shops and dairies you may be able to find cheese made with unpasteurised milk and taste the product before you buy. Normandy has some little-known goat's cheeses, from the Seine-Maritime, while the region's rich cow's milk is used to make France's finest butter at Isigny-sur-Mer.

Farm shops and farmers' markets are the best places to pick up other specialty foods, such as the *boudin noir* black sausages of the Perche area (▷ 72). Here, you can buy a variety of pâtés. Sées is famous for corn-fed poultry (▷ 73).

Normandy's orchards and apple presses mean that cider is on sale everywhere, along with Calvados (apple brandy) and Pommeau (apple juice fortified with Calvados). The best buys are to be found by following signposts to local producers or by taking official tours of major manufacturers.

In town centres, an '*épicerie fine*' is a quality grocer's store, usually selling food from small producers. A *boulangerie* is a bakery, where *baguettes* are baked several times a day and best eaten straight away. *Brasillés* are loaves made with the local salted butter. A *pâtisserie* is a cake shop and a *chocolatière* makes chocolates. A *boucherie* is a butcher, a *charcuterie* is a delicatessen

and a *poissonerie* sells fish; local favourites include mackerel, herring and oysters.

MODERN STORES

Supermarkets (*hypermarchés*) are found on the outskirts of big towns and cities. Here you find a *boulangerie*, *boucherie*, *charcuterie* and *poissonerie* under one roof, alongside clothes, electrical and household goods. The best-known names are Carrefour, Auchan and E. Leclerc. Smaller supermarkets, such as Intermarché, can be found on the roads leading to minor towns.

MARKETS

The market (*marché*) is a French institution. Large cities have at least one daily market as well as a weekly event, and even the smallest town has a market day, with traders and shoppers coming from outlying villages. These usually start between 7 and 9am and continue until noon, and are good places to find local farm produce. Apple and cheese fairs are held across Normandy, while a *foire artisanale* is a craft fair selling anything from wool to handmade jewellery.

CLOTHES

Knitwear is a Norman tradition. All ports have boutiques selling tailored woollens that appeal to both the boardwalk and catwalk markets. Cotentin even has its own label, the Tricoterie du Val de Saire, which has outlets across the region.

Many individual boutiques survive, selling fashion (*prêt-à-porter*), lingerie and shoes. The fashionable resorts have plenty of designer outlets. Department stores (*grands magasins*) include the big Parisian names, Printemps and Galeries Lafayette.

ART AND ANTIQUES

From roadside junk shops (*brocantes*) to weekend flea markets (*marchés aux puces*), you can still find bargains, such as embroidered vintage bed linen. Antiques shops in larger towns are good for Rouen's blue-and-white crockery and copper utensils. Galleries, especially in the Impressionist country around Honfleur and the Alabaster Coast, promote works by up-and-coming French artists. Country auction houses provide a day's entertainment in their own right.

ENTERTAINMENT AND NIGHTLIFE

Normandy may be best known for its rural pleasures, but it also celebrates the arts. Shows range from café-théâtre in Caen to *son et lumière* in remote ruined abbeys, summer arts festivals by the sea and opera in chateau gardens. Pick up a free local listings guide. Nightlife in Normandy invariably involves a drink, and so tends to blossom around the café and bar culture. Since clubs, concerts, cabarets and casinos don't get going until late, it is customary to start any evening, whether sporting or cultural, with a visit to a local bar.

THEATRE AND CINEMA

You will find theatres in most major cities, as well as in a surprising number of smaller towns. Normandy has several *scènes nationale* (national theatre stages), ranging from 19th-century Italianate playhouses to modern arts centres. Programmes vary from touring productions to in-house pieces, and from classical works to experimental performance art. A diverse mix of music, dance and children's entertainment may all be enjoyed. As well as a main playhouse, university towns host a number of alternative venues, from *café-théâtre* to outdoor spaces, where fringe shows are staged throughout the year. In rural areas, principal theatres often double as cinemas.

Most cities have a choice of traditional cinemas in their centre and modern multiplex options on their outskirts. The majority of foreign films will be dubbed into French (marked as 'VF' in listings), but in university towns you will often find American or British movies screened in the original language, with French subtitles ('VO' in listings).

MUSIC

Normandy has a constant musical soundtrack. From the springtime jazz festival in the orchards of the Cotentin to the mellow sounds of a city centre jazz club in winter, you can find music wherever you go. Large-scale dance productions and big-name rock concerts are staged at arenas such as Caen's Zénith, while lesser-known musicians can be discovered performing in bars everywhere. At seaside resorts, casinos have cabaret.

The former railway station at Louviers, in Eure, is now La Gare aux Musiques, a venue for performances by up-and-coming musicians, while the Brasserie Hotteterre in La Couture-Boussey, Eure, is a great spot for enjoying live music and tasting the local brew at the same time. The opening of the gardens at Champ-de-Bataille in summer 2005 saw grand opera staged in the grounds of the chateau.

Festivals provide the ideal opportunity to enjoy music in characteristic places. Deauville's swing season in July is among the biggest events, but even country food fairs provide an excuse for live music in the open air. On 21 June (or the nearest Saturday night to that date), France's national music day inspires concerts, informal jam sessions and busking in towns and villages. For a weekly waterside party, discover the tradition of the *guinguette*: On Sundays, lunch segues into evening with families taking to the dance floor, as accordions or bands play favourite tunes in a bar on the banks of the Eure, the Orne or the Seine. Some *guinguettes* open for evenings during the week.

BOOKING TICKETS

Theatre box offices are open during normal working hours through the week, and should take credit card bookings. Fnac music shops in Caen, Le Havre and Rouen (www.fnac.com) and the Virgin Megastore in Rouen (www.virginmega.fr) have in-store and on-line booking agencies handling all high-profile events. For festival information and bookings, enquire at local tourist offices.

ETIQUETTE

The French dress smartly for the theatre, even though formal wear is rarely seen outside opera premieres. Festivals are informal, but beach attire is frowned upon at evening events. Women and men should dress appropriately for concerts held in a church.

In theatres and cinemas, if an attendant escorts you to your seat,

PRACTICALITIES WHAT TO DO

197

a *pourboire* (tip) of small change is expected.

SMOKING

Smoking is now forbidden by law in all public arenas including theatres and cinemas but smaller, informal venues may be smoky. Smokers are required to go out into the street if they want to light up in public places.

CAFÉ-BARS

Night and day, the café-bar is the hub of French social life. Even the smallest village will have at least one bar where the locals gather to gossip, watch sport on TV, and have a few drinks. In the country, a single bar will be the hang-out for pool-playing teenagers, a rendezvous for cloth-capped pensioners and a refuge for farmers sharing conspiracy theories about politicians.

In cities, each crowd chooses its own bar, and there are favourite places for an early- morning coffee, an aperitif or a late-night tipple. A PMU bar is part of the French tote system, where television screens show horse-racing and the barman will take bets on the race. In contrast, cafés come into their own with the pleasures of a well-chosen table on the terrace. Drinks are sometimes slightly more expensive when served outside rather than at the bar—notices in the window will indicate both prices.

While the country café may switch on a mirror ball and disco lights for an evening's karaoke, the scene in town is much more varied. In many cases, the line between bar and club culture is blurred. Latin and salsa venues in Le Havre attract the tequila, tapas and tango set, while bars in Évreux offer a round-midnight choice of live music or a DJ.

Bars in cities may open early at around 7am for breakfast and may close as late as 2am. In the countryside and the off-season, however, they may close by 9pm. The legal age for drinking is 16 and unaccompanied minors are not allowed in bars. Youngsters aged 14–16 may drink wine or beer if accompanied by an adult.

NIGHTCLUBS

Most cities and resorts have a busy club scene, with several establishments to suit different tastes. In the more rural areas, you may find just one venue, often with a choice of dance floors to cater for the young crowd and the over-30s. While retro nights are very popular, hip-hop and techno tend to be played more commonly.

Clubs open sometime after 10.30pm, but they do not fill up until the bars close after 1am. Most venues stay open until dawn. Midweek admission is often free, while weekends usually bring a door charge of €10–15. Many offer discounted or free entry to women and students, but when there is a charge the ticket usually includes your first drink at the bar. Drinks in clubs are expensive compared to café-bars. In Rouen and Caen, 'after clubs' open at weekends from around 6 or 7am until 9.30am and offer a mellower music policy to round off the night. You will find flyers advertising these venues in boutiques, trendy bars and tourist offices.

GAY AND LESBIAN CLUBS

There is a lively gay club scene in Le Havre and Rouen, with venues proving just as popular with young straight partygoers. Caen and Cherbourg have a choice of gay bars and Caen's Club Escapades offers gay sporting and social events. There are also gay-friendly venues in Alençon and Évreux. Monthly listings are posted at www.gaynormandie.com.

CASINOS

Casinos are venues for various entertainment, from cabaret to good dining. You should dress well, but there is no need to lose your shirt; the price of admission gains you a handful of non-refundable chips. Some casinos offer a choice of English or American roulette; the odds are slightly better at the English table. Doors tend to open around 10pm and close in the small hours.

CABARET

The sequinned showgirl revue is staple entertainment at the dinner theatre rooms of the seaside casinos. Do not expect the scale of Parisian shows, but few conclude without the traditional cancan. Smaller piano bars at casinos offer more intimate entertainment.

BOWLING

Ten-pin bowling is a popular night out in Normandy. Most bowling alleys offer dinner then a session on the lanes. Book ahead at weekends.

SPORTS AND ACTIVITIES

Normandy has a great deal to offer outdoors. The coastline provides an excellent setting for wind and water sports, and horseback-riding and cycling are ideal ways of seeing the countryside. Leisure options ranging from ice-skating to go-karting burn up excess energy, while municipal sports centres in most towns house swimming pools *(piscines)*, tennis courts and other facilities at reasonable prices. For more information, visit a local tourist office (▷ 192–193). Free guides listing sporting activities are published in each district.

HIKING AND CYCLING
Normandy's countryside is ideal for walkers, who can hike along sections of the coastline or explore such regions as the Parc Naturel Régional Normandie-Maine (▷ 73). The region is marked with a wide range of Sentiers de Grandes Randonnées (long distance) and Petites Randonnées (shorter) hiking trails, which are indicated on maps published by the Institut Géographique National (www.ign. fr). You can also find topographical guides at tourist offices and in park bookstores. In addition to these routes for serious walkers, local *mairies* (town halls) and tourist offices can provide information on their own marked trails along cliffs and through woodland. The Comité Régional de la Randonnée Pédestre in Basse Normandie (tel 02 33 55 34 30) and the Fédération Française de Randonnée Pédestre (www.ffrp. asso.fr) produce specific updated information for walkers. You can also opt to *randonnée avec âne*—travel with a donkey, loading your kit in the panniers; for more information, check with the local tourist office.

Details of VTT (mountain bike) trails are available from tourist offices, many of which can also arrange bicycle rental. In July, France's leading sporting event, the Tour de France, often passes through the region—discover the route in advance at www.letour. fr and find a spot by the roadside to watch the race and enjoy the associated carnival-style roadshow.

FISHING
Hire a boat to fish the Cotentin seaboard and Alabaster Coast, or enjoy angling from the river banks. You need a permit from a tackle shop to fish privately owned stretches of rivers and *étangs* (lakes). *Départements* produce free guides to fishing.

GOLF
Normandy has an ideal climate for golf, and there are courses across the region, some with fitness centres, clifftop views, and chateaux; 37 courses are open year-round, 23 of them with 18 holes. In Calvados, you can buy a pass accessing all the region's courses.

HORSEBACK-RIDING
Le Haras National du Pin (▷ 72) and Le Haras de Préaux are two breeding stables that have won Normandy worldwide fame. Many stables are open to the public, and riding lessons and hacks are widely offered. Information can be obtained through the website of the Fédération Française d'Equitation (www.ffe.com).

WATER SPORTS
Sailing can be enjoyed from the ports and marinas along the Norman coastline—there are sailing schools *(écoles de voile)* and boatyards hiring dinghies and motorboats from Le Havre to Granville. Inland, you can go boating on the lakes of the Léry-Poses basin, southeast of Rouen in Eure, and canoe or kayak on rivers. For simpler routes, canoes or kayaks may be hired by the hour or half-day; longer itineraries often require a guide.

ADVENTURE SPORTS
Acrobranching (swinging through the trees) and paint-balling are among the treats on offer in the region's forests. There are also go-karting tracks outside major towns, and air and wind sports, such as sand yachting, can be tried along the beaches. Rock climbing and abseiling is also organized.

HEALTH AND BEAUTY
The French adore spas and health treatments derived from mineral springs and sea water. The belle époque Bagnoles-de-l'Orne, in a lakeside setting, is the biggest spa in western France, attracting 12,000 visitors a year to the spring, with its 24°C (75°F) waters. The spa season runs from mid-March to the end of October, while the winter months herald 'get back into shape' deals. Thalassotherapy sea-water treatments at resort hotels use the natural minerals in mud and seaweed. Resorts create a package centred around the basic treatment, with massage, water jets, sauna and steam baths as standard.

FOR CHILDREN

Normandy has plenty to keep children entertained, whether the traditional treats of the seaside or the option of activity centres and theme parks. There are also plenty of outdoor choices, from horseback-riding to bicycle trails. The emphasis throughout is on having fun as a family, rather than segregating kids and adults.

FAMILY ACTIVITIES

A lot of family fun may be had on Normandy's railways. Vintage trains run through scenic countryside in high season, miniature trains tour local country circuits and rail bike four-seater contraptions can be pedalled along genuine railway track through the Suisse Normande area. Normandy's agricultural tradition ensures that there are plenty of farms where children can observe cheese-making and other techniques and often meet the animals at the same time. Go-karting tracks, Cherbourg's ice-skating rink, water parks and ten-pin bowling are also all bound to keep the active family happy.

ADVENTURE PARKS, THEME PARKS AND ZOOS

Woodland adventure parks have discovery and activity trails adapted for various age groups and abilities, so that teenagers and younger children are able to explore according to their own abilities. Normandy's theme park, Festyland, at Bretteville-sur-Odon on the outskirts of Caen, has the roller-coasters and side-shows that children expect, but the theme here is Normandy's heritage, with William the Conqueror, the Vikings and other periods of local history marking out the rides and restaurants. There are also several zoos and animal parks in the region, whose occupants range from local farm breeds to more exotic species from abroad.

FESTIVALS AND EVENTS

Hundreds of events fill Normandy's festive calendar, many of them centred around food. Even the first major jazz event of the year, Jazz Sous les Pommiers, is scented with the springtime apple blossom of the Calvados orchards of Coutances.

TRADITION AND RELIGION

Joan of Arc is remembered each May in Rouen, the city of her trial and martyrdom, with a medieval market and other events. Every five years, the city also hosts its famous l'Armada, a gathering of tall ships and their crews from around the world as the Seine relives the golden age of sail; the next l'Armada is planned for summer 2013.

Also on a nautical theme, spring and summer each year bring traditional blessing ceremonies for smaller boats in fishing ports such as Honfleur and Étretat.

Christmas sees markets in the old town of Rouen and in smaller centres around the region, some of them staging nativity scenes, with villagers and farm animals re-creating Bethlehem. December brings the annual poultry fair to Sées, where people from miles away travel to choose their Christmas turkey.

ARTS

Normandy has a love of film, and several small festivals dedicated to the medium are staged during the year. Various events celebrate Asian and British cinema, but best known is Deauville's September American Film Festival, which attracts the biggest names in Hollywood to the Norman seaside.

Summer music events range from July's celebration of the big-band sound at Deauville to the concerts on the island of Tatihou in August.

FOOD AND DRINK

Cheese fairs in spring and summer, and grand apple and cider festivals throughout the autumn harvest season, are Normandy's best-known food events. The *boudin blanc* sausage is honoured in Mortagne-au-Perche and herrings and scallops are fêted along the coast. The second weekend of September sees the Automne Gourmande gathering of chefs and farmers at Bagnoles-de-l'Orne, with gourmet workshops and tastings as the town becomes a *bistrot des chefs* (tourist office tel 02 33 37 85 66).

EATING

Food fads may come and go, but this is a region where hearty eating has never fallen out of fashion. Normandy even has its own way of helping you squeeze in a bit more—the *trou normand* (literally 'Norman hole'), taken to clear the digestive system. Traditionally a shot of potent farmhouse Calvados, the *trou* is now often an alcoholic sorbet or granita.

THE FLAVOURS OF NORMANDY

'Although I did not realize it at the time, it was by way of Norman cookery that I first learned to appreciate French food.' So said Elizabeth David, one of many visitors seduced by Normandy's *crème fraîche* and *beurre d'Isigny*, its rich cheeses, coarse *rillette* pâtés and Mont-St-Michel omelettes. Fresh fish and farmyard fare dominate menus across the region, with cream and apples in most dishes. The same fruit used to make cider, Pommeau and Calvados often accompany meat dishes and appear in the ubiquitous *tarte tatin* apple tart. The cheeseboard is a key course. Camembert, Livarot and Pont-l'Évêque are served with every meal.

Each corner of Normandy has its own special dishes. Normans declare that they could be led blindfolded around the region and know each place by its food: tripe in Caen, *andouille* sausage in Vire, sole in Dieppe and the distinctive flavour of the lamb and mutton reared on the salty pastures around the bay of Mont-St-Michel.

WHERE TO EAT

Cafés, bars, brasseries, bistros and restaurants make up a confusing array of establishments, each with its own rules and traditions. Many cafés and bars will offer a *plat du jour* lunch, which is less expensive than a restaurant, and an excellent way of enjoying unpretentious home cooking.

Bistros offer a choice of simple country dishes, cooked from old family recipes, and again provide good value with their set menus. Brasseries are a half-way point between the informality of the bistro and the formality of a restaurant. They may be more flexible about opening hours. Restaurants themselves range from simple or specialist tables to grander gastronomic establishments.

MENUS

Restaurants typically offer the choice of dining *à la carte* or opting for a set menu. The set menu, or *prix fixe*, has a selection of two or three courses at a fixed price. At the top end of the scale is the *menu dégustation*, or *menu*

gastronomique, which may cost anything from €33 to €90.

The daily specials *(plats du jour)* will usually make use of the freshest seasonal ingredients. The best-value set menus are served midweek lunchtimes only, and are a good way of sampling food at top restaurants without going over budget.

WHAT TO DRINK

When choosing a wine, be guided by your waiter. Waiters in France are professionals and will be adept at selecting the best accompaniment to your meal. Let the waiter know your budget, and always consider the house wines, as in a good establishment these should reflect the taste of the restaurateur. If you are dining on traditional country food in a bistro, try a farmhouse cider.

WHEN TO EAT

Restaurant opening hours in Normandy are generally from noon to 2.30pm for lunch and from 7.30pm in the evening for dinner. However, in quiet rural areas out of season, arrivals after 1.30pm for lunch or 9pm in the evening may sometimes

MENU READER

COOKING STYLES
...à la Deauvillaise a cream and onion sauce, served with white fish
...à la meunière a method of serving fish, which is panfried and topped with butter, lemon juice and parsley
...à la Normande a white sauce made with crème fraîche, served with variety of dishes

MEATS AND POULTRY
agneau lamb
andouille de Vire lightly smoked chitterling sausage
boeuf beef
boudin black sausage from Mortagne-au-Perche
canard duck
caneton duckling
dinde turkey
jambon ham
lapin rabbit
lardons bacon pieces
lièvre hare
oie goose
porc pork
poulet roast chicken
poussin baby chicken
pré-salé lamb reared on the salt marshes of Mont-St-Michel
sanglier wild boar
veau veal
venaison venison
volaille chicken

FISH
bar sea bass
brochet pike
cabillaud cod
carpe carp
carrelet plaice
coquilles St-Jacques scallops
crabe crab
crevettes shrimps or prawns
fruits de mer seafood
hareng herring
homard lobster, best from Barfleur or la Hague
huîtres oysters
maquereaux mackerel
moules mussels
palourdes clams
raie skate
rouget red mullet
sole sole
truite trout
turbot turbot

SAVOURY DISHES
caneton à la Rouennais pressed duckling (▷ 15)
côtes de porc vallée d'Auge pork cutlets fried in butter, then flambéed with Calvados and served with a cider sauce
escalopes Cauchoise veal with cream, apples and Calvados
faisan à la Cauchoise roast pheasant flambéed in Calvados and served with sautéed apples
marmite Diéppoise a fish stew

poule au pot stewed chicken
poulet vallée d'Auge chicken in a cream and onion sauce
sole à la Diéppoise sole with white wine and seafood
sole en Matelote sole cooked in cider with mussels
tripes à la mode de Caen tripe cooked with cows' hooves, cider, Calvados and stock

DESSERTS
pommes au beurre slices of apple fried in sugar and butter
tarte aux pommes apple tart
tarte tatin upside-down tart
tergoule rice pudding

DAIRY PRODUCTS
beurre d'Isigny the finest butter in France (▷ 15)
Camembert the round creamy cheese sold from farmhouses
crème fraîche the other famed product of Isigny is a rich cream, sold in tubs or ladled from bowls
fromage frais young farmhouse cream cheese, often eaten as a yoghurt-style dessert with sugar
Livarot strong smelling and recognizable by its straw bands
Neufchâtel eaten within a fortnight of being made or as a three month-old mature variety
Pont-l'Évêque farmhouse cheese of the Pays d'Auge

be turned away. Conversely, people may dine later in resorts during the summer. It is always advisable to reserve a table in advance. Since the introduction of the 35-hour working week, some restaurateurs have been flexible with their opening hours, closing early on Monday to Friday to accommodate weekend demand. Many establishments also close Saturday and Monday lunchtimes and Sunday evenings.

DINING ETIQUETTE
» Dress smartly if dining in a gastronomic restaurant. A meal is treated as a special event in such places, and dressing well shows respect for the food, the establishment and other diners.
» Switch off mobile phones in smart restaurants.
» Address serving staff as Monsieur, Madame or Mademoiselle.
» Smoking is banned in bars and restaurants.
» Service charges are now included in the price listed on the menu, so the traditional 10–15 per cent tip is no longer expected.

VEGETARIAN FOOD
Normandy is not the most enlightened corner of France when it comes to vegetarian options. In towns and resorts, ethnic North African and Asian restaurants, chains such as Bistrot Romain and pizzerias are the best bets for meat-free meals.

From chateau luxury to simple country hospitality, Normandy has a welcome for all visitors whatever their budget, inland or along the coast. Norman hotels in are inspected and categorised with a nationally approved star rating, ranging from four stars at the top end, down to no stars for the most basic. Arguably the most authentic taste of Norman life comes through the *chambre d'hôte* (bed-and-breakfast) experience.

PRICING

Detailed prices are posted in the front windows of hotels and are always quoted per room and not per person, except in the case of full- or half-board accommodation, when the price is per guest. Smoking in not allowed in hotels.

LUXURY

Normandy's most luxurious hotels are deep in the countryside, around the Côte d'Albâtre (▷ 166–167) and in the Orne. Here you will find gastronomic treats in the restaurant. Pampering of a different sort is to be enjoyed at coastal or spa resorts.

MID-RANGE

In the middle price range are comfortable city-centre hotels, often air-conditioned in summer, and traditional seafront hotels. Inns and family-run hotels bearing the Logis de France symbol (www. logis-de-france.fr) are independent establishments renowned for their hospitality and home-cooked meals. All Logis are regularly inspected and are of a high standard. Some offer themed fishing and hiking packages.

ON A BUDGET

Chain hotels and motels are the least expensive touring option, offering basic rooms at the lowest prices. But they do not reflect the character of the region. Simple one-star hotels, often close to railway stations, can be good value if you overlook dated décor. Youth hostels *(auberges de jeunesse)* are open to visitors of all ages, provided that they are members of the Youth Hostelling Federation of their home country. Discover more online at www.fuaj.org.

BON WEEKEND

The Beaux Weekends promotion gives you two nights' accommodation for the price of one on Fridays and Saturdays at a range of hotels, together with two-for-one discounts at local visitor sights and attractions. You have to reserve your hotel through the tourist office at Le Havre.

BED-AND-BREAKFAST

While many roadside signs advertise *chambre d'hôte*, it is best to select one through the Gîtes de France organization (see below). You can stay in a farmhouse or a watermill, a converted barn or manor house. Rooms often have ensuite facilities. Breakfast will include a home-made element, such as fresh-baked bread. Many establishments are situated in rural locations and *table d'hôte* evening meals may also be offered, when you dine with the family at a very low price.

SELF-CATERING

Purpose-built holiday homes, ranging from resort complexes in towns such as Deauville to basic VVF holiday parks, are widely availble. However, the Gîtes de France organization (www.gites-de-france.fr) offers a more authentic local flavour. Note that linens and towels are rarely supplied in French self-catering properties.

CAMPSITES

Camping and caravanning are part of French life. Excellent sites where you can pitch your own van or tent, or rent tents, chalets or static caravans, are found across the region. Regional tourist offices supply listings brochures. Book in advance in summer. Sites may close in winter. Do not park motorhomes by the roadside or on beaches, and note that casual camping may be forbidden.

WORDS AND PHRASES

Even if you're far from fluent, it is always a good idea to try to speak a few words of French while in Normandy. The words and phrases on the following pages should help you with the basics, from ordering a meal to dealing with emergencies.

CONVERSATION

What is the time?
Quelle heure est-il?
When do you open/close?
A quelle heure ouvrez/fermez-vous?
I don't speak French.
Je ne parle pas français.
Do you speak English?
Parlez-vous anglais?
I don't understand.
Je ne comprends pas.
Please repeat that.
Pouvez-vous répéter (s'il vous plaît)?
Please speak more slowly.
Pouvez-vous parler plus lentement?
What does this mean?
Qu'est-ce que ça veut dire?
Write that down for me please.
Pouvez-vous me l'écrire, s'il vous plaît?
Please spell that.
Pouvez-vous me l'épeler, s'il vous plaît?
I'll look that up (in the dictionary).
Je vais le chercher (dans le dictionnaire).
My name is...
Je m'appelle...
What's your name?
Comment vous appelez-vous?
This is my wife/husband.
Voici ma femme/mon mari.
This is my daughter/son.
Voici ma fille/mon fils.
This is my friend.
Voici mon ami(e).
Hello, pleased to meet you.
Bonjour, enchanté(e).
I'm from ...
Je viens de ...
I'm on holiday.
Je suis en vacances.
I live in ...
J'habite à ..

Where do you live?
Où habitez-vous?
Good morning.
Bonjour.
Good evening.
Bonsoir.
Goodnight.
Bonne nuit.
Goodbye.
Au revoir.
See you later.
A plus tard.
How much is that?
C'est combien?
May I/Can I?
Est-ce que je peux?
I don't know.
Je ne sais pas.
You're welcome.
Je vous en prie.
How are you?
Comment allez-vous?
I'm sorry.
Je suis désolé(e).
Excuse me.
Excusez-moi.
That's all right.
De rien.

USEFUL WORDS

Yes..Oui
No..Non
There.....................................Là-bas
Here...Ici
Where..Où
Who..Qui
When...............................Quand
Why................................Pourquoi
How...............................Comment
Later...............................Plus tard
Now.........................Maintenant
Open...............................Ouvert
Closed..............................Fermé
Please.......................S'il vous plaît
Thank you...........................Merci

SHOPPING

Could you help me, please?
(Est-ce que) vous pouvez m'aider, s'il vous plaît?
How much is this?
C'est combien?/Ça coûte combien?

I'm looking for ...
Je cherche ...
When does the shop open/close?
A quelle heure ouvre/ferme le magasin?
I'm just looking, thank you.
Je regarde, merci.
This isn't what I want.
Ce n'est pas ce que je veux.
This is the right size.
C'est la bonne taille.
Do you have anything less expensive/smaller/larger?
(Est-ce que) vous avez quelque chose de moins cher/plus petit/plus grand?
I'll take this.
Je prends ça.
Do you have a bag for this, please?
(Est-ce que) je peux avoir un sac, s'il vous plaît?
Do you accept credit cards?
(Est-ce que) vous acceptez les cartes de crédit?
I'd like ... grams please.
Je voudrais ... grammes, s'il vous plaît.
I'd like a kilo of ...
Je voudrais un kilo de ...
What does this contain?
Quels sont les ingrédients?/ Qu'est-ce qu'il y a dedans?
I'd like ... slices of that.
J'en voudrais ... tranches.
Bakery
Boulangerie
Bookshop
Librairie
Chemist
Pharmacie
Supermarket
Supermarché
Market
Marché
Sale
Soldes

NUMBERS

1	un
2	deux
3	trois
4	quatre
5	cinq
6	six
7	sept
8	huit
9	neuf
10	dix
11	onze
12	douze
13	treize
14	quatorze
15	quinze
16	seize
17	dix-sept
18	dix-huit
19	dix-neuf
20	vingt
21	vingt et un
30	trente
40	quarante
50	cinquante
60	soixante
70	soixante-dix
80	quatre-vingts
90	quatre-vingt dix
100	cent
1000	mille

POST AND TELEPHONES

Where is the nearest post office/ mail box?
Où se trouve la poste/la boîte aux lettres la plus proche?

How much is the postage to...?
A combien faut-il affranchir pour...?

I'd like to send this by air mail/ registered mail.
Je voudrais envoyer ceci par avion/ en recommandé.

Can you direct me to a public phone?
Pouvez-vous m'indiquer la cabine téléphonique la plus proche?

What is the number for directory enquiries?
Quel est le numéro pour les renseignements?

Where can I find a telephone directory?
Où est-ce que je peux trouver un annuaire?

Where can I buy a phone card?
Où est-ce que je peux acheter une télécarte?

Please put me through to...
Pouvez-vous me passer..., s'il vous plaît?

Can I dial direct to...?
Est-ce que je peux appeler directement en...?

Do I need to dial 0 first?
Est-ce qu'il faut composer le zéro (d'abord)?

What is the charge per minute?
Quel est le tarif à la minute?

Have there been any calls for me?
Est-ce que j'ai eu des appels téléphoniques?

Hello, this is...
Allô, c'est... (à l'appareil)?

Who is speaking please...?
Qui est à l'appareil, s'il vous plaît?

I would like to speak to...
Je voudrais parler à …

DAYS/MONTHS/HOLIDAYS/TIMES

Monday	lundi
Tuesday	mardi
Wednesday	mercredi
Thursday	jeudi
Friday	vendredi
Saturday	samedi
Sunday	dimanche
January	janvier
February	février
March	mars
April	avril
May	mai
June	juin
July	juillet
August	août
September	septembre
October	octobre
November	novembre
December	décembre
spring	printemps
summer	été
autumn	automne
winter	hiver
holiday	vacances
Easter	Pâques
Christmas	Noël
morning	matin
afternoon	après-midi
evening	soir
night	nuit
today	aujourd'hui
yesterday	hier
tomorrow	demain
day	le jour
month	le mois
year	l'année

HOTELS

Do you have a room?
(Est-ce que) vous avez une chambre?

I have a reservation for... nights.
J'ai réservé pour... nuits.

How much each night?
C'est combien par nuit?

Double room.
Une chambre pour deux personnes/ double.

Twin room.
Une chambre à deux lits/avec lits jumeaux.

Single room.
Une chambre à un lit/pour une personne.

With bath/shower/lavatory.
Avec salle de bain/douche/WC.

Is the room air-conditioned/ heated?
(Est-ce que) la chambre est climatisée/chauffée?

Is breakfast/lunch/dinner included in the cost?
(Est-ce que) le petit déjeuner/le déjeuner/le dîner est compris dans le prix?

Is there a lift in the hotel?
(Est-ce qu') il y a un ascenseur à l'hôtel?

Is room service available?
(Est-ce qu') il y a le service en chambre?

When do you serve breakfast?
À quelle heure servez-vous le petit déjeuner?

May I have breakfast in my room?
(Est-ce que) je peux prendre le petit déjeuner dans ma chambre?

Do you serve evening meals?
(Est-ce que) vous servez le repas du soir/le dîner?

I need an alarm call at...
Je voudrais être réveillé(e) à... heures.

I'd like an extra blanket/pillow.
Je voudrais une couverture/un oreiller supplémentaire, s'il vous plaît.

May I have my room key?
(Est-ce que) je peux avoir la clé de ma chambre?

Will you look after my luggage until I leave?
Pouvez-vous garder mes bagages jusqu'à mon départ?

Is there parking?
(Est-ce qu') il y a un parking?

Where can I park my car?
Où est-ce que je peux garer ma voiture?

Do you have babysitters?
(Est-ce que) vous avez un service de babysitting/garde d'enfants?

When are the sheets changed?
Quand changez-vous les draps?

The room is too hot/cold.
Il fait trop chaud/froid dans la chambre.

Could I have another room?
(Est-ce que) je pourrais avoir une autre chambre?

I am leaving this morning.
Je pars ce matin.

What time should we leave our room?
A quelle heure devons-nous libérer la chambre?

Can I pay my bill?
(Est-ce que) je peux régler ma note, s'il vous plaît?

May I see the room?
(Est-ce que) je peux voir la chambre?

Swimming pool.
Piscine.

No smoking.
Non fumeur.

Sea view.
Vue sur la mer.

GETTING AROUND

Where is the information desk?
Où est le bureau des renseignements?

Where is the timetable?
Où sont les horaires?

Does this train/bus go to...?
Ce train/bus va à ?

Do you have a Métro/bus map?
Avez-vous un plan du Métro/des lignes de bus?

Please can I have a single/return ticket to...?
Je voudrais un aller simple/ un aller-retour pour..., s'il vous plaît.

I'd like to rent a car.
Je voudrais louer une voiture.

Where are we?
Où sommes-nous?

I'm lost.
Je me suis perdu(e).

Is this the way to...?
C'est bien par ici pour aller à...?

I am in a hurry.
Je suis pressé(e).

Where can I find a taxi?
Où est-ce que je peux trouver un taxi?

How much is the journey?
Combien coûte la course?

Go straight on.
Allez tout droit.

Turn left.
Tournez à gauche.

Turn right.
Tournez à droite.

Cross over.
Traversez.

Traffic lights.
Les feux.

Intersection.
Carrefour.

Corner.
Coin.

No parking.
Interdiction de stationner

Train/bus/Métro station
La gare SNCF/routière/la station de Métro.

Do you sell travel cards?
Avez-vous des cartes d'abonnement?

Do I need to get off here?
(Est-ce qu') il faut que je descende ici?

Where can I buy a ticket?
Où est-ce que je peux acheter un billet/ticket?

Where can I reserve a seat?
Où est-ce que je peux réserver une place?

Is this seat free?
(Est-ce que) cette place est libre?

Where can I find a taxi?
Où est-ce que je peux trouver un taxi?

MONEY

Is there a bank/currency exchange office nearby?
(Est-ce qu') il y a une banque/un bureau de change près d'ici?

Can I cash this here?
(Est-ce que) je peux encaisser ça ici?

I'd like to change sterling/ dollars into euros.
Je voudrais changer des livres sterling/dollars en euros.

Can I use my credit card to withdraw cash?
(Est-ce que) je peux utiliser ma carte de crédit pour retirer de l'argent?

What is the exchange rate today?
Quel est le taux de change aujourd'hui?

COLOURS
brown ....marron/brun
black.................................. noir(e)
red .... rouge
blue ....bleu(e)
green................................. vert(e)
yellow ....jaune

RESTAURANTS
I'd like to reserve a table for... people at...
Je voudrais réserver une table pour ...personnes à...heures, s'il vous plaît.

A table for ..., please.
Une table pour ..., s'il vous plaît.

We have/haven't booked.
Nous avons/n'avons pas réservé.

What time does the restaurant open?
A quelle heure ouvre le restaurant?

We'd like to wait for a table.
Nous aimerions attendre qu'une table se libère.

Could we sit there?
(Est-ce que) nous pouvons nous asseoir ici?

Is this table taken?
(Est-ce que) cette table est libre?

Are there tables outside?
(Est-ce qu') il y a des tables dehors/à la terrasse?

Where are the lavatories?
Où sont les toilettes?

Could you warm this up for me?
(Est-ce que) vous pouvez me faire réchauffer ceci/ça, s'il vous plaît?

Do you have nappy-changing facilities?
(Est-ce qu') Il y a une pièce pour changer les bébés?

We'd like something to drink.
Nous voudrions quelque chose à boire.

Could we see the menu/wine list?
(Est-ce que) nous pouvons voir le menu/la carte des vins, s'il vous plaît?

Is there a dish of the day?
(Est-ce qu') il y a un plat du jour?

What do you recommend?
Qu'est-ce que vous nous conseillez?

This is not what I ordered.
Ce n'est pas ce que j'ai commandé.

I can't eat wheat/sugar/salt/ pork/beef/dairy.
Je ne peux pas manger de blé/sucre/ sel/porc/bœuf/produits laitiers.

I am a vegetarian.
Je suis végétarien(ne).

I'd like…
Je voudrais…

Could we have some more bread?
(Est-ce que) vous pouvez nous apporter un peu plus de pain, s'il vous plaît?

How much is this dish?
Combien coûte ce plat?

Is service included?
(Est-ce que) le service est compris?

Could we have some salt and pepper?
(Est-ce que) vous pouvez nous apporter du sel et du poivre, s'il vous plaît?

May I have an ashtray?
(Est-ce que) je peux avoir un cendrier, s'il vous plaît?

Could I have bottled still/ sparkling water?
(Est-ce que) je peux avoir une bouteille d'eau minérale/gazeuse, s'il vous plaît?

The meat is too rare/overcooked.
La viande est trop saignante/trop cuite.

The food is cold.
La nourriture est froide.

Can I have the bill, please?
(Est-ce que) je peux avoir l'addition, s'il vous plaît?

The bill is not right.
Il y a une erreur sur l'addition.

We didn't order this.
Nous n'avons pas commandé ça.

I'd like to speak to the manager, please.
Je voudrais parler au directeur, s'il vous plaît.

The food was excellent.
La nourriture était excellente.

FOOD AND DRINK
Breakfast
Petit déjeuner
Lunch
Déjeuner
Dinner
Dîner
Coffee
Café
Tea
Thé
Orange juice
Jus d'orange
Apple juice
Jus de pomme
Milk
Lait
Beer
Bière
Red wine
Vin rouge
White wine
Vin blanc
Bread roll
Petit pain
Bread
Pain
Sugar
Sucre
Wine list
Carte/liste des vins
Main course
Le plat principal
Dessert
Dessert
Salt/pepper
Sel/poivre
Cheese
Fromage
Knife/fork/spoon
Couteau/Fourchette/Cuillère
Soups
Soupes/potages
Vegetable soup
Soupe de légumes
Chicken soup
Soupe au poulet
Lentil soup
Soupe aux lentilles

Mushroom soup
Soupe aux champignons
Sandwiches
Sandwichs
Ham sandwich
Sandwich du jambon
Dish of the day
Plat du jour
Fish dishes
Les poissons
Prawns
Crevettes roses/bouquet
Oysters
Huîtres
Salmon
Saumon
Haddock
Aiglefin
Squid
Calmar
Meat dishes
Viandes
Roast chicken
Poulet rotî
Casserole
Plat en cocotte
Roast lamb
Gigot
Mixed cold meat
L'assiette de charcuterie
Potatoes
Pommes de terre
Cauliflower
Chou-fleur
Green beans
Haricots verts
Peas
Petits pois
Carrots
Carottes
Spinach
Épinards
Onions
Oignons
Lettuce
Laitue
Cucumber
Concombre
Tomatoes
Tomates
Fruit
Les fruits
Apples
Pommes
Strawberries
Fraises

Peaches
Pêches
Pears
Poires
Fruit tart
Tarte aux fruits
Pastry
Pâtisserie
Chocolate cake
Gâteau au chocolat
Cream
Crème
Ice cream
Glace
Chocolate mousse
Mousse au chocolat

TOURIST INFORMATION

Where is the tourist information office, please?
Où se trouve l'office du tourisme, s'il vous plaît?
Do you have a city map?
Avez-vous un plan de la ville?
Where is the museum?
Où est le musée?
Can you give me some information about...?
Pouvez-vous me donner des renseignements sur...?
What are the main places of interest here?
Quels sont les principaux sites touristiques ici?
Please could you point them out on the map?
Pouvez-vous me les indiquer sur la carte, s'il vous plaît?
What sights/hotels/restaurants can you recommend?
Quels sites/hôtels/restaurants nous recommandez-vous?
We are staying here for a day.
Nous sommes ici pour une journée.
I am interested in...
Je suis intéressé(e) par...
Does the guide speak English?
Est-ce qu'il y a un guide qui parle anglais?
Do you have any suggested walks?
Avez-vous des suggestions de promenades?
Are there guided tours?
Est-ce qu'il y a des visites guidées?

Are there organized excursions?
Est-ce qu'il y a des excursions organisées?
Can we make reservations here?
Est-ce que nous pouvons réserver ici?
What time does it open/close?
Ça ouvre/ferme à quelle heure?
What is the admission price?
Quel est le prix d'entrée?
Is there a discount for senior citizens/students?
Est-ce qu'il y a des réductions pour les personnes âgées/les étudiants?
Do you have a brochure in English?
Avez-vous un dépliant en anglais?
What's on at the cinema?
Qu'est-ce qu'il y a au cinéma?
Where can I find a good nightclub?
Où est-ce que je peux trouver une bonne boîte de nuit?
Do you have a schedule for the theatre/opera?
Est-ce que vous avez un programme de théâtre/d'opéra?
Should we dress smartly?
Est-ce qu'il faut mettre une tenue de soirée?
What time does the show start?
A quelle heure commence le spectacle?
How do I reserve a seat?
Comment fait-on pour réserver une place?
Could you reserve tickets for me?
Pouvez-vous me réserver des billets?

ILLNESS AND EMERGENCIES
I don't feel well.
Je ne me sens pas bien.
Could you call a doctor?
(Est-ce que) vous pouvez appeler un médecin/un docteur, s'il vous plaît?
Is there a doctor/pharmacist on duty?
(Est-ce qu') il y a un médecin/docteur/une pharmacie de garde?
I feel sick.
J'ai envie de vomir.
I need to see a doctor/dentist.
Il faut que je voie un médecin/docteur/un dentiste.

Please direct me to the hospital.
(Est-ce que) vous pouvez m'indiquer le chemin pour aller à l'hôpital, s'il vous plaît?
I have a headache.
J'ai mal à la tête.
I've been stung by a wasp/bee/jellyfish.
J'ai été piqué(e) par une guêpe/abeille/méduse.
I have a heart condition.
J'ai un problème cardiaque.
I am diabetic.
Je suis diabétique.
I'm asthmatic.
Je suis asmathique.
I'm on a special diet.
Je suis un régime spécial.
I am on medication.
Je prends des médicaments.
I have left my medicine at home.
J'ai laissé mes médicaments chez moi.
I need to make an emergency appointment.
Je dois prendre rendez-vous d'urgence.
I have bad toothache.
J'ai mal aux dents.
I don't want an injection.
Je ne veux pas de piqûre.
Help!
Au secours!
I have lost my passport/wallet/purse/handbag.
J'ai perdu mon passeport/portefeuille/porte-monnaie/sac à main.
I have had an accident.
J'ai eu un accident.
My car has been stolen.
On m'a volé ma voiture.
I have been robbed.
J'ai été volé(e).

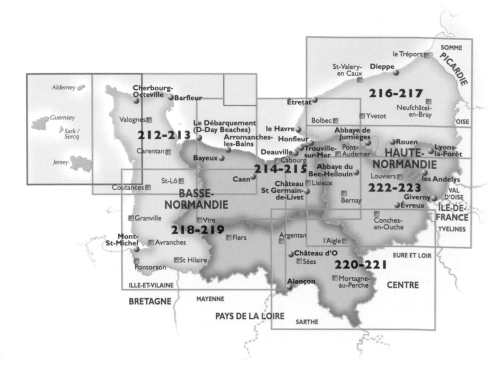

Alderney

Guernsey

Sark / Sercq

Jersey

Cherbourg-Octeville
Barfleur
Valognes
212-213
Carentan
Coutances
St-Lô
Caen
BASSE-NORMANDIE
Granville
Vire
218-219
Flers
Mont-St-Michel
Avranches
St Hilaire
Pontorson
ILLE-ET-VILAINE
BRETAGNE
MAYENNE
PAYS DE LA LOIRE
SARTHE

Le Débarquement (D-Day Beaches)
Arromanches-les-Bains
Bayeux
Cabourg

le Havre
Honfleur
Deauville
Trouville-sur-Mer
214-215
Château St Germain-de-Livet
Lisieux
Bernay
Argentan
l'Aigle
Château d'O
Sées
220-221
Alençon
Mortagne-au-Perche
CENTRE

Étretat
Bolbec
Yvetot
Abbaye de Jumièges
Pont-Audemer
Abbaye du Bec-Hellouin
Conches-en-Ouche
EURE ET LOIR

St-Valery-en Caux
Dieppe
le Tréport
SOMME
PICARDIE
216-217
Neufchâtel-en-Bray
OISE
Rouen
Lyons-la-Forêt
HAUTE-NORMANDIE
Louviers
les Andelys
222-223
Giverny
Évreux
VAL D'OISE
ÎLE-DE-FRANCE
YVELINES

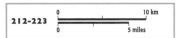
212-223   0   10 km   5 miles

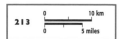
213   0   10 km   5 miles

	Toll motorway (Turnpike)			Département boundary
	Motorway (Expressway)			City
	Motorway junction with and without number		■	Town / Village
	National road			National Park
	Regional road		●	Featured place of interest
	Other road			Airport
	Railway		621 ▲	Height in metres
	Administrative region boundary			Ferry route

MAPS

Map references for the sights refer to the atlas pages within this section or to the individual town plans within the regions. For example, Caen has the reference ✚ 214 H5, indicating the page on which the map is found (214) and the grid square in which Caen sits (H5).

3

Portsmouth

B a i e   d e   l a   S e i

213

4

C ô t e   d e   N a c r e

nglesqueville-
la-Percée
Omaha
Beach
Vierville-sur-Mer
St-Laurent-
sur-Mer
Formigny
Port-en-Bessin-
Huppain
Longues-
sur-Mer
Villiers-
sur-Port
Arromanches-
les-Bains
Gold
Beach
D514
Bernières-
sur-Mer
le Paisy-Vert
Juno
Beach
St-Aubin-sur-Mer
Langrune-sur-Mer
C ô t e
D13 E46
Mosles
Maisons
Aure
Meuvaines
Ver-sur-
Mer
Reviers
Courseulles-
sur-Mer
Luc-sur-Mer
Lion-sur-Mer
Rade de Caen
Bernesq
Cussy
Tour-en-
Bessin
D6
D512
Ryes
Sommervieu
D12
Douvres-
la-Délivrande
D514
Sword Beach
Ouistreham
Cabourg
Tortonne
Bayeux
D12
Villiers-
le-Sec
Seulles
Creully
Cresserons
Hermanville-
sur-Mer
Riva-
Bella
D514
D514
le Molay
Vaux-sur-
Seulles
Château de
Fontaine-Henry
Colleville-
Montgomery
Mathieu
Merville-
Franceville-
Plage
Tournières
le Molay-
Littry
Subles
Cully
D22
Cairon
Blainville-
sur-Orne
Bénouville
Ranville
Sallenelles
Varaville
D27 Brucourt
Abbaye de
Cerisy-la-Forêt
Monteaux-
en-Bessin
N13
Loucelles
Buron
Epron
Héroouville-
St-Clair
Orne
Hérouvillette
Escoville
Vaubadon
Trungy
Audrieu
Bretteville-
l'Orgueilleuse
Rots
St-Contest
Colombelles
Ranville
Goustranville
Château de Balleroy
Tilly-sur-
Seulles
D9
St-Manvieu-
Norrey
N13
Carpiquet
St-Germain-la-
Blanche-Herbe
Giberville
Cuverille
Sannerville
St-Rich
Balleroy
Lingèvres
Fontenay-
le-Pesnil
Carpiquet
Caen
CAEN
Démouville
St-Samson
Foulognes
Marcelet
Verson
Louvigny
Troarn
Hattot-
les-Bagues
Fleury-sur-Orne
E401 A84
Tourville-
sur-Odon
Fontaine-
Etoupefour
Ifs
Soliers
Frénouville
Vimont
Argences
Missy
Feuguerolles-
Bully
St-Martin-
de-Fontenaye
Bourguébus
Chicheboville-
Secqueville
Croissanville
Moult
la Vacquerie
Briquessard
Villy-Bocage
Évrecy
May-sur-Orne
Conteville
Airan
la Lande-
sur-Drôme
Cahagnes
Amayé-
sur-Seulles
Villers-
Bocage
le Mesnil-
au-Grain
Amayé-
sur-Orne
Fontenay-
le-Marmion
St-Aignan-
de-Cramesnil
Cesny-aux-
Vignes-Ouezy
E03 E401 A84
Montigny
Clinchamps-
sur-Orne
Cintheaux
St-Sylvain
Vieux-Fumé
St-Martin-
de-Besaces
Bauquay
Aunay-
sur-Odon
Odon
Orne
Bretteville-
sur-Laize
Magny-
la-Campagne
le Mesnil-
Auzouf
le Moutier-
en-Cinglais
Bretteville-
le-Rabet
CALVADOS
Jurques
Danvou-
la-Ferrière
Thury-
Harcourt
Barberry
Quesnay
Potigny
Château de
Vendeuvre
Montchamp
Mont Pincon
Campandré-
Valcongrain
Cesny-Bois-
Halbout
Meslay
Sassy
le Bény-
Bocage
Beaulieu
St-Pierre-
la-Vieille
Caumont-
sur-Orne
St-Rémy
Mont du Père
Ussy
Villers-
Canivet
St-Pierre-Canivet
Aubigny
Morteaux-
Coulibœu
Etouvy
Estry
Presles
Clécy
St-Germain-
Langot
Falaise
Proussy
St-Christophe
Collines

219

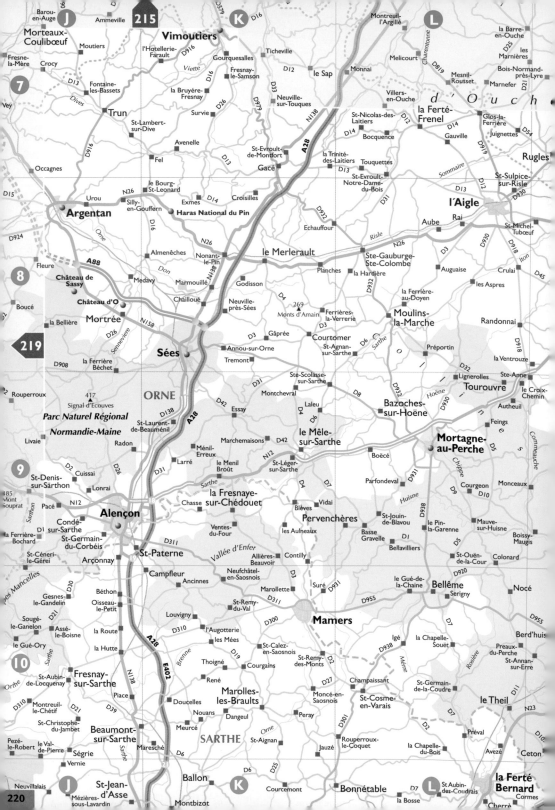

Place		
Reviers	214	H5
Réville	212	E3
Ri	219	J7
Richemont	217	Q2
Richeville	223	P5
Rieux	217	Q2
Riva-Bella	214	H5
Rive, la	218	D8
Riviere-St-Sauveur, la	215	K4
Rivière-Thibouville, la	222	M6
Rogerville	215	K4
Rolleville	215	K3
Romagny	218	F8
Romilly-sur-Andelle	223	P5
Roncey	218	E6
Ronde-Haye, la	212	D5
Ronthon	218	D7
Rosay	217	P3
Rostes	222	M6
Rots	214	H5
Rouellé	219	G8
Rouen	223	N4
Rougemontiers	222	M5
Rouge Periers	222	M6
Rouperroux	219	J9
Rousset, le	221	N8
Routot	222	M4
Rouville	216	L3
Rouxeville	218	F6
Rouxmesnil-Bouteilles	217	N2
Rue-du-Bocage, la	212	D5
Rugles	220	M7
Rumesnil	215	J5
Ryes	214	G5
Sahurs	222	N5
Sallenelles	214	J5
Salmonville	217	P4
Sannerville	214	J5
Sap, le	222	K7
Sartilly	218	D7
Sasseville	216	M2
Sassy	219	J6
Sauqueville	217	N2
Saussaye, la	222	N5
Saussay-la-Champagne	223	P5
Saussemesnil	212	E3
Saussey	218	D6
Sées	220	K8
Selle-la-Forge, la	219	G8
Sensurière, la	212	D4
Sept-Forges	219	G9
Sept-Frères	218	F7
Sept-Meules	217	P2
Serigny	220	L10
Serqueux	217	Q3
Serquigny	222	M6
Sevrai	219	J8
Sigy-en-Bray	217	P4
Silly-en-Gouffern	220	J8
Smermesnil	217	P2
Soliers	214	H6
Sommervieu	213	G5
Sommery	217	P3
Sotteville-lès-Rouen	223	N4
Sotteville-sur-Mer	216	M2
Soulanger, le	222	M5
Sourdeval	218	F8
St-Agnan-sur-Sarthe	220	L8
St-Aignan-de-Cramesnil	214	H6
St-Amand	218	F6
St-André-d'Hébertot	215	K5
St-André-de-l'Eure	223	P7
St-André-de-Messei	219	G8
St-André-sur-Cailly	217	N4
St-Annan-sur-Erre	220	M10
St-Arnoult (Calvados)	215	K5
St-Arnoult (Seine-Maritime)	216	M4
St-Aubin	217	Q4
St-Aubin-des-Bois	218	E7
St-Aubin-de-Scellon	215	L6
St-Aubin-le-Cauf	217	N2
St-Aubin-lès-Elbeuf	222	N5
St-Aubin-Routot	215	K4
St-Aubin-sur-Gaillon	223	P6
St-Aubin-sur-Mer (Calvados)	214	H5
St-Aubin-sur-Mer (Seine-Maritime)	216	M2
St-Aubin-sur-Scie	217	N2
St-Barthélemy	218	F8
St-Christophe	219	H7
St-Christophe-de-Chaulieu	219	F7
St-Clair	219	J7
St-Clair-sur-l'Elle	213	F5
St-Clair-sur-les-Monts	216	M3
St-Côme-du-Mont	212	E4
St-Contest	214	H5
St-Denis-de-Béhélan	221	M7
St-Denis-le-Gast	218	E6
St-Denis-sur-Särthon	219	J9
St-Désir	215	K6
Ste-Adresse	215	K4
Ste-Anne (Orne)	220	L9
Ste-Anne (Eure)	222	M7
Ste-Austreberthe	216	N3
Ste-Colombe (Seine-Maritime)	216	M2
Ste Colombe (Eure)	222	M6
Ste-Croix-Hague	212	D3
Ste-Croix-sur-Buchy	217	P4
Ste-Foy	217	N2
Ste-Gauburge-Ste-Colombe	220	L8
Ste-Honorine-la-Chardonne-le Poirier	219	H7
Ste-Honorine-la-Guillaume	219	H7
Ste-Marguerite-de-Viette	215	K6
Ste-Marguerite-sur-Duclair	216	M4
Ste-Marie des-Champs	216	M3
Ste-Marie-du-Mont	212	E4
Ste-Marthe	222	M7
Ste-Mère-Église	212	E4
Ste-Pience	218	E7
Ste-Scolasse-sur-Sarthe	220	K9
Ste-Suzanne	221	M7
St-Etienne-du-Rouvray	223	N4
St-Etienne-du-Vauvray	223	N5
St-Eugène	215	K5
St-Eustache-la-Forêt	215	L4
St-Evroult-de-Montfort	220	K7
St-Evroult-Notre-Dame-du-Bois	220	L7
St-Fromond	213	F5
St-Gatien-des-Bois	215	K5
St-Georges-de-Bohon	212	E5
St-Georges-de-Rouelley	219	G8
St-Georges-des-Groseillers	219	G7
St-Georges-du-Vièvre	222	L5
St-Georges-Montcocq	213	F5
St-Georges-Motel	221	P8
St-Germain-de-la-Coudre	220	L10
St-Germain-de-Tallevende-la-Lande-Vaumont	218	F7
St-Germain-de-Varreville	212	E4
St-Germain-du-Corbéis	220	J9
St-Germain-la-Blanche-Herbe	214	H5
St-Germain-Langot	219	H7
St-Germain-le-Campagne	215	L6
St-Germain-sous-Cailly	217	N4
St-Germain-Village	222	L5
St-Grégoire-du-Vièvre	222	L5
St-Hélène-Bondeville	216	L2
St Helier	213	B5
St-Hilaire-de-Briouze	219	H8
St-Hilaire-du-Harcouët	218	E8
St-Jacques-sur-Darnetal	223	N4
St James	218	E9
St-Jean-d'Abbetot	215	L4
St-Jean-de-Daye	213	F5
St-Jean-de-Frenelles	223	P5
St-Jean-de-la-Haize	218	E8
St-Jean-de-Livet	215	K6
St-Jean-des-Champs	218	D7
St-Jean-du-Cardonnay	216	N4
St-Jean-du-Corail	218	F8
St-Jores	212	E5
St-Joseph	212	D3
St-Jouin Bruneval	215	K3
St-Jouin-de-Blavou	220	L9
St-Julien-le-Faucon	215	K6
St-Lambert-sur-Dive	220	J7
St-Laurent-de-Beauménil	220	K9
St-Laurent-de-Cuves	218	E7
St-Laurent-des-Bois	221	P7
St-Laurent-en-Caux	216	M3
St-Laurent-sur-Mer	213	F4
St-Léger-aux-Bois	217	Q2
St-Léger-sur-Sarthe	220	K9
St-Léonard	216	L3
St-Lô	213	F6
St-Lo-d'Ourville	212	D4
St-Loup-de-Fribois	215	J6
St-Maclou	215	L5
St-Maclou-la-Brière	216	L3
St Manvieu-Norrey	214	H5
St-Marcel	223	P6
St-Marcouf	212	E4
St-Mards	216	N3
St-Mars-d'Ergenne	219	G8
St-Martin-aux-Buneaux	216	L2
St-Martin-d'Audouville	212	E3
St-Martin-de-Besaces	219	F6
St-Martin-de-Boscherville	222	N4
St-Martin-de-Bréhal	218	D7
St-Martin-de-Cenilly	218	E6
St-Martin-de-Fontenaye	214	H6
St-Martin-de-la-Lieue	215	K6
St-Martin-de-Landelles	218	E8
St-Martin-des-Champs	218	E8
St-Martin-des-Landes	219	J9
St-Martin-du-Manoir Gournay	215	K4
St-Martin-du-Vivier	217	N4
St-Martin-en-Campagne	217	P2
St-Martin-Gréard	212	D3
St-Martin-la-Campagne	222	N6
St-Martin-Osmonville	217	P3
St-Maurice-du-Désert	219	H8
St-Maurice-lès-Charencey	221	M8
St-Michel-de-Montjoie	218	F7
St-Michel-les-Andaines	219	H8
St-Michel-Tubœuf	220	M8
St-Nicolas-d'Aliermont	217	P2
St-Nicolas-de-Bliquetuit	216	M4
St-Nicolas-des-Bois	218	E7
St-Nicolas-des-Laitiers	220	L7
St-Ouen	222	M5
St-Ouën-de-la-Cour	220	L9
St-Ouen-des-Champs	222	L4
St-Ouen-du-Breuil	216	N3
St-Ouen-sous-Bailly	217	P2
St-Paër	216	M4
St-Pair-sur-Mer	218	D7
St-Patrice-de-Claids	212	E5
St-Pellerin	213	E5
St Peter Port	213	A4
St-Pierre-Canivet	219	J7
St-Pierre-d'Entremont	219	G7
St-Pierre-de-Semilly	213	F6
St-Pierre-des-Fleurs	222	N5
St-Pierre-des-Ifs	222	L5
St-Pierre-de-Varengeville	216	M4
St-Pierre-du-Regard	219	G7
St-Pierre-du-Vauvray	223	N5
St-Pierre-Eglise	212	E3
St-Pierre-en-Port	216	L2
St-Pierre-la-Vieille	219	G7
St-Pierre-le-Viger	216	M2
St-Pierre-sur-Dives	219	J6

PICTURES

The Automobile Association would like to thank the following photographers, companies and picture libraries for their assistance in the preparation of this book.

Abbreviations for the picture credits are as follows – (t) top; (b) bottom; (c) centre; (l) left; (r) right; (AA) AA World Travel Library.

2 AA/C Sawyer;
3tr AA/I Dawson;
3tcr AA/J Tims;
3bcr AA/I Dawson;
3br AA/C Sawyer;
4 AA/I Dawson;
5 AA/R Moore;
6 AA/C Sawyer;
7bl AA/P Bennett;
7br AA/C Sawyer;
8t © Peter Turnley/Corbis;
8b AA/I Dawson;
10 © Goélette Tapisserie de Bayeux;
11bl © Musée C Dior;
11br © Palais Bénédictine;
12bl AA/P Bennett;
12br AA/R Moore;
13 AA/I Dawson;
14 AA/R Moore;
15l AA/R Moore;
15r AA/R Moore;
16 AA/I Dawson;
17bl © Vudoiseau;
17br AA/I Dawson;
18l AA/P Bennett;
18r AA/I Dawson;
19 © Tapisserie de Bayeux;
20 AA/R Moore;
21t AA/C Sawyer;
21b Musée Dobrée, Nantes, France/ Giraudon/The Bridgeman Art Library;
22 © Peter Turnley/CORBIS;
23bl Musée Lambinet, Versailles, France, Lauros/Giraudon/The Bridgeman Art Library;
23br Musée Marmottan, Paris, France, Giraudon/The Bridgeman Art Library;
24 © Jouanneau Thomas/Corbis Sygma;
25 AA/I Dawson;
28 AA/C Sawyer;
33bl AA/P Bennett;
33br Digitalvision;
34 Photolibrary Group;

35 © Jon Arnold Images Ltd/Alamy;
36 AA/C Sawyer;
37 © SL-Convergencephotos.com;
38 AA/R Moore;
40 AA/J Tims;
41 AA/P Bennett;
42 AA/C Sawyer;
43 AA/I Dawson;
44tl AA/P Bennett;
44tr AA/C Sawyer;
45 AA/C Sawyer;
46 AA/R Moore;
47 AA/C Sawyer;
48 AA/I Dawson;
49 AA/C Sawyer;
50bl AA/C Sawyer;
50br AA/C Sawyer;
51 AA/I Dawson;
52 AA/R Moore;
53 AA/C Sawyer;
54 AA/I Dawson;
55 AA/I Dawson;
56 Neale Clark/Robert Harding;
58 AA/R Moore;
61 AA/R Moore;
62 AA/J Tims;
64 AA/M Jourdan;
65 AA/J Tims;
66 AA/P Bennett;
68 AA/C Sawyer;
69 © Office de Tourisme Alençon - Ville d'Ale;
70 AA/C Sawyer;
71 AA/C Sawyer;
72tl AA/R Moore;
72tr AA;
74 AA/C Sawyer;
76 AA/R Moore;
77bl AA/I Dawson;
77br AA/C Sawyer;
78 AA/C Sawyer;
80 AA/P Bennett;
81 AA/P Bennett;
82 AA/C Sawyer;
84 AA/I Dawson;
85c AA/I Dawson;
85b AA/C Sawyer;
86 AA;
87 © Martin Beddall/Alamy;
88 AA/R Moore;
89bl AA/R Moore;
89br AA/R Moore;
90 © CDT Calvados;
91 AA/C Sawyer;
92 AA/I Dawson;
93 AA/P Bennett;
95 AA/I Dawson;

96 AA/C Sawyer;
98 AA/I Dawson;
99t AA/I Dawson;
99b AA/C Sawyer;
100 AA/R Moore;
101 AA/I Dawson;
102 AA/C Sawyer;
103 AA/R Moore;
104 AA/R Moore;
106 AA/C Sawyer;
107 AA/R Moore;
108 AA/C Sawyer;
109 AA/I Dawson;
110 © G Wait;
114 AA/C Sawyer;
116 AA/P Bennett;
118 AA/I Dawson;
120 AA/R Moore;
121 AA/B Smith;
122 AA/C Sawyer;
123bl AA/R Moore;
123br AA/R Moore;
124 AA/P Bennett;
125 AA/P Bennett;
126 AA/P Bennett;
127 AA/P Bennett;
128 © Franz-Marc Frei/Corbis;
129 AA/C Sawyer;
130 AA/C Sawyer;
131tl AA/R Moore;
131tr AA/I Dawson;
132 AA/C Sawyer;
133 AA/P Bennett;
134 AA/C Sawyer;
135bl AA/R Moore;
135br AA/C Sawyer;
136 Roland Brierre;
137 AA/P Bennett;
138 AA/C Sawyer;
142 AA/C Sawyer;
143 Ingram;
144 AA/P Bennett;
146 AA/P Bennett;
148 AA/R Moore;
149 AA/I Dawson;
150tl AA/C Sawyer;
150tr AA/R Moore;
151 AA/R Moore;
152 AA/C Sawyer;
153bl AA/R Moore;
153br © La Cité de la Mer Sylvain Guichard;
154 AA/C Sawyer;
155 AA/C Sawyer;
156 AA/I Dawson;
157bl © ImagesEurope/Alamy;
157br © Bildarchiv Monheim GmbH/

Alamy;

158 Musée des Beaux-Arts André Malraux, Le Havre, France/Giraudon/ The Bridgeman Art Library;

159 Pictures Colour Library;

160 AA/I Dawson;

161 © OT de Rouen;

163t © SL-Convergencephotos.com;

163b AA/R Moore;

164t © B Voisin - OT de Rouen;

164b AA/I Dawson;

165 AA/P Bennett;

166 AA/I Dawson;

167c AA/I Dawson;

167b AA/R Moore;

168 AA/C Sawyer;

169 AA/R Moss;

170 AA/R Moore;

172 AA/R Moore;

174 Digitalvision;

176 AA/P Bennett;

178 AA/P Bennett;

180 AA/R Moore;

181 AA/R Moore;

185 AA/P Bennett;

186 AA/J Tims;

188t AA/P Kenward;

188b AA/J Tims;

189 AA/C Sawyer;

190 AA/P Bennett;

192 AA/C Sawyer;

195 AA/R Moore;

196 AA/C Sawyer;

197 Photolibrary Group;

198 Brand X Pics;

199 AA/I Dawson;

200 AA/R Moore;

201 © CDT Calvados;

202 AA/I Dawson;

204 © Dormy house;

211 AA/C Sawyer

ACKNOWLEDGMENTS NORMANDY

CREDITS

Managing editor
Marie-Claire Jefferies

Project editor
Bookwork Creative Associates Ltd

Design
Drew Jones, pentacorbig, Nick Otway

Picture research
Lesley Grayson

Image retouching and repro
Michael Moody

Main contributors
Nicholas Inman, Laurence Phillips

Updater
Nicholas Inman

Indexer
Marie Lorimer

Production
Karen Gibson

Published by AA Publishing, a trading name of AA Media Limited, whose registered office is
Fanum House, Basing View, Basingstoke, RG21 4EA. Registered number 06112600.
A CIP catalogue record for this book is available from the British Library.

ISBN 978-0-7495-6234-2

KeyGuide is a registered trademark in Australia and is used under license.
Colour separation by Keenes, Andover, UK
Printed and bound by Leo Paper Products, China

We believe the contents of this book are correct at the time of printing. However, some details, particularly prices, opening times and
telephone numbers do change. We do not accept responsibility for any consequences arising from the use of this book.
This does not affect your statutory rights. We would be grateful if readers would advise us of any inaccuracies they may encounter, or any
suggestions they might like to make to improve the book. There is a form provided at the back of the book for this purpose, or you can email us
at Keyguides@theaa.com

A03807
Maps in this title produced from mapping © MAIRDUMONT / Falk Verlag 2009
Transport maps © Communicarta Ltd, UK
Weather chart statistics supplied by Weatherbase © Copyright 2005 Canty and Associates, LLC.

Find out more about AA Publishing and the wide range of travel publications and services the AA provides by visiting our website at
www.theAA.com/bookshop

READER RESPONSE

Thank you for buying this KeyGuide. Your comments and opinions are very important to us, so please help us to improve our travel guides by taking a few minutes to complete this questionnaire.

You do not need a stamp (unless posted outside the UK). If you do not want to cut this page from your guide, then photocopy it or write your answers on a plain sheet of paper

Send to: **KeyGuide Editor, AA World Travel Guides**
FREEPOST SCE 4598, Basingstoke RG21 4GY

Find out more about AA Publishing and the wide range of travel publications the AA provides by visiting our website at www.theAA.com/bookshop

ABOUT THIS GUIDE

Which KeyGuide did you buy? ....

Where did you buy it? ....

When? ....,month ..... year

Why did you choose this AA KeyGuide?
☐ Price ☐ AA Publication
☐ Used this series before; title
☐ Cover ☐ Other (please state)

Please let us know how helpful the following features of the guide were to you by circling the appropriate category: very helpful (VH), helpful (H) or little help (LH)

Size	VH	H	LH
Layout	VH	H	LH
Photos	VH	H	LH
Excursions	VH	H	LH
Entertainment	VH	H	LH
Hotels	VH	H	LH
Maps	VH	H	LH
Practical info	VH	H	LH
Restaurants	VH	H	LH
Shopping	VH	H	LH
Walks	VH	H	LH
Sights	VH	H	LH
Transport info	VH	H	LH

What was your favourite sight, attraction or feature listed in the guide?

Page.................. Please give your reason ....
....

Which features in the guide could be changed or improved? Or are there any other comments you would like to make?

....

ABOUT YOU

Name (Mr/Mrs/Ms)...

Address ....

....

....

Postcode... Daytime tel nos...

Email...
Please only give us your mobile phone number/email if you wish to hear from us about other products and services
from the AA and partners by text or mms.

Which age group are you in?
Under 25 ☐   25–34 ☐   35–44 ☐   45–54 ☐   55+ ☐

How many trips do you make a year?
Less than1 ☐   1 ☐   2 ☐   3 or more ☐

ABOUT YOUR TRIP

Are you an AA member?   Yes ☐ No ☐

When did you book?.............. month................. year

When did you travel?.............month................. year

Reason for your trip?   Business ☐   Leisure ☐

How many nights did you stay? ....

How did you travel?   Individual ☐   Couple ☐   Family ☐   Group ☐

Did you buy any other travel guides for your trip? ....

If yes, which ones?...

Thank you for taking the time to complete this questionnaire. Please send it to us as soon as possible, and
remember, you do not need a stamp (unless posted outside the UK).
AA Travel Insurance call 0800 072 4168 or visit www.theaa.com

Titles in the KeyGuide series:
Australia, Barcelona, Britain, Brittany, Canada, China, Costa Rica, Croatia, Florence and Tuscany, France,
Germany, Ireland, Italy, London, Mallorca, Mexico, New York, New Zealand, Normandy, Paris, Portugal,
Prague, Provence and the Côte d'Azur, Rome, Scotland, South Africa, Spain, Thailand, Venice, Vietnam,
Western European Cities.
Published in July 2009: Berlin

The information we hold about you will be used to provide the products and services requested and for identification, account administration,
analysis, and fraud/loss prevention purposes. More details about how that information is used is in our privacy statement, which you'll find
under the heading "Personal Information" in our terms and conditions and on our website: www.theAA.com. Copies are also available from us
by post, by contacting the Data Protection Manager at AA, Fanum House, Basing View, Basingstoke, Hampshire RG21 4EA.

We may want to contact you about other products and services provided by us, or our partners (by mail, telephone, email) but please tick the
box if you DO NOT wish to hear about such products and services from us. ☐

AA Travel Insurance call 0800 072 4168 or visit www.theaa.com